W9-CFX-810

Journalism Kids Do Better

What Research Tells Us about High School Journalism

Jack Dvorak

Larry Lain

Tom Dickson

Jim,
Thanks for your
lifelong friendship,
encouragement and
support ... and I'm
proud to call you
"brother."
Love,
Jack

ERIC®

ERIC Clearinghouse on Reading,
English, and Communication

EDINFO
PRESS

Published 1994 by
ERIC Clearinghouse on Reading, English, and Communication
Carl B. Smith, Director
2805 East 10th Street, Suite 150
Bloomington, Indiana 47408-2698

Editor: Warren Lewis
Cover, Design & Production: Lauren Bongiani Gottlieb
Front Cover Photograph: Christy M. Miller

ERIC (an acronym for Educational Resources Information Center) is a national network of 16 clearinghouses, each of which is responsible for building the ERIC database by identifying and abstracting various educational resources, including research reports, curriculum guides, conference papers, journal articles, and government reports. The Clearinghouse on Reading, English, and Communication (ERIC/REC) collects educational information specifically related to reading, English, journalism, speech, and theater at all levels. ERIC/REC also covers interdisciplinary areas, such as media studies, reading and writing technology, mass communication, language arts, critical thinking, literature, and many aspects of literacy.

This publication was prepared with funding from the Office of Educational Research and Improvement, U.S. Department of Education, under contract no. RR93002011. Contractors undertaking such projects under government sponsorship are encouraged to express freely their judgment in professional and technical matters. Points of view or opinions, however, do not necessarily represent the official view or opinions of the Office of Educational Research and Improvement.

Library of Congress Cataloging-in-Publication Data
Dvorak, Jack, 1944-
    Journalism kids do better : what research tells us about high school journalism /
Jack Dvorak, Larry Lain, Tom Dickson.
       p.   cm.
    Includes bibliographical references and index.
    ISBN 0-927516-40-3 : $24.95
    1. Journalism, High school—United States. 2. Academic achievement—
United States. 3. Curriculum planning—United States. 4. Educational law and
legislation—United States. I. Lain, Larry, 1947- . II. Dickson, Tom, 1946- .
III. Title.
LB3621.5.D86 1994
373.18'974—dc20
                                        94-4006
                                          CIP

TABLE OF CONTENTS

ERIC/REC ADVISORY BOARD

IN MEMORY OF

ROBERT PATRICK KNIGHT

PREFACE

This is a book by, for and about high school journalism educators in the 1990s. Along with providing new facts and figures about the shape of scholastic journalism today, we hope to provide you with some sense of how we got to this point.

We have provided plenty of charts, graphs and numbers to better explain where we are on a national basis. But this book is not intended as a research study replete with esoteric jargon. Rather, we have tried to translate the many discoveries we've made about high school journalism into a readable, usable and—we hope—interesting format. Our purpose in compiling such a book is threefold: to help secondary school teachers and media advisers know more about our collective work; to help solve the problems that confront us daily; and to learn and grow in our jobs.

While all three of us have collaborated on parts of all the chapters and the bibliography, we have divided our work into primary areas of responsibility.

In Chapter 1, Larry Lain describes the journalism educator's role in the school and the unique position that person holds. In Chapters 2, 3, 4 and 5, Jack Dvorak summarizes several recent studies involving journalism students and teachers. In Chapter 2, he records journalism student achievements in various language arts areas compared with their counterparts who have not taken journalism. In Chapter 3, he outlines results of journalism student Advanced Placement examinations and the role of Intensive Journalistic Writing Institutes for teachers. Chapter 4 recaps the sheer numbers of journalism programs, courses and publications in the United States—and for the first time, we believe, presents baseline data for future examinations of this type. And in Chapter 5, Dvorak looks closely at advisers' situations nationally—including experience, formal education, salary, work load, job satisfaction, and many other aspects of journalism educators' unique positions within the school and community.

In Chapter 6, Larry Lain shares his recent national studies of publication financing and advertising. He continues this theme in Chapter 7, while expanding on it and linking it to various First Amendment considerations, including the crucial relationship between funding sources and editorial autonomy. This is the most authoritative study we find to date on this fascinating and most important nexus.

Tom Dickson expands on legal issues in Chapters 8, 9 and 10. In Chapter 8, he looks at the history of scholastic press freedoms from the pre-*Tinker* (1969) era through the 1970s and 1980s. Chapter 9 recaps research done following the *Hazelwood* (1988) decision of the U.S. Supreme Court, the only high school newspaper case ever to reach the nation's highest court. And in Chapter 10, Dickson examines student editor, adviser and principal attitudes about student freedom of expression in the post-*Hazelwood* years of the late-1980s and early 1990s. He uses his own extensive national studies while summarizing studies of other researchers in providing the most comprehensive look to date at the meaning and aftermath of *Hazelwood* as reflected in reliable national surveys. Larry Lain provides the final thoughts in the Concluding Thoughts section, and all three authors and ERIC bibliographers helped compile what we believe is the most extensive bibliography involving high school journalism research.

We hope our findings are helpful to all educators, curriculum designers, administrators, student journalists and others interested in high school journalism.

Our efforts in compiling such a book have been buoyed by many others. Collectively, we'd like to thank our many professional colleagues in the Scholastic Journalism Division of the Association for

Education in Journalism and Mass Communication who have provided encouragement, impetus, feedback and friendship. Your collegiality has meant much to us for many years. To the thousands of high school journalism teachers, administrators and editors who have responded to the various surveys reported in this study, we give a special thanks. To the dedicated teachers of journalism and advisers of school publications, we salute your efforts and applaud the noble and important knowledge and skills you share with so many teen-agers. To ERIC Editor Warren Lewis, we appreciate your excellent suggestions, accommodating nature and willingness to engage in spirited discourse as you steered us toward our goal. Many thanks to you and your staff for accepting and producing our ideas in book form.

Specifically, we'd each like to acknowledge some special people as we individually completed portions of this book.

—*J.D.*

—*L.L.*

—*T.D.*

~ ~ ~ ~ ~

I want to thank co-authors Larry Lain and Tom Dickson for their excellent scholarship, good natures, attention to detail, ability to meet deadlines and perseverance as we put this book together. Indeed, you epitomize what it means to be professional colleagues, and it has been a pleasure to work with each of you on the project. For help with data entry and analysis, many thanks to my associate Linda J. Johnson of the High School Journalism Institute and to Allen Li, Ph.D. candidate in Mass Communication at Indiana University. I am also indebted to the High School Journalism Institute of Indiana University for funding the national adviser survey in Chapters 4 and 5 and to the Journalism Education Association and its Commission on the Role of Journalism in Secondary Education for making possible the ACT studies cited in Ch. 2. And especially to my immediate family—my wife Cathy, and our son John—for their understanding, patience and time alone while this project was being completed, I send deepest gratitude, love and respect.

— *Jack Dvorak*

~ ~ ~ ~ ~

No one undertakes a project of any significant size alone, and no project ever stands by itself. *Everything* is cumulative. The cumulative portion of these notes is too extensive to list in its entirety but I need to mention Merle and Betty Lain of Valparaiso, IN, whose determination and persistence in the face of obstacles even now provide a model for perseverance and faith; Lou Ingelhart of Ball State, whose mentorship a quarter-century ago is probably still the greatest single influence on my philosophy; and scores of advisers across the country, many of whom are dear friends, whose collective insights have educated me for many years. More immediately, I salute my co-authors, two men easy to work with and from whom I have learned much both before and during this project. My admiration for them both is unbounded. The University of Dayton and its Department of Communication funded either directly or indirectly much of my portion of the work that is included here. I am most grateful. Finally, my inspiration, my best critic and my biggest supporter has been, as always, the friend and companion of my life, my wife Barb, without whom nothing is possible or meaningful.

— *Larry Lain*

~ ~ ~ ~ ~

I would like to thank Mark Oglesby, coordinator of Academic Computing at Southwest Missouri State University, for his assistance with the computer programs for the 1990 and 1992 national studies. I also would like to thank Susi Klug and Carol McNeil for assistance with mailing both surveys and Southwest Missouri State University for funding both projects.

I have been interested in journalism ever since my grandfather gave me a miniature printing press for my birthday—I think it was my 12th. I started a neighborhood newspaper that lasted at least two editions. If my interest in First Amendment issues doesn't go back quite that far, it goes back at least to two experiences in my journalistic life that involved prior restraint.

The first incident took place when I was co-editor of the university newspaper. I wrote an editorial in response to a lecture on campus by William Rusher, editor of the conservative *National Review*. As best I can remember, Rusher stated that academic freedom and freedom of speech on the college campus should go only so far. I wrote in my editorial that Rusher seemed to be saying that it was OK for conservatives to close a public forum to people who didn't agree with them. I saw my editorial set in type.

The lesson I got about freedom of the press that day was that you can write about anything you want as long as you don't write what the adviser doesn't want written. My recollection, however, is that I was more upset with what the adviser thought about me at the time than the fact that my First Amendment rights had been taken away. My relationship with the adviser never was the same.

My second brush with censorship was in the Army in Vietnam. I edited the newspaper for the 18th Military Police Brigade, which was responsible for most of the military police units in the country. Before we could print anything, we had to send it to military censors in Saigon. Usually, the censors cut only a word here or there; however, if we had covered more hard news, I expect more deletions would have occurred.

Those two experiences showed me a little of what it is like when an adviser rides roughshod over the First Amendment and what it would be like to be a journalist in a country with no First Amendment. Because of those incidents, I gained a little more respect for the First Amendment and for those people who fight for their own First Amendment rights and for the rights of others.

— *Tom Dickson*

CHAPTER 1

WHAT ARE WE DOING HERE, ANYWAY?

What Am I Doing Here?

When journalism teachers and publications advisers get together, discussion inevitably comes around to some variation on the theme: "What am I doing here? Nobody understands me." That's more than the mournful cry of someone caught in a mid-life crisis; it's the honest fate of practically every high school journalism teacher in America.

Almost every other person in the building has real colleagues. English teachers have legions of other English teachers to share their frustrations with: *All* of them understand the agonies of teaching students about subject-verb agreement and sentence fragments. Social studies teachers have other social studies teachers, and all social studies teachers grasp the difficulties of making students *care* about history and of making events long-past relevant to contemporary life. Even head coaches have assistant coaches to share their troubles with, and the problems of a head football coach are not dissimilar from those of a head basketball coach. They can support each other; they can just sit and talk shop.

Few journalism teachers, however, have anyone else in their buildings who *really* understands. We admit that journalism teachers do have professional colleagues in one sense: The greatest number of journalism teachers are also teachers of English, so the lone journalist can talk to the other English teachers. But "pure" English teach-

1

ers are also student journalists' greatest critics. Journalistic writing is *different* from expository writing—tighter, more direct, far more spare of adjectives, unafraid of one-sentence paragraphs. These ideas are foreign to the rest of the English faculty. All journalism teachers know that, regardless of how carefully edited the newspaper is, typos will occur; nevertheless, every school has at least one hard-nosed English teacher who delights in circling the newspaper's mistakes in red pen and sending the paper back to the staff.

Other aspects of the nature of the job sometimes tend to make journalism teachers and publications advisers feel cut off from other teachers. They spend far more time, as a rule, with their students in an *informal* setting than do most teachers, keeping them company during deadline nights or traveling to out-of-town workshops together. Journalism teachers are often closer to their students in casual ways that many other teachers would find odd, possibly imprudent, or even impudent. Articles in two newsletters that arrived in the mail within a few days of each other illustrate this point:

In *Newswire*, the national newsletter of the Journalism Education Association, 1992 national journalism teacher of the year Gloria Grove Olman described a phone call from a former student which begins, "Hi, O. Just wanted to keep in touch."[1]

Sarah Ortman, writing in a state newsletter, talked about a deadline night with her staff during which an editor said, "It's finished, Ort."[2] Larry Lain (one of the authors) recalled that as a newspaper and yearbook adviser in Indiana, he was known to his staffs—and to nobody else—as "L.B."—and that his own high school journalism teacher 10 years earlier had been tagged "Mr. B" by *his* staffs.

Few lofty English teachers tolerate this degree of intimacy with students, and most other teachers would deem such closeness inappropriate. Not all journalism teachers are this close to their staffs, but the fact that so many journalism kids across the country feel able to risk casualness with a teacher underscores the special bond that is common among journalism teachers and their students, a bond that is unusual in other school activities.

Journalism teachers share a sense of purpose with their staffs, and they are frequently more sympathetic to students' positions during the inevitable student/administration disagreements over the school newspaper. Journalism teachers often feel that their loyalties are divided, believing even that their first responsibility is to the students, not the administration. Not all journalism teachers feel that way, but many do.

If other teachers don't understand, can we hope that other activity advisers will? No one outside the group knows or cares very much what the chess club or Future Farmers chapter is doing, but the school newspaper is a high profile activity, as visible to the whole school community as is the basketball team. Even coaches, as buddy-buddy as they may be with their teams, don't understand the problems of a journalism teacher, either. The important difference between a coach and a newspaper adviser is that the coach makes the big decisions: The coach establishes the game plan, makes assignments to the players, substitutes players at will; he has power over his players; they do, or try to do, what he says. Not so with the journalism teacher.

The newspaper adviser is different. He or she functions like a coach as far as teaching the class or staff is concerned, but then the journalism adviser turns the job over to the student editor. It's the editor or other kid designated by the editor who determines the content of the paper, makes the assignments, edits the copy, lays out the pages. If the adviser subscribes to the principle of maximum freedom of expression for students, it is a fundamental precept that *students*, not teachers, make those decisions—and they are all big decisions. It's difficult for most other teachers to understand how an article they disapprove of, or even writing they consider substandard, gets into the paper. "Just *make* them do it right," the critics may say.

If only it were that easy! There is far more to teaching journalism than getting students to use inverted pyramid leads and helping them learn PageMaker. Journalism teachers may frequently disagree with their administrators, with their teaching colleagues, and even sometimes among themselves about what their proper role ought to be, but most believe that what they are doing is important at a level that goes far beyond the teaching of mechanical skills and producing a not-for-profit periodical. Most feel significant amounts of stress because they are being held accountable for things that in good conscience they feel they cannot, to a greater or lesser extent, control.

What Are We Doing Here?

Many high school publications advisers might respond to this question, "I'm not really sure. It just sort of happened!" Surprisingly enough, that's true! In Chapter 5 we talk about the absolute *minority* of journalism teacher/advisers who were actually hired for their jobs. Most were assigned the job by their principals or volunteered to take it on. It's impossible to imagine a school appointing the head basketball coach or the band director that way. Only a small minority of journalism teachers majored in journalism in college, and few have themselves worked in the field professionally. Many states do not even have a formal certification for journalism, yet there are few programs in the typical high school that are more visible and more discussed.

Most journalism teachers do an excellent job of teaching and advising their newspaper, yearbook, and magazine staffs, but they can certainly be pardoned if their role seems ambiguous sometimes. So many people have such different expectations of them. At least six different, and sometimes contradictory, functions are often ascribed to scholastic journalism programs, and there is, frankly, no way to prioritize them. *All* these functions play a role in what we do sometimes, and *all* have their proponents in every school and among professional colleagues. All are well-supported in articles on academic journalism that go back at least 80 years.

Four of the six functions are to a large extent essentially utilitarian. They concern things that people expect journalism education or the school press to *do*. Utilitarian views might be described as the four following perspectives:

- a mechanistic perspective
- a public-relations perspective
- a vocational perspective
- an informational perspective

The other views are more conceptual in nature, and they are more concerned with what press and education should be. They are these two:

- a free-expression perspective
- an integrative perspective

Utilitarian Perspectives

1. The Mechanistic View

In the mechanistic perspective, journalism is merely an extension of the English program, whose reason for existing is to provide reinforcement for the grammar and writing skills taught in other classes and, perhaps, to provide a means for students to have their writing published.

By no means do we suggest that this aim is incompatible with high school journalism! Indeed, in chapters 2 and 3, we demonstrate the enormously positive influence that a background in academic journalism has on subsequent attainment in English. Educators and school journalism organizations across the country rightfully become involved in pressing state and local boards of education to recognize journalism classes as full partners in school English curricula. Full academic credit for journalism courses ought to be awarded on the same basis as for English elective classes.

English teachers, probably, are the greatest proponents of this mechanistic view. Even the great majority of English teachers who would never red-ink the newspaper are certain to sigh inwardly at the spelling and punctuation errors that slip through the editing process, and feel that the paper reflects badly on what they have tried to accomplish in their classes. The view is an old one; Perry wrote in 1919 that newspapers should be published by English Departments, and "the paper should be studied by the department to analyze the department's own performance."[3] From this perspective, the content often seems to matter less than the form.

2. The Public-Relations View

A second, but still utilitarian, view of the school press has been, from early in this century, that of the press's role as *school citizen*. In

5

an early high school journalism textbook published in 1922, H.F. Harrington, director of the Medill School of Journalism, contended that the "duties" of a school newspaper include not only elevating to a "fascinating art" the principles of English composition but also promoting school spirit, building up respect for school and civic authority, promoting good sportsmanship and good scholarship, informing parents of school events, and working for the welfare of the school.[4]

Other educational specialists also described the role of the school press in similar terms. Foster, writing in 1925, noted the value of school newspapers to administrators in disseminating information to the student body, and—"rightly conducted"—in promoting the interest of students in producing more literary work. He also stressed the importance of the paper in community relations and in strengthening students' skills in English.[5] He cautioned schools not to "overemphasize the news value of high school publications."[6]

Probably no one who has had more than a week's experience as a school newspaper adviser would fail to recognize this community-relations function of the journalism program as a favorite of administrators. Many parents and school supporters would also agree with this conviction, and they can be quick to criticize a staff and its adviser who publish anything that they construe as negative. "Boost. Boost everything and everybody" was journalism professor Frances Perry's succinct advice to high school newspapers in 1919. "Boost!"[7]

3. The Vocational View

This is the only one of the six chief perspectives on the high school press that no longer enjoys great currency, but it was once very popular with educators.[8] Journalism was seen as possible career training for students and, even today in a few places, journalism teachers must have college-level coursework in vocational education to be eligible for journalism certification. Journalism courses and school publications work may indeed expose students to career alternatives that they had not previously considered, but no one any longer expects these academic experiences to provide the training necessary for entry into the profession.

4. The Informational View

The purposes of journalism in a school setting are considered by some people to be not greatly different from those of journalism generally. Its function is to provide useful information for its consumers and, perhaps, to serve as a vehicle for entertainment and opinion. The news function, however, is paramount in this perspective. Journalism teachers, and many other teachers, too, and most of the students in most schools probably see the journalism program in this light.

Nearly everyone understands, of course, that newspapers do more than merely provide information, and most of the other roles we are discussing here are also compatible with it to some extent. For many people, the issue is as simple as it sounds: The purpose of the journalism program is, first of all, to provide information to the school publics.

Conceptual Perspectives

If utilitarian views are focused more on outcomes, conceptual views are more concerned with processes. These concerns have more to do with learning—learning to reason, learning to think, learning to articulate one's views, indeed, learning to learn—than they do with the actual product.

5. The Free-Expression View

Despite the prominence this view takes in contemporary literature on school journalism, emphasis on the importance of school publications as forums for student expression is anything but a recent value. Perry, whose advice to "boost everything" was tempered with a warning to avoid censorship,[9] and McKown, who used the term "freedom of expression" in 1927,[10] had more company than opposition in the belief that teachers should not require nor prohibit the publication of particular material.

Probably no aspect of journalism education has been more discussed, dissected, and even litigated during the past generation, than the issue of freedom of the press at school, and the issue is still a divisive one, as we demonstrate in chapters 8 to 10. Most, but not all, journalism teachers advocate stretching the boundaries of expression permitted to high school journalists to limits comparable to those enjoyed by their collegiate and even their professional counterparts, and this is certainly the most important function of the high school press as far as most student journalists are concerned. Students have little interest in showcasing the school's English program, and few care much about providing good PR for the school in the community. Some may be interested in the training aspect—exploring a possible area to study in college. For most students, however, the great allure of working on the newspaper is probably the opportunity to express themselves, to feel like they're making a difference. Indeed, even students—maybe *primarily* students—who work on underground newspapers want the official press to matter. They want to find their voices and have a voice.[11]

Administrators, who often place a higher premium on boosterism, are often skeptical of too much freedom of the school press. A press that enjoys wide latitude in what it prints and deals more often with controversial subjects will cause the principal more headaches than a press that sticks to reporting car washes and student council election results. There are many principals who are deeply committed to an open student press, but there are probably many more who have reservations.

6. The Integrative View

Journalism and publications work are worth doing for reasons that have little to do with the actual subject matter or the types of publications produced. The kind of inquiry, clear thinking, discovery, reasoning, and writing that are necessary to good journalism—a willingness to investigate and an ability to communicate—can be taught no more effectively in any other context in the high school. The frequent and timely production of a newspaper, or the annual publication of a complex yearbook, are as effective as any other program in the school in teaching responsibility, teamwork, self-reliance, and thoroughness. Much is made of the teamwork and sense of loyalty that athletics or band engender: Those qualities are present in no smaller degree in publications work. Much is made of the discipline and critical-thinking skills that are developed in studying mathematics and foreign language: Journalism requires exactly the same thing.

A journalist, whether high school or professional, straddles the arts and the sciences, using the investigative skills of the sciences and the powers of communication—linguistic and graphic—of the humanities. All this makes journalism intrinsically worth studying.

Olman[12] pointed out that there is a renewed attention to the higher-order outcomes described in Bloom's Taxonomy of Educational Objectives.[13] Briefly, these levels of achievement are, in ascending order, as follows:

- Knowledge: recall of specific information
- Comprehension: the lowest level of factual understanding
- Application: using abstractions and technical principles
- Analysis: deconstruction into parts; seeing relationships
- Synthesis: constructing meaning; communicating abstract ideas to others
- Evaluation: judgments of value, accuracy, and truth

The steps described above are progressive: learning starts with simple knowledge and culminates with the ability to evaluate; mastery of each stage is a precondition for progression to the next.

The common complaint is that too much of the educational process focuses on the lower-order skills; too much time is spent on knowledge and comprehension functions, such as memorizing and reciting; and far too little time is allowed for students to come to grips with the *meaning* of their knowledge, i.e., the higher-order skills in the taxonomy. In 1983, the National Commission on Excellence in Education complained in *A Nation at Risk* that few high school students were able to perform higher-order skills.[14] Ernest Boyer, author of the Carnegie Commission report *High School*, charged that students' poor writing skills are indicative of their poor thinking skills.[15]

But Olman asked a journalism teacher's question that tells against the Commission's complaint: "Where are our students?" Then, Olman answered: "At . . . the highest levels. That's where we've always been. What a shock!"[16]

9

In fact, journalism education at every level, from junior high school onward, has *always* placed the highest premium on those higher-order abilities. Reporters—even student reporters—must be able to do much more than listen and repeat: They must understand, evaluate, reconstruct, and communicate clearly, or else their efforts are wasted. This is what we journalism teachers have been teaching all along, and this is exactly what the educational system purports to value the most.

What Is *This Book* Doing Here?

We said at the outset that we, as journalism teachers, often feel terribly isolated in our schools. Outside our school buildings, however, we are anything but isolated! The great body of literature that exists, much of which will be spotlighted in the coming pages, demonstrates most clearly the great scope of our field. There are thousands of places to turn to for information, support, and collegiality: Individuals, associations, university programs, and professional practitioners are there to meet our needs. *Knowing* that we are not alone can be a terrific morale-builder at 11 o'clock on a deadline night when the paper's still only half done. It may not get the pages pasted up, but somehow it's nice to know that scattered somewhere out in the darkness are hundreds of other advisers who are also staring into the night and grinding their teeth.

In this book we focus on research in school journalism and, as this portion of the chapter suggests, it's appropriate to ask what it's good for. As advisers, we're all too busy to spend a lot of time reading things just because they're interesting. What *good* is it?

Knowledge of the research in our field can do at least three things for us all, and we have put this book together with those outcomes in mind:

- Know more about our field
- Help solve the problems we have
- Learn and grow in our jobs

Let's look briefly at each.

Knowledge

The more we know about our field, the more secure we'll feel and the better we'll do our jobs. Much of the research in school journalism can provide us with that kind of background knowledge. Demographic information about high school publications has been around longer than most people realize, and while the methodology of 70-year-old studies is shaky by today's standards, the awareness of the importance of demographic study since early in the history of school journalism is valuable.[17]

The research discussed in this book tells us about the following, and more; this list could be pages long:

- Who we, the journalism advisers, are
- What our schools and publications are like
- Just how good and important is the job we do
- How our publications work
- What the law is, and how it has developed
- What editors, principals, and our colleagues really think.

Knowing the backgrounds of other advisers and the characteristics of other programs in schools like our own can serve as measures of where we stand, of what we can aspire to, of how common our problems are. Understanding the work that's been done with students like ours gives us new insights into our jobs. Our principals probably don't know, for example, that studies as early as 1982[18] demonstrate empirically just how much better journalism students do in advanced placement and honors English classes, and how much better they do on the ACT test and in college English than non-journalism students. *Journalism is not merely a vocational area any more, and it hasn't been for decades.* Journalism is an important academic discipline that enhances the ability of students to do well throughout the curriculum. As 1983 high school journalism teacher of the year John Bowen of Lakewood, Ohio, has emphasized, "[N]o other course in the high school curriculum is more basic and more necessary than journalism."[19] That is why we gave this book its name, because journalism kids *do* do better, both in school and later on.

11

One of the most significant movements of the past decade in education is the rise of competency-based or proficiency testing in several areas, particularly in mathematics and writing. The ability to write well is so foundational to academic success in almost every area, not just to English, that many state and national organizations have prepared guidelines for the competencies that students need to be able to demonstrate. Iowa's guidelines are typical. That list of proficiencies[20] includes the ability to conceptualize ideas; organize them into a coherent structure; write using correct spelling and mechanics; vary writing style for different purposes and audiences; be able to edit, revise and rewrite; and gather and write information from a variety of sources using summaries and quotations. Members of the committee that prepared the catalogue of competencies may have been *thinking* about English classes, but they were *describing* journalism classes!

Dennis Cripe, executive secretary of the Indiana High School Press Association, has emphasized that journalism forces students to *apply* what they've learned from *all* areas of the curriculum and thereby "define [their] own education and level of understanding."[21]

Problem-Solving

Journalism educators and publications advisers are concerned mostly about practical, down-to-earth issues: How to structure a journalism class, how to critique student writing, how to use computers effectively, how to make a budget for the newspaper, how to increase minority involvement in the journalism program, how much or little to become involved in the content of the paper, and so on. All these and other questions have been addressed in books and articles over at least the past 80 years.

Some of the pieces are merely descriptive, an exposition of one idea or approach that has worked for an educator in some school. Other articles are based on extensive study of hundreds of schools; they not only provide an exhaustive description of what's happening across the country but also they address, through the use of statistical analysis, more universally meaningful questions and establish relationships that are not immediately apparent. This book is rooted in such studies.

School-journalism educators have had trouble finding this kind of research information in a form that would be useful in solving the problems of our profession. A number of excellent periodicals contain dozens of articles a year on "how-to" issues, but whereas most of them also run some research-based pieces or legal reviews, the overall focus remains rather practical. *Quill & Scroll* magazine, *Trends in High School Journalism, Student Press Review*, and *C:JET* are the best-known, and the journalism educator who has developed the habit of reading them regularly knows how truly valuable they are. Since 1991, *C:JET* has published an bi-annual issue devoted to printing condensed versions of important research about scholastic journalism education, making *C:JET* one of the few sources of this information readily available to most high school teachers.

But there is much other important work out there! Our book is a compilation and review of some of the most significant recent research, assembled in as readable a form, with as complete a bibliography, as we and our friends at ERIC/REC could do. Knowing what sort of information is available is a necessary first step to gathering it; we have tried to point you in some useful directions.

Much of the most useful literature in our field is contained in scholarly journals to which high school journalism educators do not ordinarily subscribe. Other important work has never been published at all, but is to be found in papers delivered at conventions and conferences. Reproductions of most of those papers are available from the ERIC database.

Journalism advisers and educators at all levels in high schools and colleges can achieve greater insights as journalists and greater expertise as teachers by reading about the subsequent superior scholastic attainments of journalism students as contrasted to the lower performance of those who had not been journalism students. Journalism teachers need to read about, and compare, the attitudes and perceptions of principals, advisers, and student journalists. We need to read and know about the relationship between a school newspaper's sources of funding and the amount of free expression its staff has. These and other issues, both mundane and subtle, are the stuff of research in school journalism. To be well-informed about the essential matters is to grow beyond our natural preoccupation with day-to-day tasks.

Learning and Growing

Every teacher at every level knows that it is difficult to keep up with reading in the field. Teachers in journalism have a particularly difficult time because they, like other English teachers, have an enormous amount of grading to do, and the thoroughness with which they must do it takes much of the time that teachers in other areas have for professional development. Nevertheless, important things are happening in our field, and we have to make a real effort to keep as current with important issues as we can. Only in that way can we offer our students what they need in the classroom, and our staffs what they need in the newsroom.

For example, the ground rules pertaining to student expression have changed since the *Hazelwood* ruling in 1988. Advisers need to have grasped the implications of that judgment so that they may know what sort of guidance to offer to their staffs when they face controversy. Apart from the practical matter of giving advice, though, journalism educators who understand the ruling and the history of the decisions that led up to it, have a more complete sense of their jobs and their professional performance. They are working from a broader context, with a more complete understanding of the field than someone has who is less well-informed.

With regard to *Hazelwood* and on other issues, this book became for us the ideal opportunity to make it possible for knowledgeable journalism educators to point to the large and growing body of evidence that, in the words of an editor we know and the title of our book, "Journalism kids do better!" Educators who know and understand the issues involved, issues that go beyond the how-to-solve-a-particular-problem approach, are better equipped to serve their students, their schools, and their field than other educators may be.

The problem of retaining knowledgeable publications advisers is a difficult one. A substantial majority of high school journalism teachers are restricted by severely limited backgrounds in journalism, whether academic study or practical experience. They have had little of the benefit of reading about important issues in the field and discussing it with like-minded students and professors. No wonder they feel isolated! This is a situation that hasn't changed appreciably in many years; Fretwell noted in 1924 that nine of 10 advisers were wholly untrained.[22]

To make matters worse, the average professional life expectancy for high school advisers is eight years, and at least 12 percent of journalism teachers are brand new to the field each year. Too often we lose effective advisers just as they are building up an experience base that will make their own work easier and will equip them to serve effectively as resources for other advisers. That high rate of turnover is a real shame because in most cases it probably means that an experienced adviser is being replaced with someone who has no experience and who must start at the bottom of the learning curve again.

We can retain more of our veteran educators and advisers if we can help them feel less alone and if we can show them more broadly the power and importance of our field—that it's not all deadline nights and budget meetings with the principal. Significant educational principles and issues are central to our jobs, and we can be important people in the greater educational process if we are willing to be, if we are willing to confront those issues and grow in our jobs. Burnout and turnover rates are always lower among people who feel that the importance of their work goes beyond immediate day-to-day concerns and involves broader and more consequential issues.

Jim Willis wrote about the need for greater communication between the researcher and the professional journalist,[23] something that is just as true for the researcher and the high school journalism teacher. If the growing body of literature in our field is really going to improve our mutual conditions, it must be accessible, both in terms of the way it is presented and in terms of its ready availability. That is what this book is doing here.

NOTES ON CHAPTER 1

1. Gloria Grove Olman, "Value of Journalism Touted," *Newswire 21,2* (January 1993): 1.

2. Sarah Ortman, "Are You the Adviser or the Editor-in-chief?" *JAOS Journal* (Winter 1993): 6.

3. Frances M. Perry, "The Supervision of School Publications," *English Journal 8* (December 1919): 619.

4. H.F. Harrington, *Writing for Print* (Boston: D.C. Heath & Co., 1922): 170-171.

5. Charles R. Foster, *Extra-Curricular Activities in the High School* (Richmond, VA: Johnson Publishing Co., 1925): especially 144-151.

6. *Ibid.*: 147.

7. Frances M. Perry, "School Publications," *English Journal 8* (May 1919): 299.

8. For a good review of early approaches to journalism education, particularly in American colleges, see Paul L. Dressel, *Liberal Education and Journalism* (New York: Columbia University Bureau of Publications, 1960): 21-25.

9. Perry, "Supervision . . . ": 617.

10. Harry C. McKown, *Extracurricular Activities* (New York: Macmillan Co. 1927), 297.

11. John Birmingham, ed. *Our Time Is Now: Notes from the High School Underground* (New York: Praeger 1970): 7.

12. Olman: 20.

13. Benjamin S. Bloom, ed., *Taxonomy of Educational Objectives I: Cognitive Domain* (New York: David McKay Company, Inc. 1956).

14. National Commission on Excellence in Education, *A Nation at Risk: The Imperative for Educational Reform* (Washington, D.C.: U.S. Department of Education, April 1983): 18.

15. Gene I. Maeroff, "Teaching of Writing Gets New Push," *The New York Times Education Winter Survey*, Section 12, 8 January 1984: 36.

16. Olman: 20.

17. One good set of early numbers can be found in Quincy Alvin W. Rohrbach, *Non-Athletic Student Activities in the Secondary School.* (Philadelphia: Westbrook Publishing Co., 1925), especially 205-207. The information about school newspapers is only a part of a more extensive study of extracurricular activities, and the methodology is not well-described; nevertheless, the study from an earlier time does contain interesting summaries of newspaper size and format, content categories and general disposition of space, frequency of publication, cost per copy, and staff size. Also see Guy Montrose Whipple, ed., *Twenty-Fifth Yearbook of the National Society for the Study of Education, Part II: Extra-Curricular Activities* (Bloomington, IL: Public School Publishing Co., 1926).

18. John Robert Blinn, "A Comparison of Selected Writing Skills of High School Journalism and Non-journalism Students," *Dissertation Abstracts International* 43, Section A, p. 3,146 (Ph.D. dissertation, Ohio University, 1982).

19. John Bowen, "More Than a Basic," *School Press Review* (Winter 1984): 20.

20. Joint Committee on Instructional Development and Academic Articulation in Iowa, *Educational Excellence for Iowa* (Des Moines: Iowa State Board of Regents and the Department of Public Instruction, February 1984).

21. Dennis Alan Cripe, "We Are What We Write," *School Press Review* (Winter 1984): 21.

22. Elbert K. Fretwell, *Extra-Curricular Activities in Secondary Schools* (Boston: Houghton Mifflin Co., 1931).

23. Jim Willis, *Journalism: State of the Art* (New York: Praeger, 1990): 7.

CHAPTER 2

GRADES, ACT TESTS, ATTITUDES, AND INVOLVEMENT

Chapter Highlights

- Journalism kids do better in 10 of 12 major academic areas.
- Journalism kids write better in 17 of 20 comparisons of collegiate writing.
- Journalism kids value high school Journalism more highly than required English courses in fulfilling major language arts competencies.
- Journalism kids are "doers" in schools—they're more involved in co-curricular and community activities.

Do journalism students make better high school and college grades than their peers with no newspaper or yearbook staff experience? Do they earn higher scores than their peers on the ACT standardized examinations? Is their writing better? Is their opinion about Journalism's worth in language arts more positive than non-Journalism students' attitudes about their own English classes? Are they more involved in their school and off-campus communities?

Yes.

During the past decade, studies have shown a relationship between participation in high school journalism and performance on widely respected measures of academic success. While we are not prepared to ascribe direct causation, we have gathered and examined

19

a wide body of evidence that, if nothing else, points to the worth of involvement in journalism and publications as an outlet for talented language arts students. Do these results mean merely that kids who are more literate in the first place tend to develop an interest in journalism, and then do well in all their studies, or do they mean that taking part in journalistic work sharpens all their literacies and thus helps them to do better in all their intellectual endeavors? Perhaps in time, and with further study of the direct effects of taking a high school Journalism class, we will be able to draw the causal relationships more tightly.[1]

In a study conducted by the Journalism Education Association, an independent variable was selected for analysis, Item #143 from the ACT Student Profile Section that was completed when the student took the ACT Assessment as a high school junior or senior. The item was listed in the "Of Class Accomplishments" section, and students had to respond "yes, applies to me" or "no, does not apply to me" to the following item: "Worked on the staff of a school paper or yearbook." Altogether, 19,249 students who went on to 10 U.S. colleges and universities took part in the study, and 4,798 of them had served on the staff of a school newspaper or yearbook.

College and High School Grades, Standardized Tests

When former high school publications staff members went to college, they had significantly higher freshman overall grade-point averages as well as higher grades in their first English courses, as presented in Graph 2.1. While it is true that the overall GPA is close, 2.67 for publications staffers and 2.62 for non-staffers, the difference is statistically significant. Also, in their first college English course, former high school staff members had average grades of 2.82 compared with non-staffers' 2.71.

To test the validity of the findings further, Journalism Education Association commissioners and ACT officials drew another entirely different sample of freshmen from 11 other colleges and universities.[2]

In the second sample, similar results occurred, as presented on the right side of Graph 2.1. Among 6,251 students who had taken "English Composition" as their initial language arts course as college freshmen, those who had taken Journalism earned an overall 2.61 GPA, whereas the non-staffers earned only 2.51 as cumulative averages. In their first college composition course, students with high school publications backgrounds averaged 2.66 compared with non-staffers' 2.56. All these differences were, once again, statistically significant. The replication of the test verified that the differences, though small, were real. Students who had worked on a high school newspaper or yearbook had higher overall freshman college GPAs and higher grades in their first college English course, usually English Composition.

Graph 2.1

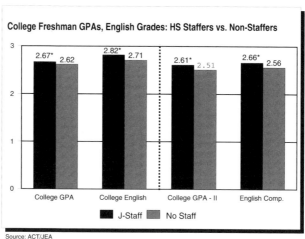

College Freshman GPAs, English Grades: HS Staffers vs. Non-Staffers

Source: ACT/JEA

(left side) J-Staff n = 4,634   No Staff n = 13,869
(right side) J-Staff n = 1,643   No Staff n = 4,294
* All Differences between J-Staff and No Staff experience significant beyond .001 level

Journalism staff members also had significantly higher high school grades than did their non-staffer peers.

In every area of analysis, the newspaper and yearbook staffers did better in their school work than did their counterparts. Graph 2.2 shows the publications students had better final-course high school grades in English, social studies, mathematics, and science. Overall GPAs for these final courses were also averaged for a cumulative score, which was also significantly higher for those with publications experience. The four-course high school average for those with publications experience was 3.31 on a 4.0 scale, compared with a mean of 3.20 for those without newspaper or yearbook experience. The high school English final-course mean grade was 3.45 for the group with publications background whereas those without that experience averaged 3.26. In social studies, the journalism staffers earned 3.49, compared with 3.36 for the non-staffers. Also, newspaper and yearbook staff members earned slightly better grades in mathematics (3.1) than did the non-staffers (3.04). In science, staffers earned 3.3 GPAs in their final course compared with non-staffers' 3.22. In all five of these comparisons, differences are statistically significant, even though they seem numerically small.

Graph 2.2

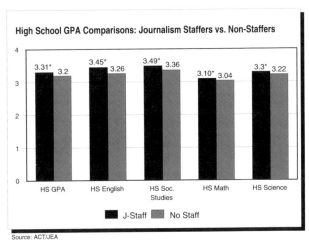

High School GPA Comparisons: Journalism Staffers vs. Non-Staffers

Source: ACT/JEA

* Difference significant beyond the .001 level

J-Staff n = 4,798   No Staff n = 14,451

Another measure of scholastic ability and potential is the ACT test, often used as one of many criteria in the college admissions and placement process.[3] Once again, high school journalism students with newspaper or yearbook staff experience performed well, with significantly higher scores on the ACT Composite, the ACT English, and the ACT Social Studies components. They had significantly lower scores on the ACT Mathematics Assessment, however, and they scored about the same as their non-publications peers on the ACT Science Assessment. Graph 2.3 shows differences between the two groups across the five ACT scores.

Graph 2.3

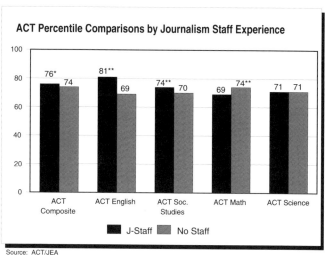

ACT Percentile Comparisons by Journalism Staff Experience

Source: ACT/JEA

* Difference significant beyond .01

** Difference significant beyond .001

J-Staff n = 4,798   No Staff n = 14,451

Newspaper and yearbook staffers who went on to college earned percentile scores about two points higher than non-publications students in the 10 colleges and universities used in the main part of this study. We double-verified the statistical significance of this finding by comparing it with a smaller sample of students from the 11 colleges referred to at the end of Endnote 2. In that study of 6,251 students, the ACT Composite score was four percentile points higher for publications staffers than it was for non-publications students. In the analysis of the larger sample, publications staffers scored in the 76th percentile, whereas non-staffers averaged in the 74th.

The largest difference, perhaps understandably, was in the ACT English score, where former publications staffers achieved the 81st percentile, compared with non-staffers in the 69th—a 12-point difference.

Graph 2.3 also shows the ACT Social Studies Assessment is four points higher for publications students (74th percentile) compared with non-journalism people (70th percentile). Mathematics was the only statistically significant lower score for publications students at the 69th percentile compared with 74th for non-staffers. ACT

Natural Science scores were about the same for each group (71st percentile).

Among the 12 major bases for academic comparison thus far, we note that those students who have completed at least one year of college and who have been on the staff of a high school newspaper or yearbook earned significantly higher scores than did their non-publications counterparts in 10 areas, namely, cumulative freshman GPA; first college English course; mean score of the final four high school courses in English, social studies, mathematics and natural science; final high school English grade; final high school social studies grade; final high school mathematics grade; final high school natural science grade; ACT Composite score; ACT English score; and ACT Social Studies score.

In only one of 12 comparisons—the ACT Mathematics score—did the group with high school publications experience show a negative significant difference. In the ACT Natural Science assessment, no significant differences were observed, as shown in Graph 2.3.

While journalism students did not fare so well in the ACT Mathematics subtest as did their non-publications peers, they did receive significantly higher mathematics grades in their final high school math courses. Similarly, no difference was found between ACT Natural Science scores between the two groups, yet journalism students had higher science grades in high school than did their non-journalism counterparts.

The discontinuity of scores in math and science could be explained in a couple of ways. Publications students are high achievers who may have applied themselves harder to mathematics and science in high school, even though their natural abilities and acquired knowledge in those areas were not so well-developed. We also think it could mean that publications students did not take advanced-level high school mathematics or science courses. By not taking elective advanced courses in these areas, or by taking a minimum number of math and science courses in high school, publications students might have been able to earn higher grades. Whatever the case, when they took the ACT Assessment, either their low math aptitude or lack of preparation caught up with them.

In the next phase of the analysis, we added the following items from the ACT Student Profile Section to the 12 academic measures just described: participated in high school radio/television; number of semesters taken of high school English; had high school creative writing published in a public magazine or book; wrote original but unpublished work in high school; worked on the staff of a high school newspaper or yearbook; won a high school literary prize for creative writing; had poems, stories, or articles published in a non-school publication; had creative writing published in a high school literary magazine or paper; and had poems, stories or articles published in a school publication.

The seven items related to out-of-class writing accomplishments were combined as one independent variable. Others were ACT Composite score; the average of the final four high school grades earned in English, social studies, mathematics and natural science; and the number of semesters that the student had taken in English. These were used to predict both the first college-English course grade and the overall GPA for freshman year.

The best predictor of success in the first college English grade was the ACT Composite score, with the high school grade point average almost as strong a predictor. Also significantly strong in predicting English class success was the out-of-class writing accomplishments component.[4]

Likewise, when the same four independent variables were used to predict freshman-year cumulative GPA, the high school GPA surfaced as the strongest predictor, followed by the ACT Composite score. Neither the out-of-class writing accomplishments nor the number of semesters of high school English were significantly related. When out-of-class writing accomplishments were separated into their seven components, and used as predictors, none surfaced as predictive of the college outcomes under consideration. That does not mean that they lacked scholastic or personal value to the students either while they were still in high school or once they got to college.

For one thing, none of the seven—including that of serving on the staff of a high school newspaper or yearbook—is related to a specific class accomplishment or activity. Because our data from ACT did not include an item directly related to a course called "Journalism," as opposed to one called "English," we could not test effects that having taken such a course might have had on this part of the analysis. Nor were we able to examine whether high school course work in similar areas such as creative writing, poetry, short-story writing, or other forms of language arts was contributive to greater academic success.

Our suspicions are strong, however, that the interactions among Journalism and other similar language arts classes, but especially classes in Journalism, do affect academic progress positively. Other parts of our study provide evidence that students value highly their classes in high school Journalism, especially when compared with non-Journalism students' attitudes about their language arts courses as preparation for college-level English and other classes.

Comparisons of Collegiate Writing Samples

Do beginning college students with high school publications experience do better on various types of written communication than do those students without secondary school Journalism staff backgrounds?

Yes.

About 1,200 college freshmen from 18 colleges and universities were involved in taking ACT assessments geared towards measuring their knowledge and abilities in general education. Three writing samples were collected from each student as part of a battery of tests taken early in the first semester. Samples were graded by English professors, and the tests were found to be both reliable and valid in measuring students' overall writing effectiveness as well as their abilities at writing for a specific audience, organizing well, and using proper language skills. In 17 of 20 major comparisons examined here, students with high school newspaper or yearbook staff experience had higher writing scores.[5]

Eighteen colleges and universities were randomly selected for which ACT had both Assessment Standard Research Service Records from high school testing as well as COMP (College Outcome Measures Program) Prospectus data.[6] The latter was developed by

ACT in 1976 both to assist post-secondary schools in efforts to improve general education and to build support for their programs. With assistance from faculty at more than 160 colleges and universities, ACT personnel identified educational outcomes thought to be critical to those students' success at graduating from colleges. Several writing components were integral parts of the program.

COMP measures process areas (communicating, solving problems, clarifying values) as well as content areas (functioning within social institutions, using science and technology, using the arts). The writing portion of the instrument incorporates these areas through three writing passages. Scoring was done at each of the 18 schools in the study by faculty members who taught writing. A sample of those writing passages was rechecked by ACT officials. The degree of agreement among raters is high, with coefficients of interrater agreement typically ranging from .80 to .95.[7]

The Assessment consists of three 20-minute writing assignments based on audio-tape stimuli material to which students listen. Each tape is two- to four-minutes long. Areas covered are social science, science, and the fine arts. Three individual letters were written, one for each topic. One letter is personal, another to a U.S. senator, and the third to a radio station. While practical in nature, the letters (writing passages) were not journalistic, but they were meant to measure standard writing competencies thought by a consensus of educators to be important for college-age students. ACT reported that the Writing Assessment provides college and university faculty with diagnostic information as well as comparisons with college freshmen and seniors in high schools at other participating institutions. New forms are introduced annually, and three versions of the Assessment are used each year.

Each writing sample includes a total possible score of 31, with maximums being 10 in Audience, 10 in Organization and 11 in Language Skills. For reporting purposes here, we have converted the raw scores into percentiles to distinguish levels between those with high school journalism staff background and those without that experience.

Evaluators were prompted to grade each section holistically with the following criteria in mind: *Audience:* appropriateness of writing form for situation and intended audience; consistency in adherence to audience perspective; reference to common experiences; use of humor, tact, flattery, and the like. *Organization:* develops the points called for in a direct fashion, with control of language and transition; written on at least two levels of abstraction. *Language:* writes in a precise or in a lively manner, with originality and effort to use interesting or clever phrases, and few scribal errors.

ACT provides the following general instructions to evaluators:

> *The examinee should show an awareness of audience and create a "voice" with a focus on explanation and persuasion: there should be a sense of organization and development, skillful use of language and sentence structuring devices (such as antithesis or parallelism), and no obtrusive scribal errors (e.g., spelling, punctuation, paragraphing and form). A special caution: No credit should be given for being "right," and no penalty should be given for a position or attitude that you cannot accept, as long as it seems to represent what the writer intended. Try to avoid credit or penalties for penmanship.*

In the three samples of writing used for analysis here, one involved marriage roles, in which writers had to write a letter to a mythical friend about defined roles of two other friends whose wedding was recent. Another sample required writers to respond to a four-minute radio news broadcast involving the federal government's development of synthetic fuels versus conservation allocations. A letter was to be written to the writer's U.S. senator supporting one side or the other. In the third writing sample, students were to listen to a two-minute selection of bluegrass music and then write the station's management, encouraging them not to drop the weekly program of traditional music.

Students coming from high school publications programs did significantly better on the overall COMP Composite Writing component than did those without journalistic background, as is evident in Graph 2.4. In the same graph, one can see that when individual parts of the Composite score are analyzed, we find that Journalism staffers did significantly better in both Audience and Language scores while scoring slightly better on the Organization portion. All 1,161 students in this part of the study had taken the COMP tests early in their freshman year of college; thus, effects of having taken a college-level writing course do not figure into the results. These students' high school writing experiences were the most likely formal academic influences on their performance on the COMP Writing component. These results will be valuable to colleges later when students are evaluated as sophomores and seniors—the standard practice among participating ACT institutions. In this study, however, results are of value because they indicate one of the first after-high school records of writing ability.

Graph 2.4

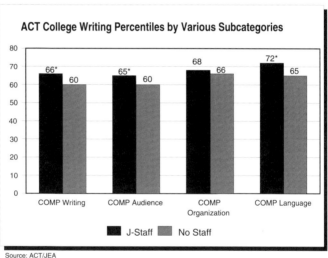

ACT College Writing Percentiles by Various Subcategories

Source: ACT/JEA

* Difference significant beyond .05 level

J-Staff n = 371   No Staff n = 790

Because publications staffers have better standardized scores in the several areas already analyzed—including the ACT English Usage component—we were fearful that these writing results were reflective of better ability generally. So in the next phase of the analysis, we divided the students according to four subgroups, based on their performance on the English Assessment of the ACT test taken while in high school. In this way, we grouped the students according to generally recognized language arts knowledge and potential, and then we compared each group's early collegiate writing samples. By looking at the results in this way, the ACT COMP Total Writing score would be more reflective of general high school writing experiences, including work on high school publications.

In Graphs 2.5 through 2.8, the following ACT English percentiles were used to group students: 1-42 Low; 43-77 Fair; 78-94 Good; and 95-99 High.

Graph 2.5

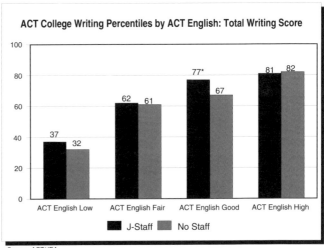

Source: ACT/JEA

*Significant beyond .005 level

J-Staff n = 57 low, 194 fair, 84 good, 36 high

No Staff n = 163 low, 404 fair, 162 good, 61 high

Graph 2.6

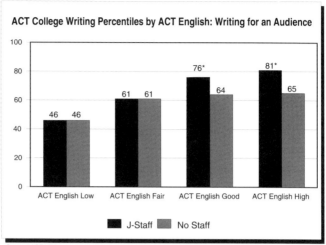

ACT College Writing Percentiles by ACT English: Writing for an Audience

Source: ACT/JEA

*Significant beyond the .05 level
J-Staff n = 57 low, 194 fair, 84 good, 36 high
No Staff n = 163 low, 404 fair, 162 good, 61 high

Graph 2.7

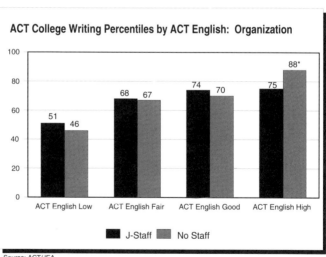

ACT College Writing Percentiles by ACT English: Organization

Source: ACT/JEA

*Difference significant beyond .03
J-Staff n = 57 low, 194 fair, 84 good, 36 high
No Staff n = 163 low, 404 fair, 162 good, 61 high

Graph 2.8

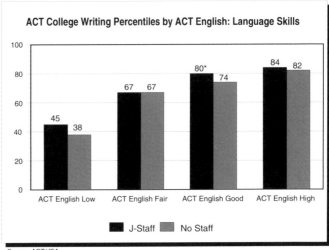

ACT College Writing Percentiles by ACT English: Language Skills

Source: ACT/JEA
*Difference significant at .001
J-Staff n = 57 low, 194 fair, 84 good, 36 high
No Staff n = 163 low, 404 fair, 162 good, 61 high

To summarize writing abilities as seen in Graphs 2.4 through 2.8, we have observed that in 20 major comparisons of freshman college student writing abilities, those with high school publications experience earned higher scores in 17 of 20 categories. In seven of those 17 categories, the staffers' scores were significantly higher. In only one of three scores in which non-staffers' scores were higher did we find a significantly higher difference.

We contend that writing experiences enjoyed by students in high school newspaper or yearbook efforts provide realism, cogency, relevance, timeliness and appropriateness. Because of their obvious applicability to real-world problem-solving, primary and secondary research skills, critical thinking and communication with peers, journalistic writing assignments in many ways fulfill the very competencies often espoused by English educators. Without these built-in objectives in their traditional high school language arts courses, non-staffers may find their writing experiences to be less meaningful and less frequent. Based on this research, the extent that former Journalism students outperform non-Journalism students when both groups are challenged with writing for general audiences at the beginning of their college careers, it seems that journalistic writing experiences teach skills transferable to other writing.

Journalism Students' Attitudes about Language Arts Courses

Our comparisons thus far have involved differences between staff members of high school newspapers or yearbooks because data were not available on the ACT Assessment that distinguished between staffers and those who took Journalism as a for-credit class. In this next segment, however, we examine the results of an ACT Language Arts Experiences Survey that measures student opinions about all of their language arts coursework in high school—required English, Journalism, and English electives such as speech, debate and drama.

Do college students who took Journalism as a class in high school think that it fulfilled well-defined language arts competencies better than required English or English elective courses? Do their free-response answers to an open-ended question support this point of view?

Yes.

Part of the work of the JEA Commission on the Role of Journalism in Secondary Education involved constructing a survey that measured opinions of college students about all of their language arts experiences, not just Journalism. The survey was refined and sent out under the auspices of ACT so that a Journalism bias would not be detected. Students understood that they were reacting to all of their formal language arts courses in high school.

The 29 items selected for the survey were based on generally accepted language arts competencies found in various national and state commissions examining curriculum reform.[8] For each of the 29 competencies, students were asked to rate their experiences in any of three categories that applied to their high school language arts classes: Required (Standard) English, Journalism Courses, and English Electives. Each was rated on a three-point scale with "3" being "helped a lot," "2" being "helped a little" and "1" being "did not help." All of the students in the survey had been on the staff of a student yearbook or newspaper in high school, but only 143 of 558 in the study had taken a class in Journalism, 125 had received credit for newspaper lab, and another 159 took yearbook lab for credit. In most of the comparisons between Required English and English Electives, non-Journalism students outnumber those with Journalism course experience by about a 4:1 ratio because several people who took a Journalism class also took newspaper or yearbook for credit as well.

Of 2,687 surveys mailed, 558 of those returned were usable.[9] The return rate was low because permanent addresses were used on the mailing, and many of the students in the study were away at college, causing parents/guardians to have to forward the mail to them. A postage-paid return envelope was provided.

Because of the low return rate, respondents were not typical of the sample selected. Nevertheless, the study was of much value because we found that those who answered the survey were in many ways academically superior to those who did not respond. The respondents were college students who have significantly higher scores in the following areas: ACT Composite scores; ACT scores in English, mathematics, social studies and natural science; high school GPA in English; and first-year college overall GPA. Another characteristic of those who answered the survey was that they tended to be female non-minority students. While a more representative sample would be ideal, this analysis is of value because it signifies the attitudes and ideas of academically superior students who have already achieved success in college.

As shown in Graph 2.9, overall results of the 29-item survey of language arts competencies show that students who had taken high school Journalism classes perceived those courses to have fulfilled more adequately language arts objectives than did any other classes. The highest rating on Graph 2.9, Journalism, reached 65.9 points. Those same Journalism students reported that Required English courses helped them fulfill language arts competencies with a rating of 60.8, and they rated their English Electives at 60.7. From the other group of students—those who had not taken a Journalism class—ratings for Required English classes were highest, with a total of 62.4, and English Electives totalled 61. Those same students who took a yearbook or newspaper lab for credit but who did not take a course in Journalism gave those lab experiences the lowest score of any comparison, 56.8.

Graph 2.9

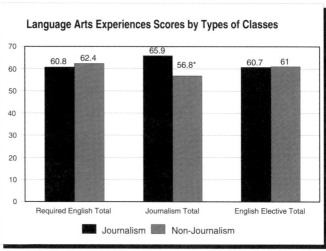

Language Arts Experiences Scores by Types of Classes

Source: ACT/JEA

*Students who took Publications Lab only, not a class
Journalism Experience n = 143 in first two comparisons; n = 88 in third
Non-Journalism n = 415 in first comparison, 162 in second, 240 in third

When ratings of competencies garnered in various language arts classes are totalled, it becomes evident that college students who have taken high school Journalism claim that it has contributed to the development of their overall competencies better than any other English classes.

Observe, further, that those students who did not take a Journalism class were more satisfied with Required English and English Electives than were Journalism students who took the same courses. The lowest rating observed in Graph 2.9—Publications Lab—is not a Journalism class per se. The low rating would indicate that these students believed that publications lab experiences for credit did not do as good a job at fulfilling the 29 language arts competencies as did either Required English or English Electives. Although those who took a Journalism class rated it more highly than any other group rated any other language arts classes, and thus one might argue that these classes might easily fulfill high school

35

English requirements or electives, some caution needs to be applied in this area when looking at publications labs for credit when they are not accompanied by a Journalism class.

Table 2.1 shows the average ratings of each of the 29 language arts competencies, with "3" being highest and "1" being lowest. Students who had taken Journalism rated it best in 15 of 29 competency areas. In one other area, Journalism tied with Required English as a top competency. Those same students with a Journalism class selected Required English as best in eight of the 29 competencies, and they chose five items as best in the English Elective category.

Table 2.1: ACT Language Arts Experiences Survey Raw Scores by High School Courses

Competency	Standard English		Journalism		English Electives	
	Journalism (n=143)	Non-Journ. (n=415)	Class (n=143)	J-Lab Only (n=159)	Journalism (n=88)	Non-Journ. (n=240)
WRITING						
1. Ability to develop topic ideas for writing	2.41	2.42	2.41*	1.98	2.21	2.45
5. Ability to vary writing style for different readers and purposes	2.02	2.07	2.51*	2.05	2.21	2.42**
8. Development of a writing style applicable to either fiction or non-fiction	2.15	1.99	1.93**	1.64	2.01	2.00
9. Ability to write non-fiction concisely, with clarity, accuracy, and objectivity	2.17	2.19	2.41*	1.97	1.94	1.97
19. Ability to write persuasively about issues related to school and non-school issues	2.02	2.14	2.54*	2.19	2.34	2.36
EDITING						
2. Ability to organize a piece of writing for a specific purpose and audience	2.42	2.44	2.56*	2.12	2.48	2.60
3. Ability to organize, select, and relate ideas, outline them, and develop them into coherent paragraphs	2.65	2.63	2.38*	1.97	2.20	2.38
6. Ability to improve writing through self-editing—correcting errors, and rewriting sentences and paragraphs	2.26	2.12	2.65*	2.24	1.98	2.00
10. Ability to edit, for a specific audience, the writing of others	1.78	1.87	2.57*	2.15	1.79	2.03
GATHERING INFORMATION / USE OF SOURCES						
7. Ability to gather information from primary and secondary sources, to write a report using this research, to quote, paraphrase and summarize accurately, and to cite sources properly	2.42	2.49	2.39*	1.99	2.12	2.34
15. Ability to identify and comprehend the main and subordinate ideas in lectures and discussions and to report accurately what others have said	2.03	2.08	2.37*	2.02	2.11	2.17

Competency	Standard English		Journalism		English Electives	
	Journalism (n=143)	Non-Journ. (n=415)	Class (n=143)	J-Lab Only (n=159)	Journalism (n=88)	Non-Journ. (n=240)
CRITICAL THINKING						
11. Ability to identify and comprehend the main and subordinate ideas in a written work and to summarize them	2.52	2.45	2.05**	1.75	1.84	2.00**
12. Ability to separate personal opinions and assumptions from those of a writer	1.99	2.15	2.37*	1.89	1.93	2.10
13. Ability to engage critically and constructively in the exchange of ideas, particularly during class discussions and conferences with instructors	2.11	2.19	2.22	2.00	2.36	2.36
14. Ability to answer and ask questions coherently and concisely, and to follow spoken instructions	2.16	2.26	2.31***	2.08	2.11	2.27
17. Ability to identify and formulate problems and to propose and evaluate ways to solve them	1.84	1.86	2.06	1.95	2.05	2.01
18. Ability to recognize and use inductive and deductive reasoning, and to recognize errors in reasoning	1.90	1.92	1.85***	1.61	1.88	1.96
20. Ability to draw reasonable conclusions from information found in various sources, whether written, spoken, or in tables and graphs	2.13	2.24	2.24*	1.84	2.07	2.14
21. Ability to comprehend, develop, and use concepts and generalization	2.41	2.38	2.13**	1.82	2.12	2.20
23. Ability to understand and synthesize main ideas from reading, lectures, and other academic experiences; and to apply information to new situations	2.29	2.28	2.12*	1.77	2.18	2.16
LANGUAGE USE						
4. Ability to write Standard English sentences in correct sentence structure using appropriate verb forms, punctuation, capitalization, possessives, plurals, word choice, and correct spelling	2.67	2.74	2.09*	1.79	1.79	1.83
16. Ability to use appropriate spoken language with diverse individuals and groups	1.94	2.07	2.12*	1.82	2.44***	2.33
24. Ability to develop specialized vocabularies, and to use them for reading, speaking, listening, computing, and studying	2.36	2.33	2.33*	1.93	2.45	2.26
AFFECTIVE DOMAIN						
22. Ability to accept constructive criticism and learn from it	2.26	2.37	2.51	2.36	2.67	2.64
25. Ability to communicate with peers and older people on a professional level	2.04	2.11	2.50	2.31	2.53	2.47
26. Ability to deal with conflicts while working with other people on a project	1.64	1.81	2.51	2.51	2.29	2.19
27. Development of a sense of responsibility, leadership, and personal maturity	1.85	1.88	2.66	2.56	2.40	2.31
28. Development of self-confidence, personal worth, and self-esteem	1.99	1.98	2.59	2.46	2.57	2.52
29. Development of a sense of accomplishment and involvement in the school and community	1.72	1.84	2.65	2.60	2.32	2.23

* within-group chi square significant beyond the .001 level
** within-group chi square significant beyond the .01 level
*** within-group chi square significant beyond the .05 level

The following areas of Table 2.1 are those in which students thought that Journalism best fulfilled their high school general language arts competencies:

2. Ability to organize a piece of writing for a specific purpose and audience

5. Ability to vary writing style for different readers and purposes

6. Ability to improve writing through self-editing—correcting errors, and rewriting sentences and paragraphs

9. Ability to write non-fiction concisely, with clarity, accuracy and objectivity

10. Ability to edit, for a specific audience, the writing of others

12. Ability to separate personal opinions and assumptions from those of a writer

14. Ability to answer and ask questions coherently and concisely, and to follow spoken instructions

15. Ability to identify and comprehend the main and subordinate ideas in lectures and discussions and to report accurately what others have said

17. Ability to identify and formulate problems and to propose and evaluate ways to solve them

19. Ability to write persuasively about issues related to school and non-school issues

20. Ability to draw reasonable conclusions from information found in various sources, whether written, spoken or displayed in tables and graphs

26. Ability to deal with conflicts while working with other people on a project

27. Development of a sense of responsibility, leadership and personal maturity

28. Development of self-confidence, personal worth and self-esteem

29. Development of a sense of accomplishment and involvement in the school and community

Journalism students also rated competency 1 on the survey as a tie between Required English and Journalism: Ability to develop topic ideas for writing.

Students who took Journalism rated nine of the remaining 13 areas as their second choices in fulfilling language arts competencies (numbers 3, 4, 7, 11, 13, 16, 21, 22, and 25 of Table 2.1). In only four of the 29 competencies did students who took Journalism rate those courses lowest of the three areas—numbers 8, 18, 23 and 24 of Table 2.1.

Within each of the three language arts areas examined— Required English, Journalism, and English Electives—chi-square tests were used to examine differences of answering patterns in the three-point scale between those students who took Journalism as a class compared with those students who had not. The most notable number of significant differences occurred within the Journalism course area. Twenty-one of 29 competencies proved to be statistically significant (numbers 1-12, 14-16, 18-21 and 23-24 of Table 2.1).

A possible explanation for such consistent differences, especially compared with relatively few found in either Required English or English Electives categories, might be that when Journalism is taught as a regular class, the teacher is most likely to hold certification or other expertise in Journalism. In many schools where this is not the case, administrators might not allow a formal class to be offered, or might call the class by some other name so as to avoid accreditation or state department difficulties. Names like "Publications," "Practical English," "Yearbook," "Newspaper," or "English Practicum" are common.

In these classes, which are often heavy in laboratory exercises or production of actual school publications, students might lack the guidance of a qualified Journalism teacher or be so consumed with production emphasis that they are not perceiving that many of the 29 competencies chosen as language arts objectives are being met. Also, these students have *not* had a formal Journalism course before their publications lab experience, and they have missed out in learning fundamental principles, theories, discipline, and practices available in a traditional classroom situation.

This does not mean that school publications are not valuable as co-curricular activities. Information presented above shows the worth of co-curricular activities and points toward significantly better performance of publications students performing in several academic areas in high school, on college entrance examinations, and in the first year of college. This means that students do not believe that publications experience alone is an adequate substitute for an academic class in Journalism when it comes to fulfilling language arts competencies; neither do they see it as being as meaningful as Required English or English Electives. We can reasonably conclude that while Journalism as a class in language arts is the strongest of all in meeting the 29 competencies, the same competencies are least met through publications experience unaccompanied, or not preceded, by a formal class.

In order to get a more simplified and unified picture of the 29 competencies at work, we subdivided them into six logical categories, each of which comprised two or more of the 29 items. Table 2.2 shows the configuration after totalling points within each of the following subdivisions:

Writing: numbers 1, 5, 8, 9, 19

Editing: numbers 2, 3, 6, 10

Gathering Information and Use of Sources: numbers 7 and 15

Critical Thinking: numbers 11, 12, 13, 14 17, 18, 20, 21, 23

Language Use: numbers 4, 16, 24

Affective Domain: numbers 22, 25, 26, 27, 28, 29

Journalism students rated four of the six category areas as having fulfilled competencies better than they did Required English or English Electives: Writing, Editing, Gathering/Use of Sources, and Affective Domain. It was a close second in Critical Thinking to Required English, and it was third in Language Use, but in this area it was almost the same as English Electives and fairly close to Required English. In the two areas in which Journalism courses did not finish first, Required English was the top choice. Perhaps because the Journalism course experience was so strong in fulfilling the competencies, Journalism students' attitudes about other language arts courses were relatively less positive.

Table 2.2: ACT Language Arts Experiences Survey Total Competency Scores by High School Courses

Competency	Standard English Journalism (n=143)	Standard English Non-Journ. (n=415)	Journalism Class (n=143)	Journalism J-Lab Only (n=159)	English Electives Journalism (n=88)	English Electives Non-Journ. (n=240)
Writing	10.53	10.62	11.35	9.34***	10.20	10.38
Editing	8.89	9.20	9.84	8.01***	7.99	8.53
Gathering / Use of Sources	4.39	4.48	4.64	3.90***	4.15	4.34
Critical Thinking	18.85	19.37	18.58	15.94***	17.42	17.89
Language Use	6.85	7.04	6.31	5.36***	6.33	6.03
Affective Domain	11.27	11.64	15.15	14.28*	14.63	13.85

* t test difference significant beyond the .05 level
*** t test difference significant beyond the .001 level

In the open-response part of the survey, students were asked to react to the following: "If you have suggestions for teachers of the high school language arts courses that would benefit future college students, please list your ideas in the space below." Of the 558 responses, 269 of them included at least one suggestion, and several included more than one.

Of those people who mentioned "Journalism" experiences, all 15 statements seem to be positive. One student wrote about the value of a yearbook experience as it related to expressing complex ideas in concrete terms and in doing research:

> *Writing style in college seems a lot different than in high school. In research analysis we have learned to write complex tasks (like factorial design experiment) in simple terms for anyone to understand. In high school we wrote with much more fillers and "jargon." College professors frown on that. I wish I had done more research in high school. I would have been more prepared. Yearbook has prepared me for college way more than any English class did.*

Another student, pleased that high school journalism preparation had been good for using grammar and a wide vocabulary, found that Journalism was helpful in applying college-level styles of writing to term papers and analysis papers.

Other important college-level abilities were nurtured through electives as well. One student wrote about debate, forensics, and Journalism in terms of immediate and long-term values:

The classes that most helped me not only throughout high school but also well into college were debate and forensics. There is no substitute for the experience these programs give the student in composing thoughts quickly and effectively, or in appearing in an interview or public speaking scenario. However, it is also important to realize that these programs force the student to accept responsibility—the instructor cannot do the student's work for him (or her). I believe that this aspect of debate and forensics can and must be applied to the "Standard English courses." It is the individual responsibility that Journalism class places upon the student that helps that student most. It is the responsibility placed on the student that best prepares him (or her) most not only for post-secondary education but also for "real life."

Another student thought English should not be taught "straight from books" but should focus on basic structures for each year of the curriculum. Other structures or types of writing included "organizing skills—spatial, chronological, etc.; choice of wording—poetic, technical, etc.; and various writing styles—business, journalism, informal, fiction, etc."

Writing of college research papers was mentioned by several students who had taken Journalism in high school. One wrote:

Students should be required to write papers often so they are prepared to do so in college. A section teaching them how to do library research would also be helpful. I recommend taking a Journalism class and also stressing more reading with class discussion. These are all helpful once you graduate whether you continue school or work.

Others had advice concerning emphasis areas or approaches to the handling of the classroom:

Emphasize a little more on grammar and writing—a little less on literature. Get students ready for college, and don't be so lenient on things such as writing and term papers. Teach students the proper way of writing these things. Journalism, Newspaper and Yearbook help a lot in learning the proper way to do these things; therefore, all three should be counted as a credit.

Similarly, one student wrote that Journalism and English Elective courses helped more than Required English: "I suggest incorporating these language arts into Standard English courses for those students who would not choose electives."

Others compared Required English and Journalism with respect to areas in the affective domain—interesting classes, broadening perspectives, and the like. One student wrote:

Teachers of Standard English classes seemed apathetic about the class—it was not challenging. I had Basic English which was required freshman year, then electives such as Speech, Journalism, and Debate for the last three years. I learned more from the elective classes because the teachers seemed more involved and the work more involved and interesting.

Another student thought Required English courses "tried to cover too many things in one term." The most beneficial courses for this person were electives "such as British Literature and Newspaper. (These were also the most interesting courses.)"

Some students stressed the importance of co-curricular activities within the school because they broadened their outlooks and allowed them to relate what they were learning to non-school situations. One person wrote: "Encourage high school students to be involved with outside activities, such as Drama, Yearbook or Newspaper staff to broaden their opinions of people and the way we utilize the English language other than in the classroom. I was greatly involved, and it has helped me in my college career."

Along this line of reasoning, another student who did not take publications and co-curriculars for credit wrote: "The Required English classes I took helped me learn the basics—grammar, punctuation, etc., but I [had] learned that in grade school. High school English was a mere repetition. Working on Debate/Speech team and Newspaper/Yearbook for no credit is what helped me TREMENDOUSLY! (Need to put Elective English classes back in the system!)"

These few comments from respondents clearly support the more formal findings of the survey: Journalism and related publications experiences powerfully accomplish the learning objectives in the many aspects of literacy and communication that students so importantly need to learn for academic success in higher education and for personal and career success in life.

High School Accomplishments and Future Directions

Are these yearbook and newspaper staffers and journalism students more likely to be involved in other school activities than their non-publications peers? Are they more likely than non-staffers to choose communications as a major in college? Are they more likely to want some type of communications career following college?

Yes.

As one might expect, high school staffers are much more likely to serve on a collegiate publications staff than non-staffers from high school.[10] In fact, by a ratio of almost three-to-one, high school publications staff members indicate that they would like to serve on collegiate newspaper or yearbook staffs, as seen in the first comparison of Graph 2.10.

Graph 2.10

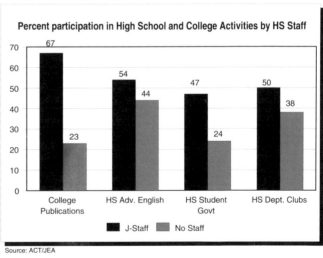

Percent participation in High School and College Activities by HS Staff

Source: ACT/JEA

J-Staff n = approximately 4,540   No Staff n = approximately 13,196

44

In other comparisons on the same graph, we note significant involvement by staff members compared with non-staffers when it comes to curricular and co-curricular activities. For example, staffers are much more likely to be enrolled—or to have been enrolled—in Advanced Placement, accelerated, or honors English courses. The second comparison in Graph 2.10 shows that while 54 percent of the staffers have been involved in these English courses, only 44 percent of the non-staffers have been.

Likewise, the third comparison in the same graph shows that almost half of all publications staffers were involved in student government during high school. Only 24 percent of their counterparts were involved in their schools' political process—nearly half as many.

And when it comes to departmental clubs like science club, foreign language club, math club, and so on, 50 percent of the journalism staffers were members compared with 38 percent of the non-staffers, as seen in the fourth comparison of Graph 2.10.

When other high school involvement in extracurriculars and leadership activities is considered, publications staffers seem to be much more active than non-staffers. For example, as seen in Graph 2.11, 52 percent of the newspaper and yearbook staffers were involved in special-interest groups like ski club, sailing club, judo club, card sections at athletic contests, drill team and the like. Only 39 percent of non-staffers were involved in those activities—a difference of about 13 percent.

In leadership positions within the school—besides publications staff membership—the journalism participants show a greater percentage of activity. The second comparison in Graph 2.11 indicates that 42 percent of the staffers were appointed or elected to student office while only 22 percent of the non-staffers were—a 20 point difference. Also, the third comparison of the graph shows that 48 percent of the staffers received an award or special recognition for leadership of some kind while in high school. Fully 14 percent fewer non-staffers received such recognition. The fourth comparison in Graph 2.11 shows that while 36 percent of the staff members were in a student movement to change institutional rules, procedures or policies, only 23 percent of the non-staffers were.

Graph 2.11

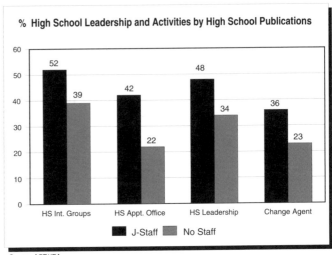

% High School Leadership and Activities by High School Publications

Source: ACT/JEA

J-Staff n = approximately 4,540   No Staff n = approximately 13,196

Some other indicators reflect the involvement in voluntary academic pursuits as well as in the community, as shown in Graph 2.12.

Graph 2.12

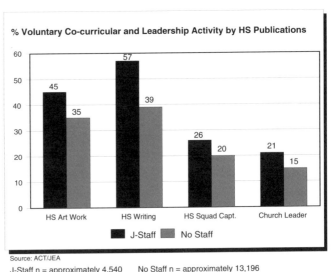

% Voluntary Co-curricular and Leadership Activity by HS Publications

Source: ACT/JEA

J-Staff n = approximately 4,540   No Staff n = approximately 13,196

For example, publications staffers are more likely to have finished a work of art—like painting, ceramics, sculpture, and the like—on their own time and not part of a course than were their non-staffer peers. Likewise, in the second comparison of Graph 2.12, we note that staffers compared with non-staffers—by a 57 percent to 39 percent margin—were more likely to have written an original but unpublished piece of creative writing on their own, and not part of a course.

Staffers are also more likely to have been appointed or elected cheerleader or captain of a varsity team than are non-staffers. In our study, 6 percent more publications students than non-staffers fit in this category, as noted in the third comparison of Graph 2.12. And in non-school involvement related to religious participation, 21 percent of the staffers indicate that they taught in a church or synagogue, or led a religious service on a regular basis, whereas only 15 percent of the non-staffers claim this type of religious leadership.

The tendency of high school yearbook and newspaper staff members to be more involved in various activities both in school and in the community can be seen in Graph 2.13.

Graph 2.13

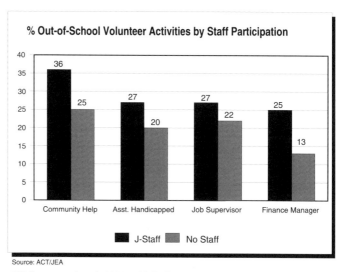

% Out-of-School Volunteer Activities by Staff Participation

Source: ACT/JEA

J-Staff n = approximately 4,535   No Staff n = approximately 13,187

About 36 percent of the staff members indicate that they were also active in programs that helped their communities or neighborhoods develop pride in themselves whereas only 25 percent of the non-staffers were similarly involved—a gap of 11 percentage points. Staffers also seem to be more involved in assisting children or adults who are handicapped mentally, physically, educationally or economically. The second comparison in Graph 2.13 shows that 27 percent of the staff members are involved in these programs while about 20 percent of non-staffers do volunteer work in this area.

Likewise, 5 percent more staffers say that while working at a job while in high school, they supervised the work of others—as shown in the third comparison of the graph. And, finally, by a margin of almost two to one, staffers seem to have managed the financial affairs of some organization while in high school compared with their non-publications peers.

Some Concluding Thoughts

While high school Journalism classes and publications activities are not designed primarily as vocational or career-influencing experiences, they nevertheless do attract a considerable number of students who later select Communications (journalism, radio or television broadcasting or advertising) as a collegiate major and as a likely career.

Our ACT data show that when a high school student has taken both Journalism as a course and has been a participant on a newspaper or yearbook staff, that person is 10 times more likely to choose Communications as a college major. About the same number indicate Communications as their career choice. Implications abound for college and university Journalism educators, media managers, and secondary school curriculum designers. University educators ought to realize the worth of high school Journalism and publications experience and accord them every possible consideration—in teacher-training, through outreach, and via other recruiting programs. From these high school programs come the next generation of college Communication majors and teachers.

Media executives ought to support secondary (and collegiate) Journalism programs because the talented and involved students described throughout this chapter are the next generation of professional journalists.

High school administrators, curriculum designers, and teachers ought to accord Journalism and publications activities a substantial place within the high school language arts curriculum. We have shown here that—whatever the reasons—publications staff members show significantly better achievement on an array of well-respected academic, individual, and social measurements than do their non-staff counterparts. Perhaps these better students naturally gravitate toward publications as an outlet for their talents. Perhaps their noted tendencies to be more active in school and community life also weigh heavily in their decisions to become involved with publications. In any event, Journalism kids do demonstrably better. Regardless of the motivations, the high degree of activity in intelligent, talented, and involved students has a correlative and reciprocating effect in Journalism students' other undertakings. Students who took a class called "Journalism" found it superior in meeting well-recognized language arts competencies than did either required English courses or other English electives. These indications from academically superior students affirm the worthiness of Journalism as a course at the heart of the language arts curriculum, not to be relegated to distant or second-class or adjunct status within the English curriculum, and not to be squeezed out during times of budget crunch. All too often, however, Journalism has been relegated to this less-than-noble place.

We propose that language arts department chairs and others involved in the English curriculum seriously consider re-evaluating any negative biases towards Journalism and school-publications activities, should such biases exist. Based on this solid statistical evidence, we can say that Journalism classes and staff work on high school newspapers and yearbooks are definitive educational experiences in students' secondary-school careers that not only carry over into higher education and future life but also make the difference for distinction and success while in high school itself.

NOTES ON CHAPTER 2

1. For a more complete analysis of the ACT study, see *High School Journalism Confronts Critical Deadline*. A Report by the Journalism Education Association Commission on the Role of Journalism in Secondary Education. Journalism Education Association: Manhattan, KS, 1987. All findings used with permission of that JEA Commission. Throughout this chapter, we are using data gathered from the American College Testing program.

2. Both sets of colleges and universities were randomly selected from among those schools that participated in ACT's Standard Research Service during 1983-1984. The majority of analyses involved 19,249 students from Auburn, Arizona State, Arkansas, Denver, Northern Illinois, Illinois, Kansas, Calvin College, Oklahoma, and Brigham Young. For verification purposes, a second set of institutions was selected from 11 participating institutions: St. Lukes (Iowa), Fort Hays (Kansas), Hutchinson Community College (Kansas), Benedictine College (Kansas), Michigan Christian, Holmes Junior College (Mississippi), Akron, Oklahoma State, Bob Jones University (South Carolina), Christian Brothers College (Tennessee), and Freed-Harman (Tennessee).

3. According to information provided by ACT in 1985, about 1 million high school juniors and seniors complete the ACT Assessment each year. The results are used by more than 2,700 colleges and universities, scholarship agencies, and state educational systems. Many of these institutions participate each year in ACT's research services, through which local normative data, predictive information, and college freshman class profiles are generated. It is the prevalent standardized test of this nature in 28 states.

4. For further description of this analysis, see Jack Dvorak, "Publications Experience as a Predictor of College Success," *Journalism Quarterly 66* (Autumn 1989): 702-706.

5. For added details on ACT writing comparisons, see Jack Dvorak, "High School Publications Experience As a Factor in College-Level Writing," *Journalism Quarterly 65* (Summer 1988): 392-398; and *High School Journalism Confronts Critical Deadline*: 70-85.

6. Institutions involved were Alabama, South Alabama, Arizona State, Arkansas, DePaul, Northern Illinois, Illinois, Kansas, Hope College

(Michigan), Detroit, Creighton, New Mexico State (Las Cruces), Ohio (Athens), Oklahoma State, Tennessee, Stephen F. Austin (Texas), Brigham Young, and Wisconsin-Eau Claire. ACT Assessment scores were gathered in the 1983-1984 school year, and COMP Prospectus data—including writing samples—were collected during students' 1984-1985 freshman college year.

7. *COMP Prospectus* booklet. American College Testing Program: Iowa City, IA, 1985.

8. See, for example, *A Nation at Risk: The Imperative for Educational Reform.* The National Commission on Excellence in Education (Washington: U.S. Department of Education, April 1983); *First in the Nation in Education.* Final Report of the Iowa Excellence in Education Task Force (Des Moines: Iowa Legislative Council, 1984); *Academic Preparation for College: What Students Need to Know and Be Able to Do* (New York: College Entrance Examination Board, 1983); and *Educational Excellence for Iowa.* Final Report of the Joint Committee on Instructional Development and Academic Articulation in Iowa (Des Moines: Iowa State Board of Regents and the Department of Public Instruction, February 1984).

9. From a representative sample of 18 colleges and universities in 14 states participating in ACT high school and collegiate testing programs, ACT personnel matched up 8,063 students for whom both high school and college records were accessible. Surveys were mailed to 2,687 college students randomly selected from this list in late March 1986. Because of time constraints, no follow-up mailing was possible to non-respondents.

10. Data were gathered from "The ACT Interest Inventory and Student Profile Section" that was completed by high school juniors and seniors as part of the ACT Assessment.

CHAPTER 3

ADVANCED PLACEMENT

Chapter Highlights

- Nearly 66 percent of students from Intensive Journalistic Writing courses pass Advanced Placement exams in English Language and Composition; all test-takers pass at an average rate 5 percentage points lower.

- Journalism students average 3.07 on Advanced Placement language tests; all test-takers average 2.90.

- African-, Hispanic-, Asian- and Native-American Journalism students do better on tests in Advanced Placement language and composition than do non-minority students.

- Females and seniors do better on the tests than males and underclassmen.

- Other topics:
  - Evolution of the Intensive Journalistic Writing programs
  - Advanced Placement test content
  - Intensive Journalistic Writing course content
  - Teacher preparation for Intensive Journalistic Writing classes

In the first four years of a national experiment, high school students from programs with specially trained Intensive Journalistic Writing teachers have shown marked improvement. They now surpass the national average for all students taking the Advanced Placement English Language and Composition Examinations offered by the College Board. Much like the results we've already examined involving journalism and non-journalism students who have taken ACT tests, the data suggest that students in journalism-related writing courses do better than non-journalism high school students when both groups are compared using College Board language and writing tests.

Background

The Advanced Placement English Language and Composition Exam is a three-hour exercise. One hour of the examination involves multiple-choice questions that address syntax, sentence structure, rhetoric, style and content. Two hours are devoted to essay-writing.[1]

When students take a high school class that helps qualify them to take the Advanced Placement exam, they are earning credit towards graduation, but they might also be earning college credit, should their scores be high enough on the AP exam. On a 5-point scale, with 5 being highest, 3 and above are passing grades. Depending on the college or university and the level of the passing score, either college credit or an exemption from one or more English Composition courses is granted.[2]

Beginning in the summer of 1988, The Dow Jones Newspaper Fund has sponsored one or more two-week workshops on various university campuses for journalism and English teachers whose school administrators had consented to offer an Intensive Journalistic Writing class during the next school year. While not designated as "Advanced Placement" courses per se, the content of these classes enable students to take the Advanced Placement English Language and Composition Examination in much the same way that traditional Advanced Placement or honors English composition courses have done in the past. In fact, Charlotte Rosen, assistant director of the Advanced Placement program for the College Board, has been quoted as saying that the journalistic course model is "a practical framework for the study of Advanced Placement Language and Composition."[3]

But the Intensive Journalistic Writing course does not officially carry the "AP" label, nor are students required to take the Advanced Placement exam. About 50 percent of the students who take the IJW classes do, however, take the AP English Language and Composition exam as a test of what they've learned.[4]

We estimate that more than 1,000 students took one of these courses in the 1991-1992 school year; 507 of them chose to take the AP exam in May 1992.

Results

The 507 students from 35 schools in 18 states who took the Intensive Journalistic Writing classes passed the 1992 Advanced Placement exam at a higher rate than those who took standard AP English classes, as seen in Graph 3.1.

Graph 3.1

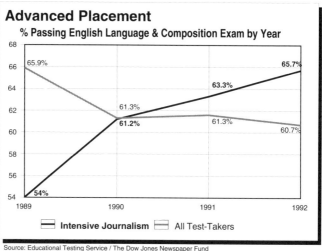

Source: Educational Testing Service / The Dow Jones Newspaper Fund

Whereas 65.7 percent of the Intensive Journalistic Writing students passed the English Language and Composition Examination, all students involved in the 1992 tests—the vast majority of whom had taken traditional English AP and honors courses—passed the same exam at the rate of 60.7 percent (N = 31,523 from 2,561 schools). The Journalism kids did better.

We note that a steady increase in percent of IJW students who pass the exam has occurred in each successive year the program has been offered. For example, in the first year of the program, 1989, only 54 percent of the IJW students passed, whereas the national average was 65.9 percent. During the second year of the program, in the 1990 testing period, IJW students passed in much greater numbers (61.2 percent), even though about half of the students came from programs in which teachers had offered the special journalism course for the first time. That was almost identical to the overall passing rate among all students who took the exam (61.3 percent). In the 1991 testing period, journalism students surpassed the national average for the first time, with 63.3 percent passing, compared with an overall rate of 61.3 percent.

Given the newness of the program, and considering that 34 of the 72 teachers involved taught IJW courses for the first time in the 1991-1992 school year, the passing rates seem quite high. Experts from the College Board and the Educational Testing Service indicate that the rate of students' passing grades increases with each year of experience that teachers have with AP-type courses.[5] Thus, with nearly half of the teachers in their first year before the 1992 testing period, the passing rates are likely to be even more positive in coming years.

Coupled with a higher-than-average passing rate, students who have taken Intensive Journalistic Writing courses at their schools also earned higher-than-average scores on the 5-point examination. Graph 3.2 shows that IJW students averaged 3.07 on the Advanced Placement Language and Composition exam whereas the average score for all test-takers was 2.90. A score of "3" is considered passing.

Journalism students from African-American, Hispanic, Asian-American, and Native-American backgrounds did better than other students on the Language and Composition Examination. For one thing, 68.8 percent of them passed the exam (compared with 65.7 percent of all IJW students, and in contrast to 60.7 percent of all test-takers). The ethnic-minority student average was 3.11 (compared with 3.07 for IJW students and 2.90 for all test-takers). Of the 507 IJW students who took the AP Language and Composition Exam, 80 of them (15.8 percent) were from ethnic-minority backgrounds.

Graph 3.2

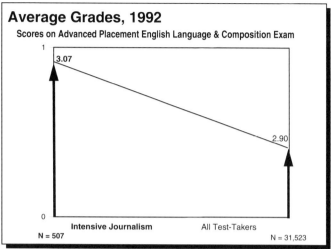

Source: Educational Testing Service / The Dow Jones Newspaper Fund

Females comprised 62.3 percent (N = 316) of all IJW students taking the exam, and they averaged 3.10—above the norm for IJW students. Males comprised 37.7 percent (N = 191) of the test-takers among IJW students, and they averaged 3.02 on the exam—lower than average for the group, yet higher than the average score among all test-takers.

As might be expected, seniors did the best on the exam, averaging 3.29 (N = 255). Sophomores were next-highest with a 3.09 average (N = 22), while IJW juniors averaged 2.82 (N = 226), which is slightly below the national norm for the Language and Composition exam. While an analysis of previous years' exams would have to be done to see if this is a pattern, it's safe to say that based on 1992 results, seniors' added years of maturity, experience, and course work make a substantial difference in IJW students' performances. Because only 4.4 percent of all IJW test-takers were sophomores, we guess that they were rather advanced students. During the four years of testing thus far, 1989 through 1992, a steady growth in number of Intensive Journalistic Writing students passing the Advanced Placement Language and Composition Exam can be noted. As seen in Graph 3.3, those gradually increasing percentages of passing scores are accompanied by large increases in the numbers of students taking the exam. This increase might be attributed to Journalism/

English teachers' added experience in teaching the Advanced Placement-type course. Here are the percentages of increase in the number of test-takers in the IJW program: 24 percent increase from 1989 to 1990; 66 percent increase from 1990 to 1991; and 79 percent increase from 1991 to 1992.

Graph 3.3

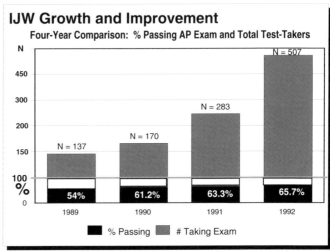

IJW Growth and Improvement
Four-Year Comparison: % Passing AP Exam and Total Test-Takers

Source: Educational Testing Service / The Dow Jones Newspaper Fund

Since its first year, test scores of IJW students have increased by almost 22 percent, numbers of test-takers have grown by 270 percent, and the numbers of IJW teachers who have attended specially funded workshops have grown from 15 in 1989 to 72 through the summer of 1991. How and why did all this happen?

Evolution of the Intensive Journalistic Writing Program

Like so many other worthwhile programs, projects and workshops that have supported school journalism, the Intensive Journalism Writing Workshop concept has been nurtured since its inception by the Dow Jones Newspaper Fund of Princeton, N.J., which began in 1959. The primary impetus in the development, coordination, and continuity was provided by Tom Engleman, Newspaper Fund executive director for more than two decades. He left the Fund in the autumn of 1992 to become an administrator at Temple University in Philadelphia.

Engleman was one of several dozen scholastic journalism leaders who met in New York at a "Summit Meeting" in the spring of 1987. The group was following up on recommendations included in a national study by the Journalism Education Association's Commission on the Role of Journalism in Secondary Education, which had just released its report following about three years of study.[6] One recommendation of the Commission that Engleman and others adopted was that "colleges and universities should lobby for the development of a performance-oriented Advanced Placement journalism education."[7]

The College Board personnel, however, were not optimistic about the addition of a journalism test to their battery of 28 tests in 15 academic areas because of cost and time involved. Engleman therefore pursued another route. He and colleagues with him from the "Summit" realized that a good Journalism course might fulfill all the same objectives that any intensive, honors, or Advanced Placement composition course would provide.[8] The College Board had such a test in place, the English Language and Composition Examination. Engleman realized that an intensive journalistic writing course, leading students to participate in that examination, would go a long way towards legitimizing Journalism as a worthwhile academic course in language arts.

Engleman wrote:

> *It became clear that one of the reasons other academic fields in the nation's high schools have achieved academic respect is due in some degree to the direct and parallel relationship their courses maintain with those disciplines at the college level. One of the strong links between high schools and college is the College Board. A bridge between high school journalism education as an academic discipline and the nation's colleges did not exist that afternoon in May (1987). It does now . . . .*

Within a short time, the Dow Jones Newspaper Fund board of directors approved funding of a two-week workshop at a university campus that would prepare certified English and Journalism teachers to offer a specialized course in Intensive Journalistic Writing that would be separate from regular school Journalism classes and publications production. In fact, the course was to be strictly "academic," and it would emphasize both non-fiction literature—including journalism—as well as a strong writing component in which students would practice writing styles but with an emphasis on Journalism. From among several proposals, the board selected Marquette University as the site of both the first and second workshop in 1988 and 1989.

Since then, workshops have been offered at Virginia Commonwealth University (1990); the University of Alabama, Ohio University, and Rutgers University (1991); and the University of Alabama, Marquette University, and Saint Michaels College in Vermont (1992). Indiana University was the site of the 1993 IJW workshop for teachers.

The Newspaper Fund has supported teachers through full-tuition scholarships that include graduate credit at the participating universities, as well as room, meals, and incidental expenses for about 115 teachers who have participated during the first six summers.

As Engleman envisioned the workshops, they would help fulfill several of the recommendations for school Journalism set forth in the JEA Commission's final report:

- that minimum standards be established for academic-based Journalism courses
- that courses be accepted both by schools and state departments of education as components of the high school English/language arts curriculum
- that these academic-based Journalism courses carry the same full high school credit given any other recognized language arts writing class, and also that these courses allow students to earn college English credit based on the passage of the College Board's Advanced Placement English Language and Composition examination
- that these courses in Intensive Journalistic Writing be accepted by colleges in the same way they accept other advanced-level writing courses[9]

Based on students' fine showings on the Advanced Placement exams thus far, it seems that Engleman's thoughts during the early phases of the project are now coming to fruition. Everybody—the teachers, the kids, the schools, and everyone else—is a winner.

Engleman wrote:

The students win because they become better writers and can earn college credit while still in high school.

High school teachers benefit because they gain respect among their colleagues and add a dimension to their careers as English and Journalism instructors.

High schools win because they are able to demonstrate how they are meeting national, state, and local pressures to intensify writing instruction.

The nation's college-level journalism schools and industry as a whole benefit because the students, professional writers of the future, will be more productive than ever before.

The Dow Jones Newspaper Fund benefits because the project directly addresses its primary purpose: encouraging young people to pursue journalism as a career.[10]

Advanced Placement Test Content

According to the College Board, the Advanced Placement English Language and Composition course, leading to the Advanced Placement examination, is meant to cover both effective writing and critical reading. The exam is intended for students who have developed their writing abilities and awareness of style and rhetoric outside the realm of fiction. "Their chief practice in composition has been the writing of expository, analytical, and argumentative essays.... (O)n the AP English Language Examination, students normally are not expected to analyze poetry or fiction; their main concern is with expository prose."[11]

Much like an Intensive Journalistic Writing course designed to establish concentrated writing competencies, the Advanced Placement exam in language and composition includes reading passages from various periods, demonstrating a variety of styles and purposes. Following each passage of reading, on the multiple-choice portion of the exam, questions are asked involving meaning, purpose, structure, tone, syntax, and diction—in other words, items that get at the heart of both the language and the composition of the passage involved. The entire objective portion of the test, which takes one hour, tests another student skill as well, namely, manipulation of syntax.[12]

The final two hours of the AP Exam involve writing three separate passages depicting different, specific types or styles of writing. One of the questions involves analysis of the rhetoric and the style of a prose passage but without the prompts offered in the multiple-choice portion of the test. Typical writing exercises also include a persuasive essay, a descriptive piece, and a narrative passage. All are to be aimed at "the common reader," and all are written under strict deadline: 40 minutes for each of the three essays.[13]

Expressed goals of the Intensive Journalistic Writing courses, developed in the early years of the IJW workshops, are entirely consistent with aims of the AP program. Seven goals have been listed that mesh the journalistic and general language arts skills that are important to college-bound students in the courses that prepare for AP examinations:

1. To teach the writing process using a journalistic process model

2. To correlate and integrate journalistic and rhetorical modes

3. To use journalistic techniques and models to teach writing forms

4. To teach students to observe, to interview, to research and to organize

5. To provide a variety of classical and contemporary models

6. To develop students' critical reading and thinking skills

7. To teach students to compose in a variety of modes for different purposes and audiences[14]

In a *Teacher's Guide* for IJW courses published by the Newspaper Fund, authors stated that the study and practice of journalism can easily fulfill stated requirements of the Advanced Placement language and composition course and examination:

> *Just as writers of fiction wrestle with verisimilitude, journalists also must balance event, action, quotation, description and background. Just as an editor at a publishing company may require an author to add more detail and to develop characterization, the daily newspaper editor may require a reporter to verify accuracy of quotation and detail, to check the library or to rewrite for a stronger lead.*
>
> *The study of narration, description, exposition, definition, argumentation and cause-effect influence the form and impact of a piece and show how the modes interrelate. All modes can be found in both (Journalism and English composition) approaches to writing.*[15]

Intensive Journalistic Writing Courses

Teachers with appropriate backgrounds, such as having taken one of the IJW workshops, do their college-bound students a great service when they offer a course in Intensive Journalistic Writing as part of the regular language arts curriculum. According to the Teacher's Guide published by the Newspaper Fund, one wants to cover three types of skills: composing skills, language skills, and interpreting skills.[16]

While studying composition, students practice the following detailed list of skills: interviewing skills; constructing questions; organizing; using quotations; punctuating and documenting direct quotations; writing editorials, reviews, and other persuasive articles; planning and writing features and other descriptive pieces; arranging details in various types of order—chronological, spatial, thematic, order of importance; creating personal narratives; writing and gathering news stories; aiming writing at specific audiences for specific purposes on specific occasions; improving writing through pre-writing, drafting and revising; selecting and maintaining appropriate point of view; adhering to proper voice; defining an idea and extending it; and participating in activities to generate ideas for writing.

Study of language use in Intensive Journalistic Writing courses covers the following skills: examining the diction of other writers in order to determine reasons for their selections; recognizing how diction helps create and maintain tone and style; relating imagery and word choice to tone and theme; citing rhetorical devices and speculating on their effects and the writer's intention in using them; identifying and differentiating between analogies, allusions, comparisons, metaphors, paradoxes, onomatopoeia and similes; identifying and explaining irony; choosing vivid verbs and verb tense; analyzing grammatical structures of sentences by other writers; identifying and using figurative language; selecting proper transitional words and devices; and understanding and using connotations.

Study of interpretation by IJW students involves the following: understanding and differentiating main and subordinate ideas in their and others' writing; locating congruent and incongruent elements; determining a passage's emphasis by proportion and placement of details; locating textual references to validate a major point; paraphrasing difficult prose; applying prototype questions to new material; making generalizations based on research and inferences; writing themes; analyzing plausibility of literary and nonfiction characters; reviewing humorous devices; identifying grammatical structures; evaluating effectiveness of various sentence and paragraph lengths; inferring authorship based on style; identifying cause-effect relationships in a nonfiction work; using specifications to evaluate news, features and editorials; identifying and writing various types of journalistic leads; identifying in journalistic writing effective uses of narration, description, anecdotes, senses, humor and organization; and evaluating specific and general qualities of excellent journalistic (and other) forms of writing.

How are IJW courses organized?

IJW teachers have thus far used the following organizational approaches in designing courses: the rhetorical, the thematic, process design, the historical, and current-events emphasis.[17]

Readings vary widely among existing courses, but among the writers who show up on a regular basis in class outlines are the following: Jane Adams, James Agee, Isaac Asimov, Carlos Baker, Russell

Baker, James Baldwin, Lois W. Banner, James Gordon Bennett, Erma Bombeck, Jimmy Breslin, Gwendolyn Brooks, Heywood Broun, Art Buchwald, William F. Buckley, Teresa Carpenter, Stephen Crane, Joan Didion, Annie Dillard, Paul Engle, Nora Ephron, Anne Frank, Ellen Goodman, Vivian Gornick, Stephen Gould, Horace Greeley, Bob Greene, Alex Haley, Ernest Hemingway, Nat Hentoff, John Hersey, Langston Hughes, and Susan Jacoby.

Pauline Kael, James J. Kilpatrick, Stephen King, John Knowles, Jack Lait, William Laurence, Fran Lebowitz, Max Lerner, Anthony Lewis, Walter Lippmann, Jack London, Joyce Maynard, H.L. Mencken, William Least Heat Moon, Toni Morrison, George Orwell, Ernie Pyle, William Raspberry, James Reston, Andy Rooney, Mike Royko, William Safire, Upton Sinclair, John Steinbeck, Studs Terkel, Lewis Thomas, James Thurber, Calvin Trillin, Barbara Tuchman, Mark Twain, Jane Van LaWick-Goodall, Judith Viorst, Eudora Welty, E.B. White, William Allen White, Tom Wicker, George Will, Walter Williams, Tom Wolfe, Virginia Woolf, and Cathy Young.

Several teachers also use collections of recent and historically respected reporting, including these: *Popular Writing in America* edited by McQuade and Atwan; *How I Wrote the Story* edited by Christopher Scanlan; *A Treasury of Great Reporting* edited by Louis L. Snyder and Richard B. Morris; various volumes of *Best Newspaper Writing of 19__* edited by Don Fry; various volumes of *The Pulitzer Prizes* edited by Kendall J. Wills; *The Literary Journalists* edited by Norman Sims; *Eyewitness to History* edited by John Carey; and *Writing Day by Day* edited by Robert Atwan and William Vesterman.[18]

Teacher Preparation for Intensive Journalistic Writing Classes

Journalistically oriented, advanced language arts classes that serve honors or Advanced Placement students well require specialized teacher preparation.

The two-week workshops that have been operating since 1988 with sponsorship by the Dow Jones Newspaper Fund and participating colleges and universities require a blend of journalism and English instruction for teachers attending. Besides practicing journalistic techniques themselves, high school teachers interact with English-education experts, College Board personnel, and participants of previous workshops who have since taught IJW courses at their schools. In addition to the specific competencies and materials already listed, each workshop has the following goals:

1. Raise critical and analytical thinking abilities

2. Improve personal communication

3. Establish journalistic forms and practices as viable additions to traditional approaches to advanced writing courses in the high schools

4. Write a course guide for an Intensive Journalistic Writing course

Attention to several specific objectives permeates the workshop program for these English/Journalism teachers as they prepare their own courses:

- Emphasize comprehension of the writing process at all stages of composition

- Identify specific techniques for individualized instruction

- Develop a body of knowledge about teaching writing

- Use journalistic forms and disciplines as a foundation for effective writing in high school; cover specific areas of gathering information, news-writing, feature-writing and opinion-writing

- Enable teachers to teach the writing process using a journalistic process model

- Assist teachers to correlate and integrate journalistic and rhetorical modes in their classrooms

- Assist teachers to develop a strategy to improve student critical reading and thinking skills[19]

Through these IJW workshops, teachers have been able to retool both their journalistic and their English teaching skills to provide students with unusually stimulating courses. This is why these students have performed as well or better than their non-journalistic counterparts on the AP English Language and Composition Examination—especially in 1991 and 1992 testing periods.

Is IJW a worthy offering for talented language arts students? Ought it have equal status with any other advanced English writing course in high school?

Yes.

The research tells us that IJW courses with a qualified instructor can assume a status in schools alongside any of the traditional honors or Advanced Placement language arts courses. Journalism students' performance on Advanced Placement exams, together with the many other academic comparisons we've examined thus far, lead us to conclude that journalism experience correlates well with some of the most highly regarded formal educational measures. Journalism kids do as well, and often they do better.

NOTES ON CHAPTER 3

1. *The Entire 1982 AP English Language and Composition Examination and Key.* (New York: Advanced Placement Program, The College Board, 1984): 1.

2. C. Zoe Smith, editor. *Teacher's Guide to Intensive Journalistic Writing Courses.* (Princeton, NJ: The Dow Jones Newspaper Fund, 1991): 5.

3. *Ibid.:* 2.

4. *Ibid.:* 6.

5. Tom Engleman, "Analysis of Advanced Placement English Language and Composition Exam Results," invited speaker at the Annual convention of the Association for Education in Journalism and Mass Communication, Secondary Education Division, Washington, DC, August 1989.

6. *High School Journalism Confronts Critical Deadline.* A Report by the Journalism Education Association Commission on the Role of Journalism in Secondary Education. (Manhattan, KS: Journalism Education Association, 1987).

7. *Ibid.:* 113.

8. Smith, *Teacher's Guide to Intensive Journalistic Writing Courses:* 3.

9. See, for example, *High School Journalism Confronts Critical Deadline*, 110; and Smith, *Teacher's Guide to Intensive Journalistic Writing Courses:* 5.

10. Smith, *Teacher's Guide to Intensive Journalistic Writing Courses:* 5.

11. George Gadda, et al., *Teacher's Guide to Advanced Placement Courses in English Language and Composition.* (New York: The College Board, Advanced Placement Program, 1985): iii.

12. *Ibid.:* 1-2.

13. *Ibid.:* 2.

14. Smith, *Teacher's Guide to Intensive Journalistic Writing Courses:* 12.

15. *Ibid.:* 12-13.

16. *Ibid.:* 14-17.

17. *Ibid.:* 37-38.

18. Specific references to authors' articles and complete bibliographic citations may be found in Smith, *Teacher's Guide to Intensive Journalistic Writing Courses:* 19-114.

19. Goals and objectives listed are based on the proposal written by Carol Lange for the Virginia Intensive Journalistic Writing Institute held at Virginia Commonwealth University in the summer of 1990. They stem from goals and objectives used by the initial IJW workshops held at Marquette University, Milwaukee, WI, in 1988 and 1989.

CHAPTER 4

JOURNALISM PROGRAMS INVOLVE ALMOST A MILLION KIDS AND TEACHERS

Chapter Highlights

- About 95 percent of U.S. high schools have some type of journalistic class or media outlet.
- More than 540,000 high school students are enrolled in Journalism.
- Nearly 720,000 students serve on school media staffs.
- 93 percent of U.S. high schools publish yearbooks.
- Newspapers are produced in 79 percent of U.S. high schools.
- Journalism educators tend to be married females in their early 40s who have two children.

Nearly 95 percent of the secondary schools in the United States have at least one of the following media-related activities: a journalism course for credit, a yearbook, a newspaper, a news magazine, or a television or radio outlet. With 94.6 percent of the nation's schools reporting some type of journalistic activity, it means that about 21,555 of the country's 22,785 high schools offer communications outlets or classes for students, as shown in Graph 4.1.

These findings, among most others presented in this chapter and the next, are based on a scientifically selected national sample of high school Journalism educators done under the auspices of the

High School Journalism Institute at Indiana University. All 22,785 U.S. secondary schools that included at least grades 10-12 and were listed in Patterson's American Education 1991 were potential sources. Personnel at Quill and Scroll International Honorary for high school journalists at The University of Iowa randomly selected 1,906 schools for the study. A seven-page survey containing 120 items was addressed to the "Journalism educator" in each school. A postage-paid, self-addressed envelope was included in each. After an initial mailing in February 1991, a follow-up to non-respondents was mailed in April 1991.

Altogether, 834 school personnel returned the survey for a response rate of nearly 44 percent. Some type of journalistic activity occurred in 789 of the schools during the 1990-1991 academic year (94.6 percent). Maximum sampling error for a random sample of this size is 3.4 percentage points at the 95 percent confidence level. Tolerances in sampling error were smaller than plus or minus 3.4 percentage points as responses moved away from the 50th percentile.

The stats break out as follows:

Graph 4.1

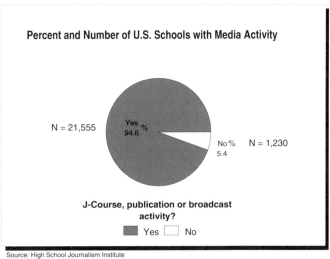

Percent and Number of U.S. Schools with Media Activity

N = 21,555 — Yes % 94.6

No % 5.4 — N = 1,230

J-Course, publication or broadcast activity?

■ Yes ☐ No

Source: High School Journalism Institute

- 75 percent of the nation's schools offer Journalism for credit in one form or another: basic, advanced classes; newspaper, yearbook, radio/TV labs.

- 91 percent of America's high schools—almost 21,000—offer media labs so student journalists can work on newspapers, yearbooks, and the broadcast media.

Graph 4.2

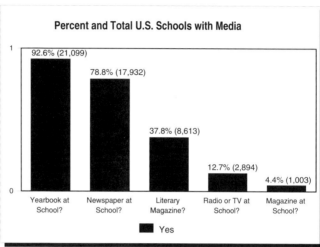

Source: High School Journalism Institute

- Almost 93 percent of high schools produce a yearbook.
- Almost 79 percent publish newspapers, and another 4.4 percent publish newsmagazines, for a total of 83.1 percent in the print journalism business.
- 37.8 percent publish literary magazines—a low figure, considering the high numbers of kids enrolled in English, literature, and other language arts courses.
- Only 12.7 percent—fewer than 2,900—high schools have TV/radio stations.
- Average size for a Journalism class is 31.5 students.
- Average size for a media lab is 34.6 students.
- About 540,000 students are enrolled in "Journalism."
- About 720,000 students staff high school media activities.

Graph 4.3

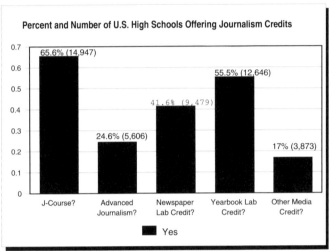

Percent and Number of U.S. High Schools Offering Journalism Credits

65.6% (14,947)	J-Course?
24.6% (5,606)	Advanced Journalism?
41.6% (9,479)	Newspaper Lab Credit?
55.5% (12,646)	Yearbook Lab Credit?
17% (3,873)	Other Media Credit?

■ Yes

Source: High School Journalism Institute

- 66 percent of high schools offer "Basic Journalism" or "Beginning Journalism," a for-credit course that lasts at least one semester.

- 56 percent offer yearbook labs for credit; 42 percent offer credit for staffing the newspaper.

- 89 percent of journalism/media programs have computers for student use. That figure now is surely well above 90 percent partly because of the convenience of desktop publishing and partly because of continued growth in computer acquisitions since the survey was taken in 1991.

- About 17 percent of schools offer broadcast and other media labs for credit.

- 86.5 percent of high schools offer credit for journalistic work.

- 13 percent offer Journalism or media labs as English requirements.

- 26 percent offer courses and labs as language arts electives.

- 43.4 percent offer courses and labs as general electives.

- 4.1 percent offer them as "other"—vocational education, social studies, and the like.

- 13.5 percent grant no credit, although they do allow lab time during the school day. Most of the publication work done at these schools, and all of it at the great majority of schools, is done by student staffers with the guidance of faculty advisers who labor long hours after school and on weekends.

Recruitment of Students for Journalism Classes

High school Journalism educators often express concern over the health of the program relative to number of students in it. Unlike most other academic subject areas, Journalism often requires recruitment of students by school personnel, ordinarily the Journalism educator. Because in so many schools Journalism does not count as a required language arts course, teachers are often known to take extraordinary measures to recruit good students. It is possible that these efforts to attract and retain good students account for some of the academic superiority of journalism kids noted in Chapter 2. It is also true that naturally talented language arts students might gravitate toward Journalism as a logical outlet for their interests, in much the same way that students interested in drama, sports, art, chorus or band find their way into those programs.

None of that is an argument against either Journalism or those other programs, of course; and because we value literacy achievement in our society, it is an argument in favor of making opportunities for talented and promising kids to exercise their gifts.

Here are the typical methods used to recruit students for Journalism classes:

- student applications (66.2 percent): An application procedure distinguishes Journalism classes from most other subjects because the others don't require a special application process. Advanced Placement or equivalent specialized courses are the exceptions.

- recommendations from English teachers (39.6 percent)

- scheduling and recommendations from guidance counselors (31.2 percent)

- Journalism teacher visits English classes to explain programs, answer questions and encourage interested students (21.1 percent)
- other (22 percent): these methods include self-selection, recommendations from peers, parents' guidance, and recommendations from teachers of subjects other than English.

Recruitment of Students for Publications Staffs

Because a fairly high percentage of schools do not offer a yearbook lab for credit (37 percent) or a newspaper lab for credit (41 percent), many schools' Journalism educators must make special efforts to recruit student leaders who will perform the tasks well and get the job done. Among those schools that do offer credit, educators have the added inducement of a grade and a structured portion of the school day in which to stimulate learning and quality production. Because of the public nature of the output of school media productions, many educators recruit carefully so that maximum benefits may be obtained by all staff members and so that the entire operation is as smoothly run as possible.

Here are some of the commonly used methods by which Journalism educators recruit staff members:

- adviser selects after students make application (61.7 percent)
- adviser selects from among those who have taken a Beginning Journalism class (29.6 percent)
- other (27.9 percent), e.g., faculty recommendations
- vote among present or outgoing staff members (7.4 percent)

Journalism as Part of the School Day

For the typical Journalism educator in a U.S. high school, the school day is comprised of 5.32 periods, of which more than half (2.81 periods) are devoted to teaching Journalism or supervising media labs. Graph 4.4 shows these relationships. By way of contrast, according to the U.S. Department of Education, a typical secondary school teacher spends a little less time per day in classes, 5.14 periods. The Department lists 6.1 total periods in an average secondary school day, with a class period averaging 51.1 minutes.[1]

Graph 4.4

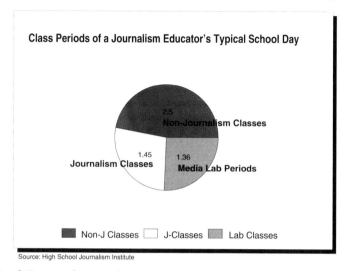

Class Periods of a Journalism Educator's Typical School Day

Source: High School Journalism Institute

The typical Journalism educator represented in this study spends about 53 percent of the school day involved with Journalism students and media staff members. The remaining 47 percent of the day involves the teaching of English, social studies, speech/drama, or some other academic area.

School Size, Type and Location

To get a better picture of the overall environment in which Journalism programs exist, we examined general characteristics of the respondents' schools. Where possible, we compared outcomes with other studies to validate further our findings about Journalism.

The plurality of Journalism educators in the study taught at schools that had grades 10-12 enrollments within the 200-500 student range (28.3 percent), whereas the next most likely size of school was one with fewer than 200 students (25.1 percent). As seen in Graph 4.5, that means that about 53 percent of the teachers in this study are employed at relatively small schools. However, this is indicative of school sizes nationally. For example, even when total student populations of the largest schools in the country are included within the comparisons, the average number of students in a typical U.S. high school is only 681.[2]

Only 1.7 percent of the teachers in this study taught at schools that were very large (more than 2,500 students). In fact, only about

25 percent of all Journalism educators in the country teach at schools with more than 1,000 students in the school population. This is typical of school enrollments generally. Graph 4.5 shows other enrollment categories represented in the study.

Graph 4.5

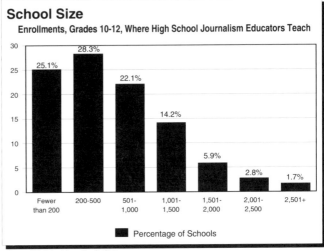

Source: High School Journalism Institute

Type of School

Further linkage may be seen between our study and the nation's schools when looking at composition of public, parochial, and private schools. Graph 4.6 shows the relationships.

Graph 4.6

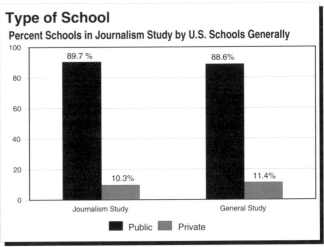

Source: High School Journalism Institute and U.S. Dept. of Education

In latest figures available from the U.S. Department of Education, we find about 1.14 million high school teachers in public schools and about 147,000 teaching in private schools.[3] Thus, about 88.6 percent of all high school teachers work in the public sector while 11.4 work for parochial or private schools. In our study of Journalism educators, we were well within the expected 3.4 percentage points of margin of error, which further validates our overall study. Graph 4.6 shows that 89.7 percent of the participants in the Journalism study are public school teachers whereas 10.3 percent teach in non-public schools. Among the latter, 5.5 percent come from parochial schools, and 4.8 percent work in other private schools.

Location of School

We know that a majority of schools have grade 10-12 enrollments under 500, so we would expect that a good share of them are in small towns and rural communities. Our findings bear this out, and are further corroborated by a study released by the National Opinion Research Center.[4]

Graph 4.7

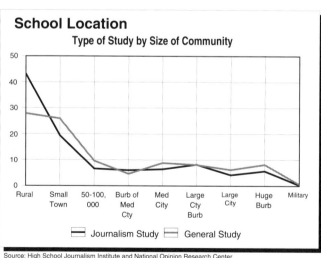

Source: High School Journalism Institute and National Opinion Research Center
N = 783 Journalism   N = 1,147 General Study

The plurality of schools in which Journalism educators teach and advise are in rural and farming areas (43.2 percent). In cities of towns of fewer than 50,000 people, we find our next highest percentage of schools (19.4 percent). More than 75 percent of all U.S.

Journalism educators work in schools that are in suburbs, cities, towns, and rural areas of less than 100,000 population. In fact, we found that only about 10 percent of the schools in which Journalism educators work to be in cities of more than half-a-million population and suburbs that surround those very large cities. Graph 4.7 shows that our study closely parallels another national study of secondary school teachers.[5]

AHANA (Minority) Participation

Participation by AHANA (African American, Hispanic, Asian American and Native American) students in journalism seems to parallel enrollment trends in the overall school population. Our study shows that journalism programs (classes and news media staffs) include 24 percent AHANA student participation, whereas total overall AHANA enrollment in the same schools stands at 23.6 percent. One percent was the mode when we examined both total school enrollment and journalism program participation by AHANA students, meaning that the most commonly selected number (1 percent) comes from these groups. About 22 percent of both the total school enrollment and the Journalism program involvement are found in schools with but 1 percent AHANA participation. However, the median related to AHANA percentages in both total school enrollment and in Journalism program involvement was 10 percent. This means that AHANA students tend to come from schools with larger enrollments.

Graph 4.8 shows other relationships pertinent to AHANA involvement:

- In nearly 33 percent of all schools studied, total AHANA enrollments are between 1 and 3 percent. That is low, but only 28.6 percent of Journalism programs are grouped in schools thus categorized with low AHANA enrollment.

- In schools with 4 to 9 percent or 10 to 28 percent total AHANA enrollments, AHANA students account for a far higher rate of participation in Journalism, and in schools where AHANA enrollment is above 29 percent, AHANA students participate in Journalism at a higher rate than does the overall student population: 31.9 percent to 25.9 percent.

- Our findings concur generally with the results of another study, conducted through the ACT Program: 10 percent of college-bound school publications staffs included AHANA students, compared with 9.8 percent of the non-staff, college-bound school enrollment.[6]

Graph 4.8

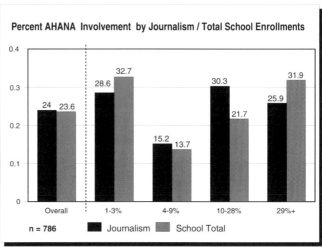

Percent AHANA Involvement by Journalism / Total School Enrollments

Source: High School Journalism Institute

Academic Credit for Journalism and Media Labs

In Chapter 2 we noted that when high school students took a class called "Journalism," they rated it higher on several language arts competencies than they rated their required English courses. Given this finding and in combination with many others presented in that chapter relating to experiences with both classes and school publications, we now examine some characteristics common among schools that offer a basic Journalism course (e.g., Journalism I, Beginning Journalism, Basic Journalism, Introduction to Journalism, and the like). In our study of 834 U.S. high schools, we found that as schools increase in size, they are decidedly more likely to offer a basic Journalism course.

- fewer than 200 enrollment: about 50 percent
- 200 to 500: about 60 percent
- 501 to 1,000: 73 percent

- 1,001 to 1,500: 79 percent

- more than 1,500: almost 84 percent

Whereas smaller schools tend to use faculty members to teach Journalism basics within a fairly well-established curriculum in language arts, larger schools have more diversified staffs, support superior technical resources, offer more electives, and tend to make a bigger place for different kinds and levels of Journalism.

Public schools (67 percent) more than parochial, and parochial schools (54 percent) more than private (40 percent), offer Journalism.

Limited resources, smaller numbers of staff, and lesser flexibility of scheduling prevent higher percentages of parochial and private schools from offering Journalism. Most private schools have smaller enrollments as well.

AHANA students are also more likely to attend schools that offer a basic Journalism course largely because a higher percentage of minority students attend large schools in large cities with larger enrollments than rural or small-town schools have.

When it comes to offering other courses and media lab experiences for credit beyond the Basic Journalism class, those schools offering that initial course are much more likely to offer other credit experiences for journalistic activities. For example, almost 43 percent of U.S. schools offering a Basic Journalism course also offer an advanced class—Journalism II, Advanced Journalism, or some other course beyond the beginning one. By contrast, only about 7 percent of the schools offer any type of advanced credit in Journalism where a Basic Journalism course is not offered.

The Basic Journalism course is also significantly related to credits being offered for yearbook and newspaper lab experiences offered in conjunction with production of those publications. Sixty percent of the schools offering the beginning course also offer credit for Newspaper Lab, and 69 percent of the schools having that course offer Yearbook Lab credit. By comparison, in schools with no Basic Journalism course, only 28 percent offer Newspaper Lab credit, though 48 percent do offer Yearbook credit.

Journalism Educators' Profiles

We turn now to an examination of the people who lead Journalism classes and who advise school media operations: Journalism educators. Here are some overall findings of our national study of high school Journalism teachers and media advisers (n=786), interspersed with results from other studies, along with running commentary:

Age: 40.9 average

Graph 4.9 shows that Journalism educators are similar in age to all other U.S. secondary school teachers (median age: 41.1).[7] By contrast, college Journalism educators, about whom educational and professional experience expectations are higher, are older (median age: 46).[8] Professional journalists in America (median age: 36), however, tend to be fully five years younger than their teaching colleagues in the high schools.[9]

Graph 4.9

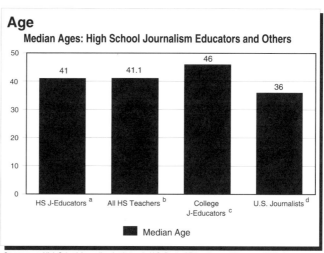

Sources: a High School Journalism Institute   b U.S. Dept. of Education   c Weaver and Wilhoit *Profile* (1988)   d Weaver and Wilhoit *The American Journalist in the 1990s* (1992)

Gender: Women comprise the majority of Journalism educators (see Graph 4.10)

- 71.5 percent women Journalism teachers, overall
- 81 percent women in the youngest (22 to 31 year old) age group

- 80 percent women in the smallest schools (fewer than 200 students)

- 74 percent women in the schools with 200-to-500 enrollment

- 76 percent of first-year Journalism teachers are women (Among older Journalism teachers, with 16 or more years of experience, males have the edge: 63 percent)

- more than 70 percent women in Journalism programs with either very high or very low participation by AHANA students

- 52 percent and 66 percent women Journalism teachers and advisers in programs with moderately low and moderately high numbers of AHANA students, respectively

Graph 4.10

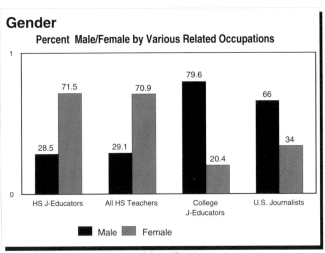

Gender
Percent Male/Female by Various Related Occupations

Sources: High School Journalism Institute; U.S. Dept. of Education;
Weaver and Wilhoit *Profile* (1988); Weaver and Wilhoit *American Journalist* (1992)

This clear majority of women is comparable to the majority of high school teachers in general, which also is women: 70.9 percent.[10] Among college Journalism teachers, an opposite situation prevailed in 1988: nearly 80 percent were males,[11] and in 1992, the majority of professional journalists in America was also men: 66 percent.[12] This tendency seems gradually to be changing, and while that change may have slowed a little, it will probably continue, for women comprise the majority (in 1989-90) of those who received baccalaureate (61.9 percent) and master's (61.3 percent) degrees (though only 44 percent of doctorates were women).[13] The journalism profession, whether as educators or as practitioners of the media arts, is turning female.

Marital status

- 72 percent married
- 11 percent divorced or separated
- 1.4 percent widowed
- 15.6 percent single, never married

Children

- 2.32 average

Religious practice (in youth)

- Jewish: 2.1 percent
- Catholic: 24.8 percent
- Protestant: 63.1 percent
- none: 3.1 percent
- other: 6.9 percent

Religious practice (in adulthood)

- Jewish: 1.3 percent
- Catholic: 20.7 percent
- Protestant: 47.5 percent
- none: 22.3 percent
- other: 8.2 percent

We note the curious drop-off in religious practice between Journalism educators' youth and current affiliation, especially among Protestants. While nearly 97 percent were introduced to religion as youngsters, only about 78 percent continue to practice as adults.

Father's occupation

- agricultural: 12.7 percent
- homemaker: 0.1 percent
- professional/managerial: 49.4 percent

- trade/technical: 37.7 percent
- other: 0.1 percent

Mother's occupation

- agricultural: 0.7 percent
- homemaker: 57.4 percent
- professional/managerial: 15.6 percent
- trade/technical: 15.6 percent

Years in Journalism education (see Graphs 4.11 & 4.12)

- years as a teacher: 14.6 average
- years teaching Journalism: 8.4 average
- in their first year of teaching: 3 percent
- in their first year of teaching Journalism: 12 percent
- in their second or third year of teaching: fewer than 10 percent
- in their second or third year of teaching Journalism: more than 19 percent

Graph 4.11

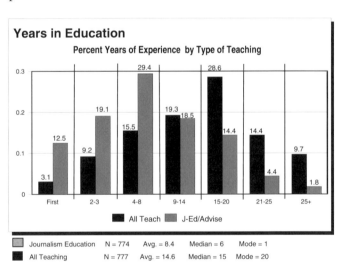

Years in Education

Percent Years of Experience by Type of Teaching

■ All Teach ▨ J-Ed/Advise

| Journalism Education | N = 774 | Avg. = 8.4 | Median = 6 | Mode = 1 |
| All Teaching | N = 777 | Avg. = 14.6 | Median = 15 | Mode = 20 |

86

Graph 4.12

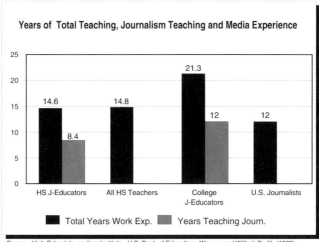

Source: High School Journalism Institute; U.S. Dept. of Education; Weaver and Wilhoit *Profile* (1988); Weaver and Wilhoit *The American Journalist* (1992)

Ethnicity (see Graphs 4.13 & 4.14)

- African Americans: 1.9 percent
- Asian Americans: 0.8 percent
- Caucasians: 95.3 percent
- Hispanic Americans: 0.6 percent
- Native Americans: 1 percent
- Other: 0.4 percent

Graph 4.13

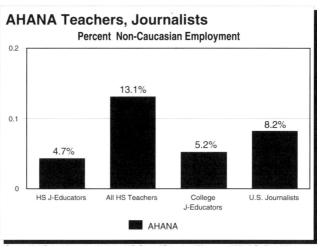

Source: High School Journalism Institute; U.S. Dept. of Education; Weaver and Wilhoit *Profile* (1988); Weaver and Wilhoit *Portrait* (1992)

Graph 4.14

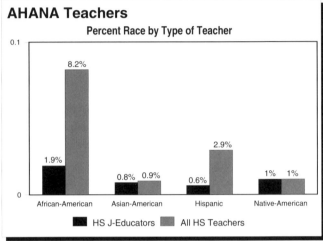

AHANA Teachers
Percent Race by Type of Teacher

Source: High School Journalism Institute; U.S. Dept. of Education

Income (see Graphs 4.15 & 4.16)

- annual salary (basic contract): $29,675 average
- yearbook stipend: $1,096 average
- newspaper stipend: $1,055 average
- news magazine stipend: $1,453 average
- TV/radio stipend: $443 average
- literary magazine stipend: $600 average
- family income (1990): $53,212 average

Graph 4.15

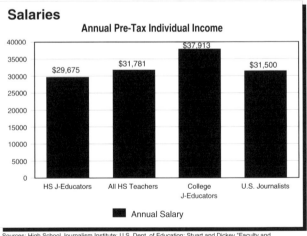

Salaries
Annual Pre-Tax Individual Income

Sources: High School Journalism Institute; U.S. Dept. of Education; Stuart and Dickey "Faculty and Administration Faculty Survey" (1991); Weaver and Wilhoit *The American Journalist* (1992)

Graph 4.16

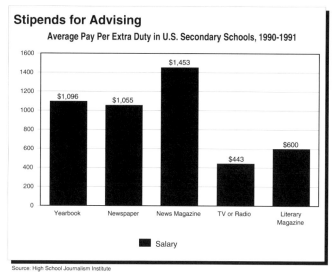

Source: High School Journalism Institute

Salary and school enrollment

school size	% of Journalism teachers who make $40,000 to $65,000 per year
under 200	1.7 percent
201–500	10.6 percent
501–1,000	22 percent
1,001–1,500	26 percent
more than 1,500	38.2 percent

school size	% of Journalism teachers who make less than $25,000 per year
under 200	60.5 percent
201–500	31.9 percent
501–1,000	23.2 percent
1,001–1,500	14.4 percent
more than 1,500	10.5 percent

The trend evident in Graph 4.11 shows that many Journalism educators begin their teaching careers as specialists in other areas, most notably English, and then are later assigned to teach Journalism or to advise publications. While the largest number of people indicate that they have been involved with education in general for between 15 and 20 years, the largest cluster of Journalism educators shows that they have been involved in Journalism teaching and media advising for between four and eight years. After this large clustering of Journalism experience tops out after the eighth year of experience, it quickly drops off in successive years. By contrast, total teaching experience seems to have a more gradual growth and decline rate, as seen in Graph 4.11.

These trends indicate the likelihood that people are apt to be involved with Journalism for a lesser time than their total teaching experience. They start their Journalism duties later than when they started teaching, and then they drop them earlier in their careers while continuing to teach other subjects.

And as Graph 4.12 shows, people now teaching-advising in high school journalism programs have almost identical total teaching experience (14.6 years) as do all secondary school teachers (14.8 years) even though their time in Journalism education is but 8.4 years.[14] By way of comparison, collegiate Journalism educators have about 12 years of teaching experience combined with other media experience totaling 21.3 years of professional activity altogether.[15] The latest data collected on U.S. journalists show that they have been practicing their craft for about 12 years (median).[16]

The percentage of AHANA students in high school journalism programs is about the same as it is for the overall secondary school population in the U.S., about 24 percent. This number is also identical to the 1990 U.S. Census estimate of the overall AHANA population percentage. However, teachers and advisers in those media programs are decidedly from Caucasian backgrounds, as shown in Graph 4.13.

Compared with all non-college teachers from AHANA backgrounds (13.1 percent),[17] only 4.7 percent of high school Journalism educators come from African-American, Hispanic, Asian-American, Native-American or other non-Caucasian backgrounds. College Journalism educators are close to the same small proportion of AHANA faculty (5.2 percent) as found among high school ranks.[18] In a 1992 study of American journalists, Weaver and Wilhoit found that 8.2 percent come from AHANA backgrounds, which was more than double the percentage of ethnic-minority journalists found in their study a decade earlier.[19]

We see that the same massive efforts will be needed to recruit ethnic-minority Journalism educators that have helped professional Journalism become more in line with the AHANA composition of society. All four groups represented in Graph 4.13—high school Journalism educators, all high school teachers, collegiate Journalism educators, and professional journalists—need to expand their members with AHANA people in order to approach the 24 percent racial and ethnic composition of their students or their readers, viewers and listeners.

A more careful look at the individual racial and ethnic makeup of the teacher groups is shown in Graph 4.14. When comparing high school Journalism educators with all pre-college faculty members, we find disparities among two of the four specific racial ethnic groups. For example, 8.2 percent of all secondary school teachers are African-American, but only 1.9 percent of the Journalism educators are African-American.

The greatest disproportion of representation in view of population trends, however, is Hispanics. Although Hispanic-Americans are our fastest growing ethnic minority, only 2.9 percent of all secondary school teachers are from Hispanic backgrounds, and an infinitesimally small 0.6 percent of U.S. high school Journalism educators are Hispanic.[20]

Nearly 1 percent of Asian American teachers and 1 percent of Native Americans make but a tiny representation in Journalism classrooms as well as non-Journalism classrooms.

We also find an inequity of distribution of AHANA Journalism teachers among types of schools: public, parochial, private. Of all public school Journalism educators in this study (n = 694 schools), only 4.3 percent come from ethnic-minority groups. Not one AHANA teacher represented the 42 parochial schools in this part of the study, whereas 12.5 percent AHANA Journalism teachers can be found in other private schools. These percentages may not tell the complete story, for only 32 schools in this part of the study are non-parochial private schools.

Another significant relationship is observed when we examine the percent of AHANA students in journalism programs and the racial or ethnic background of teachers.

In school Journalism programs having 9 percent or fewer AHANA students involved (206 schools), we find only three teachers-advisers who are from AHANA backgrounds, which is only 1.5 percent. Even when we look at the group of schools with 10-29 percent AHANA student composition, we find merely 3.4 percent of those programs headed by a teacher/adviser from a non-Caucasian background. In schools with a large AHANA student involvement in Journalism, where the percentage is 30 percent and above (122 schools in the study), we note that the percentage is somewhat better with nearly 16 percent of those programs being headed by an ethnic-minority teacher/adviser.

Clearly, these discrepancies indicate the need for recruitment and retention of AHANA Journalism educators in all kinds of schools so that a closer relationship can exist between the multicultural makeup of Journalism students and their teachers-advisers.

Salaries and Other Income. High school Journalism teachers seem to be lagging behind, by more than $2,000, in contracted school-year salaries when compared with all U.S. secondary school teachers.

Graph 4.15 shows Journalism teachers earning $29,675 in annual pre-tax salary ($28,000 median) compared with $31,781 for all public and private high school teachers.[21] College Journalism educators' salaries are about $37,913 per year for the 1989-1990 school year.[22] However, it should be pointed out that collegiate educators' average ages are five years older, and their years of professional experience average about six years longer than their high school counterparts. It should also be noted that the current high school study was based on the 1990-1991 school year, so a greater disparity might be expected if college educators' salaries were adjusted to reflect an additional annual increase.

Likewise, in the final figure shown in Graph 4.15, professional journalists' salaries in 1991 were $31,500 (with a median of $31,297).[23] The periods of comparison between high school educators and professional journalists are slightly different because the educators' incomes were based on the 1990-1991 academic year (9- or 10-month), not on the 1991 calendar year. We might expect a slight upward adjustment for the Journalism educators for strict comparative purposes. However, we also note that professional journalists' salaries are based on those with an average age of 36 who have 12 years of professional experience.[24] High school Journalism educators are five years older and typically have two added years of work experience than do "typical" professional journalists.

Many of the high school Journalism educators in the survey also received added school-year income through stipends the schools paid for media advising. In fact, 85 percent of the educators received a stipend for advising one or more media outlets. Graph 4.16 shows the average stipend for each.

Yearbook and newspaper stipends are virtually the same at $1,096 and $1,055 respectively. While the news magazine compensation appears, at $1,453, considerably better than those of any of the others, one must take into account that only 4.4 percent of the schools in the study had news magazines. Generally, schools with news magazines are in larger and more affluent school districts. Lowest annual stipends among news media outlets are in radio or TV advising with an average of $443. But because only 12.7 percent of the schools have broadcast media, the actual number of schools represented in this part of the study might be too small to judge stipend size accurately.

School literary magazine advising, generally not considered the prerogative of Journalism educators, pays $600 annually. Nearly 38 percent of U.S. schools offer literary magazine experiences to students.

Salaries and Related Issues. Not surprisingly, we find that school size is significantly related to salaries. Generally speaking, greater numbers of teachers in higher salary levels are found in the larger schools.

Much the same pattern emerges when we look at salary levels of Journalism educators coming from public or private schools. Whereas only 29.2 percent of public school Journalism teachers make less than $25,000 annually, more than 58 percent of the parochial and private school teachers earn that amount or less per year. At the higher end of the scale, more than 17 percent of all public school Journalism educators make more than $40,000 annually while only 4.4 percent of the parochial and private school teachers do. While a few of the private schools in the study are affluent boarding schools, many others are church-related schools that traditionally pay teachers at less than the public school scale.

Summary

Journalistic activities are fairly common in U.S. high schools, with nearly 95 percent of them offering a Journalism class or some type of media outlet for student staff members and their audiences. More than half-a-million students take a course called "Journalism," and more than 700,000 serve on publications staffs. Yearbooks are published in 93 percent of the nation's schools, and newspapers are produced in 79 percent. Journalism educators typically spend more than half of their school day teaching or supervising media-related classes or labs. At 40-something, they are roughly the same age as other secondary school teachers; they have about the same number of years of teaching experience, almost 15; but they have been involved with Journalism teaching or advising for only about half that time.

NOTES ON CHAPTER 4

1. *Digest of Education Statistics 1990*. U.S. Department of Education Office of Educational Research and Improvement, Washington, D.C., 1991, 138. (Data collected 1988).

2. *Ibid.:* 107.

3. *Ibid.:* 75.

4. Penny Sebring, et al., *The National Longitudinal Study of the High School Class of 1972, Fifth Follow-up (1986).* (Chicago: National Opinion Research Center, 1987): 35.

5. *Ibid.*

6. *High School Journalism Confronts Critical Deadline.* A Report by the Journalism Education Association Commission on the Role of Journalism in Secondary Education. Manhattan, KS: Journalism Education Association, 1987.

7. *Digest of Education Statistics 1990:* 75.

8. David Weaver and G. Cleveland Wilhoit, "A Profile of JMC Educators: Traits, Attitudes and Values," *Journalism Educator* 43 (Summer 1988): 11.

9. David Weaver and G. Cleveland Wilhoit, "The American Journalist in the 1990s," A Preliminary Report of Key Findings from a 1992 National Survey of U.S. Journalists. Bloomington, IN: Indiana University School of Journalism, November 17, 1992: 4.

10. *Digest of Education Statistics 1990:* 75.

11. Weaver and Wilhoit, "A Profile": 11.

12. Weaver and Wilhoit, "The American Journalist in the 1990s: A Preliminary Report": 4.

13. Lee B. Becker, "Annual Enrollment Census: Comparisons and Projections," *Journalism Educator* 46 (Autumn 1991): 57.

14. *Digest of Education Statistics 1990:* 75.

15. Weaver and Wilhoit, "A Profile": 16, 28.

16. Weaver and Wilhoit, "The American Journalist in the 1990s": 3.

17. *Digest of Education Statistics 1990:* 75.

18. Weaver and Wilhoit, "A Profile": 12.

19. Weaver and Wilhoit, "The American Journalist in the 1990s": 5.

20. *Digest of Education Statistics 1990:* 75.

21. *Digest of Education Statistics 1990:* 83.

22. Elnora W. Stuart and Elizabeth B. Dickey, "Faculty and Administration Salary Survey and Analysis," *Journalism Educator 46* (Summer 1991): 64.

23. Weaver and Wilhoit, "The American Journalist in the 1990s": 15, 8.

24. *Ibid.:* 3.

Chapter 5

TEACHERS MAKE IT WORK, BUT HOW?
CERTIFICATION, SATISFACTION, PROFESSIONAL LIFE

Chapter Highlights

- Only about 28 percent of high school journalism teachers/advisers are certified in Journalism.

- Fewer than 8 percent have a major in Journalism or Mass Communication.

- About 43 percent have been assigned to the Journalism program by an administrator, but most made an early commitment to teaching language arts.

- Certified teachers are more likely to be found in larger public high schools.

- Journalism teachers/advisers are as satisfied as, or happier than, their non-Journalism colleagues.

- Job satisfaction predictors are faculty morale, annual salary, amount of freedom administrators allow in advising, and age.

- More than 80 percent say they wish to remain in teaching until retirement.

- About 25 percent have college or professional media experience; 40 percent were on high school media staffs.

- Journalism people have a demanding work load but are quite involved in professional organizations.

- They tend to be right of center ideologically but more likely to be Democrats than the population at large.

- They are likely to value student press freedoms more highly than do either their non-Journalism colleagues or the general public.

With the strong academic showing by student journalists, as described in Chapters 2 and 3, one might assume that high school Journalism educators are well-qualified academically to teach Journalism and advise publications. Not so.

Yes, there are several wonderful teachers and programs around the country, but in general, we find that those who teach Journalism courses and who advise various media in the nation's schools are not certified in Journalism by their states. Neither are their academic credentials strong in Journalism.

We assume that outstanding student performance must be strongly related to some quality inherent within journalistic study and practice itself—and perhaps to well-intentioned and hard-working educators who make up for academic deficiencies through a strong commitment to their own lifelong learning. In any event, however, the widespread successes of journalism students in high school and college language arts cannot be linked to teacher certification or formal academic training.[1]

State Certification to Teach Journalism

For example, a mere 28.2 percent of the country's Journalism educators hold state certification in Journalism, and Journalism requirements state-by-state are varied, with some states having no Journalism course work as requirements and others having minimal standards for certification.[2] For example, 22 states, among them Alaska, Connecticut, and Georgia, do not have Journalism certification requirements at all. Another 21 states, including Illinois, Michigan, Oklahoma and Washington, require minimal formal academic background to earn certification.[3]

So it is conceivable that several of the 28.2 percent of educators in this study who hold state certification credentials might have taken only one or two Journalism courses, accompanied by a teaching major in some other related field like English, but nevertheless still qualify for state certification in Journalism. In other states, language arts background suffices. Some educators come from states with no certification requirements, but they are well-qualified to teach Journalism, but this is an exception rather than the rule. Graph 5.1 shows the top four areas of certification among U.S. Journalism educators.[4]

Graph 5.1

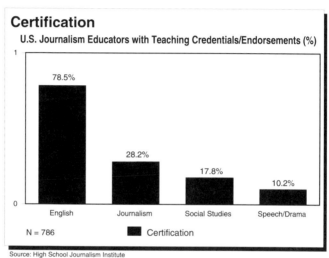

Certification
U.S. Journalism Educators with Teaching Credentials/Endorsements (%)

78.5%	English
28.2%	Journalism
17.8%	Social Studies
10.2%	Speech/Drama

N = 786 ■ Certification

Source: High School Journalism Institute

Among those people teaching Journalism in the nation, 78.5 percent of them hold English/language arts certification whereas another 17.8 percent have credentials to teach social studies. Another 10.2 percent of the Journalism educators have earned state certification to teach speech/drama.

One possible explanation for the relatively small incidence of formal certification among Journalism educators can be found by looking at the time during which they first considered going into Journalism education. In answer to the question "When did you first think about getting involved in Journalism education?" the largest response, 43.2 percent, was this: "after assignment by an administrator." Thus, while a high percentage of current Journalism educators knew they wanted to be teachers before and during college, a substantial portion of them had no inclination toward Journalism teaching/advising until they drew that assignment while under a teaching contract that included a subject area of their first choice, namely, English.

Graph 5.2 also makes plain some other interesting factors about Journalism educators' initial interest in teaching in general and in Journalism in particular. We observe that 85.4 percent of the Journalism educators knew that they wanted to teach before their college graduations, but only about 39 percent of them had even considered Journalism during the same time period. We do observe that almost one-quarter of the teachers considered Journalism education while they were still in high school, perhaps a testimonial to their own secondary school journalistic experiences. More than 50 percent of them had considered teaching careers before they went to college.

Graph 5.2

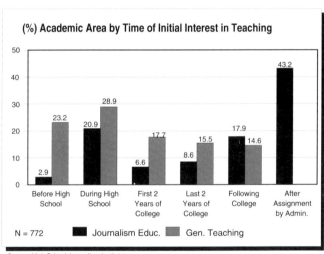

(%) Academic Area by Time of Initial Interest in Teaching

N = 772 ■ Journalism Educ. ▨ Gen. Teaching

Source: High School Journalism Institute

On the other hand, collegiate influences don't appear as strong. About 15 percent of current Journalism educators considered Journalism teaching/advising while in college, but more than 30 percent of them decided to be high school teachers while in college.

We see a decided commitment to teaching as a career choice fairly early among the educators, but we see nowhere near the same commitment to Journalism education until either after college or until after being assigned by an administrator, once the teachers are under contract.

Degrees

Given the lateness of entry into Journalism education, it is not surprising that few educators hold a major in Journalism. We find only 7.8 percent of all earned degrees are in Journalism. However, the educators in our study hold many degrees, with more than 53 percent of them holding master's degrees and 10.1 percent of them possessing post-master's degrees (education specialist and doctoral). Graph 5.3 shows the breakdown of each degree category and the percentage of journalism majors in each:

- 11.1 percent associate (2-year) degrees, 8 percent in Journalism
- 97.2 percent bachelor's degrees, 8.5 percent in Journalism
- 53.3 percent master's degrees, 5.5 percent in Journalism
- 10.1 percent post-master's degrees, 12.7 percent in Journalism.

Graph 5.3

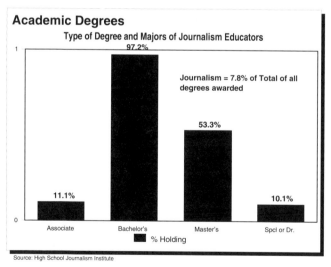

Academic Degrees

Type of Degree and Majors of Journalism Educators

Journalism = 7.8% of Total of all degrees awarded

Source: High School Journalism Institute

Motivations for Entering Teaching

Even though it wasn't journalism that attracted most current media educators to the field, some subject matter did (primarily

101

English/language arts). Nearly 63 percent of the respondents cited "interest in the subjects taught" among their three top reasons for entering teaching.

The second-most cited reason turned out to be "desire to work with young people," with 59.7 percent of the educators claiming this as one of their strong motivators for entering the field. Next in line are "importance of education to society," 38.1 percent; "desire to serve others," 33.7 percent; and "work schedule (hours, vacation, etc.)," 32.4 percent. Besides the academic attraction, we see a certain altruism running through the top motivators.

Our study in many ways is similar to one taken of 1972 high school graduates who have pursued secondary and elementary school teaching careers, as seen in Table 5.1. Because the teachers in the general study are all about the same age, their motivations might be slightly different from those in the Journalism educator study, which represents ages 22 through 73. (Even so, the average of Journalism teachers is 41, nearly the same as the teachers in the general study).[5]

Table 5.1: Motivation to Enter Teaching
Summary of Most Important Reasons for Becoming a Teacher

Item	J-Ed.	Rank	All Ed.	Rank
Interest in the subjects	63.1%	1.	49%	2.
Desire to work with young people	59.7%	2.	67.2%	1.
Importance of education to society	38.1%	3.	34%	3.
Desire to serve others	33.7%	4.	27.9%	4.
Work schedule (hours, vacation, etc.)	32.4%	5.	25.9%	5.
	n = 754		n = 1,011	

Source: High School Journalism Institute, National Opinion Research Center

We note that the Journalism teachers were most attracted to "interest in the subjects." Most of these people knew that they wanted to be secondary school language arts teachers whereas teachers in the general study knew that they wanted to be teachers on either elementary or secondary levels, but they did not have the same dedication to a subject area. Nonetheless, they selected this as their second-most frequent reason for entering teaching. Their primary motivation was "a desire to work with young people," which was the second-most common reason among Journalism educators. In all other comparisons of Table 5.1, we find the rank ordering and the general percents of each group to be similar, showing a consistency of motivations for entering a teaching career.

Influence of Former Teachers

Many current Journalism educators have been drawn to teaching generally (not necessarily to Journalism teaching in particular) by their former teachers. Influences from these role models might seem obvious.

When asked to rate "very important" or "important" reasons for wanting to enter teaching as a career, more than 67 percent chose the influence of a former high school teacher (non-Journalism); more than 24 percent specifically mentioned a high school Journalism teacher; 42 percent selected a non-Journalism college teacher; 17 percent mentioned a college Journalism educator. Thirty percent of the current high school Journalism educators rated former elementary school teachers as being "very important" or "important" influences in their own decisions to opt for careers in education.

Even though influences of former teachers are important to those now in the field, however, they were not among the most crucial influences, as mentioned earlier (See Table 5.1).

Certification: Other Considerations

We find many interesting relationships related to teachers' having or not having Journalism certification.

For example, it is significantly more likely that we will not find certified teachers in the smaller schools of the nation (e.g., under 500 enrollment) while being more likely to find them in schools of 1,001 and higher enrollments.

We also find the greater likelihood that certified teachers can be found in public schools as opposed to parochial or private. The parochial schools were least likely to employ a certified Journalism teacher (only 9.3 percent of them had one on the faculty) whereas in public schools we find about 28.4 percent of all Journalism teachers to be certified in the field. In 20 percent of the nation's non-parochial private schools, certified teachers are involved in the journalism program.

Certification becomes more problematic when examining schools that offer a credit course called "Journalism," "Beginning Journalism," "Journalism I," or something similar. Even though almost 66 percent of the schools in the U.S. offer such a course, in only 34 percent of those schools are the instructors certified to teach Journalism. A 1990 study by the U.S. Department of Education found that about 20 percent of secondary school teachers are involved in instructional areas in which they are unqualified.[6] Journalism is certainly an area that far exceeds the already high portion of uncertified high school teachers generally.

The problem could be even more severe than this because it is a fairly well-known practice for administrators to fudge on course names for purposes of skirting state department or accreditation guidelines. Thus, we might actually find a much higher percentage of uncertified Journalism teachers were we to include those Journalism courses called by some other name ("Practical English," "Vocational Writing," "Writing Lab," and the like).

Another significant difference may be found when examining Journalism certification among schools that offer some type of advanced Journalism course for credit. In almost 25 percent of U.S. high schools, a course in Advanced Journalism is offered. Of those rather specialized Journalism courses, only 46 percent are taught by certified Journalism teachers.

Likewise, in the 42 percent of the nation's schools offering a newspaper lab for credit, only about 41 percent have a certified Journalism educator in charge. Among the 56 percent of schools that give credit for yearbook lab, only 36 percent of those programs are headed by a state-certified Journalism educator. While each of these comparisons shows a significantly higher number of certified teachers available for students in schools wherein publications lab credits are granted, one can see that the percentage of academically qualified instructors is abysmally low.

To their credit, Journalism teachers go back to school in direct proportion to the time they remain in media education. About three times as many first-year teachers are not certified compared with those who are. By the time teachers reach 4-8 years experience, this trend neutralizes, and we find a 50-50 split among those having certification and those who don't. For those who stay at it more than eight years, a decidedly higher percentage of Journalism educators have earned certification than those who have not earned it during all those years. We suspect that some of these educators got "assigned" to the Journalism program, became more and more interested in it, and went on to become certified. With others, the scenario is a bit more threatening and comes from administrative edict: "Become certified or get pink-slipped." Whatever the case, the longer teachers remain in Journalism the greater the tendency there is for them to go to summer school, to attend workshops for credit, and to take correspondence courses toward earning their certification stripes.

As could be expected, those who first think about going into Journalism education while in high school or during their college careers are far more likely to be certified than those who come into the field after teaching other subjects first or after being assigned by an administrator. More than 73 percent of the teachers in the latter categories lack certification, but by contrast, 71 percent of those who have certification initially considered attaining it while in high school or in college.

Obviously, the ideal recruiting methods for future high school Journalism teachers and publications advisers ought to be concentrated during the high school years, and definite encouragement ought also be made among college freshmen and sophomores now in language arts teacher education sequences. Opportunities would seem plentiful if current English majors who also have an interest in and affinity for Journalism would become certified in both subject areas while attaining their teaching degrees.

If all U.S. high schools that now offer credit were suddenly to require that certified people actually teach the Journalism courses, there would be an enormous teacher shortage. Colleges currently offering Journalism education sequences would be filled to capacity. About 10,000 new Journalism teachers would be needed immediately if 100 percent of the current programs offering credit but not now having a certified teacher were to add one. If all the schools in the country offering some type of activity, whether for credit or not, were to seek a certified Journalism educator for the next school year, college Journalism education programs would have to graduate 15,500 people immediately.

Given that about 414 U.S. colleges and universities offer programs in Journalism or Mass Communication,[7] and assuming that all of them would offer sufficient credits combined with Education Department courses in order to prepare students for such jobs, it would mean that each institution would have to graduate 37 Journalism education students this next year. This is highly unlikely, of course, because many colleges offering Journalism do not also provide the course work or personnel necessary to support those wishing to earn certification. To illustrate, the most recent listing of U.S. Journalism programs in *Journalism Educator* provides an enrollment and graduation rate among 18 subdivisions offered in specific departments (e.g., "News-editorial," "Broadcast news," "Public Relations," "Advertising," and the like),[8] but "Secondary School Journalism education" is not listed at all. This indicates that a relatively small number of students, in only a small percentage of these programs, are interested in Journalism education at this time.

One other relationship involving certification worth noting involves standards and mandates. We divided states according to Marilyn Weaver's 1988 findings about Journalism certification requirements into three groups: states with no requirements (N=22), states with low requirements (N=21) and states with moderate-to-high endorsement expectations (N=10). American Samoa, the District of Columbia, and Puerto Rico bring the total to 53.[9] Graph 5.4 shows the relationships of the three major grouping of states and the accompanying percentages of teachers in the current study who have certification.

Graph 5.4

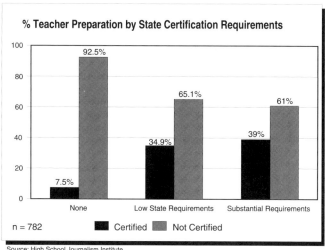

% Teacher Preparation by State Certification Requirements

n = 782 ■ Certified ▨ Not Certified

Source: High School Journalism Institute

It appears that as state certification requirements become more rigorous, teachers are more likely to acquire, or possess before being hired, state-mandated endorsement in Journalism. Perhaps when these mandates are well-known, or at least a minimum requirement is expected, administrators are more careful to hire qualified people. Nevertheless, at a 39 percent certification rate among Journalism teachers in the 10 states requiring fairly substantial academic background, the number is well below what most administrators, parents, educators and students would expect of teachers in other academic courses such as English, mathematics, social studies, and science. Our guess is that if these areas were as poorly staffed in terms of the formal education of teachers, the public would be in an uproar.

Job Satisfaction

Depending on which study is used for comparisons, U.S. high school Journalism educators appear to be at least as satisfied with their jobs as non-Journalism teachers, if not more so.

Graph 5.5 shows degrees of satisfaction of Journalism educators compared with all public school teachers,[10] college Journalism educators,[11] and U.S. journalists.[12] Almost 84 percent of the high school Journalism educators claim to be satisfied with their present careers. In contrast, 86 percent of all public school secondary teachers claim to be satisfied. Almost the same percentage of college Journalism teachers say that they are satisfied, 86.2 percent; but only 77.6 percent of professional journalists in the U.S. indicate being satisfied with their jobs.

Graph 5.5

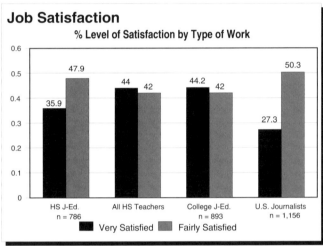

Job Satisfaction

% Level of Satisfaction by Type of Work

Source: High School Journalism Institute; U.S. Dept. of Education; Weaver and Wilhoit *Profile*; Weaver and Wilhoit *American Journalist in the 1990s*

In an earlier study of the high school graduating class of 1972 who went on to become elementary and secondary school teachers in public and private schools, their level of satisfaction with teaching stood at only about 70 percent, significantly lower than high school Journalism educators in the current study.[13] This could be because all those in that 1987 study were graduated from high school in 1971 and are about the same age. Our current study includes a wide range of ages.

Graph 5.5, on the other hand, does also signify that high school Journalism educators show less intensity of satisfaction than do their non-Journalism counterparts. About 8 percent more of the non-Journalism teachers claim to be "very satisfied" (44 percent vs. 35.9 percent for Journalism educators). This same approximate difference in "very satisfieds" exists when comparing high school Journalism educators and collegiate educators. However, we find that only about 27 percent of current U.S. journalists claim to be "very satisfied," a considerably lower percent than high school Journalism educators, all public school teachers or college Journalism educators.

Another indicator of satisfaction with present teaching jobs is found in Graph 5.6. Asked if they would choose to pursue teaching if they could start back in college again, almost 64 percent of the secondary school Journalism educators said that they would start over again, compared with only about 49 percent of the non-Journalism high school teachers. Also, almost double the number of non-Journalism teachers say they would not teach again, given another opportunity (30.5 percent vs. 16.3 percent of the Journalism teachers).[14]

Graph 5.6

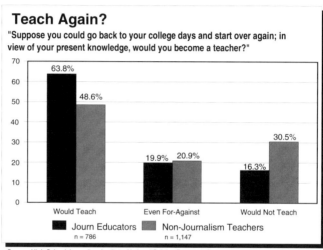

Teach Again?

"Suppose you could go back to your college days and start over again; in view of your present knowledge, would you become a teacher?"

Source: High School Journalism Institute; National Opinion Research Center

Several other factors would appear to be at work in effecting an atmosphere for teacher satisfaction. As pertains to high school Journalism educators, we now lay out several of the basic findings of our national study before looking at several relationships among them.

Future Plans

Of all U.S. secondary school Journalism educators, more than 60 percent wish to remain in teaching until retirement. Roughly 21 percent say they will probably continue in teaching unless something better comes along. Less than 4 percent indicate that they definitely plan to leave teaching as soon as possible, and nearly 15 percent are undecided about their long-term prospects in teaching.

Publication Advising Freedom

The vast majority of Journalism educators believe they are operating in schools in which administrators allow them to do most of the decision-making with regard to the publications they advise. When asked, "How much freedom do your school administrators usually allow those who advise student publications?" more than 83 percent claimed "almost complete" or "a great deal." Only 15.4 percent said "some," and 1.1 percent claimed to have "none," a prospect that seems rather unlikely but nonetheless would seem to indicate severe restrictions for this very minor portion of our respondents.

Teaching Freedom

Academic freedom is another aspect that could contribute to a teacher's sense of job satisfaction. Almost 48 percent of the Journalism educators feel they have "almost complete freedom" when it comes to deciding how to teach their courses. This accompanies another 41 percent who claim they have a great deal of freedom in approaches to teaching their classes. About 10 percent say they have "some" freedom, while only 1.7 percent claim "none at all."

Faculty Opinion of Journalism Programs

Another measure of satisfaction, we feel, is the Journalism educator's assessment of how other school colleagues view the journalism program. Generally, the Journalism educators thought their colleagues saw communications programs as equal to or better than other departments. More than 52 percent thought other faculty evaluated journalism as "about the same as other units," and almost 28 percent thought colleagues' opinions of journalism were higher than other units. Among 19 percent of the respondents there was a perception that colleagues' opinions of the journalism program were lower than other units in the school. Thus, by and large, journalism programs seem to be fairly well thought of by colleagues of Journalism educators, as measured by the educators' self-assessments.

Faculty Morale

Besides faculty opinion of the journalism program, another measure of educator satisfaction may be measured by examining the faculty morale at the school. Journalism educators come from schools in which the following levels of overall faculty morale exist, as measured by Journalism educators' responses: Excellent 8 percent; Good 35.3 percent; Fair 36.4 percent; Poor 12.7 percent; and Very Poor 7.6 percent. Thus, we find more than 42 percent thinking faculty morale is at least good while only about 20 percent think it poor.

We also asked a question related to morale change to see how present-day attitudes compare with those formerly held. Journalism educators feel there has been deterioration in faculty morale in the last few years. More than 54 percent of them indicate that either slight or substantial deterioration in morale had occurred. By contrast, only about 24 percent think improvements have been noticed. And 22 percent claim "no change" in morale during the past few years.

School Improvement

Related to morale, in a sense, is the opinion educators in our study have of the public schools in their communities with regard to improvement or lack thereof. More than 29 percent indicate schools have improved during the past five years; almost 27 percent say they have gotten worse; nearly 37 percent say they have stayed the same; and almost 8 percent claim they don't know. These responses are nearly identical to public high school teacher responses collected in a 1989 Gallup Poll.[15] (However, in that study, 42 percent indicated that schools stayed about the same—rather than the 37 percent we found.)

Tenure

Nearly 67 percent of the U.S. high school Journalism educators have earned tenure at their respective schools.

Leave Teaching

Journalism educators seem more strongly committed to remaining in teaching than do their non-journalism colleagues. We asked a series of five questions that dealt with changing careers or leaving their current teaching positions for other school-related employment.

About 55 percent of the Journalism educators say they would not leave teaching if offered a position in educational administration. However, 37 percent of public and private school teachers say they would not leave teaching for an administrative post.[16]

When we compare the same two groups on non-administrative jobs, the differences are less noticeable. If offered a full-time non-teaching job (12 months, 40 hours per week) for $5,000 more per year than the current teaching salary, 45 percent of the Journalism educators and almost 47 percent of the other educators say they would not leave teaching, but 34 percent of the Journalism teachers say they would consider leaving while only 27 percent of the other educators would. But 27 percent of the non-Journalism educators say they would "probably" or "definitely" leave teaching for such a non-teaching job whereas only 21 percent of the Journalism educators would do so.[17]

What about being offered a teaching job in an elite private school at the current teaching salary? Forty-three percent of the Journalism educators would not take such a position while more than 48 percent of the non-Journalism teachers would not take it. However, more than 23 percent of the Journalism educators say they would "probably" or "definitely" leave for this other unique teaching job, but only about 15 percent of the non-Journalism educators say they would leave.[18]

What if offered a non-teaching job in a field in which they were interested? About 18 percent of the Journalism educators and 22 percent of the other educators would not leave their current teaching jobs for such a non-teaching job. But nearly 55 percent of the Journalism teachers would consider leaving while only 47 percent of the other educators would consider it. Close to 30 percent of each group would definitely or probably leave teaching for this new job.[19]

The final area involving commitment to teaching involves the proposition of a non-teaching job at current teaching salary but with greater possibilities for promotion. Basically, the two groups are virtually the same on this item. Answers and percentages of each group follow: Would not leave teaching: 37 percent Journalism educators, 40.8 percent other educators. Would consider leaving teaching: 38.1

percent Journalism educators, 34.8 percent others. Would "definitely" or "probably" leave: 24.8 percent Journalism educators, 24.9 percent others.[20]

In sum, we note the following trends about Journalism educators when compared with their colleagues in other departments: They are less likely to leave current jobs for administrative posts, they are less likely to be attracted to 12-month non-teaching jobs at higher salaries; they are more likely to leave current teaching jobs to teach at an elite private school for the same salary; they are more apt to leave if offered a non-teaching job in a field of interest; and they are no more attracted than are fellow faculty to a non-teaching job that has better promotion possibilities.

Predictors of Job Satisfaction

Many of the rather complex number of variables we have looked at thus far, as well as others examined later, we submitted to multiple regression analysis to determine the most significant factors that lead to job satisfaction. In the final analysis, four of the variables surfaced as powerful predictors of on-the-job satisfaction among Journalism educators: faculty morale, annual salary, amount of freedom allowed by administrators in advising school publications, and age of the educator.[21] We will examine each more closely as it relates to job satisfaction.

Satisfaction/Faculty Morale

Journalism educators' perception of overall faculty morale at the school is the primary variable leading to job satisfaction. In taking a closer look, we find that in schools where teachers/advisers are dissatisfied, they perceive faculty morale to be low. Conversely, among very satisfied educators, we find that their perception of faculty morale is that it is high. Graph 5.7 shows some of the relationships when we grouped advisers according to their job satisfaction as well as to the faculty morale at their schools.

Examining the "very satisfied" Journalism teachers/advisers, we find that a large percentage of them (65 percent) can be found in schools with high faculty morale. On the other hand, we find the opposite tendency among the largest group of dissatisfied teachers/advisers: The largest group of them (55.2 percent) is clustered in schools where morale is deemed to be "poor."

Graph 5.7

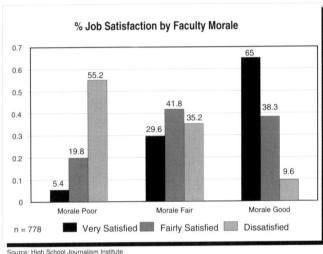

% Job Satisfaction by Faculty Morale

Source: High School Journalism Institute

Cramer's V = .338 p<.0000

A number of factors contribute to school morale, but we note that various studies support the common perception that administrative leadership is a major contributor to an upbeat atmosphere.[22] Perhaps Journalism educators have little control over serving in schools with enlightened administrators who would be sensitive to building a positive atmosphere; nonetheless, prospective teachers might be able to probe this important and obvious area of job satisfaction before they sign a contract.

Satisfaction/Annual Salary

A significant relationship is found between job satisfaction and annual salary. In addition to the analysis above showing that salary is a predictor of happiness, we determined, by grouping Journalism educators according to salary levels and degrees of satisfaction, that those in higher income brackets tend to be more satisfied than those at the lower end of the scale. To illustrate, of those teachers earning more than $40,000 annually, 53 percent are "very satisfied" with their jobs whereas only 22 percent of those earning $20,000 or less claim to be "very satisfied." In the highest group, only 12 percent claim to be "dissatisfied" whereas more than 18 percent of the lowest-paid educators claim to be unhappy with their jobs.

Satisfaction/Advising Freedom

Another strong predictor of job satisfaction among Journalism educators is the freedom allowed by school administrators in the publications advising process. Where job satisfaction increases, an accompanying greater amount of freedom has been granted by administrators. Advisers in these freer circumstances enjoy a "hands-off" policy on the part of administrators when it comes to advising student publications. For example, 60 percent of very satisfied advisers claim "almost complete" freedom whereas only about 33 percent of dissatisfied advisers make the same claim. On the other hand, only 9 percent of very satisfied advisers say that they have minimal freedoms in making advising decisions whereas about 32 percent of the dissatisfied advisers say they have minimal freedoms.

Satisfaction/Age

Higher percentages of older Journalism educators appear to be very satisfied with their jobs. In our study, nearly 45 percent of teachers older than 45 are "very satisfied" with their jobs whereas about 33 percent of those under 32 show the same degree of satisfaction. Among those between 32 and 38, only 28 percent are "very satisfied."

Advising Freedom/Other Variables

Because freedom in advising school publications was identified as important to an adviser's job satisfaction, we looked at this aspect of administrative behavior a bit more closely.

Faculty Opinion

A tendency exists for advisers to sense that they have more freedom in working with school publications as they perceive faculty opinion of the journalism program's quality to be higher than that of other units. As degrees of administrative freedom lessen, so also does the tendency lessen for advisers to believe that other faculty members perceive the publications program to be of high quality.

115

Plans to Stay in Teaching

As the amount of administrative freedom granted advisers increases, so does the tendency of the Journalism educators to indicate their desire to remain in teaching until retirement.

Teaching Freedom

A similar tendency exists when advisers are grouped according to degrees of advising freedoms and degrees of teaching freedoms. We find that in schools where administrators allow great freedom for the adviser in handling publications, those administrators are also more likely to allow teachers to have wide latitude in selecting teaching methods, classroom techniques and publications management.

Faculty Morale

When Journalism educators are granted administrative freedom to advise publications without interference, a much stronger likelihood exists that those same advisers perceive faculty morale at the school to be much better than is the case when administrators restrict publications advising.

Age

As might be expected, there's a significant tendency for advising freedom to be more prevalent among those who are older.

Journalism Educators' Professional Lives

Today's high school Journalism educators seem to contradict the disparaging adage that "those who can, do; and those who can't, teach." Despite the well-documented weaknesses in formal Journalism education, many Journalism educators have other media-related experiences that strengthen them in the performance of their current educational duties.

Graph 5.8 shows us that more than 40 percent of today's high school Journalism teachers/advisers served on the staffs of publications while they were high school students. Their average number of years on the staff was 3.1.

Nearly 27 percent of the Journalism educators worked on college publications for an average of 2.7 years.

Graph 5.8

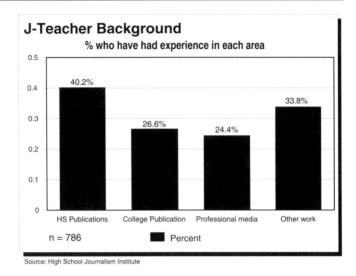

J-Teacher Background
% who have had experience in each area

n = 786 ■ Percent

Source: High School Journalism Institute

One rather surprising finding about media experiences is that more than 24 percent of today's high school Journalism educators have spent time working in some aspect of professional journalism, on average for nearly five years.

In addition to these media-related experiences, which no doubt help educators bring depth and breadth to their high school class-rooms, more than one-third of them have worked at non-teaching jobs following their college graduations. Of the 33.8 percent who reported doing non-school-related work, the average time spent not teaching is 10.2 years.

Workload

Earlier, we described the typical U.S. high school Journalism educator's workload as 5.32 classes per day, with about 53 percent of that being devoted to media-related classes and labs.

Beyond these formal class and lab times totalling 26.6 hours per week, teachers report spending 7 hours each week advising students in their publications or media work outside the school day.

Here's the remainder of a typical (and busy) work week for a Journalism teacher/adviser:

- 3.9 hours on hall duty, study hall, supervising detention
- 2.9 hours completing forms and administrative paperwork

117

- 10.5 hours preparing lessons, lectures, composing tests, grading papers
- 4.2 hours doing background reading in various subject areas
- 2.1 hours contacting employers on students' behalf and visiting students at worksites
- 2.1 hours conducting makeup work for students
- 3 hours per week counseling students
- 10.6 hours coaching athletics
- 5.4 hours directing non-athletic extracurricular activities (non-journalism)
- 3.8 hours participating in non-school sponsored activities with students (such as service and church/synagogue)
- 3.2 hours tutoring

In sum, a "typical" week of teaching, advising, preparing, supervising and doing other school-related tasks totals 85.3 hours. We suspect that this self-assessment of time might be a tad inflated; yet it is the perception Journalism teachers/advisers have of their workloads. Indeed, we know of several high school teachers—both journalism and non-Journalism educators—who routinely put in these types of hours during the school year. A national study of elementary and secondary school teachers by the National Opinion Research Center shows an average week of about 53.5 hours.[23]

Professional Memberships

Given memberships or other involvement in educational, media or student-related associations, we conclude that high school Journalism educators value participation in these professional groups and that they are considerably involved.

Listed below are the percentages of Journalism educators who claim to be involved with each of the named groups. Because 786 teachers/advisers answered this part of the survey, one could roughly calculate the total number of U.S. advisers active in each of the groups by multiplying the percentage by 21,474—the baseline number of schools represented by the teachers/advisers taking part in the study.

- 52.3% State teachers association
- 50.8% National Education Association (NEA)
- 37.7% Other teacher associations
- 30.2% Quill and Scroll International Journalism Honorary Society
- 27.9% State press association
- 21% Journalism Education Association (JEA)
- 16.2% Columbia Scholastic Press Association (CSPA)
- 12.6% National Scholastic Press Association (NSPA)
- 10.2% American Federation of Teachers (AFT)
- 7% Other media associations
- 4.5% Phi Delta Kappa (PDK)
- 2.8% Society of Professional Journalists (SPJ)
- 2.2% Southern Interscholastic Press Association (SIPA)
- 1.5% Association for Education in Journalism and Mass Communication (AEJMC)

Interestingly, the top three organizations represented are oriented toward the teaching profession in general, not Journalism or Mass Communication specifically. Likewise, the top two organizations, enrolling more than half of all U.S. high school Journalism educators, serve the teaching profession in general, not specifically the Journalism or Communications guild. By contrast, Weaver and Wilhoit found in their 1988 study of college Journalism educators that no more than 4 percent of them belonged to a non-communication professional association. The American Association of University Professors (AAUP) was the only one of 21 such professional organizations listed that involved education generally. However, more than half of the college educators in the study belonged to a Journalism education group, AEJMC.[24] In a 1992 study, the same authors found that only 36 percent of all U.S. professional journalists, by contrast, belonged to any professional organization.[25]

Comparing these figures, we see a strong commitment by high school Journalism educators (and college Journalism educators) to membership in professional organizations, more so, at any rate, than full-time journalists.

Of the media organizations, secondary school Journalism educators are most involved with Quill and Scroll, an international honorary society for high school journalists that has chapters in all states and in more than 40 foreign countries. Thus, while Quill and Scroll probably has more active involvement of teachers than shown above because of its international nature, we would project that about 6,485 teachers/advisers work in schools with active Quill and Scroll chapters. Given our 3.4 percent maximum margin of error, we would estimate that between 5,755 and 7,215 teachers/advisers in the United States are now working with a Quill and Scroll chapter. That same formula may be applied to figures above for further estimates of numbers of teachers actually involved.

Some of the groups, for example the Columbia Scholastic Press Association and the National Scholastic Press Association, are organizations that register schools and publications rather than teachers; however, their services are aimed primarily at students. Teachers take active roles in them by attending conventions with students, making sure publications are critiqued for students, and encouraging other types of student involvement in activities sponsored by the national and state organizations.

A further sign of active involvement by high school teachers in these organizations is that nearly 24 percent of the teachers have held an office in one or more of the associations.

Professional Reading

Journalism educators seem to read a wide variety of journals related to secondary school media teaching and advising. No doubt they read many other books and journals related to their personal interests as well as those connected with their classes. Here, we look strictly at Journalism-related reading.

With a higher percentage of schools having yearbooks than newspapers, and with professional yearbook companies blanketing the markets with their publications, it is not surprising that the two periodicals best-read by Journalism educators are produced by year-book publishers.

In the chart following, Journalism educators' responses to the following question have been logged: "Which Journalism education periodicals listed below do you read regularly?" The percentage of readership among 786 respondents is listed before each periodical. To get an approximate number of total educator readership in U.S. schools, multiply the percent by 21,474, the baseline number of educators represented in this part of the analysis. (Readership should not be equated with subscriptions. Some readers may use a library copy rather than a subscription.)

- 40.5% *Adviser* (Jostens Yearbook Co.)
- 34.4% *Taylor Talk* (Taylor Publishing Co.)
- 32.6% *Quill & Scroll Magazine*
- 22.9% State press association publications
- 21.8% *Student Press Review* (CSPA) (formerly *School Press Review*)
- 17.7% *Student Press Law Center Report*
- 17.6% *C:JET* (*Communication: Journalism Education Today*) (JEA)
- 7.8% Other media publications
- 7% *Trends* (NSPA publication)
- 6.5% *Journalism Educator* (AEJMC)
- 5.1% *Journalism Quarterly* (AEJMC)

Of the non-profit organizations that produce periodicals for teachers (and students), *Quill & Scroll Magazine* is the most widely read. Publications produced by state high school press associations are the next best read of the journals. Most of these include monthly or quarterly newsletters and other specialized publications directed at Journalism teaching/advising and student publishing.

Writing

About 4.7 percent of the Journalism educators indicate that they have written an article for one or more of the professional journalism periodicals. Applied to the entire country, this means that about 1,000 teachers have taken an active role in writing various types of articles, columns, or other instructional pieces to share with a wider audience.

Use of News Media

High school Journalism educators appear to be regular users of local and national news media, and probably include it among their class preparation time, given the 80+ hours they claim to work each week.

In terms of use, here are the usual number of days each week that a Journalism educator uses each medium:

- local newspaper, 5.5 days per week
- cable or early evening network TV news, 5.6 days per week
- local newscasts on TV, 5.6 days per week
- local radio newscasts, 5.4 days per week
- national radio network news, 5.1 days per week

In addition to local media, 83 percent of the high school Journalism educators listed general-interest magazines that they read regularly (that is, almost every issue):

- *Time*, 29.8 percent
- *Newsweek*, 26.8 percent
- *Reader's Digest*, 10.2 percent
- *U.S. News and World Report*, 9 percent
- *National Geographic*, 7.9 percent
- *People*, 5.7 percent

Aside from local newspaper reading, 54 percent of the Journalism educators read at least one non-local newspaper regularly (at least once a week). Among the top non-local newspapers in terms of readership are

- *USA Today*, 26.5 percent
- *New York Times*, 15 percent
- *Wall Street Journal*, 8.1 percent

Journalism Educators' Political Concerns

High school Journalism teachers tend to be politically about as middle-of-the-road as it gets. Our survey found that on a scale of 0 to 100, with 0 being extreme left and 100 being extreme right, Journalism educators' average score is about 52, putting their average a bit to the right, but not much. The median and the mode are 50.

When compared with public school teachers generally, we find the Journalism educators to be a bit more liberal. Larger percentages of Journalism educators see themselves as middle-of-the-road politically, and a smaller percentage see themselves as conservative; in both groups, however, the conservatives outnumber the liberals among the journalists and the non-journalists alike.

To illustrate, The Carnegie Foundation found in a study of more than 20,000 U.S. elementary and secondary public school teachers that 29 percent of the teachers classified themselves as liberal, 29 percent middle of the road, and 42 percent conservative. Converted to a 100-point scale, the average score is approximately 54.[26] Our study of Journalism educators shows that about 27 percent see themselves as liberal, 42 percent as middle of the road, and 31 percent as conservative. The average is 52.

By contrast, college journalism faculty are somewhat more left of center politically, averaging 44.2 on the scale of 100 (median of 45 and mode of 50).[27]

Political Affiliation

High school Journalism teachers tend to list themselves more so as Democrats (43.4 percent) than as Republicans (34.2 percent). As shown in Graph 5.9, the number of Democrats among them is similar in percentage to college Journalism teachers (1988)[28] and to professional journalists (1992), and all three groups register 5 to 10 percentage points higher than do Democrats in the general population as a whole.[29]

High school Journalism educators, however, are about two times more likely than either college Journalism teachers or U.S. journalists to affiliate with the Republican Party, with about one-third of the teachers claiming membership compared with only about 15 percent of college educators[30] and about 16 percent of professional journalists.[31] High school teachers/advisers are also much less likely to claim that they are Independents politically than are college Journalism educators or professional journalists. We observe in Graph 5.9 a striking similarity of party affiliation between the college Journalism educators and professional journalists, even though those surveys were taken about five years apart.

Graph 5.9

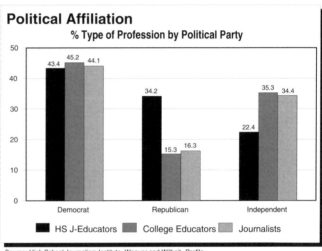

Source: High School Journalism Institute, Weaver and Wilhoit *Profile*,
Weaver and Wilhoit *American Journalist* (1992)

Journalism Educators and Freedom of the High School Press

We address legal issues in more detail in later chapters. In the national study described in this section, we did, however, survey secondary school Journalism educators to find out where they stand on the question of freedom of the school press.

Specifically, we asked this question that involved the *Hazelwood v. Kuhlmeier* case: "The U.S. Supreme Court (in 1988) ruled in favor of more authority for high school principals to censor school-sponsored student publications. Do you believe that this was a good ruling or a bad ruling?" As shown in Graph 5.10, almost 33 percent of the Journalism educators thought *Hazelwood* was a good ruling, a considerably lower percentage than their non-journalism public high school teacher colleagues, who agreed at a 71-percent rate that the ruling was good.[32]

Graph 5.10

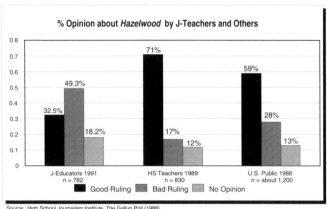

% Opinion about *Hazelwood* by J-Teachers and Others

Source: High School Journalism Institute, The Gallup Poll (1988)
and The Second Gallup/Phi Delta Kappa Survey of Teachers (1989)

The public in general (59 percent) was less likely than non-Journalism teachers to agree with the new restrictions on the school press, but they were much more likely than Journalism teachers to agree that the decision was a good one.[33]

We find it curious in Graph 5.10 that a high percentage (18.2 percent) of Journalism educators had no opinion about *Hazelwood*. By contrast, public school teachers in 1989, and the public in general in 1988, had much lower percentages of those who responded "don't know." One possible explanation is that the question was asked of Journalism educators in the spring of 1991, fully three years after the Supreme Court decision. We have seen that a high percentage of teachers are new to Journalism, so a considerable number of them might not have taken note of the ruling. Given the high number of teachers/advisers who are not certified, who have been assigned journalistic duties by an administrator, who did not take a Journalism major in college, and who did not aspire to teach Journalism when they first considered education as a career, it is reasonable to expect that a substantial percentage of them would show a certain indifference to the *Hazelwood* decision.

No matter what the reason, slightly more than 50 percent of Journalism programs in 1991 were headed by teachers who either thought that the restrictions of *Hazelwood* were good or did not know one way or the other. Only 49.3 percent of the Journalism educators thought that it was a bad ruling.

Change in Freedoms

A related question was asked of Journalism educators: "How has the U.S. Supreme Court decision in 1988 (*Hazelwood v. Kuhlmeier*) affected student freedom of expression as applied to their work on official school publications in your school?" Graph 5.11 shows percentages of today's Journalism teachers/advisers in relationship to the degrees of freedom they believe they now have in the wake of *Hazelwood*.

Graph 5.11

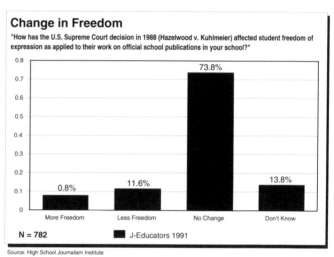

Change in Freedom

"How has the U.S. Supreme Court decision in 1988 (Hazelwood v. Kuhlmeier) affected student freedom of expression as applied to their work on official school publications in your school?"

N = 782   J-Educators 1991

Source: High School Journalism Institute

The largest percentage of Journalism educators, almost 74 percent, believe that no changes in freedoms of students have occurred related to their work on school publications. Nearly 12 percent, however, claim that less freedom is now available for students. Less than 1 percent claim "more freedom" is enjoyed by students, and almost 14 percent either don't know or don't have an opinion.

We find that advisers' attitudes about the rightness of the *Hazelwood* Supreme Court decision are related to several other factors that we've explored thus far and that are worth exploring in more detail.

Type of School

Legally, *Hazelwood* applies only to those students, teachers, and administrators within public schools among the 45 states currently affected by the decision.[34] Parochial and other private schools were not affected by the decision, though it is of interest for us to examine reactions of teachers from those schools. We assume that for optimum learning experiences for students in such schools, many teachers and administrators in the private sector would want to consider allowing an atmosphere in which students could express themselves freely.

Public school teachers are much more likely to be in disagreement with the *Hazelwood* decision than are parochial or private school teachers. Almost 51 percent of the public school teachers believe that it was not in the students' best interests for the Supreme Court to have limited press freedoms in the schools. But 43 percent of parochial school teachers and 25 percent of private school teachers believe the decision was a bad one.

Annual Salary

A direct, significant relationship exists between teachers' salaries and their opinions of the *Hazelwood* decision. Those who make more money are more apt to think that it was a bad ruling than those who make less. Many more advisers in the $40,000+ income brackets were likely to be in favor of greater student freedoms of the press than those in the $25,000-and-under category.

Tenure

High school Journalism educators with tenure are more likely to disagree with the *Hazelwood* restrictions on student freedom of the press than are those without tenure. Of the educators who think the restrictions are bad for the student press, almost 71 percent have tenure whereas only about 29 percent who do not have tenure think the decision was wrong.

Certification

Also significantly related to each other is the relationship between the Journalism educators' attitudes about the *Hazelwood* decision and whether or not they are certified to teach Journalism. We found a much higher incidence of disagreement with the deci-

127

sion among those with certification than among those who have not attained it. Graph 5.12 shows the relationships.

Graph 5.12

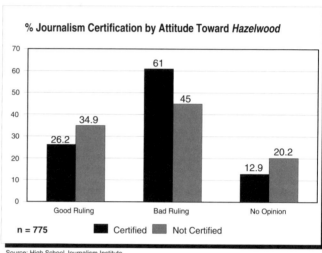

% Journalism Certification by Attitude Toward *Hazelwood*

n = 775 ■ Certified ▨ Not Certified

Source: High School Journalism Institute

We assume that knowledge of journalistic practice and principles that accompany certification might lead to a teacher's greater sense of independence and resistance to a meddlesome decision of the Supreme Court that actually interferes with instruction.[35] For example, only 45 percent of those without certification thought it was a bad ruling whereas 61 percent of those with certification thought it was bad. We also find that more than 20 percent of those without certification do not have an opinion about the case—or don't know about it—compared with about 13 percent who have certification. Graph 5.12 also shows that among those who think *Hazelwood* was a good decision, almost 35 percent are uncertified teachers whereas only about 26 percent of the certified teachers think it was a decision in the best interests of students' freedoms.

Faculty Morale

We found that faculty morale was the single most important predictor of the Journalism educator's job satisfaction. Faculty morale is also significantly related to educators' opinions about *Hazelwood*. Those Journalism teachers/advisers who think the restrictive nature of the Supreme Court's decision was good also tend to see morale at the school as being good. The same is true for those who have no opinion or don't know about the case. Among those teachers who thought the decision was bad, there is a much stronger likelihood that they evaluate morale at school as also being "poor" or "fair" than those who think the decision was a good one.

Morale Change

We also wanted to see if the 1988 court decision limiting student freedom was related to the Journalism teacher/adviser's notion of change in faculty morale during the past few years. Similarly, we find that those who are in agreement with the restrictive nature of the decision are more likely to see either no change or actual improvements in faculty morale in recent years than are those who do not like the decision. Nearly 60 percent of the educators who think the decision was bad also see a deterioration in morale during the past few years whereas only 45 percent of those who think the ruling was good agree that morale has deteriorated.

Teaching Methods

Journalism teachers who do not agree with the *Hazelwood* decision are less likely than those who agree with it that they have a great deal of, or almost complete, freedom in deciding how to teach their courses. For example, nearly 58 percent of those who agreed with the ruling claim they have "almost complete freedom" in their classroom methodology. Only 43 percent of those who think *Hazelwood* a bad decision make the same claim.

Advising Freedom

Among advisers who think *Hazelwood* is a bad decision there is a much greater tendency to say that there is "less freedom" now than there was before the decision. Also, a much lower percentage of them (71.3 percent) believe that there has been no change since the decision compared with those who agree with the decision and who also see no change (81.3 percent).

Holding Office

Journalism educators who are involved in professional organizations as office holders are more likely to disagree with the *Hazelwood* decision than are those who are not involved as officers. We find that those who disagree with the ruling are about twice as likely to hold an office in an organization.

Political Ideology

Not surprisingly, Journalism teachers who claim to be left of center politically are more likely than their conservative colleagues to think *Hazelwood* a bad decision. By contrast, educators with a right-leaning political philosophy are much more likely to agree with the Supreme Court in *Hazelwood* than their left-leaning colleagues. Also, those who affiliate with the political right are more likely to have "no opinion" on the Court's decision than are their more liberal counterparts.

Political Party

In Graph 5.13, we see that Journalism educators affiliating with the Democratic Party disagree with the *Hazelwood* decision in a much greater percentage (almost 51 percent) than do Republicans (28 percent). Just about the reverse is seen when we note that Republican educators tend to favor the decision that restricts student press freedoms (almost 46 percent) compared with just less than 32 percent of the Democrats.

Graph 5.13

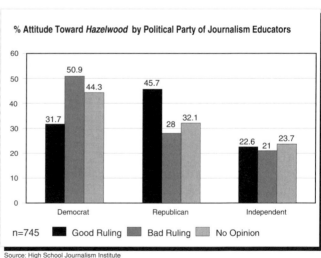

% Attitude Toward *Hazelwood* by Political Party of Journalism Educators

n=745 ■ Good Ruling ▨ Bad Ruling ▨ No Opinion

Source: High School Journalism Institute

130

Summary and Recommendations

Even with nearly 95 percent of all U.S. high schools having a class in Journalism or some type of media outlet, only about 28 percent of the teachers and advisers are certified Journalism educators. Considering that many states have few, if any, requirements for Journalism certification, this percentage is all the more perplexing. Furthermore, fewer than 8 percent have a major in Journalism or Mass Communication, but as length of time in Journalism education increases, so does the likelihood that teachers/advisers return to school for additional credits in Journalism. Many of them, while dedicated to the profession of teaching, did not choose Journalism as a content area. About 43 percent have been assigned to the Journalism program by an administrator, and another 18 percent thought of teaching Journalism after they completed college. However, more than half of them knew they wanted to be teachers (mainly high school language arts teachers) while in high school, and more than 85 percent of them made that choice before finishing college.

Certified Journalism teachers are more likely to be found in large public high schools rather than in smaller schools or private schools. Even with an average week that finds them working many more hours than their teacher colleagues, U.S. high school Journalism educators are as satisfied as or happier than their colleagues. More than 80 percent say they wish to remain in teaching until retirement. Predictors of job satisfaction are faculty morale, annual salary, amount of freedom administrators allow in advising, and age. We find that they bring some solid background in Journalism despite rather minimal formal educational credentials: About 25 percent have college and professional media experience; 40 percent were on high school media staffs; and more than one-third of them have held non-media jobs outside the secondary school environment. They are quite involved in professional organizations, both educational and media-related. Journalism educators tend to be in the center ideologically but more likely to be Democrats than the population at large. They are likely to value student press freedoms more highly than either their non-Journalism teaching colleagues or the general public.

Given these findings, we recommend the following:

- Administrators should urge uncertified Journalism educators to professionalize their credentials.

- Journalism educators who lack certification should seek workshops or summer, Saturday, correspondence or evening courses that lead toward state licensing in Journalism.

- Journalism educators who lack a major or minor in Journalism or Mass Communication should consider adding that teaching area to their credentials or seeking a master's degree in it.

- Administrators should take note of the extremely demanding schedules of Journalism teachers/advisers and attempt to improve those persons' situations through assignment of adequate preparation time and stipends.

- School administrators doing job searches for Journalism educators, particularly at smaller schools where there exists a greater tendency for a non-certified Journalism teacher to fill a vacancy, should make contacts with nearby universities, colleges and state press associations for names of qualified candidates.

- Administrators should provide an atmosphere in which trust, freedom and faculty morale prosper, for in these situations greatest job satisfaction of Journalism educators occurs.

NOTES ON CHAPTER 5

1. Other than endnoted data, results in this chapter are based on the same survey reported in Chapter 4. Findings are based on a random sample of 22,785 United States' secondary schools. Altogether, 834 of 1,906 school personnel returned a survey sent in winter 1991, with follow-ups to non-respondents in spring 1991. The response rate was nearly 44 percent. Maximum sampling error for a random sample of this size is 3.4 percentage points at the 95 percent confidence level. Tolerances in sampling error were smaller than that as responses moved away from the 50th percentile.

2. See, for example, Marilyn Weaver, "A Summary of Journalism Certification Requirements: A National Assessment," paper presented at the Mid-winter Meeting of the Secondary Education Division, Association for Education in Journalism and Mass Communication, Knoxville, TN, Jan. 16, 1988.

3. *Ibid.*: 14.

4. In this study, "certification" is defined as the subject-area endorsement or credentialing system used by each state's Department of Education in the licensing of secondary school teachers. This should not be confused with the Journalism Education Association's professional certification programs. These are strictly voluntary and are meant to help professionalize Journalism education, especially in states where credentialing requirements are minimal or non-existent. JEA offers a Certified Journalism Educator program as well as a more advanced Master Journalism Educator recognition. Details of each may be obtained through the association at JEA headquarters, Kansas State University, Manhattan, KS.

5. Penny Sebring, *et al.*, *The National Longitudinal Study of the High School Class of 1972, Fifth Follow-up* (Chicago: National Opinion Research Center, 1987): 73-74.

6. *Digest of Education Statistics 1990.* U.S. Department of Education. Washington, DC: Office of Educational Research and Improvement, 1991: 79.

7. Gerald M. Kosicki and Lee B. Becker, "Annual Census and Analysis of Enrollment and Graduation," *Journalism Educator* 47 (Autumn 1992): 62.

8. *Ibid.*: 66.

9. Marilyn Weaver, "A Summary of Journalism Certification": 14.

10. *Digest of Education Statistics 1990:* 83.

11. David Weaver and G. Cleveland Wilhoit, "A Profile of JMC Educators," *Journalism Educator 43* (Summer 1988): 22.

12. David Weaver and G. Cleveland Wilhoit, "The American Journalist in the 1990s: A Preliminary Report of Key Findings from a 1992 National Survey of the U.S. Journalists," Bloomington, IN: Indiana University School of Journalism: 10.

13. Penny Sebring, *et al.*, "The National Longitudinal Study of the High School Class of 1972," 12. See also Jack Dvorak, "Job Satisfaction and Working Conditions of Today's High School Journalism Educator," *C:JET (Communication: Journalism Education Today) 26* (Spring 1993): 2-5.

14. Non-Journalism educator data used in comparisons with Journalism educators are taken from a study by Penny Sebring, *et al.*, "The National Longitudinal Study of the Class of 1972": 33.

15. Stanley Elam, *The Second Gallup-Phi Delta Kappa Survey of Public School Teacher Opinion: Portrait of a Beleaguered Profession.* Bloomington, IN: Phi Delta Kappa, 1989: 26.

16. Non-Journalism educator data found in Penny Sebring, et al., "The National Longitudinal Study of the High School Class of 1972": 123.

17. *Ibid.*

18. *Ibid.*

19. *Ibid.*

20. *Ibid.*: 124.

21. Using hierarchical multiple regression, we submitted four different blocks of variables to analysis using job satisfaction as the dependent variable (n cases = 786). The first block included certain demographic variables (church or synagogue affiliation, age, ethnic background, marital status and gender). The second block added the following: certification of adviser, hours spent advising each week, type of school (public, private, parochial), freedom of the school press, motivations to enter teaching, longevity as a teacher, size of school, state certification

requirements, and years in advising. The third block included these additional items: methods of teaching, school improvements, extent of Journalism classes, faculty morale changes, faculty opinion of Journalism department, advising freedom, and morale of faculty. In the final block, we added family income and opinion of the *Hazelwood* court decision. Beta weights of significant items are .50 faculty morale, .35 annual salary, .29 advising freedom, and -.24 teacher/adviser's age. R-Square = .58. Significance of F <.001.

22. See, for example, Andrew W. Halpin and Don B. Croft, "The Organizational Climate of School." In *School Administration: Selected Readings*, edited by Sherman H. Frey and Keith R. Getschman. (New York: Thomas Y. Crowell Company, 1968): 248-253.

23. Penny Sebring, et al., *The National Longitudinal Study of the High School Class of 1972:* 97-100.

24. Weaver and Wilhoit, "A Profile of JMC Educators": 30-31.

25. Data were gathered for, but not reported in, David Weaver and G. Cleveland Wilhoit, "The American Journalist in the 1990s: A Preliminary Report of Key Findings from a 1992 National Survey of U.S. Journalists."

26. *The Condition of Teaching: A State-by-State Analysis, 1990.* Princeton, NJ: The Carnegie Foundation for the Advancement of Teaching, 1990: 15.

27. Weaver and Wilhoit, "A Profile of JMC Educators": 14.

28. *Ibid.*

29. Weaver and Wilhoit, "The American Journalist in the 1990s": 6.

30. Weaver and Wilhoit, "A Profile of JMC Educators": 14.

31. Weaver and Wilhoit, "The American Journalist in the 1990s": 7.

32. Stanley Elam, *The Second Gallup/Phi Delta Kappa Survey:* 26.

33. *Ibid.*

34. California, Massachusetts, Colorado, Iowa and Kansas currently have laws that grant students press freedoms broader than those allowed by the *Hazelwood v. Kuhlmeier* decision in 1988. In March 1993 several other state legislatures were in the process of considering similar legislation for their young citizens.

35. For a discussion of effects of *Hazelwood* on the Journalism curriculum, see, for example, Jack Dvorak and Jon Paul Dilts, "Legacy of *Hazelwood v. Kuhlmeier:* Academic Freedom vs. Administrative Authority," *Journalism Educator* 47 (Autumn 1992): 3-12.

CHAPTER 6

WHO PAYS THE PIPER?
SOURCES OF NEWSPAPER BUDGETS

Chapter Highlights

- There's almost no difference in the amount of money public and non-public schools spend on their newspapers, but larger schools and schools in larger cities spend much more.

- Schools spend about the same total amount of money on their papers no matter how many issues they publish.

- Nearly 40 percent of newspapers get at least half their money from the principal.

- Only three in five school papers run ads, but more than half of those who do generate most of their budgets that way.

- Newspapers that sell ads are much more likely to make a profit than those that don't.

The Purposes of a Newspaper

What's the basic purpose of a professional newspaper? Many ideas come to mind:

- To inform people about what's going on in the world
- To entertain
- To serve as a forum for public opinion
- To influence citizens on issues of public importance

- To promote democracy through an educated citizenry

Those are excellent answers that express ideals any journalist can agree with. Those ideas form the very core of every Journalism class in America, from junior high to graduate school. Journalists—both student and professional—are taught how to write leads, news stories, features, and editorials; how to interview sources and use public records to obtain information; and how to package the news product graphically to lure readers into every corner of every page.

As much as those ideals drive the newspaper business and the actual work of the staff, the newspaper industry thinks of them largely as a means to a greater end: The *fundamental* purpose of a commercial newspaper, publishers will tell you, is to make money for the people who own it.

If that seems like a cynical and utilitarian view of the press, it's true nevertheless. Consider the *National Observer*. The *Observer* was one of the finest weekly newspapers ever produced. It was an exciting and innovative paper in every respect: Its articles were lively and insightful, its design was bold and original, its opinion columns were thoughtful and well-reasoned. It was published by Dow Jones, the same folk who publish the *Wall Street Journal*, so there was plenty of money behind it. Yet it flopped.

Good as it was, and it was very good indeed, it never caught on with readers, so it lost money by the truckload. Even Dow Jones couldn't afford to keep it afloat, and the *National Observer* is now nothing more than a fond memory. Any high school senior taking Economics comes to understand that our system is largely based on enterprises that pay their own way or else, and that the less they rely on subsidies from government, the more free they are to chart their own courses, free of suffocating regulation. Money means freedom: Financial independence means freedom from control by outside interests and forces other than the owners of the newspaper.

Purposes of the Scholastic Press

A school newspaper, by contrast, is not so profit-driven as a commercial paper. We have other ambitions besides making money for our school publications. The brief catalogue of newspaper aims at the beginning of this chapter most certainly applies to high school papers as much as it does to commercial newspapers. Moreover, school newspapers serve an educational function that commercial papers do not supply: The high school newspaper is a tool for teaching about information access in a democracy, for sharpening language skills, even for providing a social outlet for the student staffers.

None of those aims, however, is incompatible with making money. On the contrary, the school press is *stronger* when it is able to provide its own money than it is when it depends on principals or school boards for the funds it needs to operate. That's why, even though making money isn't the prime purpose of *school* newspapers, financial strength is important for schools that want to offer their students the best and freest press possible.

Who Controls the Checkbook?

Even if the purpose of the school press is not primarily to make money, it's far better to show a profit than a loss at the end of the year. School papers are not in business to lose money, either!

Most high school publications advisers have little training in Journalism, and even among those who do, their training typically includes little or nothing about financing a publications program. Financial policies and decisions are left to school administrators, who may make decisions for publications based on what's best for the school financially, not on what's best for the publication journalistically.

Financial decisions are best made, though, by the people most closely affected by them. As employees, we would—rightly—bristle at the notion of our boss determining how our household budgets should be allocated: The boss at work has no real idea what our needs are at home. Similarly, most school administrators have no real idea what the needs of a student-run press are, either. It's hard to act in a newspaper's best interests when you don't know what those best interests are.

A school press is most effective when it takes responsibility itself for its total product, and that means not only its editorial content but also its financial affairs. There is no reason to insulate student journalists and their advisers from the financial implications of the decisions they make, or to deny their programs the rewards that prudent attention to the bottom line can bring. This, too, is education in Journalism and for life. Publication staffs that control their own budgets will be stronger financially and freer editorially than those who don't, and that makes finances worth learning about.

Balancing the budget of a school newspaper is no more complicated than balancing the family bank account. Most of us have incomes and household budgets that vastly exceed any publications budgets for which we may be responsible. A first step in getting a handle on finances might be to see what *other* schools are doing so that we get a feel for how typical our own situation is. That's what this chapter helps you do by outlining briefly what newspaper budgets at other schools look like.

Good information is lacking on the ways in which the high school press is financed. Publications on school journalism and secondary school administration do deal with some issues piecemeal in how-to articles on increasing advertising revenue, sales ideas that work, and so on.[1] Several handbooks give ideas for surviving, even thriving, financially.[2] Few attempts have been made, however, to study systematically the sources of revenue for representative samples of the student press.

In 1982 a study of the student press in Iowa[3] offered assurances that high school newspapers that were members of the state scholastic press association were not suffering from budget cutbacks so badly as had been feared, although schools that were not members of the association were not studied. Nearly half of the papers in that study published their newspapers as a school page in the local community paper, something much less common in other states. Of the papers published separately, about 40 percent accepted advertising and about the same number received direct administrative subsidies. Only 15 percent sold either subscriptions or single copies.

Mary Benedict[4] found that 45 percent of high school principals favored direct school subsidy of newspapers, with advertising second (26 percent), followed by subscriptions (13 percent), and activity fees (6 percent).

In 1986, an Ohio study[5] found that only 30 percent of schools in the study received administrative subsidies and 6 percent received activity fee money, while 62 percent of the newspapers received advertising revenue, typically covering more than 40 percent of their annual budgets in that way. Single-copy sales accounted for over one-fourth of most budgets. That paper suggested, but did not attempt to demonstrate, that a school newspaper that raised its own revenues rather than relying on money from the school would probably have fewer restrictions placed on its content.

That is the point, quite apart from its more utilitarian interest in allowing schools to compare their financial performance with that of other school newspapers, that makes school publication funding of particular interest. Do, in fact, school papers have more freedom to publish if they're not reliant on the school administration for the financial wherewithal that it takes to publish a newspaper? The first task is to determine just where the money *does* come from.

The Cost of Newspaper Publishing

No two schools are alike; they differ in size, in religious orientation, and in countless other ways. They can be arranged according to categories, though, and then we can look for the ways in which schools similar to each other operate. That is what was done in the 1992 national study on which much of the rest of this chapter is based. As we look first at how much schools are paying to publish their papers, we pay the most attention to whether they were public or non-public/parochial, to their enrollment, to the size of the community in which they were located. We also consider how often a staff published its paper, whether each school's newspaper staff received academic credit for its work, and how well they had done financially the previous year.

The study was based on a sample of 434 randomly selected high schools from throughout the country which were studied during the winter of 1991-92. Schools received a four-page questionnaire addressed to the "Journalism Teacher (or Principal)" and a pre-paid reply envelope; schools which did not respond within three weeks received a follow-up letter and another copy of the questionnaire.

More than half the schools returned the questionnaire, and demographic results corresponded well with the samples in larger studies, a good indication of reliability.

In 1991-92 the average high school newspaper budget was $2,664. but that's a meaningless statistic because it lumps everybody together. A few schools listed no budget at all, and 6 percent listed less than $100, while a few papers reported budgets of at least $10,000 a year, with two schools coming in at $14,400. Because school papers vary so widely, it's necessary to break those figures down to provide any meaningful comparison.

Public/Private

There is little difference between public schools and private/parochial schools in their overall budgets: public school papers spend about $2,667 a year, whereas non-publics average $2,658. About half of all public schools with newspapers spend more than $2,000 a year on their papers whereas 55 percent of non-public schools spend that much. But non-public schools have a slightly larger share of the smallest budgets: 30 percent spend less than $1,000 a year whereas just 25 percent of public schools do.

Enrollment

Not surprisingly, a much better predictor of the size of a school's newspaper budget was the size of its enrollment. Papers at larger schools, whether public or non-public, had significantly larger budgets than papers at smaller schools.

Papers at schools with 250 or fewer students had an average budget of $966 per year; nearly 30 percent spent less than $250 per year, and less than 18 percent had budgets of $2,000 or more.

At schools with 251 to 500 students, newspaper budgets averaged $2,466. While 40 percent of those schools spent no more than $1,000 a year, 18 percent spent over $4,000. Newspaper budgets averaged $3,004 a year at schools with 501 to 1,000 students. More than a quarter of those schools spent at least $4,000 a year, and less than 10 percent spent less than $250.

The largest schools, those of more than 1,000 students, also had the largest newspaper budgets, averaging $3,486. More than one-fourth of those schools spent more than $5,000 a year whereas just 2 percent spent less than $500.

Community Size

Where a school is located also makes a difference: Schools in large cities spend much more on their newspapers than rural schools do. Urban schools are also frequently larger, but urban schools do spend more than rural schools of comparable size.

More than a quarter of rural schools spend less than $250 a year on their papers, and the average was $1,466. Seventy-one percent of rural school papers spent less than $2,000 a year. Papers in small towns of up to 25,000 population averaged budgets of $2,500.

Schools in cities of up to 100,000 population spent much more on their newspapers: More than a quarter spent over $4,000 a year whereas just 9 percent spent less than $500. The average was $3,421.

Newspapers published at schools in cities of more than 100,000 people had the largest budgets, an average of $3,633. None spent less than $1,350 a year, and almost 20 percent spent at least $5,000 per year.

Frequency of Publication

There is no clear relationship between a newspaper's budget and its frequency of publication. Schools that publish their papers just two or three times per semester spend fewer actual dollars than do other schools, of course, but they spend an average of $314 per issue. Schools that publish every two weeks have budgets more than twice as large, but they spend an average of only $221 per issue. The explanation is probably that schools that publish their papers less often produce larger, and consequently more expensive, issues.

The most frequent publication cycle for high school newspapers is monthly, accounting for more than half of the schools in the study. Those papers spend the most per issue, an average of $331.

Staff Credit

Eighty percent of the schools in this national study gave academic credit to students for their work on the newspaper. Not only do the students in those programs get the credits but also they have more money to work with. Newspapers in the credit-bearing programs have an average budget of $2,740 per year; papers that are entirely extracurricular average $2,258.

Financial Stability

During the 1991 school year, about 23 percent of the school newspapers in the country made money whereas 21 percent lost money. A little over half broke even. Public school newspapers were more likely to finish in the black than those in non-public schools, although they were equally likely to lose money. Most non-public schools just broke even.

Small schools seldom turned a profit—just 4 percent did so—whereas nearly 30 percent of schools larger than 500 students made money. Rural schools were more likely to show a profit than those in any other sort of community, more than 29 percent finishing with a balance at the end of the year. Twice as many rural and big-city schools made money as lost it.

Staffs that published a paper on an extracurricular basis were almost twice as likely to lose money as those which received academic credit. Nearly one-third of those papers lost money whereas only 18 percent of the credit-granting programs did so. Schools appeared to be more willing to subsidize papers that gave academic credit.

Who Pays the Bills, and How Much Do They Pay?

School newspapers have traditionally relied on at least five sources of income:

- money from activity fees paid by all students
- subscription sales
- single-copy sales
- direct subsidy from school administrators
- advertising revenue

There are also other financial bases, of course: bake sales, candy sales, car washes, and so on, but these generally raise relatively little money, and they vary quite a bit from year to year. In this section we look at the extent to which the different sorts of programs we're discussing rely on each of these five most common ways of raising money. Only three schools in the study reported significant proportions of their revenues to have come from sources other than these, and all were papers with very few dollars to spend. Percentages have been adjusted, therefore, to eliminate those sources to make comparisons easier.

Activity Fees

Some schools charge their students a fee which entitles them without further cost to a smorgasbord of activities like admission to athletic events, availability of certain extracurricular activities, occasional dances, and so on. A copy of each issue of the school newspaper might be one of the things paid for by this fee. Money collected from the fee is distributed to the sponsors of the activities, the school paper included, and is used to defray all or part of their expenses.

In general, activity fees are not a major source of revenue for most high school papers; only one in five school newspapers receives any activity fee money at all, but in the minority of cases where papers do receive this sort of income, it is often substantial. More than 44 percent of the schools that receive money from activity fees generate at least half their budgeted income this way, and for 4 percent of schools it was their only source of income.

Public/Private

Public schools were less likely to get money from activity fees than were non-public schools. Twenty percent of non-public schools rely on such fees for at least three-quarters of their income whereas only 5 percent of the public schools received that much support. Overall, non-public schools received 23.9 percent of their income from activity fees whereas public schools averaged 10.8 percent.

Enrollment

Papers at larger schools appear to get somewhat more activity fee money than do those at smaller schools but the differences are significant only for schools of 501-1,000 students. More than 10 percent of those schools generate at least three-quarters of their budgeted income from activity fees and nearly 30 percent of them get some activity fee money. Only 10 percent of the smallest schools receive any such fees, however.

Community Size

On the other hand, the size of the community in which the school is located appears to make a more important difference. Whereas rural schools report only 8.3 percent of their money coming from activity fees, the figure is about 12 percent in towns of under 100,000 population and 20.9 percent in cities larger than 100,000. Activity fee money is more important for the rural schools that receive it, but less than 10 percent do so; but more than one-third of the big city schools give activity fee money to school newspapers.

Staff Credit

Not surprisingly, newspapers that were published as an extracurricular activity received a much larger proportion of their budgets from activity fees than did papers published as part of a class. Extracurricular papers drew about 32 percent of their budgets from activity fees whereas credit-bearing newspapers received an average of only about 8 percent of their budgets from such fees.

Financial Stability

Newspapers that rely heavily on activity fee money aren't doing themselves any favors financially; in fact they seem to be worse off than most other papers. While only one-fifth of all the newspapers in the study lost money, the figure rose to about 60 percent among the papers that relied on activity fees for most of their budgets. On the other hand, among papers that received no activity fee money, less than 18 percent ran a deficit. So not only does activity fee money apparently not help school newspapers balance their budgets, it seems to work against it, either by providing a false sense of financial security because of the early lump-sum cash infusion it supplies, or by providing administrators with an excuse to deny papers other, more lucrative, avenues for revenue.

Subscription Sales

Few school newspapers sell subscriptions any more: Less than 9 percent of the schools sold them at all, and just 2 percent derived half or more of their budgets that way. Larger schools and public schools seem to take in a slightly larger share of their budgets from subscriptions, but the number of schools involved is too low and the differences too slight for any of them to be of any statistical significance. No general category of school represented in the study exceeded 5 percent of its budget by selling subscriptions.

Single Copy Sales

Sales of single copies of the newspapers was somewhat more important—about as important as money from activity fees. More than 75 percent of schools received no single copy sales money at all, but 8.3 percent received half or more of their money this way. One paper in twenty supported itself entirely through sales of copies.

Only two notable differences among types of schools were noteworthy: Medium-sized schools, those with enrollments between 250 and 1,000, received about 12 percent of their income from single copy sales; larger and smaller schools averaged about 3 percent. And size of community made an important difference. Rural schools relied on individual sales for more than 20 percent of their income; towns of less than 100,000 averaged just over 7 percent, whereas schools in cities of more than 100,000 people took in an average of just 1 percent of their newspaper income from single sales.

Administrative Subsidy

Direct administrative financial support is an important source of revenue for most school newspapers. More than half of the papers in this and other studies[6] received subsidies, and the amount was usually substantial. Nearly 40 percent of the schools received at least half of their budgeted income from the administration, and about 22 percent, more than one in five, got all of their money from the principal or school board.

Using the principal's money to publish a newspaper is not necessarily incompatible with good journalism. A study of award-winning newspapers in the annual CSPA critical service evaluations[7] found that the most noticeable difference between contest winners and nonwinners was in funding; winners received significantly more school funding than non-winners did. Other research, however, reveals some potential dangers in subsidy money. In the next chapter, we address some of these concerns, but we do not question the importance of the school administration's cash in subsidizing the publication of school newspapers.

Public/Private

Non-public school newspapers are normally either heavily subsidized or receive nothing. Forty-five percent of the schools studied received no administration money at all, but 35 percent were completely funded by the school. Public schools received a little less, on the average. Half of public schools received no administration money and just 20 percent were fully funded; about 40 percent of the public school papers receiving money generated less than half their budgeted income that way.

Enrollment

Clear differences emerge among schools of different sizes in how much money their papers received from administrative subsidies. Fully half of the newspapers at the smallest schools, 250 or fewer students, were completely paid for by administrators, but only 10 percent of the papers at schools of more than 500 students received full funding from the principal. In fact, more than half of those larger schools received no administrative money at all.

Newspapers at larger schools are generally larger and more costly than papers at smaller schools, of course, and it's not surprising that administration provides a smaller percentage of the newspaper's revenue. Large schools may have avenues of income open to them that small schools lack, a larger advertising base or more potential subscribers, for example. But Chapter 7 shows that regardless of school size, administrative subsidy is at best a mixed blessing.

Community Size

Few real differences showed up here. Schools in rural areas did appear to receive more administration money than the others, but differences among other types of communities were small.

Staff Credit

In programs where the school newspaper is an activity for which students receive academic credit, normally in conjunction with a Journalism class, a large share of the paper's income derives from direct school subsidy, typically more than 40 percent. Wholly extracurricular papers receive less; an average of 29.7 percent of their annual budgets come from administrative grants.

Financial Stability

It may be surprising at first glance that the newspapers most likely to make a profit were those which also received no administrative subsidy at all; almost 72 percent of the papers that took in more than they spent received nothing from their principals. Schools are not likely to bankroll papers that make money without administrative subsidy, and staffs who know they can't count on the school for their operating revenue may work harder at generating their own sources of income. Schools that received the heaviest administrative subsidies were most likely to break even.

Advertising

The second-most-important source of revenue for school newspapers is advertising, but the degree to which schools depend on it varies tremendously. More than 43 percent of school papers don't carry ads at all, many citing school policies against it. Nearly one-third of school papers, however, earn more than half their money through ads; for more than 10 percent, advertising is the only source of revenue.

Public/Private

Advertising is much more important to public school newspapers than to private school papers, accounting for about 40 percent of their income, compared with just 21.5 percent of the income of non-public schools. About 12 percent of public school papers support themselves entirely through advertising, while only 5 percent of the non-publics reported doing so. More than one-third of public school papers counted on ads for more than half their income, whereas 15 percent of the non-publics earn that much through ads.

Enrollment

The extent to which school newspapers use advertising to pay their bills is clearly related to the size of the school. Schools of no more than 500 students used ads for 22 percent of their revenues, whereas schools larger than that took in more than 46 percent of their money from the sale of ads.

Community Size

The size of the community in which the school is located, on the other hand, appears to play little role in the use of advertising. While rural schools do make less use of advertising—about 27 percent of their revenues, on the average—schools located in cities and towns of all sizes from less than 25,000 to more than 100,000 all earn an average in the vicinity of 42 percent of their budgets through advertising. The use of ads is probably the result of the availability of nearby businesses as potential advertisers, something characteristic of towns of all sizes but largely absent in rural areas.

Staff Credit

Staffs that receive academic credit for their newspaper work sell more ads. About 40 percent of the budgets of those papers is typically covered by advertising. Papers that are extracurricular activities do far less well in ad sales: Only about 22 percent of their incomes are generated by ads.

Financial Stability

The more a newspaper relied on advertising for its revenue, the more likely it was to finish the year in the black. Profit-generating newspapers earned an average of 61 percent of their budgets through ad sales whereas papers that lost money averaged only 38 percent. Papers that reported breaking exactly even earned 29 percent of their budgets through ads; these were, of course, the most heavily subsidized by administrators and had, perhaps, the least incentive to sell ads or the strongest injunctions against doing so.

Graphs 6.1 through 6.5 show the relative importance of the income sources described in this chapter to different sorts of programs. Graph 6.1 shows that activity fees are a significant source of revenue only to non-public schools—more important than advertising, although only half as important as administrative subsidies. Public schools get about the same amount of money from both advertisers and administrators.

Graph 6.1

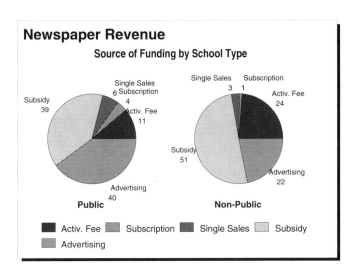

Larger schools rely most heavily on advertising (Graph 6.2), which accounts for nearly half their income. Newspapers at the smallest schools, on the other hand, are heavily dependent on administration money.

Graph 6.2

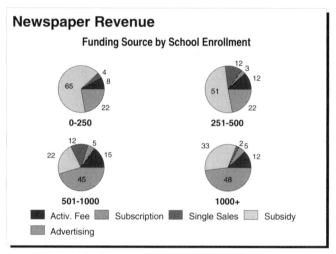

Newspaper Revenue
Funding Source by School Enrollment

Schools in larger communities make more use of advertising revenue than do schools in towns of less than 25,000, and rural schools depend very heavily on administrative subsidies, as shown in Graph 6.3.

Graph 6.3

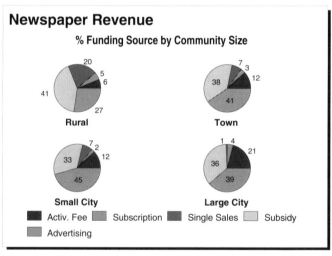

Newspaper Revenue
% Funding Source by Community Size

Graph 6.4 shows the much heavier reliance on advertising of papers produced by credit-bearing classes. Extracurricular newspapers rely most heavily on a school activity fee and take in less than one-quarter of their budgets from ads. This is the only type of paper in which something other than advertising or administrative subsidy is the principal source of a newspaper's income.

Graph 6.4

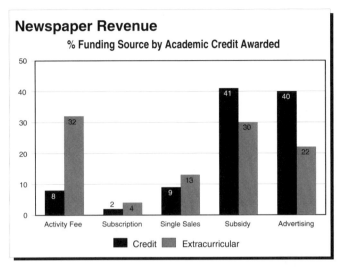

Newspaper Revenue
% Funding Source by Academic Credit Awarded

We will see in the next chapter that it appears to help the cause of free expression for a newspaper to make some profit. Among papers that made a profit, advertising was terribly important and accounted for nearly four times larger a share of revenue than administrative subsidy. (Graph 6.5) Papers that lost money showed a larger share of administrative money and activity fee money.

Graph 6.5

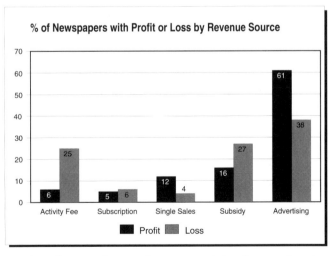

% of Newspapers with Profit or Loss by Revenue Source

Each of these five financial ingredients—activity fees, subscriptions, single copy sales, administrative subsidies and advertising—has been used as the principal method of funding outstanding high school newspapers, papers that are excellent journalistically, that are successful financially, and that meet the highest standards of free expression for their staffs and readers. But which one is best?

Simply in terms of considering which funding method produces the most money, it's a two-horse race between administrative subsidy and advertising. Activity fees are usually supposed to replace the little day-to-day participation fees in the schools that assess them: club dues, athletic admissions, newspaper subscriptions, and so on. But most schools don't have activity fees and among those who do, there's little serious money in it for the newspaper; in fact, papers that rely on fee money are more likely than others to lose money.

The subscription costs they were supposed to replace never amounted to much themselves. Few publications at any level from scholastic to commercial actually support themselves with revenue from subscriptions or single copy sales, so schools that use activity fees to replace money earned by selling the paper still are not making their newspapers any healthier financially: They're just streamlining circulation. The few papers in the study that relied heavily on subscriptions or sales were not particularly successful financially; only newspapers that are printed virtually free—on mimeograph or on the office photocopier, for instance—can hope to avoid losing money if they rely mostly on circulation fees for their income.

Advertising and administrative subsidy are the methods that bring in really useful money for most papers. They generate roughly equivalent amounts of money, but unless a newspaper's only concern is with the bottom line, they are not equally good. It's easy to rely on administration money. If you don't actually stand in the hall and wait for the principal to deliver the check, at least you rely on the school bookkeeper to let you know how much money is being transferred into the newspaper's account this year. Advertising takes more work and sets up another series of tasks for students and adviser to do: preparing client lists, running off rate cards and insertion order forms, working the phones or the street making sales calls, keeping records, invoicing, checking off payments as they come in. Is it worth all the fuss?

Yes, for three reasons. There are important lessons to be taught to student journalists about aspects of the newspaper business other than editorial production. Newspapers, indeed virtually all agents of the mass media, are profit-driven enterprises in this society. We do live in a society that professes to value initiative and capitalism, and divorcing the production of a newspaper from the financial implications of the enterprise doesn't make either journalistic or educational sense.

Second, we've seen in this chapter that papers that rely most heavily on advertising were those most likely to make a profit. Making a profit, however small, is important, even in a school setting, because it opens some possibilities for the staff that might not exist otherwise, maybe the purchase of a new piece of equipment, or the ability to afford front-page spot color in some issues, or a trip to the state scholastic press association convention. Those extras can do wonders for staff morale and can contribute to a better newspaper.

There is a third, more important, reason to favor advertising money over the administration's money: It looks as though newspapers that support themselves are more free than those that don't. An earlier study[8] suggested the following:

> *Some advisers do not want money from administrators, however. Student newspapers which are financially independent have a better chance of remaining editorially independent, they maintain, and of avoiding the pressures which even some of the best principals exert to publish or withhold certain stories.*

The school press is subject to the law and the courts, like all presses, but there may be a *psychological* climate for editorial control by the administration when administration dollars are going into the editorial product. Perhaps the best way to minimize that is to accept less administrative money. In the next chapter, we will discuss in greater detail the way in which the possible correlation between the funding of the school press and limits on free expression.

NOTES ON CHAPTER 6

1. Readers can find such articles in almost every issue of the major scholastic journalism magazines like *Quill & Scroll, Communication: Journalism Education Today, Student Press Review,* and *Trends in the High School Media.* The Bibliography contains a list of numerous such articles.

2. See, for example, Frank E. Heaston, *A Practical Guide to Advertising in Scholastic Publications* (Norman, OK: American Student Press Institute, 1984); Larry Lain, *ASK: The Advertising Survival Kit,* 2nd ed. (Iowa City: Quill and Scroll Foundation, 1992); Rob Melton and Sunny Stautz, *Advertising A-Z* (Portland, OR: Rob Melton and Associates, 1991); Billy I. Ross and Ralph L. Sellmeyer, *School Publications: The Business Side,* (Branson, MO: Molatex Press, 1989).

3. Jack Dvorak, "High School Newspaper Financing: An Assessment," paper presented to the Mid-Winter Meeting of the Secondary Education Division of the Association for Education in Journalism, Norman, OK, January 1982.

4. Mary Benedict, "Two Views of the High School Newspaper: A Comparative Study of the Perceptions of the Role of the High School Newspaper in Nine States," paper presented to the Secondary Education Division of the Association for Education in Journalism Annual Convention, East Lansing, MI, 11 August 1981.

5. Laurence B. Lain, "The Funding of Secondary School Newspapers in Ohio Schools," paper presented to the Secondary Education Division of the Association for Education in Journalism and Mass Communication Annual Convention, Norman, OK, August 1986.

6. James A. Vornberg, James J. Zukowski, Vance W. Gipson, J. Stephen Southern, "A Model for Organizing Your School's Activity Program," *NASSP Bulletin* 67,467 (October 1983): 86-90.

7. Thomas Edward Blick, Jr., "High School Newspapers: Factors Significant in Achieving High Ratings," paper presented at the Annual Meeting of the Association for Education in Journalism, Athens, OH, August 1982.

8. Lain, 1986.

CHAPTER 7

WHO CALLS THE TUNE? LINKING BUDGET SOURCES AND FREE EXPRESSION

Chapter Highlights

- Newspapers which lost money the previous year were more likely to have stories killed by the principal.

- Papers which make a profit are less likely to be reviewed by administrators before publication.

- About 44 percent of principals never reviewed copy before publication but more than 14 percent always did so.

- Few schools say they cannot publish stories on drugs or sex anymore, but political and school board endorsements would never be permitted in at least half the newspapers studied.

Freedom from Administrative Control: A 25-Year Battle

Between the *Tinker*[1] decision in 1969 and *Hazelwood* in 1988,[2] scores of cases concerning student press rights entered the legal system. Some were resolved out of court; of those which went to trial, student journalists found themselves winning more than they lost. Since the Supreme Court upheld a Missouri principal's right to control the content of his school's newspaper in *Hazelwood*, however, an awareness has grown that the battle for freedom of expression in school publications must turn increasingly from the courtroom to the classroom. What the courts are now reluctant to grant as a

Constitutional right in a single judgment must perhaps be won anew in individual school districts, working inside the school system rather than inside the legal system.

That is the battle, or rather, these are the battles, for which we want to help lay the groundwork in this chapter. The courts have broadened the kinds of circumstances in which a principal is *permitted* to censor school newspapers, but the courts have not said that he or she *must* do so. Regardless of the state of the law, regardless of local district policies, the school press will inevitably feel pressure from time to time to publish certain stories or to refrain from publishing stories about particular topics. So another area to pay some attention to might be on elements *outside* the legal and policy areas that seem to have some effect on free expression, and which newspapers might be able to influence.

Strategies for Protecting Free Expression

While one battle for free expression remains in the broader legal arena and another focuses on locally adopted policies, there is much that school newspaper staff members and advisers can do to create a *psychological* climate that makes administrators less likely to interfere with the paper.

One obvious strategy is to produce a newspaper that is as professionally and competently done as possible. It's not a foolproof answer, of course, for some of the best school papers in the country have felt the administrative heat and censor's scissors from time to time. Nevertheless, a staff that does its job well will give its principal far less cause to watch over its shoulder than a staff that does its job poorly.

Other factors have been suggested as promoting a higher degree of freedom for school papers. The type of community in which a school is located could be important; principals in larger, more heterogeneous communities might tend to take a more liberal approach than principals in smaller, closer-knit communities.

The adviser's background, training, and experience might be important in building the confidence of a principal that the job is being done right and there's no need to interfere. And, as was suggested in Chapter 6 of this book, money is usually important. Papers published with school funds may be more closely watched than papers that do *not* rely on the school for their budgets.

If it is possible to increase our understanding of the factors that seem to promote higher levels of autonomy in high school publications, we may, by encouraging the development of those factors, be able to help the lawyers and policy-makers in the battle to foster a free student press. While it may not be possible to do much about the environmental factors under which school newspapers operate, e.g., school and community size, public or private, etc., many elements are subject to influence. How school newspapers are funded, and how advisers are hired, trained and compensated—these and other factors can be studied and over time modified in directions that appear consistent with greater measures of free expression.

Campbell[3] recognized that few high school newspaper advisers had adequate backgrounds in Journalism, and the college courses they had taken had little to do with their advising responsibilities. Boyd[4] reported that Journalism teachers in Indiana were seldom hired specifically for the job and that they had little training in the field. Pettibone[5] said much the same thing 10 years later. Driscoll[6] emphasized the importance of school press and advisers' organizations to the school publication program, and a special issue of the *NASSP Bulletin*[7] ran a series of articles designed to help principals hire, train, and keep effective advisers. A study by Trager and Dickerson[8] pointed up the lack of a consistent approach to high school journalists but affirmed the importance of community size. Gallinger[9] provided recent information on levels of cooperation between the scholastic and the commercial press.

Most of the literature is based on state or regional studies; national samples are less common, but Click and Kopenhaver[10] provided some national information on principals' attitudes toward student press freedom immediately prior to the *Hazelwood* decision, and they included good demographic data about many characteristics of the school press nationally. Most of Dickson's[11] later work dealt with the immediate post-*Hazelwood* era, and he provided valuable attitudinal and demographic information from national samples about the high school press. Much of this literature is reviewed in the following chapters.

While studies involving adviser or community characteristics are not uncommon, there has been little investigation of the role, if any, played by the funding of the school press regarding the question of free expression. That work has been limited largely to the descriptive studies reviewed in Chapter 6.

Some Characteristics of School Newspapers

Our purpose here is to identify some of the traits of schools, publications, and advisers that are most often associated with certain types of autonomy found in high school newspaper programs. The word "autonomy" is used here not to suggest a wholly independent press, accountable to no one, but a press that is responsible for making its own decisions about content and coverage, free from pre-publication review by school authorities.

Few people suggest that there is, or can be, such a thing as a completely *independent* high school press, something that's rare even in colleges and universities. As a practical matter, it is usually necessary for schools to provide a teacher/adviser for Journalism students as well as facilities and equipment for the newspaper. Where academic credit is given for work on the paper, those requirements are obvious. Financial and academic support do not, however, have to imply editorial control.

There aren't many high school football coaches who would appreciate having to consult the principal before calling each play or to have their game plans approved by school administrators every Friday afternoon for the Big Game that night. Few band directors would stay at a school where the music was selected by the School Board. Such actions would never occur to most principals, even to those who insist on checking proofs of the newspaper.

Few principals, however, would simply assign the new biology teacher the job of coaching the football team; the band director invariably has formal training in music. Moreover, most of the costs of those activities are covered by paid admission to athletic events and by band and sports boosters. The financial situation with the school newspaper is frequently much different.

The student press is vulnerable to pressures from many sources, both inside and outside the school. We classify these styles of pressure in these ways:

Environmental variables are those effects that arise from the general nature of the school, community, and newspaper:

- The type of school: public or non-public
- School enrollment in grades 10-12
- Size of the community in which the school was located
- Frequency of publication of the newspaper
- The extracurricular or for-credit nature of the paper

Most of these were examined in detail in Chapter 4.

Adviser variables arise from adviser backgrounds and professional affiliations in seven ways:

- The extra pay, if any, that advisers receive for advising
- Advisers' undergraduate degree major
- Advisers' graduate degree major, if any
- How advisers acquired their jobs:
  - Were they hired for the position?
  - Were they assigned the job after hiring?
  - Did they volunteer?
- Years of advising experience
- Type and duration of personal experience in the media
  - college
  - part-time
  - full-time
- Membership for themselves or their staffs in various scholastic and professional journalism organizations

A breakdown of these kinds of demographic information was found in Chapter 5 of this book.

Financial variables measure the extent to which the papers rely on various sources of funding and on their recent financial health, using the factors discussed in Chapter 6:

- The newspaper's annual budget
- Money from activity fees
- Money from subscription sales
- Money from single-copy sales
- Money from administrative subsidies
- Money from sale of advertising
- Whether the newspaper made or lost money last year

These variables were used in a 1991 study[12] as independent, or antecedent, variables. That is, these conditions that existed at each of the schools in the study were either outside the newspaper's control (school size or adviser's education) or represented the paper's way of managing its affairs (the organizations it belonged to or where its money came from).

Administration Control and Newspaper Autonomy

Autonomy variables, a fourth type of variable measured in the study, describes some of the roles of staff, advisers, and school officials in establishing the content of the paper. Seventeen questions were asked of advisers in the study, in the search to determine some of the constraints under which their staffs operated.

To learn something about who influenced the content of the newspapers, and to see what sorts of stories could and could not be covered, there were two general types of questions about constraints.

- First, seven questions asked about who influenced the editorial process:
    - How often did an administrator read copy for the newspaper before publication?
    - Must potentially controversial articles be cleared with the administration before publication?
    - How often has an administrator killed an article before publication?

- How often does the adviser read copy for the newspaper before publication?

- How often has the adviser killed an article or required a rewrite for reasons of content, not for mechanical reasons?

- Are teachers permitted to review articles about themselves or their organizations before publication, and what changes may they make?

- Must the principal select or approve the choice of the newspaper's student editor?

• Next, advisers were given 10 general story types and asked whether each would definitely or probably be killed by the principal, would definitely or probably be killed by the adviser, probably would run in the school's newspaper, or that a similar story had run in the paper in the previous year. Advisers were told to evaluate only by subject matter and to assume that the pieces were otherwise well-written and well-researched. The story types were as follows:

- Birth Control

- Abortion

- Endorsement of a candidate for local office

- Endorsement of a candidate for school board

- Story critical of the school board

- Story critical of school administration

- Story critical of a school sports team

- Story critical of teachers in general

- Drug problems in your school

- General story about teen, sex, and pregnancy

In general, environmental, adviser, and financial variables were considered independent or antecedent variables with autonomy variables considered as dependent or criterion variables.

Because researchers have not agreed on a definition of editorial autonomy for school newspapers, and there is no standard way of

measuring it, one could argue whether adviser responses to a catalogue of questions about both observed and hypothetical practices is
the best way to go about this task. But the results do provide some
useful directions for research into the freedom of the school press, a
matter that we believe is an important purpose served by this book.
For the time being, the associations reported in this chapter are the
best information available on relationships between many of the
antecedent variables (especially the *financial* variables) and the criterion variables.

Who Influences the Editorial Process?

Some differences on most of the autonomy variables could be
statistically associated with some of the environmental, financial or
adviser variables. In this section we report those differences on the
first type of autonomy variables, i.e., those bearing on who screens or
otherwise influences the editorial process.

Principals never screen copy for the paper at 44 percent of the
schools in the study, but they always do so at 14.5 percent of the
schools. (See Graph 7.1) About a third do so only on request of the
advisers. Newspapers that lost money the previous year were more
likely to have their papers screened by administrators.[13] Papers that
had made a profit the previous year were less likely to have stories
killed by administrators,[14] and were less likely to permit teachers to
review stories about themselves or their organizations before publication.[15] More experienced advisers were less likely to have their
papers screened by the principal.[16]

About one-third of principals required that controversial articles
be cleared with them prior to publication. More experienced advisers
were less likely to work under that requirement in their schools.[17]

Two-thirds of advisers reported that their principals had never
killed a story. (Graph 7.2) A quarter said it happened rarely, and just
7 percent said it happened sometimes or often. Papers whose advisers
had no college or professional experience in Journalism were more
likely to have stories killed by the principal.[18]

Graph 7.1

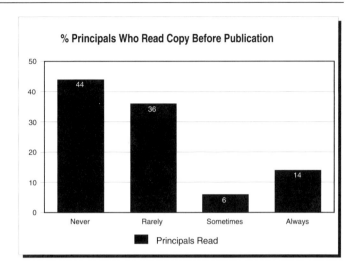

Graph 7.2

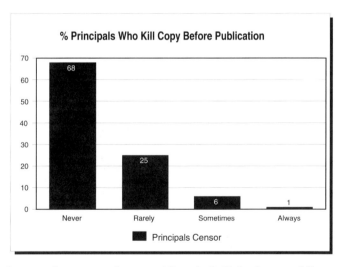

Advisers almost always read copy (Graph 7.3) before publication: Just 6 percent read less than every issue. Only a third of advisers had never killed a story (Graph 7.4), but they were more likely to have killed stories than the principal—probably because many questionable stories never made it past the adviser's desk to the principal's office. Chapter 10 will look at that conduct in greater detail.

Graph 7.3

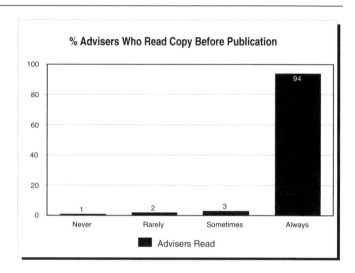

Graph 7.4

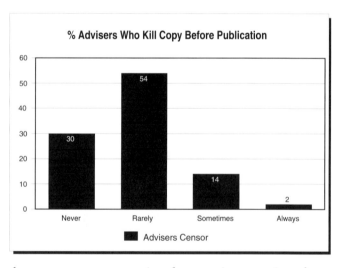

Other teachers are never permitted to review stories about themselves or their organizations at 41 percent of the schools reporting. At 42 percent they may review stories for facts only, and at 17 percent they may require changes in any content. Papers that rely most heavily on single-copy sales are most likely to allow teachers to approve stories about themselves,[19] as are papers that lost money the previous year.[20] Advisers' activity in professional organizations was also significant, with more active advisers less often permitting teachers pre-publication access to the stories.[21]

In Chapter 1 we listed six functions of high school journalism: mechanistic, public relations, vocational, informational, free expression forum for students, and integrative. We pointed out that traditional definitions of the role of the school press relied heavily on the first three of those. For more than 20 years, however, journalism teachers and associations have stressed the *last* three functions, i.e., that the school press ought to operate as much as possible like its commercial counterpart and should serve as an honest voice for student thought. In doing so, it will best perform its integrative function of leading students to better analyze, synthesize, and evaluate the world around them.

Administrators and teachers too often focus only on the mechanistic and public relations roles of the school press, however, and may attempt to control its content to promote those roles. That's why the answer to the question *"Who influences the editorial content?"* is important.

A well-meaning friend asked the authors about what he called the bias against the principal reading copy. "The school newspaper is an educational tool," he said. "Why shouldn't a teacher help a kid do a better job?" Most teachers *do* read student copy, 94 percent in this study. They do it as part of their teaching role. That is part of the *mechanistic* function of the school press, but there are higher functions. For those functions to be realized, students, not teachers or principals, must determine the content of the newspaper.

Just because a principal screens copy before publication does not mean that censorship will surely follow. The very fact that the principal reads the copy, however, can produce a chilling effect on what stories students will cover and how they will write—even in editorials and personal columns in which they are supposed to be able to express opinion! If, as most journalism teachers believe, the integrative function of the school press is best promoted by the informational and free expression functions, then the staff of the newspaper itself should determine the content of the paper, not the principal or the adviser. Allowing principals or teachers to *edit* copy, i.e., to decide what goes into the newspaper, will certainly reduce the number of typographical and grammatical errors, thereby enhancing the mechanistic function of the press, but it may badly inhibit the integrative function, and that would be a steep price to pay for good spelling.

Results described in this chapter suggest that school newspapers which make a profit are less likely to have to be approved by the principal than newspapers that do not make a profit. Advisers who have more training or experience operate under fewer restrictions than advisers with less. If it is important to minimize interference with the newspaper from school authorities, then newspapers that make a profit and that have well-trained and experienced advisers would seem to have the best chance.

Who Publishes Controversial Stories?

Dozens of different types of stories have been spiked by school officials over the years, and many advisers are given the word early on that certain types of stories "just won't go over very well in our community, so let's just leave them alone." Topics relating to sex, politics, and drugs are often considered too hot to handle or inappropriate for student discussion; sports, the band, and the faculty are frequently accorded sacred-cow status in schools, making them immune to any suggestion of criticism. Every adviser has at least a mental list of subjects that he or she knows will rock the administrative boat, but it's a list that may vary quite a lot from school to school.

Advisers in the study were asked whether they could run stories on 10 hot topics in the school paper or whether those stories would probably be killed either by the principal or the adviser. The story types mentioned were similar to many of those used in other studies cited. All of the story types are controversial, and even those *most* likely to run, we found, would be killed at 14 percent of the schools that took part in the study.

Advisers were asked to consider *only* the subject matter of the stories, and to assume that all stories were well-researched and well-written. Below are the 10 story types and what the study showed about the sorts of school papers that probably would run each story. Table 7.1 shows the relative frequency with which these stories would run or by whom they would be killed.

Table 7.1: % Stories Allowed to Run in Your Newspaper

Story Subject	Could Run	Killed by Adviser	Killed by Principal
Birth Control	69	12	19
Abortion	72	13	15
Political Endorsement	52	35	13
School Board Endorsement	41	42	17
Criticism of School Board	59	20	21
Criticism of Administration	61	23	16
Criticism of Sports Team	62	27	11
Criticism of Teachers	57	32	11
Drugs in School	86	5	9
Sex and Pregnancy	86	7	7

1. Birth control

More than 30 percent of the advisers said that this story would probably by killed by either the adviser or the principal. Private schools (mostly church-supported) would be significantly less likely to run a birth-control story,[22] as also would smaller schools.[23] Staffs that received academic credit for their work were more likely to be able to run such a story.[24] Furthermore, newspapers that paid more of their own expenses through advertising sales are more likely to be able to run such a story.[25] Adviser experience also mattered: Papers with more experienced advisers were better able to run a birth-control story.[26]

2. Abortion

Over a quarter of the schools indicated that any abortion story would definitely or probably be killed. Private schools would more often forbid such a story,[27] and papers generating more advertising revenue were more likely than others to be able to run the story.[28] Papers whose advisers were hired for the position were more likely to run the story than papers advised by appointees or volunteers[29] as also were papers whose advisers were active in associations.[30]

3. Political endorsements

Endorsement of candidates for local office is apparently a dangerous subject: Such a story would be killed at nearly half the schools responding. Papers whose advisers were active in professional associations were somewhat more likely to run political endorsements.[31]

4. School Board endorsements

This was the story most likely to be killed; almost 59 percent of the schools in the study would forbid its publication. None of the antecedent variables was statistically associated with this variable.

5. Story critical of the school board

About 40 percent of respondents said that this story would probably be killed; however, it would be more likely to be run in the school of an adviser active in professional associations.[32]

6. Story critical of the administration

Here, too, more than 39 percent of advisers said that a story critical of the school's leadership could not run in their papers, but there were more variables associated with those schools in which the story could run. Papers that bring in more advertising revenue would be more likely to run it,[33] as would schools in which advisers are better paid for their work.[34] Schools whose advisers had a bachelor's degree in Journalism, Education, or Social Science appeared more able to run a story critical of the school's administration,[35] as did schools whose advisers had a master's degree in any field.[36] Schools with advisers who belong to professional associations were also better able to run this story.[37]

7. Story critical of a sports team

Both because criticism of other students is often considered inappropriate and because sports programs are a special focal point of student life in many places, stories that criticize athletic teams are relatively rare. More than 38 percent of the respondents said that such a story could not run in their newspapers. But advisers with bachelor's degrees in Journalism reported that they were more likely to be able to do so,[38] as did advisers who themselves had had college-level or better experience in Journalism.[39] Advisers active in professional associations were also more likely to have papers that could run stories critical of school sports teams.[40]

8. Story critical of teachers in general

A story critical of teachers could not run in nearly 43 percent of the schools in the study, with advisers reporting that they would be about three times more likely to kill the story than the principal would be. Two variables are associated with this story. Advisers who were paid more for their publications work were *less* likely than others to have a paper that would run the story[41] but advisers who were active in professional associations were more often associated with a paper that would run the story.[42]

9. Story about drug problems in your school

Stories about drugs are seldom a problem any more: About 14 percent of the respondents said such a story would not be permitted in their papers. Only two variables were significantly associated with this kind of story: Advisers who were hired for the job were more likely to run it in their papers than were appointees or volunteers,[43] as also were advisers active in professional associations.[44]

10. Story about teens, sex, and pregnancy

Stories like this have become almost routine; only 14 percent of the papers in the study did not permit them. Papers that generate more advertising dollars are more likely to be able to run a story about teens and sex,[45] but papers that rely more heavily on administration subsidies are less likely to run it.[46] Papers whose adviser had an undergraduate degree in Journalism or Education are more likely to run the story,[47] as also were papers whose advisers were hired specifically for the job.[48] The newspapers of more experienced advisers were more likely to run such a story,[49] as also were those whose advisers belonged to professional associations.[50]

The influence of the factors of school type and size, and of the adviser's experience and memberships, have long been understood as important elements in the degree to which student journalists enjoyed high levels of free expression. More experienced advisers in this study were less likely to have their newspapers' copy reviewed by administrators before publication and less likely to be required to seek clearance before running controversial articles. Stories about birth control were more likely to run in their papers.

Advisers who were active in professional associations were less likely than others to allow other teachers to screen stories about themselves or their organizations before publication, and their papers were more likely to run eight of the 10 hypothetical stories; only stories on birth control and endorsements for school board candidates did not appear connected with membership in organizations.

Aside from experience and affiliation, a few other adviser characteristics were important in some features of the study. Whether advisers were hired specifically to advise Journalism programs or were obtained in some other way, was related to the ability of their newspapers to publish articles on abortion, drugs, and sex. The academic degrees they held and their major fields were associated with their papers' publication of stories about sex, criticism of the administration, and athletics. Advisers who had worked for newspapers either in college or professionally were more likely to be able to run stories critical of athletics and were less likely to have stories killed by administrators.

Links Between Finances and Free Expression

Newspaper finances are a significant factor in a school publication's ability to achieve autonomy. Papers that supported themselves largely through advertising were more likely to be able to run stories on birth control, abortion, sex, and pregnancy, and stories that were critical of school administration. Moreover, papers that had made a profit the previous school year were less likely than others to be screened by administrators before publication. Profit-generating papers were less likely to have stories killed by administrators before publication, and they were less likely to allow teachers to screen stories about themselves.

The ability to turn a profit may not be a matter of life and death for school newspapers in the same sense that it is for their commercial cousins, but clear links do exist between profitability and free expression. The ability of a paper to pay its own way is important for its autonomy and freedom.

If that's the case, what is the best way for a newspaper to generate as much of its own money as possible?

Advertising.

Other sources of revenue just don't do the job. Subscription and single copy sales bring in too little cash. Few schools have activity fees. Administrative subsidies have too many subtle strings attached. Nothing else works as well as advertising.

Papers that rely more heavily on advertising are much more likely to produce a profit-making newspaper than are papers that rely on administrative subsidy. Among newspapers that take in half or more of their revenues from advertising (Graph 7.5), 42 percent make a profit and only 19 percent lose money, whereas papers that collect half or more of their budgets from administrators (Graph 7.6) are as likely to lose money as not. Among papers that finance themselves entirely through advertising, 68 percent make a profit and just 11 percent lose money. Administrative subsidies at that level allow most papers to break even but not, of course, to make a profit. Across the sample, level of advertising support was strongly associated with a newspaper's ability to make a profit.[51] That's important, because more profitable newspapers were also more autonomous newspapers.

Graph 7.5

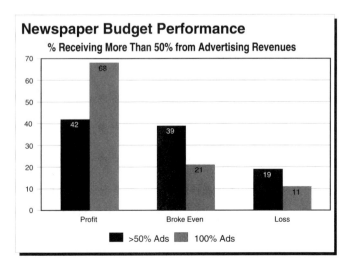

173

Graph 7.6

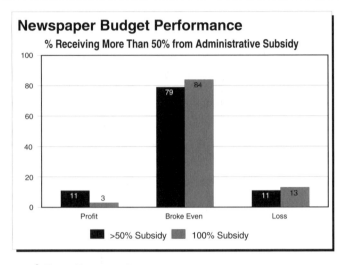

Newspaper Budget Performance

% Receiving More Than 50% from Administrative Subsidy

The Battle Lines of Free Expression

Three fronts are already well-understood as those on which the battle for freedom of expression for America's high school journalists must be fought; the fourth has newly emerged as a result of this study.

First, the shock troops are those fighting the *legal battles* to minimize the damage caused by the *Hazelwood* precedent and the decisions that are liable to be based on it. We discuss this aspect in the remaining chapters.

Second, one of the most important efforts of journalism organizations and associations is that of working state by state and school district by school district to enact *local laws and policies* protecting student free expression. The process is lengthy and tedious, but each success adds to the momentum for the next challenge.

The third battle line to be drawn is that of *adviser training and involvement*, a front which is reinforced by this study. Advisers with appropriate degrees and journalistic experience can provide their students with sound training in the professional, legal, and ethical issues that confront them. Few school systems would consider hiring a football coach or band director who had no background in sports or music, but less than 37 percent of the newspaper advisers who responded to the survey had been hired specifically for a job in high school Journalism. Thirty-one percent had volunteered and 32 percent were given no choice: They were assigned the job by their administrators. Both for the sake of better teaching and of greater freedom of the high school press, the effort must be made by teacher groups and press associations to persuade school officials that appointing underprepared teachers in Journalism is no more appropriate than is hiring untrained coaches in sports or unschooled teachers for Music. Journalism students are as entitled to qualified instruction as any other students in the school.

Moreover, advisers hired for their jobs stay on those jobs longer. A strong relationship was evident between years of advising experience and the way that advisers were hired.[52] More than 53 percent of the advisers with more than 10 years experience were originally hired for their jobs, more than twice the rate of appointees or volunteers. Because greater adviser experience is associated with several autonomy characteristics, it would seem to be in the interests of scholastic Journalism organizations to do what they can to encourage policies in favor of hiring teachers with appropriate backgrounds as Journalism advisers.

Advisers who join press associations or journalism education organizations also appear in some ways to fare better than those who don't. It is impossible to overstate the value of state, regional, and national press associations in educating and assisting their members. Where advisers and staffs are involved with their colleagues elsewhere, strong and active programs are all the more likely.

A fourth battle line for free expression for high school journalists has emerged from this study, that of *financial stability*. Newspapers that take responsibility for raising the greater part of their operating budgets seem to enjoy greater latitude in several respects than their administratively subsidized counterparts.

If further investigation confirms the apparent relationship between free expression and self-funding, this perception will signal a new ingredient to be added to the college courses and workshop sessions that advisers need. Advisers usually receive little training in business practices. They are taught an assortment of writing, editing, and layout skills, perhaps some computer or photography applications, legal and ethical issues, and a good deal about lesson plans and teaching methods. In the light of the evidence presented here, it seems that the time has come to make sure that Journalism education classes in teacher certification programs include a strong unit in business practices and advertising sales. State and national associations ought to make adviser sessions on budget, finance, and fiscal self-determination an important part of their programs at every convention. Financial self-sufficiency is not the only route to ensuring a free and self-reliant school press, of course, and is not even the most important factor. Economic autonomy is a contributor to freedom of the high school press, however, and its importance needs to be recognized. The study of school press finances ought to be added to the agendas of those who seek to understand the ways in which the student press can be brought to its full potential. Money is a driving force in the commercial press: We should not be surprised to learn that money is also an important dimension of the school press.

While research here and elsewhere shows that some differences exist in the amount of freedom students enjoy based on the size and type of their school and community, the adviser can do little to change those built-in factors. Free expression does exist at every level of the high school press, however, and that's where the battles *can* be fought.

The campaign for economic autonomy is the one battle front which can be opened anew with each issue of the newspaper; it is a battle that can be won every month. The legal and Constitutional contests are fought on state and national fronts. The struggles to get state and district adoption of policies favorable to the school press usually require carefully planned and well coordinated strategies leading up to a single big push. Hiring policies for journalism teachers are in the hands of administrators. Economic health, however, is within the control of newspaper advisers and staffs.

We believe this chapter suggests two important things that advisers can do to help themselves and their students achieve editorial autonomy. First, advisers need to become active in professional associations. Not only do those organizations lead the fight on the legal and policy-making battle fronts, they can help advisers make up for the gaps in their own backgrounds by providing conventions, workshops, publications, and personal contact with battle-wise veteran advisers. This and other research shows the greater freedom enjoyed by staffs whose advisers are more experienced in the craft and better connected to the profession.

Second, advisers must put the economic side of Journalism on an equal footing with the editorial side. The two are not separated in the "real" world, and there is no reason for them to be in the scholastic world. Newspapers which sell ads aggressively and watch spending carefully will find it easier to control their own editorial destinies as well.

Principals have an important role to play, too. They *must* understand the importance of hiring qualified professionals as advisers of school publications, and the urgency of encouraging advisers to become active members of professional organizations. Students who are taught by teachers who really *know* their subject matter are surely less likely to violate legal and ethical standards than are students who are taught by someone who may not be certain of what those standards are. Thousands of advisers without formal training in Journalism have done splendid work with student journalists, but most of those advisers have plugged the gaps in their own backgrounds by working hard to do their learning on the job.

Principals must also *encourage* school newspapers to pay for themselves, whether by helping the staff wean itself from the administrative pocketbook, or by shelving outdated policies that prohibit the sale of advertising. Newspapers that sell ads not only make economic sense, they make good educational sense: Students will not *really* understand the role of mass communication in their society unless they understand the economic realities of the media.

NOTES ON CHAPTER 7

1. *Tinker v. Des Moines Independent School District.* 89 S.Ct. 733, 393 U.S. 503 (1969).

2. *Hazelwood v. Kuhlmeier.* 108 S.Ct. 562 (1988).

3. Laurence R. Campbell, "Training Sponsors for High School Journalism," *Journalism Quarterly 16*,4 (December 1939): 366-70.

4. John A. Boyd, "High School Journalism Instruction in Indiana," *Journalism Quarterly 37*,4 (Autumn 1960): 586-87.

5. John Pettibone, "Summer Workshops Offer Training for Nation's Publications Advisers," *Quill and Scroll 44*,4 (April-May 1970): 8-9.

6. Carol K. Driscoll, *First Amendment and the High School Press Adviser*, .Journalism Education Association report (January 1976).

7. Articles included in this issue of the NASSP Bulletin 72:511 (November 1988) were by Molly Clemons, "When Will Principals Have No Need to Worry about Publications?" pp. 9-10; John Bowen, "Responsibility: The Key to Scholastic Journalism," pp. 19-20; and Thomas Eveslage, "Publications Guidelines: A Way to Avoid Conflict and Courtrooms," pp. 21-26. See also Lynn Shenkman, "Publications Advisers—What Are Their Competencies, Skills?" *NASSP Bulletin* 68:468 (January 1984): 75-78.

8. Robert Trager and Donna L. Dickerson, "Prior Restraint in High School: Law, Attitudes and Practice," *Journalism Quarterly 57*,1 (Spring 1980): 135-138.

9. Nancy Gallinger, "Still Captive Voices? High School Journalism in New England Needs Help," *Newspaper Research Journal 11,2* (Spring 1990): 12-27.

10. J. William Click and Lillian Lodge Kopenhaver, "Principals' and Newspaper Advisers' Attitudes Toward Freedom of the Student Press in the United States," paper presented to the Secondary Education Division of the Association for Education in Journalism and Mass Communication, Annual Convention, Norman, OK, August 1986. By the same authors, also see "Principals Favor Discipline More than a Free Press," *Journalism Educator 43,2* (Summer 1988): 48-51.

11. For information on principals' attitudes, see Thomas V. Dickson, "Attitudes of High School Principals about Press Freedom after

Hazelwood," *Journalism Quarterly* 66,1 (Spring 1989): 169-173. For emphasis on advisers, and for good demographic information, see Thomas V. Dickson, "How Advisers View the Status of High School Press Freedom Following the Hazelwood Decision," paper presented at the Association for Education in Journalism and Mass Communication national convention, Washington, DC, August 1989.

12. Laurence B. Lain, "A National Study of High School Newspaper Programs: Environmental and Adviser Characteristics, Funding and Pressures on Free Expression," paper presented at the Annual Meeting of the Association for Education in Journalism and Mass Communication, Montréal, Québec, August 1992.

13. X^2=17.08 with 8 df, p<.05. The X^2 (Chi-square) test compares the actual frequency of a response with the frequency that would result purely by chance. The test produces a number which can be checked for its probability level (p). A probability level of .05 or smaller is accepted by most researchers as an indication that the results are statistically significant, that is, that the results are not due merely to chance. A probability level of .05 means that the results would be obtained by chance only 5 percent of the time.

14. X^2=16.68 with 8 df, p<.05.

15. X^2=12.71 with 4 df, p<.01.

16. X^2=34.62 with 16 df, p<.01.

17. X^2=20.24 with 4 df, p<.001.

18. X^2=28.95 with 12 df, p<.01.

19. X^2=19.35 with 10 df, p<.05.

20. X^2=12.71 with 4 df, p<.01.

21. X^2=16.24 with 6 df, p<.01. Membership in JEA, CSPAA, NSPA and CSPA were all significant at at least the .05 level.

22. X^2=14.91 with 5 df, p<.01.

23. X^2=30.86 with 15 df, p<.01.

24. X^2=21.79 with 10 df, p<.02.

25. X^2=40.92 with 25 df, p<.02.

26. X^2=40.88 with 20 df, p<.01.

27. X^2=15.91 with 5 df, p<.01.

28. X^2=48.61 with 25 df, p<.01.

29. X^2=25.59 with 15 df, p<.05.

30. X^2=25.57 with 15 df, p<.05. Quill & Scroll and JEA are both significant at at least .01.

31. X^2=26.25 with 15 df, p<.05.

32. X^2=26.27 with 15 df, p<.05.

33. X^2=43.47 with 25 df, p<.01.

34. X^2=27.50 with 15 df, p<.02.

35. X^2=72.07 with 40 df, p<.001.

36. X^2=60.84 with 40 df, p<.02.

37. X^2=33.93 with 15 df, p<.01.

38. X^2=57.16 with 40 df, p<.05.

39. X^2=28.21 with 15 df, p<.02

40. X^2=28.79 with 1 df, p<.02.

41. X^2=28.19 with 15 df, p<.02.

42. X^2=29.46 with 15 df, p<.01.

43. X^2=34.27 with 15 df, p<.01.

44. X^2=30.01 with 15 df, p<.01.

45. X^2=43.97 with 25 df, p<.01.

46. X^2=37.44 with 25 df, p<.05.

47. X^2=69.48 with 40 df, p<.01.

48. X^2=37.21 with 15 df, p<.001.

49. X^2=31.87 with 20 df, p<.05.

50. X^2=27.75 with 15 df, p<.02.

51. X^2=31.21 with 10 df, p<.001.

52. X^2=27.14 with 12 df, p<.01.

CHAPTER 8

THE RUGGED ROAD TO SCHOLASTIC PRESS FREEDOM

Chapter Highlights

- Research suggests that most principals and advisers before the 1960s did not think that the First Amendment applied to student publications.

- Beginning in 1969, a number of federal court cases provided school publications considerable First Amendment protection.

- Studies during the *"Tinker* Era" (1969-1988) found that advisers continued to censor publications because they believed it was their duty to the school.

- Studies during the 1970s and early 1980s suggested that direct censorship was causing student journalists to censor themselves and had turned student publications into little more than public relations sheets for their schools.

- By the early 1980s the Supreme Court was signaling that a change was coming in regard to what First Amendment rights it was willing to grant student journalists.

Does the First Amendment apply to the secondary school press? Researchers say that the place of the First Amendment in the secondary school was not really an issue until the unrest of the late 1960s swept over U.S. colleges and secondary schools. That unrest led to the first of two Supreme Court cases that are used as dividing lines separating three eras of school journalism. *Tinker v. Des Moines Community School District*, the first case, is discussed in this chapter. The second case, *Hazelwood School District v. Kuhlmeier*, which lends its name to the current era, will be discussed in Chapter 9. We will call the three eras the pre-*Tinker* era (1948-1968), the *Tinker* era (1969-1987), and the *Hazelwood* era (since 1988).

Robert P. Knight, whose 30 years of work in secondary school journalism arched all three eras, wrote that the pre-*Tinker* era was a time when students did not question the authority of school officials or, if they did, they did not get away with it. The rapid change that swept the country in the 1960s resulted in greater independence and greater problems for youth, and it led to the Supreme Court's determination in 1969 in the *Tinker* case that students' First Amendment rights did not stop "at the schoolhouse gate." Professor Knight wrote about the first two eras:

> *The pre-*Tinker *era, 1948-1968, was an in loco parentis environment in which things were placid, rules were rules and daily dangers for teenagers were the exception. Teachers considered themselves publication "sponsors," and some had proprietary feelings about their newspaper or yearbook. Some thought they could achieve editorial independence with advertising and money-making projects. Principals did not see themselves as publishers, for they rarely had students trying to sneak things past the sponsor....*
>
> *In this* Tinker *era, 1969-1987, veteran "sponsors" wondered at the new breed of publications "adviser," who put greater stress on students' press rights and who let student editors determine content. They taught responsibility and ethics, but they gave students opportunities to get into hot water if they wished.*[1]

Despite the *Tinker* ruling, researchers continued to conclude that principals still thought of the newspaper as a public relations tool, that advisers thought that they owed it to the school to keep controversial material out of the newspaper, and that students rarely questioned the rules. According to researchers, prepublication restraint had been used on occasion, but researchers usually found that it was not often necessary because students were intimidated into submission. They concluded that school newspapers were little more than bland bulletin boards filled with good news.

A question to be answered in this chapter is whether advisers in the 1970s and '80s did give students opportunities to get into hot water if they wished, or whether they used prior restraint and intimidation that resulted in apathetic students and bland content. In trying to answer that question, we have attempted to determine whether principals and advisers followed the letter and the spirit of the law in regard to the Supreme Court's *Tinker* ruling and subsequent lower court rulings.

A Problem of Definitions

The term "censorship" has been used in nearly all studies reported here; however, few researchers have stated the definition they used in their research, and it appears that a variety of definitions were used. One dictionary definition of censorship is "the act of examining and removing or prohibiting anything considered objectionable." This definition does not include intimidation and must include prior review only if restraint followed the review.

A definition used by some researchers is "any official interference with student control of the newspaper." That definition includes both prior review and prior restraint as well as intimidation or suggestion that likely would be acted upon because of the position of the person interfering; however, it would not include deference by students. Thus, any advice given by an adviser might be seen as censorship because students could feel intimidated, or they might merely comply out of respect for the adviser or for the position that the adviser occupies.

Yet another definition that researchers have used is "any official interference by intimidation or coercion with student control of the newspaper." While this definition might cover content prohibitions, it does not seem to include the most obvious type of censorship: overt censorship; that is, prior restraint by administrative fiat.

Another definition researchers have used is "specific incidents of cutting controversial material and any policy or atmosphere of intimidation that causes students to refrain from printing certain materials in the school newspaper." This definition is probably the best of these definitions because it seems to include content prohibitions; however, it is not always clear whether students are refraining from publication because of an atmosphere of intimidation or merely from deference to, or out of respect for, authority.

It is clear from court cases that school press censorship cannot be defined so broadly as to cover prior review if prior restraint is not involved. Even in the *Tinker* era, federal courts ruled that mandated prior review did not violate the Constitution, and prohibitions on content were allowed as long as satisfactory procedural guidelines were in place before prior restraint was used. Regulations, however, had to "clearly set out what is forbidden and establish administrative procedure by which students can challenge decisions to censor."[2] Of course, even at schools where prior review is not mandated, students have no right, constitutional or otherwise, to keep the adviser or principal from looking at a school-sponsored newspaper in advance of publication.

The next problem concerns the definition of "self-censorship." A definition of that term could include any of the reasons for student self-restraint: because of intimidation, because of deference for whatever reason, because of a desire not to be controversial for whatever reason, because of a desire not to invade people's privacy or embarrass them, or even because of a lack of interest or knowledge. Use of self-censorship for several of these purposes (such as not publishing the names of juveniles accused of crimes or the names of rape victims or witnesses to a crime) are seen as traits of responsible journalists, and thus they cannot be equated with self-censorship resulting from intimidation; however, most researchers have not attempted to make such distinctions.

Professor J.C. Merrill, a scholar on journalism ethics, commented about law, ethics, and self-restraint:

> *Ethics has to do with "self-legislation" and "self-enforcement"; although it is, of course, related to law, it is of a different nature. Although law quite often stems from the ethical values of a society at a certain time (i.e., law is often reflective of ethics),*

law is something that is socially determined and socially enforced —or should be.... It has always been difficult to discuss ethics; law is much easier, for what is legal is a matter of law. What is ethical transcends law, for many actions are legal, but not ethical. And there are no 'ethical codebooks' to consult in order to settle ethical disputes.[3]

Because of these definitional problems, we use the term "censorship" when the researcher uses it, and we will supply the researcher's definition when available. In other contexts, we use the specific term for the particular component of censorship involved: content prohibition, prior review, prior restraint, adviser suggestion, or adviser intimidation. We also will use the relevant term for the type of student response we are analyzing: self-restraint, deference, or self-censorship.

Causes and Results of Administrative Censorship

The most extensive, and possibly the most critical as well as the most criticized, study of secondary school press freedom was published in 1974 by the Commission of Inquiry into High School Journalism (the Kennedy Commission). The commission concluded that the strongest push for censorship came from those at the top of the school system: principals, superintendents, and boards of education. The commission found that censorship affected not only the student press, but also the entire academic environment:

> *Not only does direct administrative censorship stifle the free expression of ideas in specific cases, but also it creates an atmosphere in which faculty and students alike know that to deal with controversial issues is to court official disapproval and perhaps disciplinary action. It breeds faculty censorship and self-censorship by students who otherwise would be more inclined toward participating in a free press.*
>
> *The result usually is an unquestioning attitude among students, an unhealthy acquiescence in pronouncements of school authorities no matter how unfair or oppressive they may be....*[4]

Research by the Kennedy Commission and others found that advisers were censoring stories with considerable zeal for their work.

The studies suggested that censorship was just one tool to assist advisers in completing the assigned mission of the school newspaper—to promote the values of the school. Not only advisers but also teachers in general were found to be supportive of censorship. A National Education Association survey, for example, found that 62 percent of secondary school teachers supported censorship of the student newspaper.[5]

Such statements as "unpopular material should not be aired in a student newspaper" and "the newspaper should reflect the school's public relations" did not seem unreasonable to advisers participating in at least one newspaper workshop in the early 1960s.[6] However, the Kennedy Commission reported a decade later that "neither a stated nor an implied policy of censorship is necessary in some cases for advisers to censor the papers. They do it as a duty to the school."[7] The Kennedy Commission referred to what took place in authoritarian schools, which it concluded were the norm:

> *(S)tudent rights are routinely denied, with little or no protest by the students. The cost of such controls is not only the absence of a free student press, but also bland, apathetic students who are unaware or uninterested in their rights.*[8]

Theories of Press Freedom

What are the prevailing theories of press freedom? What rights are guaranteed the press by the First Amendment? And to what extent, in the definition of the courts, does First Amendment freedom apply to the school press?

Theorists have classified the press (though other types of media would be included) into four broad types: authoritarian, libertarian, social responsibility, and communist or totalitarian.[9] According to Fred Siebert, Theodore Peterson, and Wilbur Schramm, the press in an authoritarian system is usually privately owned but is controlled by the government through licenses (either written or unwritten) that can be revoked if the press becomes unruly and criticizes the government.

In a libertarian system, the owners of the press determine content, and the restrictions on what can be published are minimal, though punishment is allowed for publication of some types of content. In theory, responsibility is not required, and truth is expected to win out because an enlightened public is expected to be able to distinguish the truth from the many divergent views presented in the multitude of publications available. In practice, some social responsibility is good policy under the system because punishment after publication is allowed for some types of content, such as libel or invasion of privacy.

In a system operating under the social responsibility theory, the press (and other media as well) is both expected and required to be ethical and responsible, as opposed to the libertarian system, in which responsibility is desirable but not enforced. If a publication fails to meet the level of responsibility required by the government, it can be forced to act responsibly or be closed for lack of compliance. Because social responsibility is defined by the government, critics of such a system charge that it may be hard to distinguish between a social responsibility system and an authoritarian or totalitarian one if the government decides to close or take over a media operation that it does not think is acting responsibly.

In a communist or totalitarian system, responsibility is not only required but also enforced through total ownership by the government or the ruling political party. The Soviet Communist system no longer exists, but totalitarian systems can be found in many places throughout the world.

The authoritarian theory was typified by England before the advent of democracy and by Nazi Germany. The totalitarian theory was typified by the media in Communist bloc countries. The libertarian theory has been best represented by the press in the United States. The social responsibility theory, arguably, has been instituted for the electronic media in the United States through licensing and content controls authorized by the Congress and the Federal Communications Commission.

Press Freedom According to the First Amendment

When the Bill of Rights was ratified in 1791, the Freedom of the Press clause of the First Amendment gave the American press freedom from prior restraint by the federal government, but a proposal in 1789 to require the states to provide freedom of speech and press was rejected. It was not until the 20th Century that the Supreme Court decided that the First Amendment did apply to actions of the states as well as the federal government. Until then, residents of individual states had to rely upon their state constitutions to protect them from state action to restrict freedom of speech and freedom of the press. The Supreme Court ruled in 1925 that the "due process clause" of the 14th Amendment ("nor shall any state deprive any person of life, liberty or property, without due process of law") requires the states to protect their residents' First Amendment rights.[10] By extension, actions of entities created by the states—such as cities and school boards—also are covered by the First Amendment.

The protection guaranteed U.S. citizens under the First Amendment has been strengthened over the years to assure that journalists are free of most government censorship. The U.S. Supreme Court ruled in 1931 that a state could not use prior restraint except when a publisher intends to aid the enemy in time of war, to print obscene material, to incite people to carry out violent acts, or to incite people to overthrow the government.[11] In addition, courts have allowed governmental restrictions on the time, place, and manner in which information is distributed.

The media also are accorded First Amendment protection from government punishment for printing truthful information obtained legally from the public record. A series of cases in the 1970s culminated in a 1979 case that involved the publication of the name of a junior high school student who was shot in the school's parking lot.[12] The Court ruled that if a newspaper "lawfully obtains truthful information about matters of public significance," it is unconstitutional for state officials to punish the publication of the information except to further "a state interest of the highest order."

Protection from prior restraint by the government was expanded in several cases concerning commercial advertising. In a 1980 case, the Supreme Court said the government's power to regulate any commercial message that was not misleading and did not concern unlawful activity is limited.[13]

The media can be punished if found guilty of libel or invasion of privacy; however, courts have ruled that advocacy of illegal activities (such as advocating smoking of marijuana or overthrowing the government) or use of offensive or foul language is not justification for prior restraint.[14]

Whether a publication is covered by the First Amendment rights outlined above depends upon whether it is a public forum. Under the forum theory, once a forum is opened to the public, it cannot be closed by government action unless sufficient procedural safeguards are adopted to protect First Amendment interests. Courts previously have ruled that a student publication in a public school is a public forum when it (1) publishes news, student editorials and letters to the editor; and (2) is distributed outside the journalism classroom.[15]

The forum theory was upheld by the Supreme Court in 1975.[16] Although it featured brief nudity, the play *Hair* was found in that case not to be obscene and, thus, the city of Chattanooga could not keep it from being shown in the public auditorium. Courts traditionally have found some rights of access to government-sponsored publications that are public forums; however, public officials do not have to allow access to government-sponsored publications that are not seen as public forums.

Freedom of the High School Press Under the First Amendment

Against that background, let us consider what system best typifies the secondary school press in the United States. The heart of the issue is whether the publication is a public forum. It is clear that school officials are not allowed to censor contents of a school-sponsored publication that is a public forum. When the publication is a public forum, student editors are expected to determine what news stories and editorials are accepted for publication and what advertisements are run.

If the publication is a public forum, school officials cannot ban such things as advertising that promotes a political cause, but school officials can prohibit ads for things that students are not legally allowed to purchase. For example, officials can stop publication of ads for illegal drugs or liquor when the students are below the legal drinking age, and they may prohibit ads promoting illegal acts, such as discrimination based on race or sex.

If no public forum exists, school officials can regulate content of the publication as they see fit, for they are the publishers. Such a publication, then, operates under some theory other than a libertarian one—either a totalitarian or a social responsibility theory. Press systems at public schools often are called authoritarian, but we will use the term "totalitarian" to apply to government-operated media. While that name has a harsh sound to us, it is a press theory that might be used in a closed-forum situation where the press is operated for the benefit of those responsible for the publication. The government in a totalitarian system can provide as much press freedom as it wishes. In a social responsibility system, considerable freedom is expected.

From 1969 to 1988, the question of whether or not school-sponsored publications were public forums usually was fairly easy to answer. School-sponsored publications at public schools were public forums when they published student-gathered news, student editorials, and letters to the editor and were distributed outside the journalism classroom. As in any libertarian system, the publication's content could be restricted legally only for a few specific reasons and only when certain procedural guidelines were met. Beginning in 1988, however, the question became harder to answer, as we discuss in Chapter 9.

High School Press Freedom in the 1960s

A study by Don Horine[17] is a good starting place for looking at the amount of censorship that took place in the 1960s. Like other studies of high school press freedom during that period, the stimulus for Horine's study was research about whether Journalism students wanted to seek careers in journalism.

Horine undertook his study, published in 1966, to determine whether censorship was prevalent at secondary schools in southern

California. He wanted to look at policies and practices of high school newspapers in order to understand why previous research[18] had shown that only one out of five high school students working on school publications intended to undertake a career in journalism. He suspected that the lack of press freedom experienced by student journalists was a factor in their choosing some other career.

As was the case in other studies in the 1960s and 1970s, the sample was limited to a relatively small area of the country. Horine sent questionnaires to principals, school newspaper advisers, and newspaper editors at the 148 public and the 76 parochial high schools in Los Angeles County. He received responses from about 40 percent of each of the groups surveyed. In his results, he combined responses from private and public schools.

Horine looked at such things as whether the newspaper was seen as a public relations tool for the school, whether advisers and editors read copy before publication, whether censorship was being practiced (though he did not define the term in his article, he presumably meant prior restraint), and whether school officials thought that press freedom existed at the school. He found that not only principals and advisers but also students considered the newspaper to be a means for promoting the school. His key findings are reported in Table 8.1.

Table 8.1: Responses of Los Angeles County Public and Parochial Senior High School Principals and Advisers to Questions about Press Rights (Horine, 1966)

	Principals	Advisers	Editors
How often do principals and advisers read copy prior to publication? (Principals: N=91; Advisers: N=91)			
Always	7%	88%	-
Frequently	2%	9%	-
Occasionally	71%	3%	-
Never	20%	0%	-

Table 8.1 (continued)	Principals	Advisers	Editors
How often do principals and advisers say they censor news stories? (Principals: N=91; Advisers: N=92)			
Frequently	1%	3%	-
Occasionally	44%	61%	-
Never	55%	36%	-
How often do principals say they influence the editor's editorial positions? (N=91)			
Frequently	1%	-	-
Occasionally	52%	-	-
Never	47%	-	-
How often do advisers say they edit copy? (N=92)			
Always	-	45%	-
Frequently	-	23%	-
Occasionally	-	30%	-
Never	-	2%	-
Why advisers and editors think the adviser approves copy in advance (Advisers: N=92; Editors: N=94)			
To correct grammar, spelling	-	86%	83%
To make copy more readable	-	74%	52%
To guard against libel	-	53%	35%
To guard against principal, faculty criticism	-	43%	33%
To guard against vulgar, obscene writing	-	43%	27%
To write headlines	-	16%	7%
The newspaper should criticize the principal and administration.			
Agree	8%	12%	26%
Disagree	92%	88%	74%
The newspaper should criticize the faculty.			
Agree	8%	13%	16%
Disagree	92%	87%	84%

Table 8.1 (continued)	Principals	Advisers	Editors
The newspaper should criticize students and student government.			
Agree	70%	82%	78%
Disagree	30%	18%	22%
(Principals: N=91; Advisers: N=92; Editors: N=94)			
In the past year, the newspaper has criticized which of the following?			
Principal	8%	4%	2%
Faculty	14%	8%	10%
Administrative policy	21%	27%	18%
Student government	59%	60%	53%
Educational policies	13%	22%	20%
School activities	70%	64%	64%
District school board	1%	1%	0%
(Principals: N=91; Advisers: N=92; Editors: N=94)			

While school officials thought they had the power to censor, they stated that they did not use the power very often. Horine found that students as well as principals and advisers thought of the newspaper as a public relations tool. All but one of the 277 principals, advisers, and editors responding thought that the newspaper ought to be a public relations tool of the school. Moreover, most respondents in each group thought that the school newspaper was doing a good job at its public relations mission.

Prior Review. As many later researchers would find as well, Horine found that nearly all advisers read copy before publication and that a majority of principals read it at least occasionally.

Censorship. All principals and advisers responding said that they had the power to censor the publication, but they stated that they did not use the power often.

Press Freedom. Despite their other responses, seven out of nine advisers stated that they gave the student newspaper "considerable freedom," and one in nine advisers stated they gave the newspaper "complete freedom."

Horine concluded from his study that advisers held "a tight rein" over student newspapers and that both advisers and principals supervised the newspaper closely. Horine noted:

> *In the eyes of the principal, adviser and editor, the high school newspaper has two primary functions: promotion and bulletin board. Thus, both the principal and adviser in this study closely supervised the paper....*
>
> *Yet most advisers, editors and principals were wholly satisfied with their newspapers' overall performances. They felt news coverage was good and that editorials were moderately strong.*[19]

Horine concluded with a question that some critics say is just as pertinent today:

> *An important question remains: Is the school newspaper too closely controlled, to the extent that it creates misconceptions of journalism after high school?*[20]

Atwood and MacLean (1967)

Like Horine, L. Erwin Atwood and Malcolm S. MacLean Jr.[21] investigated why researchers[22] had found that many staff members on Iowa school publications were not planning a career in journalism. They surveyed an unspecified number of students at the 1965 Iowa High School Journalism Workshop, and they sent surveys to the students' parents. They also surveyed an unspecified number of principals and advisers at Iowa high schools in April of that year. From the responses, they formed samples of 120 principals, advisers, and students, as well as 107 parents.

As Atwood and MacLean noted, the samples were not necessarily representative of all Iowa high school principals, advisers, student journalists, or parents of Journalism students. They thought the samples were large enough, nevertheless, to pinpoint the basic types of attitudes toward journalism among the four groups studied. The researchers used factor analysis of 48 opinion statements by respondents, which resulted in three distinct types of principals and parents and two types of advisers and students.

According to Atwood and MacLean, Type I (opponents) are generally negative toward high school journalism, high school publications, and journalism careers. Type II (public relations) are generally favorable to journalism and high school journalism training, but they have some reservations about high school publications and journalism as an academic subject. Type III (Proponents) were generally favorable toward all aspects of journalism. All three categories applied to principals and parents. Journalism students were either proponents or opponents. The correlation between advisers who were public relations types and those who were proponents was .99, making it impossible to differentiate between the two types.

Atwood and MacLean concluded that there was a tendency for opponent- and proponent-type principals to express a preference for the yearbook over the newspaper. Neither type of principal advocated strict control of publications content. Public Relations-type principals were generally favorable to both the newspaper and the yearbook, like proponents and opponents; however, they favored the newspaper over the yearbook.

In contrast to proponent and opponent principals, Atwood and MacLean noted that public relations-type principals saw the primary purpose of the high school newspaper as providing good public relations for the school and the community. They felt that there should be no criticism of school policy and no publication of anything that would reflect negatively on the schools or principal. They also thought that they themselves were best qualified to decide what should go into the publications.

The two researchers found that some principals saw a conflict between their practices and their preferences. For example, proponent-type principals thought that the student newspaper should be used primarily as an outlet for the student. At the same time, however, they saw the newspaper as a means for providing good public relations for the school. The researchers concluded that conflicts about the newspaper's role in the school could work against development of high school Journalism programs.

Max James (1970)

Max James conducted a study in Arizona in the fall of 1969 to determine, among other things, what type of censorship was being practiced in the state's schools.[23] James obtained responses from 89 Arizona high schools with student newspapers; however, he did not state whether only advisers responded to his survey. While he did not define his terms and discussion of his research methods does not allow a determination about the survey's scientific reliability or verifiability, his findings on types of censorship do not seem to differ much from what other researchers of the period were reporting.

James' found that four different means of censorship were being used in Arizona: (1) "understood" prohibitions developed through previous years; (2) specific prohibitions issued yearly by the administration; (3) reading of pre-published copy by an administrator; (4) cutting off or threatening to cut off funds for the publication.[24]

James' key findings are shown in Table 8.2. He stated that most of the schools reported either censorship activities or punishment for what was published, and most of the remaining schools showed a potential for censorship. He noted that advisers often were pressured by the principal to control content and were made responsible for any material found objectionable. One adviser responding to James' survey stated as follows:

> *I have been firmly told by the [administration] that although the students put out the paper, the adviser is responsible. I don't believe advisers should be blamed for mistakes made by students. Students themselves should learn what it is like to have to answer for their own errors. And isn't this what we teachers are supposed to be teaching?[25]*

Table 8.2: The Extent of Censorship and Potential for Censorship at Arizona High Schools from 1966 to 1969 (James, 1970)

What censorship problems have occurred? (N=89)

Post-publications problems have occurred	32%
Some censorship has occurred	29%
Certain topics could lead to problems	27%
No problems with censorship have occurred	11%
Only criticism by faculty has occurred	1%

The First Amendment Gets inside the Schoolhouse Gate

Many advisers in the 1960s felt a responsibility to ensure that the contents of student publications promoted a positive image of the school, often because they found themselves under considerable pressure from the principal to do so. Students' First Amendment rights were not a concern. While few educators questioned the assumption that school authorities had absolute control over the contents of their school's publications, many of them felt that considerable press freedom existed there.

Reports of this state of affairs in the late 1960s and early 1970s led researchers at the time to wonder whether freedom of high school press was being abridged, so they researched the subject. A 1968 report by the American Civil Liberties Union and another in 1970 by the American Bar Association expressed concern about the amount of censorship of high school newspapers that was taking place. A survey by the National Education Association found that 62 percent of high school newspaper advisers favored censorship of the high school press.[26]

The assumption that the First Amendment did not apply to students in a secondary school setting was dealt what seemed to be a devastating blow when the Supreme Court ruled in the 1969 case of *Tinker v. Des Moines Independent Community School District*.[27] While the case involved not the press rights of student journalists but the freedom of speech of any student, it had a far-reaching effect on the secondary school press.

The case began when three students—ages 13, 15, and 16—were suspended from school for wearing black armbands to protest the Vietnam War. In its ruling, the Supreme Court enunciated the students' right to participate in symbolic speech through protesting by stating that "it can hardly be argued that either students or teachers shed their constitutional rights to freedom of speech or expression at the schoolhouse gate."[28]

The Court also stated that schools should not be "enclaves of totalitarianism" and that school officials "do not possess absolute authority over their students." The Court did say, however, that the rights of students and adults were not coextensive. The point at which student rights end, the Court said, was when their actions "materially and substantially" interfere with the maintenance of discipline.

As a result of *Tinker*, the First Amendment rights of secondary school students were upheld in more than a dozen decisions by federal courts of appeals in the 1970s and 1980s. Courts allowed students freedom of the press for several broad content categories. According to two First Amendment scholars, those categories of speech included the following:

- features on premarital sex and the problems of teen-age sexuality, including such controversial topics as birth control and abortion

- articles about drug abuse, including advocacy of reform of drug laws

- criticism of school policies or personnel

- unsigned articles

- material that was "offensive to good taste" or which presented a "negative" image of the school

- stories on such "non-school related" topics as the draft or the war in Vietnam, civil rights, integration and racism[29]

Courts in the 1970s and 1980s upheld student press rights even when the newspaper was published as part of a class while under the supervision of a faculty member and paid for entirely with school funds. The main argument used by school officials, that they had the right to control the content of student publications because the publications were school-sponsored, was not supported by any court.[30] In virtually all cases in which students brought suits over prior restraint by school officials, courts found that schools had not provided adequate safeguards to protect the students' First Amendment rights. Because courts required that sufficient procedural safeguards be in place before disruption of school activities could be used as a reason for prior restraint, students lost few cases. The court usually found little potential for disruption at the school.

While few school policies for prior restraint were found to be entirely satisfactory, a few courts said that something similar to the safeguards required for censoring motion pictures would be required. Those safeguards mandate a timely hearing before censorship would be allowed.[31]

An analysis in 1980 by Robert Trager and Donna L. Dickerson determined that federal courts of appeals in the 1970s and 1980s were divided three ways on the issue of student press rights: those that held that prior restraint is acceptable if precise guidelines concerning the review procedures were in place; those that insisted on explicit guidelines stating what content would not be acceptable for distribution; and a single court which specifically rejected those two approaches and held that prior restraint is no more permissible in public high schools than in the community at large.[32]

The Seventh Circuit Court of Appeals followed the third route and overturned the expulsion of students who had distributed an underground newspaper.[33] Even though school officials had testified that they thought disruption would occur because of the newspaper, the justices determined that the threat of disruption could not be used as an excuse for prior restraint.

While rulings in the various federal circuits in the 1970s and early 1980s were not consistent, they gave students who wrote articles for school or off-campus publications, or who distributed underground newspapers, substantial protection against arbitrary actions by school officials. The court rulings made it clear, however, that students could be punished after publication for some types of content. In addition, some courts allowed prior restraint at a high school for articles thought to be libelous.

According to the Student Press Law Center, guidelines for prior review under *Tinker* had to meet the following requirements:

- Regulations had to offer criteria and specific examples as to what was considered disruptive, obscene or defamatory so that students would understand what expression was proscribed.

- Regulation also had to provide definitions of all key terms used, such as "disruption," "obscenity," "defamation," and "distribution."

- Guidelines had to have detailed criteria by which an administrator might reasonably predict the occurrence of "substantial disruption."

- Publication guidelines had to be included in the official school publications or circulated to students in the same manner as other official material.

- When publications guidelines allowed for prior review by school officials, they had to specify to whom the material was to be submitted for approval.

- Any system of prior review had to give students the right to a prompt hearing before the decision-maker to argue why disruption should be allowed.

- Procedural due process also required that publication guidelines limit the time which the official had in which to reach a decision on whether to prevent distribution.

- Any system of prior review had to include an expeditious procedure for appealing an administrator's decision to suppress student expression.[34]

By the mid-1980s, the student press was riding high on a series of supportive court decisions. A student press supporter wrote triumphantly:

> *The inescapable conclusion from the forum cases...is that school officials may not exercise the powers of a private publisher over student publications. They cannot tell students what they may and may not publish; they cannot withdraw funding; they cannot fire staff members at will.*[35]

Studies of Student Press Freedom after *Tinker*

Research conducted in the decade following the *Tinker* decision tended to find that fewer school officials thought that they had the complete power of censorship, contrary to the situation before the *Tinker* decision. Researchers also found that the decision had not led

200

to as much of an increase in student press freedom as might have been expected as a result of the *Tinker* ruling. A number of studies suggested that principals, advisers, and students were not aware of the extent to which student publications were protected by court rulings. Also, differences in the extent of student press freedom were found based upon the size and location of the school.

Laurence Campbell (1971)

Laurence Campbell conducted a study of publications advisers not long after the *Tinker* ruling. Because his article does not state when the study was conducted, which advisers were surveyed, or what the response rate was, there is no way to determine its validity. The responses, however, do give us some idea of the condition of secondary school press freedom shortly after the *Tinker* ruling. His findings are reported in Table 8.3.

Table 8.3: Percent of Advisers Agreeing with Statements Concerning Press Freedom Following the *Tinker* Decision (Laurence Campbell, 1971)

(Sample size not reported)

The adviser should invariably read all editorial copy.	75%
The school newspaper should be in a position to publish any news about the school that local newspapers publish.	73%
The editor should be appointed by the adviser.	69%
The adviser should invariably read all galley proofs.	68%
Nothing should be put in the newspaper to impair the school's image.	32%
Content the adviser doesn't like should be eliminated.	31%
The adviser should be a censor who decides what copy to accept or reject.	28%
Content the principal doesn't like should be eliminated.	21%
Nothing should be put in the newspaper that may hurt the school.	15%

Prior Review. Most advisers thought they should read all copy, and most thought the advisers always should read galley proofs.

Prior Restraint. A minority of advisers stated that they ought to determine what copy should and should not be published, and a minority stated that material the principal does not like should not go into the paper.

Content Prohibitions. Most advisers stated that the student newspaper should be able to publish any news about the school that the local newspaper could publish; however, a minority of the advisers stated that nothing should go into the newspaper that would hurt the school's image. A few advisers stated that nothing should go into the newspaper that could hurt the school. A small minority of advisers thought that the newspaper should avoid editorials and columns dealing with controversial topics.

The First Amendment. Few advisers disagreed with a statement that "Congress should make no law abridging the freedom of the press."

Most advisers surveyed by Campbell agreed that student journalists should be free to exercise their craft with no restraints beyond the limits of legal and ethical responsibility; are as free as other responsible citizens to probe every facet of the high school, community, state, nation and world; and should have advisers vested with the mandate of defending the student's right in the pursuit of journalistic truth.

Despite advisers' strong vocal support for student freedom, Campbell concluded as follows:

> *(T)he newspaper consists of what advisers approve or approve strongly, and it does not consist of what they disapprove or disapprove strongly.*
>
> *The same statement may be made with regard to the principal as one of the human variables in school newspaper publishing. Usually he speaks for the board of education, parents, teachers— the academic establishment.*
>
> *The same statement may not be made with regard to the staff. Its members work under an authoritarian or libertarian policy. Adults may or may not grant them freedom with which to develop responsibility.*[36]

Kennedy Commission (1974)

The most ambitious study of school press freedom was that sponsored by the Robert F. Kennedy Memorial in a book titled *Captive Voices*.[37] The Commission of Inquiry into High School Journalism undertook public hearings, consultative meetings, surveys, content analysis of high school newspapers, and review of published research papers and judicial decisions. Critics charged that, among other things, principals were not involved sufficiently in the study.

The commission surveyed students in 42 high schools in 30 states and conducted surveys of Journalism teachers and of faculty advisers. Of the 2,755 student questionnaires distributed, 1,630 usable surveys were returned. Coordinators were asked to distribute them at selected high schools in order to achieve "reasonable balance among student respondents in terms of sex, grades in school, and race."[38] The 786 journalism students and publications staff members in the sample were asked several additional questions.

As noted by the commission, the student survey did not meet the rigor required by professional polling organizations because schools were not selected randomly. Eighty-two percent of the schools had more than 1,000 students, more than two and one-half times more large schools than would be expected in the population. Also, 41 percent of the communities had a population of more than 150,000, a group almost four times larger than would have been expected by chance. Surveys also were sent to 700 members of the Journalism Education Association and 700 members of the National Council of Teachers of English. The teacher samples, thus, were biased to an unknown degree because members of two teacher organizations were surveyed.

Faculty advisers' responses are reported in Table 8.4. Students' responses to key questions are reported in tables 8.5 and 8.6. While responses would not be expected to be representative of students, advisers, and teachers as a whole, the studies do provide some valuable information about the groups surveyed. Much like previous studies, the Kennedy Commission's report concluded that censorship and self-censorship were not only rampant but also an inhibiting factor to good high school journalism. The apparent meaning of "censorship" used by the commission is prior restraint, though the commission sometimes used clearer terms, such as "overt censorship."

Table 8.4: Responses of Journalism Faculty Advisers to Questions Concerning First Amendment Issues (Kennedy Commission, 1974)

Who in school has final right of approval of articles
to be published in the paper? (N=388)

School administration	17%
Publications adviser	67%
Student editor	16%

Do you place any limitations on subject areas covered in the paper? (N=388)

Yes	37%
No	63%

Does school administration place any limitations on subject areas? (N=388)

Yes	30%
No	70%

Table 8.5: Comparison of Responses of Student Journalists and Student Readers with an Opinion to Questions Concerning the Student Newspaper/Publications (Kennedy Commission, 1974)

	Student Journalists	Student Readers
Is the school publication representative of student opinion? (Staff: N=723; Readers: N=701)		
Yes	67%	64%
No	33%	36%
Are issues or topics adequately covered by the school's publication? (Journalists: N=692; Readers: N=650)		
Yes	31%	26%
No	69%	74%

Table 8.5 (continued)	Student Journalists	Student Readers
Is the publication used to create a good impression outside of school? (Journalists: N=684; Readers: N=658)		
Yes	69%	65%
No	31%	35%
Does the publication accurately reflect everyday school life? (Journalists: N=723; Readers: N=734)		
Yes	53%	52%
No	47%	48%
Do you enjoy reading the publication? (Journalists: N=762; Readers: N=751)		
Yes, read with interest	66%	52%
No, indifferent/read with little interest	34%	48%

Table 8.6: Responses of Publications Staff Members to Questions Concerning First Amendment Issues (Kennedy Commission, 1974)
(N=312)

How is the editorial policy of the publication determined?

By students, with supervision of faculty adviser	58%
Solely by students	18%
By the faculty adviser	11%
Other	13%

Much like previous researchers had concluded, the commission determined that the amount of overt censorship depended mainly upon "the extent to which students attempt to deviate from the house organ concept of the paper."[39] It also concluded that censorship was the greatest factor in negatively affecting the "quality and relevance" of high school newspapers.[40] One adviser told the commission this:

> *Administrators look on the paper as an educational tool,*
> *depending on the administrator and how well he communicates*

with sponsors. Most items he desires are those that show the best side of the school, listing winners and spreading joy and sunshine. Administrators look on the paper as a house organ and rightfully so. Paper staff should do its darndest to uphold the administrators and present them in the best possible light. However, the staff also has the right to investigate administrative mistakes or injustices because staff is part of the administration. This right is just as long as the staff conducts its investigation in a mature reportive fashion. We are not censored. Period. I am the censor.[41]

The commission concluded that obscenity, libel, or potential disruption at the school, while the basis for most publication guidelines, seldom were the cause of censorship. The three issue areas that caused the most problems, according to the commission, were (1) controversial political issues, (2) criticism of school administrators, faculty policies, or the image of the school itself, and (3) lifestyles and social problems (such as birth control and drug abuse).

The commission's report commented individually on the three types of censorship it found: administrative censorship, faculty censorship, and student self-censorship.

Administrative Censorship. The Kennedy Commission concluded that "generally the strongest force for censorship comes from the top—principals with support of superintendents and boards of education." It added:

> *Not only does direct administrative censorship stifle the free expression of ideas in specific cases, but also it creates an atmosphere in which faculty and students alike know that to deal with controversial issues is to court official disapproval and perhaps disciplinary action. It breeds faculty censorship and self-censorship by students who otherwise would be more inclined toward participating in a free press.*
>
> *The result usually is an unquestioning attitude among students, an unhealthy acquiescence in pronouncements of school authorities no matter how unfair or oppressive they may be.*[42]

Adviser Censorship. Just as studies a decade earlier had found, the commission concluded that advisers were eager to work as censors whether or not written guidelines stated that censorship was allowed because "(i)n their eyes, the paper belongs to the administration, not to the students." It also stated as follows:

> *While a written policy is a clear warning to the faculty, neither a stated nor an implied policy of censorship is necessary in some cases for advisers to censor the papers. They do it because they believe it is their duty to the school.*[43]

Self-Censorship. The commission concluded that self-inflicted censorship by students was the most pervasive form of censorship found. It found that Journalism students were quick to learn what is acceptable content. The commission stated that a major reason for self-censorship was a lack of knowledge by students of press law and of their rights.

The commission reported the following about student self-censorship:

> *In the restrictive climate that prevails at most schools, students who dare to rebel at censorship policies know they face official punishment, a factor which the Supreme Court has called a "chilling effect" on the exercise of First Amendment rights and an unconstitutional restraint on the student press.*

> *Such a chilling effect discourages most students and results in the most pervasive form of censorship—that imposed by students on themselves. The result is apathy and passivity.*[44]

The Kennedy Commission reported 12 findings concerning censorship and the high school press. They are:

1. Censorship and the systematic lack of freedom to engage in open, responsible journalism characterize high school journalism. Unconstitutional and arbitrary restraints are so deeply embedded in high school journalism as to overshadow its achievements as well as its other problems.

2. Censorship of journalism is a matter of school policy—stated or implied—in all areas of the country, although in isolated schools students enjoy a relatively free press.

3. Censorship persists even where litigation or administrative action has destroyed the legal foundation of censorship; such

decisions are either ignored or interpreted in such a way as to continue the censorship policy.

4. Repressive policies are used against school-oriented media published off campus as well as within schools; many of the several hundred alternate or "underground" papers that have sprung up in recent years have been actively opposed by school officials.

5. Although substantive and investigative journalism and controversial or image-damaging information are most severely censored, policies of censorship apply regardless of whether the material is substantive or controversial.

6. Even advisers or journalism teachers who in private favor a free student press often succumb to bureaucratic and community pressures to censor school newspapers.

7. As part of the day-to-day operation of high school journalism, censorship generally is accepted by students, teachers, and administrators as a routine part of the school process. This has developed into the most pervasive kind of censorship, that imposed by students upon themselves.

8. Self-censorship, the result of years of unconstitutional administrative and faculty censorship, has created passivity among students and made them cynical about the guarantees of a free press under the First Amendment.

9. Fear of reprisals and unpleasantness, as well as the lack of a tradition of an independent high school press, remain the basic forces behind self-censorship.

10. Censorship is the fundamental cause of the triviality, innocuousness, and uniformity that characterize the high school press. It has created a high school press that in most places is no more than a house organ for the school administration.

11. Where a free, vigorous student press does exist, there is a healthy ferment of ideas and opinions, with no indication of disruption or negative side effects on the educational experience of the school.

12. The professional news media do not take seriously the First Amendment problems of high school journalism and do little to help protect the free press rights of students.

Not only school officials but also professional journalists came under attack by the Kennedy Commission. The commission blamed the news media for not doing more to protect student press rights. Key findings about professional journalists are reported in Table 8.7. The commission surveyed a random sample of 465 managing editors at daily newspapers. It found that only a minority of the editors surveyed favored full First Amendment rights for student journalists. About half supported First Amendment rights for student journalists under some situations. Approximately an equal number of newspaper editors thought student journalists in high schools in their community were allowed enough editorial freedom as were uncertain about the situation. A majority of the editors were not even aware of the *Tinker* decision. Also, more than a third of the editors stated that high school journalism was of little value.

Table 8.7: Responses of Managing Editors at Daily Newspapers to Questions Concerning First Amendment Issues (Kennedy Commission, 1974)

(N=180)

Are students in most schools in your area permitted to exercise First Amendment rights in the production of school publications?

Yes	26%
No	28%
Uncertain	46%

Do you consider that First Amendment rights should apply to high school students producing school publications?

Yes	35%
No	10%
Under certain conditions	52%
No opinion	3%

Are you aware of the recent court decision in favor of high school students in censorship cases, e.g., *Tinker v. Des Moines,* etc?

Yes	43%
No	57%

Louis Ingelhart, then chairman of the Secondary Education Division of the Association for Education in Journalism, criticized the report on several fronts. He charged that the recommendations were based on inadequate data from too few organizations involved in secondary school journalism, that survey percentages were not computed correctly, that the content analysis was weak and biased, and that the report indiscriminately mixed information about high school and college publications. He concluded that the report "produces greater confusion instead of clarifying legal matters for the high school level."[45]

Laurence Campbell (1976)

Laurence Campbell conducted a study soon after the Kennedy Commission's report was released. To some extent, his study was a response to that report. He studied 145 principals and 317 newspaper advisers who participated in critical and evaluation services by Quill and Scroll in 1974. Like the Kennedy Commission's samples, Campbell's samples were not randomly drawn, so we do not know how representative the results were of the opinions of all principals and advisers in the country.

Campbell, director of Quill and Scroll Studies at the time, criticized *Captive Voices* in his report. After noting the Kennedy Commission's first two findings, that "censorship and systematic lack of freedom...characterize high school journalism" and that "censorship of journalism is a matter of school policy...in all areas of the country," Campbell stated:

> *Obviously many friends of student journalism believe that censorship of the school press is much too common—as data before the 1970s revealed. Yet it is a flagrant affront to both publication advisers and understanding administrators to spread an exaggeration of this magnitude, that is, to assert that virtually all take an authoritarian role.*

As early as 1936 Quill and Scroll conducted a nationwide study of 613 publication advisers and 306 principals, but despite this precedent, the Captive Voices *did not invite principals in any significant number to express their viewpoints directly.*[46]

Campbell attempted to rectify that oversight in his study. He called the study "a modest inquiry," however, and noted that the data do not justify sweeping generalizations because of the nature of the sample. He suggested, though, that respondents probably were more supportive of student journalism than principals and advisers not represented because they were undertaking evaluation by a national organization for student journalism.

The research question for the study was this: "Who is responsible for the quality of high school newspapers—teenagers alone or principals and advisers as well?" His definition of quality was based upon the five-point evaluation form for judges in the Quill and Scroll's newspaper and newsmagazine evaluation. The first four items deal with adviser qualifications, course offerings, financial support, and facilities provided, which are not the focus of this chapter. The fifth item, respondents' attitude toward censorship, is pertinent, however. Though not stated, Campbell presumably defined censorship as prior restraint. Campbell excerpted portions of court rulings supporting press freedom and asked whether advisers and principals agreed with them. As Table 8.8 shows, in most cases only a moderate proportion of advisers and principals did agree.

Table 8.8: Percent of Principals and Advisers Agreeing with Court-Approved Concepts of Freedom of Speech and of the Press (Campbell, 1976)

(Principals: N=143; Newspaper advisers: N=317; Yearbook advisers: N=142)

"The risk taken if a few students abuse their First Amendment rights of free speech and free press is outweighed by the far greater risk run by suppressing free speech and press among the young. The remedy for today's alienation and disorder is not less but more free expression of ideas."

Newspaper advisers	51%
Yearbook advisers	51%
Principals	46%

Table 8.8 (continued)

"It would be incongruous and dangerous...to hold that students who wish to express their views on matters intimately related to them through traditionally non-disruptive modes of communication, may be precluded from doing so."

Newspaper advisers	61%
Principals	58%
Yearbook advisers	46%

"Students may not be confined to the expression of those sentiments which are officially approved."

Newspaper advisers	71%
Principals	67%
Yearbook advisers	58%

"In the absence of a specific showing of constitutionally valid reasons to regulate their speech, students are entitled to freedom of expression of their views."

Newspaper advisers	65%
Principals	60%
Yearbook advisers	54%

"The vigilant protection of constitutional freedom is nowhere more vital than in the community of American schools."

Yearbook advisers	60%
Newspaper advisers	58%
Principals	58%

"In our system, state-operated schools may not be enclaves of totalitarianism."

Principals	62%
Newspaper advisers	52%
Yearbook advisers	48%

As Table 8.9 shows, Campbell also found fairly strong support for limitations on the student press. For example, most principals and advisers thought that understood prohibitions were not a sign of censorship. Principals and advisers tended to think that their schools had press freedom; however, the way some questions were worded makes the responses difficult to analyze.

Table 8.9: Percent of Principals and Advisers Agreeing with Statements about Press Freedom at the School. (Campbell, 1976)

(Principals: N=143; Newspaper advisers: N=317; Yearbook advisers: N=142)

Censorship and lack of freedom to engage in open and responsible journalism may characterize some schools—but not ours.

Principals	68%
Newspaper advisers	59%
Yearbook advisers	49%

There is no censorship in our school though it is simply understood that some kinds of content will not be published in student publications.

Yearbook advisers	58%
Principals	57%
Newspaper advisers	49%

No student publication in our school has created a clear and present danger of the immediate and substantial physical disruption of our school.

Principals	83%
Newspaper advisers	68%

Students should be afforded experiences in exercising concepts in the freedom of the press.

Principals	81%
Yearbook advisers	63%
Newspaper advisers	62%

Teenagers—as well as teachers and other adults—are entitled to express spoken or written views without fear of retaliation.

Yearbook advisers	75%
Principals	72%
Newspaper advisers	71%

Students who participate as editors and staff members should be given the opportunity to gain educational and realistic experience in the concepts of the First Amendment to the Constitution, which asserts the freedom of speech and press.

Principals	81%
Newspaper advisers	64%

Despite his criticism of the Kennedy Commission's findings, Campbell concluded from his study that the First Amendment was not at all secure at the secondary schools in his sample and that "the situation in schools in which principals and advisers do not respond probably is less encouraging." He noted that the differences in attitudes of principals and newspaper advisers "were not as great as might have been predicted," however, and that they "are not on a collision course." He concluded, though, as follows:

> *To some extent, then, both principals and newspaper advisers repudiate the idea that "students should be afforded experiences in exercising concepts in the freedom of the press."*[47]

Despite his criticism of the Kennedy Commission's findings, Campbell's conclusion seemed as critical of principals and advisers as was the commission's. He commented:

> *It is probable that the First Amendment to the U.S. Constitution would not have been adopted today if it were left up to representatives of the participating principals and advisers, many of whom reflect the attitudes of summer soldiers and patriots.*[48]

James J. Nyka (1976)

The publication of *Captive Voices*, and the considerable criticism questioning the accuracy of the study that followed, prompted James J. Nyka to study press freedom in Illinois.[49] Nyka sent surveys to 171 Illinois principals and newspaper advisers. He asked questions concerning the rights of high school journalists, prior review of controversial material by school administrators, maturity of student journalists, distribution of controversial material, the need of school newspapers for guidance from administrators, and the role of the adviser. He received 123 responses, a 72 percent response rate. Table 8.10 reports Nyka's findings.

Nyka found that advisers were more likely than principals to believe that First Amendment rights should be the same for high school and professional journalists. In addition, more principals than advisers thought that special circumstances of public high schools require principals to restrict distribution of sensitive stories.

Table 8.10: Responses of Illinois Principals and Advisers with an Opinion to Questions about School Press Freedom (Nyka, 1976)

	Principals	Advisers
Do you believe that First Amendment rights to freedom of expression are the same under the law for high school and professional journalists? (Principals: N=65; Advisers: N=51)		
Yes	58%	62%
No	42%	38%
Do you believe that First Amendment rights to freedom of expression should be the same for high school and professional journalists? (Principals: N=65; Advisers: N=51)		
Yes	54%	78%
No	46%	22%
Do student journalists at your high school have as much freedom of expression as professional journalists have? (Principals: N=66; Advisers: N=52)		
Yes	50%	67%
No	50%	33%
Do you feel that the special circumstances of public high schools make it necessary for principals to restrict distribution of material which focuses on matters that may be sensitive in the community? (Principals: N=53; Advisers: N=48)		
Yes	62%	35%
No	38%	65%
Do you feel students in your high school are mature enough to publish a school newspaper without guidance from the administration? (Principals: N=60; Advisers: N=47)		
Yes	55%	81%
No	45%	19%

Nyka concluded from these and other findings, as well as from previous research by others, that high school students in Illinois and elsewhere in the country "enjoy only a limited amount of journalistic freedom" despite the *Tinker* ruling. He wrote:

> *Many newspaper advisers and administrators appear to be either unaware of students' constitutionally protected rights of free expression, or have simply chosen to ignore them, hoping that the legal pendulum will swing the other way and that the courts will whittle down to the size of impetuous children the "persons" created by Tinker and its successors.*

> *The results of the present survey seem to indicate that a considerable number of teachers and principals still consider all high school journalists to be nothing more than "impressionable adolescents," incapable of coping with controversial ideas that are at variance with those commonly accepted in the community....*

> *In order for students to benefit from their experiences as high school journalists, not only will many of those who run the schools have to reverse their notions of adolescents' capabilities and sense of responsibility, but they will also have to reexamine their idea about what the function of the school press really is.*[50]

Broussard and Blackmon (1978)

Studies by the American Civil Liberties Union in 1968, the American Bar Association in 1970, and the Kennedy Commission in 1974 found little support among educators for students' First Amendment rights. Those studies led E. Joseph Broussard and C. Robert Blackmon to investigate whether school officials and Journalism students knew much about students' constitutional rights as defined by federal courts following the *Tinker* decision.[51]

In their study, released in 1978, the researchers selected 10 cases involving student press rights. They asked the adviser, the student editor, and the principal of 126 randomly selected high schools in 31 states how they thought a judge would rule in each case. The cases involved the principal's power to censor the student newspaper or underground newspapers and to suspend students for writing articles or distributing the offending newspaper. Forty-two principals, 61 advisers, and 48 student editors responded. While the number of respondents was too small for a reliable national survey, the results are worth discussing.

Advisers gave correct answers to 48 percent of the cases, students to 38 percent, and principals to 33 percent. Using chi square as a test of statistical significance, however, Broussard and Blackmon found that student editors did significantly better in their analysis on three of 10 scenarios involving press freedom. Advisers and principals did not do significantly better than the other two groups in their analysis of any of the law cases. Editors were more likely correct concerning whether the principal could stop the distribution of an underground newspaper on campus, whether the principal could stop publication of a newspaper containing "four-letter words," and whether school officials could stop publication of a story in the school newspaper that stated that sexually active students at the school were not using contraceptives.

While principals as a group scored lower than did students and advisers, principals who had taken courses in Communications Law or Education Law scored even lower than principals who had not taken such courses. In addition, principals as a group gave divergent analyses of two cases that involved the same aspect of the law.

Principals scored high on their analysis of a case involving whether the principal could stop a story that attacked the way the police handled "a situation at the school." They scored extremely low on a case involving whether the principal could stop a story that unintentionally contained "incorrect information of a damaging nature to the superintendent of schools and School Board members for some of their public actions." The researchers concluded, however, that principals tended to respond according to what they thought they would do rather than what the law allowed them to do. The authors proposed that schools provide training in communications law for administrators, advisers, and students.

According to Broussard and Blackmon, the knowledgeable teacher or adviser could be described as follows:

- had a degree in education, usually a Bachelor of Science in Education
- pursued an undergraduate major or minor in Journalism

- had a master's degree in Journalism or had taken graduate courses in Journalism
- had studied Communications Law and Education Law
- taught only Journalism or Mass Communications courses, introductory and advanced
- was adviser to the school newspaper
- received supplemental pay as newspaper adviser
- had had experience as a professional journalist

Trager and Dickerson (1980)

Robert Trager and Donna Dickerson, like Broussard and Blackmon, found that students were better versed on their constitutional rights than were advisers and principals. The two researchers assumed that the amount of student press freedom would be greater in the Seventh Circuit than in other federal circuits because of the 1972 *Fujishima* case,[52] which gave the student press there the same rights as the non-school press.[53]

In the spring of 1976, Trager and Dickerson sent a questionnaire to each school in the circuit (composed of Illinois, Indiana, and Wisconsin). The surveys were sent randomly either to the principal, the adviser, or the student editor at 1,215 schools. Though not stated in the article, it appears that responses were obtained from 146 student editors (35 percent), 158 advisers (38 percent), and 170 principals (41 percent) for a total of 474 usable surveys. Table 8.11 reports on Trager and Dickerson's major findings.

Table 8.11: Percentage of Principals, Advisers, and Student Editors in the Seventh Circuit Agreeing to Statements about Student Press Freedom (Trager and Dickerson, 1980)

(Editors: N=146; Advisers: N=158; Principals: N=170)

Administrators have the power to review material prior to publication.

Principals	81%
Advisers and editors	67%
Respondents at small schools	86%
Respondents at medium-sized schools	76%

Respondents at large schools   60%

Advisers without journalism degrees   81%

Advisers with journalism degrees   41%

Advisers without professional journalism experience   74%

Advisers with professional journalism experience   53%

All printed material is reviewed by administrators before publication.

Principals, advisers, and editors overall   9%

All material in the school paper is reviewed by administrators before publication.

Principals, advisers, and editors overall   6%

Controversial material is reviewed by administrators.

Principals, advisers, and student editors overall   50%

Respondents at large schools   65%

Respondents at small schools   42%

Respondents at medium-sized schools   40%

High school and college students' rights are the same under the law.

Principals, advisers, and editors overall   58%

High school and college students' rights should be the same under the law.

Principals, advisers, and editors overall   61%

High school and college students have the same rights of freedom of expression in practice.

Principals, advisers, and editors overall   33%

High school students' and professional journalists' rights are the same under the law.

Principals, advisers, and editors overall   46%

High school students' and professional journalists' rights should be the same under the law.

Principals, advisers, and editors overall   54%

High school students and professional journalists have the same rights of freedom of expression in practice.

Principals, advisers, and editors overall   20%

First Amendment rights to freedom of expression should be the same for high school and professional journalists.

Student editors   68%

Advisers   60%

Principals   43%

Student Press Rights. The researchers found that nearly half of those responding to the survey stated that the rights of high school and professional journalists were the same under the law and slightly more than half said rights of the two should be the same; however, only a small minority responded that rights of student journalists at their schools actually were the same as those of professionals. Student journalists in the Seventh Circuit were significantly more likely than advisers, and advisers more likely than principals, to think, correctly, that First Amendment rights of students in the circuit were the same as rights of professional journalists.

Use of Prior Review. Most principals, advisers and student editors thought that the principal had the power of prior review, which the principal legally did not have. A statistical analysis of the data determined that significantly more principals than advisers and students thought that the principal had the right of prior review.

The authors found that the smaller the school and the smaller the community, the more likely respondents were to state that the principal had the authority to use prior review. Advisers without a Journalism degree were more likely than were advisers with the degree to think that principals had the power of prior review. Also, advisers without Journalism professional experience were significantly more likely than advisers with professional experience to think that the principal had the power of prior review.

Although most respondents thought that the principal had the power of prior review, few of them stated that the principal actually used that power. Half of the respondents, however, stated that the principal reviewed controversial material. Principals in large schools were significantly more likely to review controversial material than were principals in small schools. The researchers also found that the likelihood of school officials to review controversial material differed from state to state in the circuit.

Changes in Prior Review. Trager and Dickerson found that the amount of prior review of newspaper content had not changed since the *Fujishima* ruling. Contrary to what some proponents of prior restraint had expected would happen, the number of underground newspapers had not increased since the ruling either. Few principals and advisers who responded knew of the case by name, and the researchers concluded that most principals and advisers were not aware of the ruling. The authors found differences in responses based upon size of school, size of community, and the amount of the advisers' advising and professional experience.

Trager and Dickerson concluded from their study:

> *The finding of a lack of consistency in freedoms believed in and granted within one circuit shows that the state of First Amendment protection granted high school students remains based on the whim of those in charge, not the law.*[54]

Nicholas Kristof (1983)

The most reliable national study of editors in the *Tinker* era was conducted by a Harvard University student for his senior thesis.[55] Nicholas D. Kristof wanted to determine how much freedom editors had and what school and community characteristics were most closely related to censorship. He defined censorship as "any official interference by intimidation or coercion with student control of the newspaper";[56] however, he did not define the term on his questionnaire and it might be expected that students considered it to mean prior restraint.

Kristof sent questionnaires to editors at 500 public schools in October 1980. Of that total, 358 surveys were returned. Kristof phoned another 27 schools for a total of 385 responses, a response rate of 77 percent. Of the questionnaires returned, 278 were completed by student editors and were analyzed. The rest were completed by advisers or were from schools without a student newspaper. His findings are reported in Table 8.12.

Table 8.12: Student Editors' Responses to Questions about Censorship and Self-Censorship (Kristof, 1983)

(N=278)

Has there been any censorship of a student publication at the school in the previous three years?

No censorship	48%
One or two incidents	33%
Three to 10 incidents	13%
Repeated and continual censorship	6%

Has the school newspaper been censored in the previous three years?

Yes	43%
No	57%

Does the newspaper adviser or school administration discourage the newspaper from probing into controversial areas?

Yes	33%
No	67%

How restricted is the newspaper in covering sensitive subjects?

Completely unrestricted	18%
Somewhat restricted	77%
Very restricted	5%

Does the administration at the school think the editor has any legal rights of freedom of the press?

Yes	64%
No	7%
Not sure	29%

Is the editor familiar with the legal rights of high school journalists?

Very familiar	15%
Somewhat familiar	63%
Not familiar	22%

How do editors describe the newspaper?

Not controversial	29%
Sometimes controversial	68%
Often controversial	3%

If the paper is not often controversial, why is the newspaper not more controversial?

I don't think a school newspaper should spend much time criticizing the school or people who work in it.	24%
We're not allowed to be more controversial.	14%
Other	62%

What rights do editors think they should have?

The same rights as adult newspaper reporters and editors	54%
Some rights, but under supervision of the school administration	43%
The administration should have final authority over the newspaper.	2%

If a conflict arose at the school between the administration and the newspaper staff, whose side would the adviser take?

Administration's	11%
Students'	45%
Would not take sides	15%
Don't know	29%

Who has the final right of approval of articles and advertisements in the school's newspaper?

Adviser	62%
Students	14%
Administration	18%
Don't know	6%

Who assigns articles for the newspaper?

Editor alone	47%
Editor and adviser	37%
Adviser alone	10%
Other	6%

Does the adviser as well as the student editor edit articles?

Yes	78%
No	22%

How is the newspaper editor selected?

Appointed by newspaper adviser	57%
Elected by newspaper staff	16%
Chosen by outgoing editor	8%
Other	20%

Publications Policy. Only about one in seven schools had a written publications policy.

Prior Restraint. Just under half of the student editors reported no censorship in the past three years, and one-third reported only one or two incidents. The editor in few schools report repeated or continual censorship. Of those students reporting censorship, most noted that the censorship involved the student newspaper.

Only a small minority of editors stated that they had the final right of approval of newspaper content, and only a minority of the student editors stated that they were completely unrestricted and could not imagine any censorship taking place. Very few editors, however, reported being very restricted.

Controversial Content. Most editors stated that their newspaper was sometimes controversial, containing some news or editorials critical of school staff.

Intimidation. A minority of the student editors reported that school officials discouraged their newspapers from probing into controversial areas. In few schools did student editors report that they were completely unrestricted in covering sensitive subjects.

Self-Censorship. One-fourth of the student editors who stated that their newspapers were not often controversial stated that a school newspaper should not spend much time criticizing the school or the staff. Only about one editor in seven said that the newspaper was not more controversial because the staff was not allowed to be.

Student Press Rights. Most of the student editors stated that they were somewhat or very familiar with the rights of student journalists. Slightly over half of the editors stated that student journalists should have the same rights as adult journalists.

Adviser Support. Of student editors with an opinion, most thought that the adviser would take the students' side if a conflict arose between the newspaper staff and the administration.

Variables Related to Censorship. Like Trager and Dickerson three years earlier, Kristof determined that the smaller the school, the more likely censorship was to have taken place. Censorship also tended to increase as the size of the community decreased. In addition, Kristof found less censorship in the West and about the same amount in the Central region, the East, and the South.

Kristof concluded that editors were discouraged from aggressive reporting by "implicit or explicit threats or discipline that results in stifling self-censorship by the students themselves." Kristof concluded that student editors were "deferential and submissive" and that "a lack of conflict over censorship in a school is as likely to indicate a deferential and submissive editor as it is a tolerant principal."[57]

Like Trager and Dickerson, Kristof suggested that the amount of censorship had decreased little since the *Tinker* decision. He also estimated that only 7 percent of the schools indicated no potential for censorship. He isolated three factors that explain the "vapid flavor" of many high school newspapers:

> *First, many schools experience censorship at its most blatant form, where the adviser or principal prohibits publication of specific articles or editorials. Second, the principal or adviser may, without actually forbidding publication of specific articles, cultivate a climate of intimidation in which the cruder form of censorship is unnecessary. Third, many editors in traditional communities possess a stultifying deference that keeps them away from anything that might offend or shock a reader.*[58]

John Bowen (1985)

John Bowen attempted to see how much change had taken place since the release of *Captive Voices*.[59] He was able to undertake a longitudinal study by replicating research he did 10 years previously for a master's thesis. In his first study, Bowen sent surveys to 175 schools. In his 1985 study, he sent surveys to principals, advisers, and editors at 100 schools. It is not clear from the article how the sample was selected and whether it was random. Also, for a national study, the sample size and number of returns are rather small for reliability. Only 17 editors, 23 advisers, and 13 principals returned the questionnaires.

Though we cannot be sure that the findings are reliable, Bowen's conclusions are worthy of mention. Bowen reported three conclusions from his two studies:

- Many student editors were less willing to tackle potentially sensitive topics, and they were more conservative than they had been 10 years earlier.

- Administrators gave lip service to students' First Amendment rights until there was a conflict, and then they pulled back.

- Advisers continued to give strong support to students' First Amendment rights. In fact, the advisers appeared to be more liberal than their students.

Bowen wrote:

There appears to have been some improvement in the position of student editors, but that movement may well have been, for many, in just the opposite direction the investigators of Captive Voices *would have liked to have seen.*

While there has been recognition of student First Amendment rights and responsibilities in the 10 years since publication of Captive Voices, *substantive change may still be too evasive and fleeting. The changes resemble apathetic, passive and self-censoring students that led to* Captive Voices *originally.*

For advisers who believe in the essential concept of a free and vigorous press, the fight may now be swinging to the position of convincing student editors to practice responsible student press freedom.[60]

Click and Kopenhaver (1988)

A study that, in conjunction with Kristof's study, gives us a picture of attitudes toward secondary school press freedom in the early 1980s was conducted by J. William Click and Lillian Lodge Kopenhaver.[61] The two researchers conducted a national survey of principals and advisers at 492 public and private high schools over a 12-month period from October 1984 to September 1985. Responses were obtained from 191 advisers and 144 principals.

Click and Kopenhaver found that advisers were more protective of student rights than were principals. In reporting their data, the two researchers did not differentiate between public and nonpublic schools. Nonpublic schools do not have First Amendment restraints, however. As we reported in Chapter 5, public school teachers appear more supportive of press freedoms than do private and parochial school teachers.

In their discussion, Click and Kopenhaver reported opinions that were strongly held and omitted neutral and slightly agree/slightly disagree responses.[62] Table 8.13 reports their main findings.

Table 8.13: Percentages of Principals and Advisers Who Agreed or Agreed Strongly to Statements about Student Press Freedom (Click and Kopenhaver, 1988)

(Principals: N=191; Advisers: N=144)

	Principals	Advisers
Articles critical of the school board should never be published.	20%	10%
Articles critical of local politicians should never be published.	21%	14%
Articles critical of teachers and administrators should never be published.	30%	22%
Guarantees of freedom of expression in the student newspaper outweigh public relations considerations.	19%	37%
A student newspaper is more a learning tool than a vehicle for expression of student opinion.	59%	40%
Student newspaper adviser should review all copy before it is printed.	97%	89%
Having school administrators read student copy is a form of censorship.	56%	70%
Advisers should correct factual inaccuracies in copy even if students cannot be told in advance of publication.	66%	71%
An adviser who knows that the newspaper will publish something that will put the school in a bad light should see that it isn't published.	36%	18%
Newspaper advisers who do not read student copy before publication should be held personally responsible for complaints about the newspaper.	68%	66%
It is more important for the school to have a good image than an uncensored newspaper.	49%	45%
The adviser is obligated to inform the administration of any controversial stories before the newspaper goes to press.	75%	41%
If the student newspaper takes one side of a controversial issue, it should be required to publish the other side.	70%	63%

Student Control. Most principals and advisers thought that a free press is fundamental to American society. Whereas most principals did not think students should be allowed to exercise that freedom, a minority of advisers held that position. Most principals disagreed with the statement that students should have full control of all editorial content of the newspaper after they have been trained in press responsibility. Most advisers agreed that students should have full control, however.

Prior Review. The authors found that most principals and advisers thought that prior review by administrators was a form of censorship. Nearly all principals and advisers stated that advisers should read all copy.

Prior Restraint. Principals were much more likely to want to use prior restraint on constitutionally protected but distasteful speech. Most principals but only a minority of the advisers agreed that administrators should be able to stop publication of articles they thought were harmful, even though not libelous, obscene, or likely to cause disruption.

Responsibility. Most principals and advisers thought that the student newspaper should be required to publish both sides of controversial issues.

Prior Notification. Most principals but only a minority of advisers agreed that the adviser should inform the administration of controversial stories before the newspaper goes to press.

Public Relations. About half the principals and nearly half of the advisers in Click and Kopenhaver's study thought the school's good image was more important than an uncensored school newspaper. Only a minority of principals and advisers stated that the adviser has a professional obligation to see that an article that would put the school in a bad light not be published. About half of the principals and a minority of the advisers stated that the student paper should not be allowed to print stories that would hurt the school's reputation, even if the story is true.

Discipline vs. Freedom. Principals were more likely than advisers to think that the maintenance of discipline was more important than having press freedom. Nearly half of the principals but few of the advisers thought that it was more important for the school to function smoothly than for the student newspaper to be uncensored. Most principals but only a minority of advisers agreed that maintaining discipline in the school was more important than a free press.

Personal Attacks. Only a minority of principals and advisers stated that stories critical of the school board or local politicians and stories critical of teachers or administrators should not be published.

Correcting Copy. Most principals and advisers thought the adviser should correct misspellings and factual errors in stories.

Adviser Liability. The two groups also were in agreement about the adviser's liability in case a problem arose. Click and Kopenhaver found that most principals and advisers stated that a newspaper adviser who had not read copy before publication should be held personally responsible if complaints should arise over an article.

Click and Kopenhaver concluded that the opinions of the principals and advisers reported in the study "do not suggest a fostering of a free student press in American high schools."[63]

Like Campbell in his study of principals and advisers, the authors concluded that the amount of disagreement in many instances was not as large as they had expected.

The two researchers noted three findings that strongly suggested to them that U.S. high schools were not promoting freedom of the press: that nearly all principals and advisers thought the adviser should review copy before publication; that most principals and a good-sized minority of advisers stated that administrators should stop publication of articles that they thought were harmful though not libelous, obscene or disruptive; and that a quarter of principals responded that they did not think it was censorship for administrators to read copy before publication.

Click and Kopenhaver commented:

> *One would assume that principals are likely to be concerned about the image of their schools and that their views may tend to be more restrictive of press freedom. One would also assume that advisers should understand the principles of press freedom and*

ethics (and) would tend to differ significantly from principals in defending and ensuring student press freedom. However, the degree of disagreement between the two is not very strong in many instances.[64]

Click and Kopenhaver concluded the following:

Even though most advisers and principals agree that a free press is fundamental to American society, both groups' reactions to student press freedom belie this contention.[65]

Summary and Conclusions

At the beginning of this chapter, we asked two questions:

(1) Did principals and advisers in the *Tinker* era follow the letter of the law in regard to the Supreme Court's *Tinker* ruling and subsequent lower court rulings? (2) Did they follow the spirit of those rulings? We can conclude that a number of principals and advisers did not do well at upholding either aspect; however, they were the minority. Advisers did a much better job upholding the letter and the spirit of the law than did the principals.

Not only pre-*Tinker* but also post-*Tinker* studies indicated that a number of principals and advisers continued to see the school newspaper as a public relations instrument as well as a school bulletin board. In addition, large numbers of both groups thought that the adviser had the duty to try to persuade students to withhold some types of content. Some principals and advisers also thought they had the duty to use prior restraint on potentially objectionable material.

Post-*Tinker* studies also suggested that many principals and a number of advisers either did not realize that courts had granted students considerable First Amendment rights or they chose to ignore that fact. Researchers, in essence, noted that if principals and advisers did not want objectionable contents to go into the newspaper, those contents did not go into it. Most often, however, principals and advisers used self-restraint instead of prior restraint.

In addition, studies showed that some students before and after *Tinker* often did not question authority, and a number of them also seemed to agree with school officials' public relations goals for the newspaper. Studies also showed that overt censorship often was not necessary because students resorted to self-censorship—either because of intimidation, because of deference, because they did not find anything controversial to write about, or because they themselves believed that the newspaper should not be controversial. Whatever student journalists' reasons may have been not to cover controversial topics, researchers concluded that the content of the newspapers was bland.

The results of these studies, however, are open to differing analyses depending upon one's definitions of censorship and self-censorship and the level of press freedom expected or thought to be desirable. If censorship is defined as "any official interference with student control of the newspaper," then it apparently is censorship for an adviser to read the newspaper before publication or for an adviser to correct misspellings and factual errors. That definition of censorship could also cover not only intimidation but also any suggestions for story content that an adviser might make. Under a strict definition of censorship, very few school newspapers were free from censorship. If censorship is defined as the actual deletion of passages or entire articles because of controversial content, the amount of censorship in the *Tinker* era was fairly limited.

The amount of self-censorship used also is problematic. What some school officials and some student journalists would see as responsible journalism also could be called self-censorship. If the definition of self-censorship includes refraining from publishing stories without being threatened or being told by the adviser to withhold a story, then student journalists during the *Tinker* era might be seen as apathetic and passive. If other reasons for self-restraint besides intimidation (such as deference or responsible journalism) are not seen as self-censorship, then the amount of self-censorship found was somewhat limited.

We also set out in this chapter to determine whether the *Tinker* era was one in which advisers "taught responsibility and ethics but ... gave students opportunities to get into hot water if they wished," or whether the student press's rights were "routinely denied, with little or no protest by the students." Our conclusion is that the truth is somewhere between those two extremes.

The *Tinker* era certainly was a period of increased emphasis on freedom and responsibility for students in some schools. Several researchers found such factors as school size, community size and location, and adviser characteristics had a lot to do with how much freedom of the press was practiced at a school. Student characteristics also were found to be important.

Based upon the degree of press freedom allowed by federal courts, the amount of prior restraint, intimidation, and self-censorship found during the *Tinker* era was excessive. Based upon strict libertarian standards, any prior restraint, intimidation, or self-censorship would be objectionable. Most advisers during the *Tinker* era were supportive of press freedom, and Journalism students thought their advisers would side with them rather than with their principals, if problems arose. Moreover, no prior restraint was found at a majority of schools, and only sporadic instances of prior restraint were reported elsewhere.

The press system in operation during the *Tinker* era more closely resembled a system based upon the social responsibility theory than one based upon libertarian or totalitarian concepts. Paraphrasing Laurence Campbell, it is an exaggeration to assert that virtually all principals and advisers took an authoritarian role. One's conclusion about student press freedom in the *Tinker* era will depend greatly upon how much press freedom one thinks ought to exist. The question of whether any restriction upon the free exercise of student expression should be tolerated is open to debate.

Courts throughout the 1970s and into the 1980s continued to provide considerable support for students who charged that their schools' restrictions upon press freedom were excessive. Because of differing rulings by the various courts of appeal, proponents of full First Amendment rights for students looked to the Supreme Court to abolish prior restraint, if not intimidation. What happened when the Court finally did take up the matter of freedom of the secondary school press was not what First Amendment supporters had expected, however. That is a matter we will take up in the next chapter.

NOTES ON CHAPTER 8

1. Robert P. Knight, "The Post-Hazelwood High School Press," *Journalism Educator 43* (Summer 1988): 42-43.

2. Student Press Law Center, *Law of the Student Press* (Washington, DC: Student Press Law Center, 1984): 54-55.

3. Quoted by Bruce D. Itule and Douglas Anderson, *News Writing and Reporting for Today's Media* (New York: McGraw-Hill, 1991): 636.

4. Jack Nelson, *Captive Voices: The Report of the Commission of Inquiry into High School Journalism* (New York: Schocken Books, 1974): 24.

5. *Ibid.*: 29.

6. Don D. Horine, "How Principals, Advisers and Editors View the High School Newspaper," *Journalism Quarterly*, 43 (1966): 339.

7. Nelson, *Captive Voices*: 29.

8. *Ibid.*: 24-25.

9. Fred S. Siebert, Theodore Peterson, and Wilbur Schramm, *Four Theories of the Press* (Urbana, IL: University of Illinois Press, 1963.)

10. *Gitlow v. New York*, 268 U.S. 652 (1925).

11. *Near v. Minnesota*, 383 U.S. 697 (1931).

12. *Smith v. Daily Mail Publishing Co.*, 99 S.Ct. 2667 (1979).

13. *Central Hudson Gas and Electric Corp. v. Public Service Commission*, 100 S.Ct. 2343 (1980).

14. Student Press Law Center, *Law of the Student Press:* 31.

15. *Ibid.*: 15.

16. *Southeastern Promotions, Ltd. v. Conrad*, 420 U.S. 546, 95 S.Ct. 1239 (1975).

17. Horine, "How Principals, Advisers and Editors View the High School Newspaper": 339-345.

18. Penn T. Kimball and Samuel Lubell, "High School Students' Attitudes Toward Journalism as a Career: II," *Journalism Quarterly 37* (Summer 1960): 413-422.

19. Horine, "How Principals, Advisers and Editors View the High School Newspaper": 344-345.

20. *Ibid.:* 345.

21. E. Erwin Atwood and Malcolm S. MacLean Jr., "How Principals, Advisers, Parents and Pupils View Journalism," *Journalism Quarterly 44* (Spring 1967): 71-78.

22. Unpublished studies by Dr. Richard W. Budd, director of the Mass Communication Research Bureau of the Iowa School of Journalism, cited in Atwood and MacLean, *ibid.*

23. Max H. James, "Propaganda or Education? Censorship and School Journalism," *Arizona English Bulletin, 13*:1 (October 1970): 37-41.

24. *Ibid.:* 38.

25. *Ibid.:* 39.

26. Nelson, *Captive Voices:* 29.

27. *Tinker v. Des Moines Independent Community School District,* 393 U.S. 503 (1969).

28. *Ibid.,* at 506.

29. J. Marc Abrams and S. Mark Goodman, "End of an Era?: The Decline of Student Press Rights in the Wake of the Kuhlmeier Decision" (paper presented at the convention of the Association for Education in Journalism and Mass Communication, Portland, OR, July 1988), 6-7.

30. Student Press Law Center, *Law of the Student Press:* 14.

31. *Freedman v. Maryland,* 380 U.S. 51 (1965).

32. Robert Trager and Donna L. Dickerson, "Prior Restraint in High School: Law, Attitudes and Practice," *Journalism Quarterly 57* (Spring 1980): 135.

33. *Fujishima v. Board of Education,* 460 F. 2d 1355 (7th Cir., 1972).

34. Student Press Law Center, *Law of the Student Press:* 55.

35. *Ibid.:* 20.

36. Laurence R. Campbell, "The Role of the High School Newspaper," *Quill and Scroll,* February-March 1971.

37. Nelson, *Captive Voices.*

38. *Ibid.:* 171.

39. *Ibid.:* 43.

40. *Ibid.*: 44.

41. *Ibid.*: 29.

42. *Ibid.*: 24-25.

43. *Ibid.*: 29.

44. *Ibid.*: 37.

45. Louis E. Ingelhart, "A Look at Captive Voices," *NASSP Bulletin.* 59 (February 1975): 12.

46. Laurence R. Campbell, unpublished paper, "Principals' Attitudes Toward Student Journalism and Freedom of the Press." Quill and Scroll Society, 1976: 8.

47. *Ibid.*: 21.

48. *Ibid.*: 25.

49. James J. Nyka, unpublished paper, "Censorship of Illinois High School Newspapers," 1976.

50. *Ibid.*: 39.

51. E. Joseph Broussard and C. Robert Blackmon, "Advisers, Editors and Principals Judge First Amendment Cases," *Journalism Quarterly 55* (Winter 1978): 797-799.

52. *Fujishima v. Board of Education.*

53. Robert Trager and Donna L. Dickerson, "Prior Restraint in High School: Law, Attitudes and Practice": 135-138.

54. *Ibid.*: 138.

55. Nicholas D. Kristof, *Freedom of the High School Press* (Lanham, MD: University Press of America, 1983).

56. *Ibid.*: 2.

57. *Ibid.*: 4.

58. *Ibid.*: 32.

59. John Bowen, "*Captive Voices:* What Progress, Change Has Occurred in 10 Years?" *Quill & Scroll* (February-March 1985): 14-15.

60. *Ibid.*: 16.

61. J. William Click and Lillian L. Kopenhaver, "Principals Favor Discipline over Free Press," *Journalism Educator 43* (Summer 1988): 48-51.

62. Click and Kopenhaver provided seven possible responses on their questionnaire, but they reported only the "agree," "strongly agree," "disagree," and "strongly disagree" responses in their article, omitting "slightly agree" and "slightly disagree" responses as well as "neutral" responses.

63. *Ibid.:* 51.

64. *Ibid.*

65. *Ibid.*

CHAPTER 9

HAZELWOOD: THE SUPREME COURT SETS UP A DETOUR

Chapter Highlights

- The Supreme Court stated in *Hazelwood v. Kuhlmeier* that the principal can regulate the contents of a school-sponsored newspaper "in any reasonable manner" if the newspaper is not a forum for public expression.

- While many professional journalists thought the Court's ruling was sound, most journalism education experts disagreed with the ruling.

- While a number of observers assumed it would result in more censorship, researchers conducting surveys in the months after the ruling concluded that few advisers anticipated changes in their publications because of the ruling.

- A longitudinal study of principals and advisers in one state found no significant increase in censorship of school newspapers a year after the decision and no apparent change in newspaper content.

- A national study two years after the ruling found that most advisers noticed no change in censorship or content since the ruling.

For more than 15 years after the *Tinker* decision, the Supreme Court declined its opportunities to clarify the confusion between various federal circuits, ordinarily by declaring cases brought by students to be moot because the student involved had graduated. When the Court finally ruled directly on the First Amendment protection given the public school press, it was not faced with a divided nation and anti-war demonstrations on college and high school campuses as it had been when *Tinker* was decided. Instead, the country was united under a popular conservative president, and the Supreme Court was decidedly more conservative than the one that had decided the *Tinker* case.

That the Court would be taking a more conservative direction when it ruled on student press rights was evident in a case that had been decided in 1986, *Bethel School District v. Fraser*.[1] The case involved a student who had been disciplined because of a speech he gave in support of a candidate running for a student body office. While not using obscenities, Fraser included a number of sexual innuendos in his speech. In his opinion for the Court, Chief Justice Warren Burger concluded that the case was different from *Tinker*, in which students were engaged in political protest. Burger wrote that "simply because the use of an offensive form of expression may not be prohibited to adults making what the speaker considers a political point, [does not mean] that the same latitude must be permitted to children in a public school." He wrote:

> *The undoubted freedom to advocate unpopular and contro-versial views in schools and classrooms must be balanced against the society's countervailing interest in teaching the students the boundaries of socially appropriate behavior. Even the most heated political discourse in a democratic society requires consideration for the personal sensibilities of the other participants and audiences.*[2]

When the Supreme Court finally ruled in a case concerning the student press, it took *Fraser* for its model instead of *Tinker*. In its decision released on January 13, 1988, the Court differentiated the case from the *Tinker* decision because that case involved student speech that merely occurred on school property and was not school-sponsored.

The case resulted from action during the 1982-83 school year by the principal at Hazelwood East High School in suburban St.

Louis, Missouri, to stop the school newspaper from publishing articles that he said invaded the privacy of students and parents. The newspaper was written and edited by a Journalism class and, thus, was part of the school curriculum.

When the adviser submitted page proofs to the principal, he objected to a story about teen pregnancy because he thought that students would know the pregnant girls even though their names were not mentioned in the story. He also thought that references to sexual activity and birth control were not appropriate for younger students at the school. He objected to an article about divorce because the page proof identified a student who complained about her father's conduct; however, the adviser had deleted the name from the final version. The principal thought that the parents should be invited either to respond to the remarks or to consent to their publication. Deciding that there was no time to make changes before the end of the school year, he ordered the two pages containing the articles to be withheld from publication.

The federal district court ruled that the editor's First Amendment rights had not been violated, but the decision was overturned on appeal. The U.S. Supreme Court, however, ruled that the principal had acted reasonably and that his action was not unconstitutional because "First Amendment rights of students in the public schools are not automatically coextensive with the rights of adults in other settings" and that "a school need not tolerate student speech that is inconsistent with its basic educational mission, even though the government could not censor similar speech outside the school."

The determining factor in the Hazelwood case was that the school's newspaper was not seen as an open forum for student expression. Because the newspaper was not a forum for public expression, the Court stated, the principal could regulate the contents of the school-sponsored newspaper "in any reasonable manner." It gave the following definition of a public forum:

> (S)chool facilities may be deemed to be public forums only if school authorities have "by policy or by practice" opened the facilities "for indiscriminate use by the general public," or by some segment of the public, such as student organizations.[3]

The Court's definition differed from the one usually used by lower courts, which stated that a forum for student expression existed when a publication printed such things as student editorials and student letters as well as student-written stories and when the publication is distributed to students outside the Journalism class.[4] Under the Supreme Court's definition, schools presumably would have to allow "indiscriminate" use by the general public or by school organizations.

The Supreme Court in the Hazelwood case, however, said that the Hazelwood East's *Spectrum* newspaper was not a public forum because the adviser was the "final authority with respect to almost every aspect of the production and publication of *Spectrum*, including its content." In addition, each issue was reviewed by the principal prior to its publication.

The Court noted that the written policy of the school board was that the school newspaper "accepts all rights implied by the First Amendment" and that "school sponsored publications will not restrict free expression or diverse viewpoints within the rules of responsible journalism." It concluded, however, that the board did not intend to make *Spectrum* a public forum because the policy also noted that school publications were "developed within the adopted curriculum and its educational implications." The Court said that school officials had not indicated an intent "to open the paper's pages to indiscriminate use by its student reporters and editors, or by the student body generally."

Justice White stated that it did not matter whether school publications that are not public forums according to the Court's definition are part of a class or an extracurricular project "so long as they are supervised by faculty members and designed to impart particular knowledge or skills to student participants and audiences." The ruling meant that the *Tinker* standard applied only between the school-yard gate and the school's front door. White's opinion made the totalitarian theory the appropriate model not only for student newspapers but also for all other speech during school-sponsored activities. Echoing Fraser, White wrote:

> *(E)ducators do not offend the First Amendment by exercising editorial control over the style and content of student speech in school-sponsored expressive activities so long as their actions are reasonably related to legitimate pedagogical concerns.*[5]

Justice Brennan, writing in dissent, disagreed with the distinction made between school-sponsored publications and student speech taking place in other school settings, and he charged that *Tinker* had been abandoned. He challenged the three "excuses" upon which the majority based its decision: "the public educator's prerogative to control curriculum; the pedagogical interest in shielding the high school audience from objectionable viewpoints and sensitive topics; and the school's need to disassociate itself from student expression." He noted that the *Tinker* case addressed the first concern, that the second concern was not a legitimate one, and that the third could easily be achieved by other means, such as by the publication of a disclaimer. Even Brennan, however, rejected a libertarian theory for the secondary school press and espoused a social responsibility theory instead. Brennan concluded that poor grammar, bad writing, or faulty research could be targets of prior restraint because they would detract from the purpose of the Journalism curriculum.

Journalists' Reaction to the *Hazelwood* Ruling

The chairman of the Freedom of Information Committee of the Society of Professional Journalists, Paul McMasters, said the ruling "cuts the First Amendment legs off the student press."[6] The executive director of The Dow Jones Newspaper Fund also was critical of the ruling. As might have been expected because of the Kennedy Commission's findings more than a decade earlier, professional journalists' support for the school press was limited, however. Dorothy Bowles found that newspaper organizations were split on the issue and that most newspaper editorials applauded the ruling.[7] She found that a few newspapers opposed the ruling. The St. Louis *Post-Dispatch*, for example, criticized the opinion for giving the school board too much latitude, and the headline of the Miami *Herald* editorial was "High Court Flunks."

Whereas articles by Richard Schmidt and Frank Wiggins[8] and by Fern Valentine[9] questioned the lesson being taught by the Court in its ruling, the publication of the American Society of Newspaper Editors ran articles on both sides of the issue. The publication of the American Newspaper Publishers Association, which did not join in the lawsuit because its members were divided, also ran articles supporting each side.[10] Whereas the *Columbia Journalism Review* ran a story critical of the decision, the *Washington Journalism Review*'s article did not take a stand.

An article in *Editor and Publisher* concluded that most newspapers' supported the decision. It noted: "Unlike some media lawyers and journalism association heads who last week denounced the High Court decision as a 'First Amendment disaster,' the editorials, in general, seem to say, 'That's life, kids.'"[11] Supporters of the decision included *The New York Times* and the *Washington Post*, the *Cincinnati Enquirer*, the *Detroit News*, the *Philadelphia Inquirer*, and the *Chicago Sun-Times*. A *Chicago Tribune* editorial agreed with the decision while simultaneously questioning the Court's reasoning in reaching it.

Why the lack of support among professional journalists for the freedom of the secondary school press? Journalists tended to see principals as having the role of publisher, ignoring the function of principals as agents of the state. The logic of editorial writers basically followed the viewpoint expressed in the following *Philadelphia Inquirer* comment:

> (I)f the students had won their case, student editors around the country would have ended up with greater rights than their counterparts in the adult world, where editors at many newspapers often have to fight against timid owners to get controversial articles into print.[12]

Whereas journalists usually shield themselves behind the First Amendment so as not to be forced to follow someone else's standard of social responsibility, some journalists rejected the need of student journalists for such protection. They saw school officials' actions not as malevolent, but altruistic. *The New York Times*, for example, commented that it thought the ruling meant not censorship but responsibility. "The decision is a challenge to educators to help their students tell the story fairly and accurately," the editorial stated, "not to squelch them."[13]

School Officials' Responses to the Ruling

Some secondary school officials who supported the ruling did so because they felt the school newspaper should represent the school and its policies. Others agreed with many newspaper editors that school officials had a right to require that the student press be responsible based upon a school official's determination of what was responsible. Some school officials held the opinion expressed by a number of editorial writers that the principal is the publisher. Others assumed that the school and school board are legally responsible for all newspaper content even if the school did not exercise prior review. They thought, therefore, that school administrators must protect themselves from lawsuits by using prior review and prior restraint.[14]

All of those views were represented in comments of the National School Boards Association and the National Association of Secondary School Principals. Ivan Gluckman, counsel for the principals' organization, said that school officials "are responsible for what comes out in the newspaper. No reporter has an unfettered right to publish what he wants in the paper." The president of the school board members' organization said: "It is not the student who is sued; it is the school board."[15] He said it took school districts out of a position "between the rock and the hard place" by giving them the rights of a publisher to determine what will be printed in the school newspaper. The deputy general counsel of the school board members' association stated that if the *Hazelwood* case had gone against the principal, schools "would have had either anarchy or no student newspapers at all."[16]

Most of the readers (presumably mainly school board members and principals) responding to a survey published in *The American School Board Journal* in April 1988 supported the *Hazelwood* decision. Eighty-five percent of the readers participating in the unscientific survey responded that they welcomed the decision, and 71 percent agreed that "schools must teach student journalists to exercise free speech responsibility before bestowing it on them." Only 14 percent of readers responding, however, replied that the decision "merely gives school people the freedom to control editorial content that newspaper publishers already enjoy."

One Pennsylvania board member wrote: "Rights and responsibility go hand in hand. People—such as school board members—who have responsibility for protecting others must protect everyone's rights." A Texas board member responded: "Journalism classes are paid for with tax dollars. They are used as instructional tools and not primarily as sounding boards for students who wish to make statements to their classmates." A New Jersey principal noted:

> *Freedom of speech in the school context applies to the publisher and not the individual. The school is the owner and publisher of the newspaper, not the students. Youngsters are free, if they wish, to write their own newspaper—on their own time and at their own expense and liability.*[17]

Among the 15 percent of respondents who did not support the ruling, a board member from Washington State asked: "How can students learn responsibility if the principal takes responsibility for what appears in the newspaper?" A school board member from Illinois wrote: "Now that we know for certain what our authority is, we must be very careful not to be heavy-handed or dictatorial. Otherwise, we'll wind up demonstrating the need for the First Amendment."[18]

Teachers' and Students' Responses to *Hazelwood*

Editor-in-Chief Jeff Massey was quoted in an article in the January 29, 1988, *Panther Press* at Mountain Grove, Missouri, High School as saying: "It's pretty much been like this anyway. Last year when we wrote on a touchy subject, we always cleared it with the principal first."

Kevin Henderson, editor-in-chief of the *Prairie News* at Kickapoo High School in Springfield, Missouri, wrote in the January 29, 1988, issue:

The recent Supreme Court decision regarding the Hazelwood case, and censorship in general, was justice due to the circumstances. Controversial items aren't the best news around and are too often used for their shock effect....Kickapoo News will not shirk away from any issues that are hard-hitting as long as they can be covered tastefully and on a purely factual basis.

A high school journalist in the St. Louis suburb of Ladue—which, like *Hazelwood*, is located in St. Louis County, Missouri—wrote a full-page editorial about the ruling in the February 12, 1988, edition of his school newspaper, the *Panorama*. The student, David Bianco, stated:

The decision will hurt schools, because anytime freedom of expression is limited, creativity is dampened and enthusiasm for journalism is diminished. It will hurt students, because not only will vital information on important issues be withheld, but also high school newspapers in some school districts will either become propaganda for the school's beliefs or they will become void of real news, filled with only sports articles and fashion pages. Most importantly, however, the case will hurt freedom of expression throughout America. The ruling will, without a doubt, serve as a precedent for future cases, and a whole generation of journalists may just grow up under the specter of the principal's veto.

After noting the Ladue School District had a strong publications policy that was reviewed each year, Bianco added:

The Hazelwood *decision is clearly wrong, as it will diminish student rights to intelligent discussion of the issues. I'm just lucky I live in Ladue and not in Hazelwood, or you probably wouldn't be reading this.*

Other Reactions to *Hazelwood v. Kuhlmeier*

Student press groups, Journalism educators, and civil liberties organizations led an outcry against the ruling. The Secondary Education Division of the Association for Education in Journalism and Mass Communication and the entire membership of the AEJMC, composed mainly of college Journalism educators, passed resolutions condemning the ruling.

Jean Brown, a Michigan college professor, wrote that the decision "strikes an ominous blow to the whole issue of the essential purpose and value of education as it is conceived in this country."[19] Scott McNabb, an instructor at a Michigan junior college, noted: "The Supreme Court decision in *Hazelwood* is a mandate for mediocre education."[20] College professor Nathan Essex, however, noted that the decision does not mean that administrators "may arbitrarily suppress student speech" but that they must have "compelling evidence to demonstrate that the content of the publication does in fact create a disruptive influence on the school's program."[21]

First Amendment scholar Louis E. Ingelhart analyzed the majority and minority opinions in the *Hazelwood* ruling and each citation.[22] He found 28 things the Court did not rule on or did not understand. He stated that the court ignored the equal protection and due process provisions of the 14th Amendment and ignored the First Amendment rights of students to read or to receive information or to share viewpoints.

Ingelhart also noted that the ruling ignored a variety of other facts: that children can be treated like adults in court, that 16-year-olds may marry, 18-year-olds may vote and serve on juries, and that 17- and 18-year-olds may see R-rated movies; and that many girls can become pregnant by age 11. He noted that the ruling also established liability for school officials without requiring that a system of prior review be established. In addition, he stated that the Court failed to deal with academic freedom for faculty members who might disagree with the principal about what should be prohibited in the newspaper.

Ingelhart attacked Justice White's determination that the clause in *Tinker* that allows school officials to censor only student speech which would "substantially interfere with the work of the school or impinge upon the rights of other students" was not the standard to be used for student expression sponsored by the school.[23] Ingelhart commented:

> *This is an astonishing view to come from the nation's highest court which apparently dismisses legal provisions so that it can find non-legally based viewpoints as a basis for deciding legal,*

even constitutional, issues.... White differed sharply with a state-
ment attributed in a school board policy which proposed that "only
speech that materially and substantially interferes with the
requirements of appropriate discipline can be found unacceptable
and therefore prohibited."[24]

Thomas Eveslage, a First Amendment scholar and a member of the Student Press Law Center Board of Directors, called the language used by the Court "frighteningly broad and repressive" and stated that "the Court has stirred smoldering cinders that threaten to erupt in damaging ways."[25] He noted that the ruling that school officials could censor student publications did not especially "surprise or alarm" advisers, administrators or students, because most of them thought censorship was allowed or, at least, operated as if it were. However, he said, the decision presents more problems for the student press than were obvious in wire service summaries of the decision.

Eveslage noted that the Court answered three previously unresolved questions about student press rights: Who is responsible for school-sponsored student speech? (Answer: School officials.) Is the student newspaper a public forum and, therefore, free from censorship by school officials? (Answer: Not unless school policy says so and the school "behaves accordingly" and, in practice, follows the policy.) Does it matter if the student speech is in a publication produced by a class or if it is produced outside of a formal classroom setting? (Answer: School officials are allowed to control any school-sponsored activity not involving a public forum, whether inside or outside a classroom.)

Eveslage stated that the answers to the questions were not as much of a threat to student rights as was the way the Court answered the questions. First, the Court did not define what it meant by regulation "in a reasonable manner." Second, the school may censor without having specific written guidelines to let students know what school officials think is objectionable. Third, the school can set standards for the student press that are higher than those required by professional journalists. Fourth, schools may censor articles written by students who have not "mastered" all aspects of Journalism curriculum concerning the handling of controversial topics, the right to privacy, and the "legal, moral and ethical restrictions" on journalists. Fifth, school officials may censor student expression that they think does not support the school's educational mission if it is likely that members of the public might think the school is endorsing the viewpoint put forth in that expression. "Obviously, the Court has gone far beyond the central questions of liability and curriculum control," Eveslage stated.[26]

A 1988 article in the *Phi Delta Kappan* magazine noted that *Hazelwood, Bethel School District v. Fraser,* and *New Jersey v. T.L.O.* (in which the Court said that only "reasonable suspicion" and not "probable cause" was necessary for school officials to search student lockers for illegal drugs) indicated a major change in the Court's attitudes about the rights of students. The article stated:

> *It will take time and subsequent court decisions to determine the impact of the* Kuhlmeier *[i.e.,* Hazelwood*] decision. Since there is no evidence to suggest that the status of student newspapers is a major issue in most high schools across the country, it may be that initial reactions are more spirited than is justified. That remains to be seen. What is certain is that the Supreme Court has, in its three recent decisions dealing with student rights, fixed new boundaries within which those rights are to be considered.*[28]

The article noted that courts taking student press cases still could look to *Tinker* as well as *Hazelwood* because the Supreme Court distinguished between them. However, the *Kappan* article concluded that the *Hazelwood* decision would mean fewer student press cases would be going to court because of the decreased likelihood that decisions by school officials would be overturned.

The *Kappan* author reasoned that the three cases showed that the school could control activities if the school would be seen to have responsibility for those activities, particularly if those activities would send the wrong kind of message about the nature of the school. Only "reasonableness" is required of the actions of school officials under the three school cases. However, the author appeared to disagree with Eveslage in stating that policies restricting students' rights must be "grounded in clearly enunciated policies and rules, the contents of which have been communicated to students."[29]

Phi Delta Kappan's 13 Conclusions about Student Rights Based upon *Hazelwood, Bethel,* and *T.L.O.*

(Source: *Phi Delta Kappan*, February 1988, pp. 6-7.)

1. The guarantees and protections provided by the Constitution of the United States are applicable to students; however, these rights will be interpreted in terms of the unique environment that prevails in the public schools.

2. School officials, in carrying out certain disciplinary functions, are agents of the state and must act in accord with substantive and procedural guarantees provided in the U.S. Constitution.

3. Students have a legitimate right to privacy; however, this right must be balanced against the state's right to maintain a school environment that is conducive to learning.

4. The standard test that school officials must meet in search-and-seizure activities is one of "reasonableness." This is not as severe a test as the "probable cause" standard that prevails in adult criminal settings.

5. School officials are not required to obtain a warrant before searching a student under their authority.

6. The First Amendment free-speech rights of students are not as extensive as those provided for adults.

7. Schools and parents have a recognized interest in regulating student speech to prevent language that is sexually explicit, vulgar, lewd, or obscene.

8. The decision as to what speech is appropriate in the public school properly rests with the school board.

9. School authorities do not violate First Amendment rights of students in exercising control over the style and content of student speech in school-sponsored expressive activities as long as their actions are reasonably related to legitimate educational concerns.

10. The courts will intervene to protect the First Amendment rights of students only when the school's decision to censor student expression is made without a valid educational purpose.

11. The school can disassociate itself from speech and/or actions that are inappropriate in the school setting.

12. The school is not a public forum unless school officials have, by policy or by practice, opened the schools indiscriminately for use by the public.

13. Once the decision is made that the school is not a public forum, school officials may impose reasonable restrictions on the speech of students, teachers, and other members of the school community.

Although the *Hazelwood* ruling concerned rights of administrators as well as of students, other researchers have noted that it also concerned the rights of teachers. Mike Simpson, an attorney with the National Education Association's Office of General Council, stated that the Supreme Court's "broad decision may adversely affect not just student press advisers but all teachers, threatening their ability to expose students to controversial ideas." He noted that the Court's minority in *Hazelwood* wrote that the school's responsibility to "inculcate moral and political values is not a general warrant to act as thought police," and he called the ruling "a stunning defeat for the rights of student journalists." Concerning the way the rights of all teachers could be infringed because of the ruling, he wrote:

> *What impact will the Hazelwood case have on the rights of teachers? For starters, journalism advisers will now have to kow-tow to principals who want to keep sensitive or controversial issues off the pages of student publications. NEA has argued that an adviser can refuse to obey an administrator's order to censor the school paper because to do so would violate the constitutional rights of students. Such an argument is no longer viable. Advisers who fail to wield a heavy blue pencil may find their jobs at risk because the principal objects to what their students write.*

More important, the Court's ruling has dire implications for the rights of all teachers. While the Supreme Court has never ruled on whether teachers enjoy a right to academic freedom ... the legal reasoning used in Hazelwood *could be applied to severely limit the right of teachers to speak freely in the classroom or to assign outside readings.*[31]

After noting that "a school arguably has an even greater interest in controlling what's said to a captive classroom audience or assigned for required reading," he concluded:

In short, if school officials can censor articles in an official publication because they're sensitive, controversial, or age-inappropriate, then they can also censor reading lists, library books, and teachers themselves.[32]

Jack Dvorak and Jon Paul Dilts also concluded that the *Hazelwood* ruling endangers teachers' freedom of expression and could lead to conflict between teachers and administrators. They noted that because the Court all but overlooked the adviser's role as teacher, "it has moved the debate about the uses of a free press in schools from an issue concerned with student rights to an issue concerned with teachers' rights."[33] Because of the ruling, they cautioned, a teacher who decides to fight censorship can appeal "only to her own limited claims to academic freedom or, more in the spirit of *Hazelwood,* to the needs of journalism pedagogy."[34]

Dvorak and Dilts noted that if the ruling "does not mean an end to journalism education as a means of teaching democratic values, then it must mean that journalism educators are in a pedagogical quandary."[35] They noted a basic conflict for an educator in trying to teach the importance of press freedom while students live with the reality of state-sponsored censorship in the school. The two researchers wrote that "only under remarkably narrow circumstances could one imagine teaching the value of free speech by censoring it." They added:

(I)nherent contradictions result when a public school journalism adviser teaches about protections from government censorship and secrecy while at the same time serving as a state censor—or standing idly by as the school principal censors....(T)he simulation

of Constitutional freedom—whether created by school policy, state law, or the needs of pedagogy—is a teaching method vital to the success of a journalism curriculum.[36]

Censorship: Promoting Propaganda or Good Educational Policy?

Max James suggested in 1970 that those who advocated censorship of student publications as well as those who opposed it thought their actions furthered identical education goals—"the liberation or fuller development of the humanity of the individual, for his own betterment as well as that of society."[37] Thus, while some educators see censorship as fostering propaganda, others—and the Supreme Court—see it as promoting good educational policy. James, who took the view that fostering propaganda cannot be good educational policy, stated:

> *What seems to be most at stake is this fundamental question: Should the taxpayers' money be used to support a school newspaper which is essentially a propaganda sheet presenting a rosy, cozy view of the school, the community, and the world at large and thus protecting its readers (whether students, faculty, parents, or community taxpayers) from controversial matters which might divide or from unpleasant realities which might defile or corrupt, or should the taxpayers' money spent on school newspapers be expected to contribute to the intellectual growth and development of both newspaper staff and the readers of school newspapers by allowing the staff responsible freedom in the handling of all news (pleasant or unpleasant) in the best tradition of a well-defined publisher-editor relationship found in all good professional journalism? That is, should school newspapers exist for propaganda or education?*[38]

The issues on both sides of that argument were set forth in two papers presented at the 1988 summer meeting of the Association for Education in Journalism and Mass Communication, an organization for college and university Journalism educators. In their paper, Professors Louis Day and John Butler concluded that the *Hazelwood* decision was sound educational policy and represents a "restoration of the proper balance between the pedagogical mission of the public schools and the role of the student press."[39]

Day and Butler presented three reasons why *Hazelwood* is good constitutional law and good educational policy: (1) The ideas espoused in the *Hazelwood* decision are historically well-grounded in libertarian philosophy and educational ideology; (2) The general thrust of the *Hazelwood* majority opinion is compatible with a large body of legal precedent recognizing the "limited capacity" of juveniles to exercise fully the rights and privileges accorded to adults; and (3) At the least the *Hazelwood* case represents a pragmatic view of the role of scholastic journalism within the public school curriculum. The two authors added:

> [Hazelwood *was] not just a move by a conservative Court to restrain individual liberties but represents a belief by a majority of the justices that school officials should be accorded substantial deference in their formulation and implementation of educational policy.*[40]

Day and Butler saw the ruling as the reemergence of the "cultural transmission ideology," which emerged in the United States with the mass arrival of immigrants from around the world but which has its roots in the classical Western academic tradition. The ideology states that "schools had to help synthesize people around a demand for a new, functional, and positive conception of the school's role in society."[41] They also saw the ruling as the demise of the "progressive" educational theories of John Dewey and others.

Day and Butler argued that when the exercise of liberty runs counter to the educational mission of the school, the school's mission should prevail "in the interest of teaching ethical and moral standards." They wrote that the ruling at least "represents a pragmatic view of the role of scholastic journalism within the public school curriculum." They added:

> *High school newspapers are not public forums established to facilitate an unfettered marketplace of ideas. These school-sponsored publications are educational tools, designed to teach journalistic knowledge, skills and ethical behavior. Administrative restraints on articles which the principal feels are in poor taste,*

contain objectionable material or are likely to violate the interests of third parties do not abridge the general free speech rights of student reporters and editors....(A)dministrators and journalism teachers must have flexibility in formulating and implementing policies regarding the ethical and legal "standards" to be incorporated into scholastic journalism instruction.[42]

Day and Butler presented a five-point rationale for supporting the *Hazelwood v. Kuhlmeier* decision: (1) The underlying values of free speech are not as important in the public school as in society at large; (2) Some control of the high school press is essential to maintain academic standards; (3) Decisions regarding high school publications should be based upon local educational objectives rather than on a national constitutional standard; (4) The lack of maturity of high school students justifies a "limited capacity" free speech right; (5) Student journalists are not completely denied their rights of expression; there are alternative channels of communication.

In their paper about the *Hazelwood* decision, lawyers J. Marc Abrams and S. Mark Goodman concluded that the Supreme Court was in error in its conclusion that the *Hazelwood* East High School newspaper was not a public forum and that such school-sponsored publications do not have constitutional protection.[43] They reasoned that *Spectrum* was a public forum because of the school district's publication policy, because students not in Journalism II class could contribute letters and other material for publication, and because around one-fourth of the newspaper's revenue was generated by sales. They concluded that "*Spectrum* was by intention and in fact a student newspaper for the presentation of student news, view and opinions."[44] They noted that in 1983[45] the Supreme Court established three types of public forums: the quintessential public forum; the limited public forum; and the non-public forum. Abrams and Goodman argued that *Spectrum* fell under the second category because it was open for unrestricted use by a particular group—*Hazelwood* East students. They stated:

> *[T]he Supreme Court has sent a message not merely to those journalists but to all public school students. On the one hand, the Court has told those students that the educational system exists to*

inculcate in tomorrow's leaders "the fundamental values necessary to the maintenance of a democratic political system." The Court has also stated that public education serves to prepare the youth of our nation to deal with "our increasingly complex society and... the duties of citizenship in our democratic Republic." The Court, however, is telling students that these values must be received passively, without significant opportunity to debate on a school-wide basis the issues and concerns of the day. It blithely presumes that there will be other equally efficient mechanisms such as local news media by which students in a public high school may receive the information they need to make their own choices.[46]

Expectations About the Impact of the *Hazelwood* Ruling

A number of advocates for school Journalism made dire predictions about the contents of school publications and the future of the secondary school press following the *Hazelwood* ruling. For example, Mark Goodman, the executive director of the Student Press Law Center, said after the *Hazelwood* ruling that he expected "many more students will be subtly intimidated to no longer cover topics like pregnancy, divorce, AIDS, or others of vital importance to them."[47] A Michigan college instructor remarked:

Some [educators] will use it to limit students' freedom of speech as they see fit. Anything they find offensive will become a 'legitimate pedagogical concern' and disappear from students' newspapers. Others will use it to shut down student papers completely or slowly strangle them until they contain nothing of any interest so that students quit and go away.

And others will continue to do what they've always done, at least until someone with more authority stops them: to provide students with a realistic and valuable learning experience, and to teach them writing, editing, judgment skills, civics, ethics, and responsibility on one of the most meaningful situations the public schools ever had the guts to offer.

However, providing that meaningful experience just got a hundred times harder and, in some schools, impossible.[48]

Louis Ingelhart suggested that the decision had considerable potential effects on student speech far beyond the school newspaper.[49] Ingelhart stated that the decision authorized complete control by public school officials of all student and faculty expression "anywhere or anytime on the school campus." He said that "the right to read or see or hear ideas, information, or viewpoints can be denied." He came up with a list of 64 types of content specified in the Court's decision as something that could be censored: from advocating the use of alcohol to vulgarity; from content lacking fairness to content that is not responsible journalism; from content revealing intimate concerns of individuals to particulars of teen-age sexual activity in high school; from content unrelated to legitimate pedagogical concerns to content inappropriate to adolescents or readers within the school.

On the other hand, Tom Eveslage said that the case could end up strengthening high school journalism. While noting that "conciliation is preferable to a courtroom challenge," he provided advisers with some suggestions for living with *Hazelwood*.

First, advisers should "(e)stablish areas of agreement and build (their) case for student press rights on that foundation." He noted that the adviser could find support in Justice Brennan's dissent that "exposure to offensive or contradictory messages introduces students to valued diversity of ideas."

Second, the Court did not require censorship, and school officials have several reasons not to censor: (1) The burden of proof still remains on the censor, and schools officials must show that the censorship was "reasonable" and for "valid educational reasons"; (2) Officials who regulate their student publications have a financial liability that they did not have when they were public forums; (3) More restrictions on school-sponsored newspapers may encourage students to begin underground publications that are more difficult to control; and (4) Journalism courses, which help improve students' writing and critical thinking, may become less appealing to students.[50]

Robert P. Knight noted three reasons for concern among postsecondary Journalism educators about the ruling: (1) They could lose the brightest young minds because students will reject *Hazelwood-*

type journalism in their high schools; (2) They could be faced with reshaping scholastic journalists who accept the *Hazelwood* philosophy; (3) All public school students might be deprived of real understanding of the role of the press in a free society.[51]

From a post-*Hazelwood* perspective, Knight wrote that it was evident that advisers in the *Tinker* era had become de facto publishers, maintaining control over budget, personnel, and circulation but having only minimal control over editorial content. In the meantime, students were using investigative reporting techniques and turning newspapers that previously had been little more than bulletin boards into real newspapers. At the same time, student journalists were engendering conflict with school officials.

Because the option is allowed under *Hazelwood* for schools to allow their newspapers the status of public forum, Knight wrote, the ruling established several possible situations along a continuum. The continuum ranges from Justice White's majority position, which allows for almost total restriction of newspaper content, on one end, to Justice Brennan's minority position, which allows what Knight saw as almost total press freedom, on the other. Knight wrote about the challenge of the post-*Hazelwood* situation:

> *Let's be honest about this one. For almost 20 years, we would not say the teacher was acting as publisher or—heaven forbid— editor. We evaded the intriguing question in the public school setting: Who is the publisher if the agents of the state cannot control content?*
>
> Hazelwood *implies that in American public schools a continuum on the scale of control is possible. It ranges from strong control by the principal/publisher to light-handed,* Tinker-*like management. In either case, students would have as much or as little control as has existed for private and parochial school publications, whose principals are not agents of the state.*[52]

Abrams and Goodman feared the effect of the ruling on choices that student journalists would have to make. They stated that students interested in journalism would have to choose between remaining with the school-sponsored newspaper or going to an unofficial publication. They concluded as follows:

[T]he serious student who wishes to be a journalist, or merely wishes to learn to write better, will recognize the clear advantage in having access to a journalism adviser, particularly if that adviser has formal experience or training in writing and journalism. For students such as these, the asset of a trained teaching professional overseeing their writing and the development of their reporting skills is incalculable. The student who maintains ties with the student publication subsequent to the Kuhlmeier *[*Hazelwood*] decision, in order to gain these advantages, will merely have to sacrifice any thoughts of absolute editorial freedom.*[53]

The two lawyers feared that most school officials would conclude that the ruling gives them the authority to censor the student newspaper unless they decide to call it a public forum. They questioned, however, why schools would want to take control over a previously uncensored student newspaper. In doing so, the school takes responsibility for all material published, which means financial liability if a lawsuit results from what is published. State officials, by not exerting prior review take on no such financial liability because they would be in no position to prevent publication of the material. Thus, Abrams and Goodman concluded, "To convert a student newspaper that is a forum for student expression after *Kuhlmeier* [*Hazelwood*] into a non-forum publication could be a serious financial mistake."[54]

If a school publication policy declares the newspaper to be a public forum as defined by the Court in *Hazelwood*, on the other hand, the First Amendment provides protection to student editors. Many First Amendment experts would argue that the ruling also would not apply at high schools (or possibly even junior highs) at which publications had traditions of being public forums and where prepublication review did not normally occur. State law or the state constitution can provide further protection to students. By the fall of 1993, five states (California, Colorado, Iowa, Kansas, and Massachusetts) had passed such laws, providing varying amounts of protection to the student press. In all such situations, legal experts say, the principal could not censor because of content except under the *Tinker* guidelines (that is, if disruption was likely or, in some cases, because of the maturity level of students), and school officials could not withdraw financial support or dismiss editors.

Abrams and Goodman, like the *Phi Delta Kappan* article, argued that many procedural rights given students in previous court rulings remain in spite of the *Hazelwood* case. Those rights include the provision that procedures must be in place so that students know exactly what is not to be published and that, under *Hazelwood*, such regulations must be "reasonably related to legitimate pedagogical concerns." They said that such guidelines also must describe the procedures involved in the review process and provide students the right to a prompt hearing and a timely appeal of the administrator's ruling. Because of those protections, they saw the ruling as a significant step backward for school press freedom, "but not the end of the debate." They concluded:

> *[M]any student publications remain unaffected by* Kuhlmeier *and many more can be protected through state and local rather than federal mechanisms. Keeping this in mind, there is no reason to believe that student journalism will not remain a valid and vital force in the years ahead as long as its contributors continue to stand up for what they believe in and to speak about the great issues that affect their constituencies.*[55]

Thus, predictions concerning the effect of the *Hazelwood* ruling ranged across the spectrum of opinion. Some commentators thought it would result in a bland school press, whereas others held the opinion that the school press already was bland. For example, the executive director of the Gannett Center for Media Studies, Everette Dennis, noted that "the school press already was timid. It was always a captive voice and now is more captive." The executive director of the National Scholastic Press Association, Tom Rolnicki, stated, on the other hand, that "the principal is not interested in sticking his or her finger into the newspaper business." He predicted that the effect of the ruling would be limited largely to schools where animosity between the administration and the newspaper already existed.[56]

Early Research on the Effect of the *Hazelwood* Ruling

As we saw in Chapter 8, studies of high school press freedom in the *Tinker* era suggested that a number of school officials used prior review, prior restraint, intimidation, and written or unwritten content prohibitions to keep objectionable content out of the school newspaper. They also found that overt prior restraint was not necessary because students used self-censorship because of adviser intimidation or because of the students' own deference or like-mindedness with their school authorities. Thus, researchers found that students at some schools were pressured to change stories, to withdraw them voluntarily, or not to write them in the first place.

While methodological rigor was not apparent in some of the earlier studies, the evidence overwhelmingly suggests that principals and advisers during the *Tinker* era were routinely ignoring court rulings requiring First Amendment rights for students. That conclusion was supported by a 1988 study of Iowa advisers in which Jane Peterson found that advisers agreed more with principals on student press rights and responsibilities than they agreed with student editors.[57]

Tom Eveslage (1987)

In a study at about the same time as Peterson's research, Tom Eveslage compared social studies, language arts, and journalism teachers' views of their students' knowledge in five areas: understanding of responsible citizenship, awareness of free speech issues, appreciation of societal values, support for American institutions, and critical thinking.[58]

Eveslage found students were less aware of free speech issues than they had been five and 10 years earlier and that teachers rated students lower in all areas except for their support of American institutions.

Kay Phillips (1989)

Kay Phillips conducted a study that included interviews with a group of principals and advisers before and after the *Hazelwood* ruling and with student editors after the ruling. The schools were chosen because the advisers had attended the North Carolina Scholastic

Press Association Workshop in June 1987. Therefore, they may not be representative of all North Carolina editors. In her study, Phillips defined censorship as "any official interference with student control of the newspaper."

Because Phillips' study was not quantitative, she was able to draw only general conclusions from her research. She found both student deference to advisers and adviser deference to principals. She concluded: "Fear for their jobs, born largely of uncertainty in their roles, and deference to the principal's authority long before *Kuhlmeier*, characterize these advisers."[59] She noted that the advisers' lack of knowledge about student press law was the basis of much of their insecurity, and she found that principals were equally unaware of the law. She concluded the following about the role of advisers and principals:

> *In all schools, advisers exert subtle pressure, and, in practice, most of them are censors by the definition applied in this study: both cutting controversial material and instituting a policy or atmosphere or intimidation that caused students to refrain from printing certain material in the school newspaper. Clearly, persistent student editor deference to such authority has a stultifying effect on the student press.*[60]

Researchers conducting surveys in three states in the months after the *Hazelwood* ruling concluded that few advisers anticipated changes in their publications because of the ruling.

Renfro, Renfro, and Bennett (1988)

Within a few days after the *Hazelwood* ruling, Paula Renfro, Bruce Renfro, and Roger Bennett sent questionnaires to the principal, the newspaper adviser, and the newspaper editor of all 300 high schools belonging to the Texas Interscholastic League Press Conference, a statewide high school journalism organization.[61] Of the 900 questionnaires, 343 of them were returned and usable. As noted by the authors, the schools were not necessarily typical of all Journalism programs in Texas.

Support for *Hazelwood*. Whereas nearly all of the principals with an opinion approved of the ruling, only a small minority of the advisers approved, a statistically significant difference. (See Table 9.1.) Advisers who had majored in Journalism in college were more likely to favor the ruling than were those with a journalism minor or no journalism hours. Also, advisers who had been advising more than 10 years were significantly more likely to approve of the decision than were other advisers. (See Table 9.2.)

Table 9.1: Attitudes toward *Hazelwood* Ruling Held by Principals and Advisers Who Had an Opinion (Renfro, Renfro, and Bennett, 1988)

	Approve	Disapprove
Principals (N=139)	94%	6%
Advisers (N=90)	17%	83%

Table 9.2: Attitudes toward *Hazelwood* Ruling Held by Advisers Who Had an Opinion, Controlling for Years of Service as an Adviser (Renfro, Renfro, and Bennett, 1988)

(N=90)

	Approve	Disapprove
10 years or less	10%	90%
More than 10 years	31%	69%

Expected Change. Few respondents expected any change in the character of the newspaper because of the ruling. Nearly all principals and most advisers and editors expected no change would take place because of the ruling. Only a few advisers believed the ruling would have a chilling effect on freedom of expression. (See Table 9.3.)

Table 9.3: Expectations of Change in the Newspaper Because of the *Hazelwood* Ruling (Renfro, Renfro, and Bennett, 1988)

	Expect change	Expect no change	Not Sure
Principals (N=148)	1%	97%	1%
Advisers (N=100)	4%	76%	20%
Editors (N=95)	4%	78%	18%

The researchers concluded from their survey:

> *Control of the high school newspaper has been taken out of the hands of the students who produce it and advisers who work closely with them. It has been given to high school principals who have no journalism training and sometimes little sympathy for the concept of a free press....The degree to which public high school newspapers after* Hazelwood *deal with the real issues affecting high school students depends now entirely on these principals.*[62]

Dorothy Bowles (1989)

In mid-March 1988, Dorothy Bowles sent a 30-item questionnaire to publications advisers at the 109 schools that belonged to the Tennessee High School Press Association.[63] Publications advisers at just over 29 percent of the schools (32) responded. Because the sample consisted only of members of the press association, it may not reflect the situation in all Tennessee schools. The low number of responses reduces their reliability; however, Bowles' findings are similar to what other researchers at the time were reporting.

Support for *Hazelwood*. Most Tennessee advisers who responded said they were undecided about the ruling. One-quarter of the advisers disagreed with the ruling, and half as many agreed with it.

Expected Change. Only one adviser expected the decision would result in more censorship than in past years. Two advisers expected more prior review but not more censorship.

Extent of Press Freedom. Nearly two-thirds of advisers ranked their publications high for the amount of press freedom allowed them.

Self-Censorship. Bowles concluded that self-censorship was the norm for student journalists in Tennessee, even before the ruling. She suspected that students were given a free hand as long as they were not attempting to be controversial. Bowles concluded that the results of her study would be disappointing to scholastic press advocates. She wrote, reminiscent of Laurence Campbell's comments well over a decade earlier:

> *If advisers who demonstrate enough interest in the scholastic press to enroll their publications in the state high school press organization and to participate in workshops are lukewarm in*

*their support for students' First Amendment rights, then non-
participating advisers could be expected to be even less supportive.*[64]

Tom Dickson (1988)

Two months after the ruling, Tom Dickson conducted a mail
survey of principals[65] and advisers[66] at 100 randomly selected high
schools in Missouri, the state where Hazelwood is located. The sample accounted for more than one-sixth of the state's public high
schools. Seventy-four percent of the questionnaires sent to principals
and 56 percent of the questionnaires sent to advisers were returned.
Virtually all of the schools from which questionnaires were returned
had a yearbook, and more than 90 percent of those schools also had a
student newspaper.

Publication Policies. Dickson concluded that a stated policy was not
an important tool in determining content. He found that few
Missouri principals had written policies about what was suitable content for publications. A majority of Missouri principals stated that
their student newspapers were public forums, however.

Prior Restraint. Most Missouri principals said they had not made
use of prior restraint. Most principals, however, said that they would
suppress some content if it was objectionable. Most principals also
said they expected the adviser to notify them of anything that might
be objectionable.

Dickson concluded that most principals did not necessarily use
prior restraint as part of a policy of prior review of the newspaper.
Instead, they were more likely to have become aware of questionable
material by reacting to problem content brought to them by advisers.

Dickson found that most control by advisers of the newspaper's
content was by suggestion. Prior restraint was used as a last resort.
Though most advisers did show potentially controversial articles to
the principal, it was usually as a precaution or as a courtesy rather
than because they were required to do so.

Newspaper Content. As he expected, Dickson found that school
size was related to whether the newspaper had covered potentially
controversial topics. Significantly more advisers at Missouri high

schools with more than 500 enrollment said that the newspaper had covered the topics of sex, AIDS, student pregnancy, and divorce than was the case at schools with fewer than 500 students.

The greatest differences between responses based upon school size involved whether stories about sex, student pregnancy, and divorce had been published within the previous year. A statistically significant difference also was found for whether their newspapers had run stories about AIDS and drugs. In addition, advisers at larger schools were less likely to say that their newspapers were "good-news" publications and were more likely to say that they were open forums.

Expected Change. Dickson's study indicated that the *Hazelwood* ruling would not have much effect on the contents of school newspapers in Missouri. A large majority of advisers said that they did not plan to look any more closely at the content of the newspaper, and an even larger majority said that their principals did not seem to be more interested in the content of the publication than before the ruling.

Dickson concluded from his 1988 study that advisers would be under continued pressure to be on guard against potentially objectionable material, and they would be more likely than they had been to check with principals about questionable copy. He commented:

> *It seems likely that advisers will continue to respond to principals' reactions to the content of articles by seeing that questionable stories are not printed. If principals do become more interested in the content of articles because of* Hazelwood, *advisers might be more likely to bring questionable material to them for their prior review to limit after-publication queries from irate principals. Such possible courses of action would not necessitate a change in procedure.*[67]

Dickson concluded that most Missouri high schools had been operating under *Hazelwood*-type guidelines before the Supreme Court ruling. He wrote:

> *What principals and the Court may agree on most is the matter of "appropriateness." One respondent's statement reflects*

comments by several principals. He stated: "I feel that you will find most administrators have no desire to control free expression of opinion as long as that expression is appropriate to the school setting." That appears to have been the viewpoint of most Missouri principals before and after the Hazelwood ruling.[68]

Tom Dickson (1989)

A year later, Dickson conducted a study of advisers and principals at another 100 randomly selected Missouri high schools. He wanted to determine what change had taken place in advisers' and principals' attitudes toward press freedom, and he wanted to discern whether changes had taken place in the amount of prior restraint used or in the content of newspaper.

Of the 58 advisers responding to Dickson's mailing, 12 advised only the yearbook and the rest advised the newspaper or both the newspaper and yearbook. Of the 75 principals returning surveys, 55 were at schools with a student newspaper.

Dickson found that whereas some changes in advisers' attitudes were evident from 1988 to 1989, most changes were minimal and none was statistically significant. Table 9.4 compares advisers' responses in 1988 and 1989.

Table 9.4: Advisers' Responses Concerning School Press Freedom in Missouri Immediately after the *Hazelwood* Ruling and a Year after the Ruling (Dickson 1988 and 1989)

	1988	1989
Do you see the newspaper as being an open forum for student expression? (N=44)		
Yes	-	64%
No	-	36%
What do you see as the most important purpose of the newspaper?		
As a classroom teaching tool	1st	1st
As a "good-news" publication for the school	2nd	3rd
As an open forum for student expression	3rd	2nd
As an extracurricular activity for students	4th	4th

	1988	1989
Do you, as adviser, have a stated policy that guides students writers as to what topics are not to be included in the newspaper? (1988: N=52; 1989: N=46)		
Yes	33%	41%
No	67%	59%
Does the school have a policy about what should go into the newspaper? (1988: N=48; 1989: N=46)		
Yes	33%	22%
No	67%	78%
Is there a written policy? (1988: N=56; 1989: N=58)		
Yes	11%	9%
No	89%	91%
If no school policy exists for determining appropriate content, would you support the establishment of a policy? (1988: N=38; 1989: N=36)		
Yes	74%	69%
No	26%	31%
Have you ever submitted individual stories or photos to the principal to get his opinion about their suitability? (N=49)		
Yes	69%	-
No	31%	-
Do you ordinarily submit the newspaper to the principal for his review before publication? (1988: N=51; 1989: N=45)		
Yes	18%	16%
No	82%	84%
Did you ordinarily submit the newspaper for the principal's review before the *Hazelwood* decision? (N=45)		
Yes	-	14%
No	-	86%

	1988	1989
Has the principal ever asked you to let him/her review the entire paper, stories or photos that may be controversial? (N=51)		
Yes	14%	-
No	86%	-
If you do not ordinarily submit the newspaper for review, has your principal asked you since the *Hazelwood* decision to let him review the entire paper, individual stories or photos that may be controversial? (N=38)		
Yes	-	5%
No	-	95%
Does the editor determine the topics of stories to be published? (N=54)		
Yes	11%	-
No	89%	-
Because of the *Hazelwood* ruling, do you plan to look more closely at the content of your paper? (N=48)		
Yes	33%	-
No	67%	-
Because of the *Hazelwood* ruling, have you looked more closely at the content of the school newspaper? (N=44)		
Yes	-	45%
No	-	55%
Have you been able to determine that your principal has become more interested in the content of the school newspaper since the *Hazelwood* decision? (N=50)		
Yes	14%	-
No	86%	-
Has your principal become more interested in the content of the school newspaper since the *Hazelwood* ruling? (N=41)		
Yes	-	24%
No	-	76%

	1988	1989
Since the *Hazelwood* case, have you recommended to an editor or student that a particular story or photo should not be published because of content? (N=42)		
Yes	-	52%
No	-	48%
Have you ever had to suppress a story or photo? (N=52)		
Yes	52%	-
No	48%	-
Have you had to suppress a story or photo during the past 12 months? (N=40)		
Yes	37%	-
No	63%	-
Since the *Hazelwood* decision, have you yourself had to censor a story or photo over the objections of the editor? (N=44)		
Yes	-	27%
No	-	73%
Since the *Hazelwood* ruling, has there been a change in the amount of censorship you have used? (N=44)		
An increase	-	8%
A decrease	-	3%
No change	-	89%
If you have had to suppress a story or photo, what is the reason?		
Possible libel	1st	2nd
Invasion of privacy	2nd	1st
Too controversial	3rd	3rd
Obscenity	4th	4th
"Dirty language"	5th	5th

	1988	1989
Percent of newspapers having covered topics during the previous year:		
Alcohol	-	80%
Drugs	-	59%
Smoking	-	46%
AIDS	-	39%
Sex	-	34%
Student pregnancy	-	30%
Divorce	-	9%
Please rank the following types of articles or topics in order of importance for the newspaper:		
School activities	-	1st
Editorials, staff-written columns	-	2nd
Educational issues affecting students	-	3rd
Societal issues affecting students	-	4th
School administrators' views	-	5th
Letters to the editor	-	(tie) 5th

Policy Changes. According to advisers, their schools' publications policies had not changed much in the year after *Hazelwood*. Advisers were more likely in 1989, however, to state that the most important purpose of the student newspaper was as an open forum and less likely to state that being a "good-news" publication was the most important purpose of the newspaper.

Advisers in 1989 were somewhat more likely than those in 1988 to have a policy concerning what topics were not appropriate for the student newspaper, but Dickson found no change between 1988 and 1989 in the percent of schools with a written policy. Also, advisers in 1989 were slightly less likely to support the establishment of a policy on appropriate content in 1989 than they had been in 1988.

Prior Review. Dickson found only a slight increase in the amount of prior review from 1988 to 1989. He found a negligible decrease in the number of advisers who said that they ordinarily submitted the newspaper to their principals for review. Advisers in 1989 who did submit the newspaper for their principals' review most often did so "as a courtesy" or "in case problems arise" instead of "because the principal has asked me to," "because I know the principal wants to review it," or "because of a written school policy."

Prior Restraint. Dickson found little difference between the amount of prior restraint taking place in 1989 and what had been reported in 1988. For example, he found no noticeable change from 1988 as to the percent of advisers who said their principals had suggested to them that they not publish a particular story or photo.

Fewer advisers in 1989 than in 1988 said that they had suppressed a story or photo in the previous year. Moreover, 90 percent of advisers in 1989 said that no change in the amount of prior restraint had occurred in the 12 months since the *Hazelwood* ruling as compared to the 12 months before the ruling. One adviser stated that the amount of prior restraint had even decreased.

Some change was indicated in the reason for prior restraint, however. While potential libel had been a slightly greater cause of prior restraint than privacy or embarrassment to students in 1988, privacy was more likely to be the cause of restraint in 1989. Dickson found that advisers in 1989 were more likely to state that they had used prior restraint for "journalistic reasons" and "because the stories were harmful to students" rather than "because the principal would object."

Changes in Newspaper Content. Dickson thought that the content of the newspaper might change even if the amount of prior restraint had not, either because of increased pressure on students or because of increased student deference. Dickson knew that advisers had considerable input into story topics because Dickson had found in his 1988 survey that most advisers said that they chose story topics.

Despite expectations, he found that the contents of Missouri's newspapers had not changed much since the ruling, and he found little indication of increased editor deference or increased adviser pressure for less-controversial content. Advisers in 1989 were no less likely to state that the newspaper had covered any of the potentially controversial issues listed in the 1988 survey except for divorce. Advisers were slightly more likely to state that the newspaper had run a story about drugs and about smoking. Newspapers, however, were no less likely to have run stories about student pregnancy, sex, and AIDS.

Stories that were seen as an invasion of privacy or embarrassing to students were most likely to cause an adviser to suggest that a story or photo not be published. They were followed by stories containing possible libel and "dirty language." Controversial topics were least likely to result in pressure on the editor. Few advisers had suggested that a story not run because it was too controversial.

Dickson found that while some changes in principals' attitudes were evident from 1988 to 1989, most were minimal and none was statistically significant. Table 9.5 compares principals' responses in 1988 and 1989.

Table 9.5: Principals' Responses Concerning School Press Freedom in Missouri Immediately after the *Hazelwood* Ruling and a Year after the Ruling

	1988	1989
If your school has a student newspaper, do you see it as being an open forum for student expression? (1988: N=67; 1989: N=57)		
Yes	61%	47%
No	39%	53%
What do you see as the (most important) purposes of your newspaper?		
As a classroom teaching tool	-	1st
As a "good-news" publication for the school	-	2nd
As an extracurricular activity for students	-	3rd
As an open forum for student expression	-	4th
Because of the *Hazelwood* ruling, do you foresee any change in the procedure concerning the content of the student newspaper? (N=67)		
Yes	19%	-
No	81%	-

	1988	1989
Have you looked more closely at student publications because of the *Hazelwood* ruling? (N=58)		
Yes	-	28%
No	-	72%
Has it been the usual practice at your school for you to review the yearbook before publication?(N=74)		
Yes	22%	-
No	78%	-
If you have a student newspaper, has it been the usual practice at your school for you to review the student newspaper before publication? (N=68)		
Yes	32%	-
No	68%	-
If you have a student newspaper, was it the usual practice before the *Hazelwood* case for you to review the newspaper before publication? (N=58)		
Yes	-	40%
No	-	60%
Since the *Hazelwood* case, has it been your practice to review the newspaper before publication? (N=58)		
Yes	-	36%
No	-	64%
Is there a written policy requiring the newspaper adviser to submit copy or photos for your review? (1988: N=70; 1989: N=48)		
Yes	4%	6%
No	96%	94%
Have you ever had pressure from any of the following to suppress content of the student newspaper? (N=74)		
Superintendent	12%	-
School Board	8%	-
Community	12%	-

	1988	1989
Would you expect the adviser to talk with you if she/he had any question about the appropriateness of some material? (1988: N=72; 1989: N=66)		
Yes	99%	100%
No	1%	0%
Before the ruling, did you ever have to censor the student newspaper? (N=75)		
Yes	-	37%
No	-	63%
Since the ruling, have you had to censor the student newspaper? (N=55)		
Yes	-	18%
No	-	72%
Because of the *Hazelwood* ruling, are you more concerned about the appropriateness of the contents of any of the student newspaper (N=55)		
Yes	-	22%
No	-	78%
What type of subject matter do you think you might suppress in a student publication if you found them objectionable? (1988: N=74; 1989: N=75)		
"Dirty language"	89%	97%
Invasion of privacy	-	76%
Sex	61%	76%
Drugs	57%	59%
Student pregnancy	42%	42%
AIDS	37%	38%
Problems related to divorce	34%	33%

Publications Policies. None of the principals in 1989 stated that a school policy had been put in place since the *Hazelwood* ruling requiring the adviser to submit copy or photos for the principal's review.

Changes in Prior Review. Dickson found no statistically significant change between 1988 and 1989 in the percent of principals who stated that they looked at the newspaper or yearbook before publication.

Prior Restraint. Few principals in 1989 said they had used prior restraint on the newspaper since the *Hazelwood* ruling. All principals without a policy requiring the adviser to submit the newspaper to them for prior review said in 1989, however, that they expected their advisers to keep material that might be objectionable out of the newspaper.

Objectionable Content. Dickson found virtually no change from 1988 to 1989 in the type of stories that principals thought they would suppress if they found them to be objectionable. Fewer than half of the principals either year said they likely would suppress a story about student pregnancy, AIDS, or problems related to divorce.

Dickson concluded that the *Hazelwood* decision had little immediate effect upon Missouri public high schools. Advisers continued to advise students about suitability of content, but they were no more likely to suppress stories. Principals were less likely to see their newspapers as public forums, but they were no more likely to review the paper before publication. They were not practicing much prior restraint, but most of them appeared to be ready to do so if necessary.

The response of an adviser to Dickson's 1988 study is representative of comments about many school officials' attitudes about the school newspaper:

> *The recent decision will have little impact on the content of our school paper. It has always been ultimately controlled by the administration/board. They pay for it.*[69]

Kopenhaver, Martinson, and Habermann (1989)

Findings similar to Dickson's in Missouri were reported by researchers in Florida at about the same time. Prompted by reports that the Student Press Law Center had noted a sharp increase in requests for assistance in the fall following the *Hazelwood* ruling, Lillian Lodge Kopenhaver, David L. Martinson, and Peter Habermann undertook a study of principals and advisers at the 62 public high schools in four Florida counties in the Miami-Palm Beach area.[70] They did not, however, state exactly when the study was undertaken.

The researchers used a seven-point scale for respondents to note their level of agreement with statements about scholastic press freedom. They received responses from 41 advisers and 29 administrators, and all but three surveys were usable.

Nearly all administrators and advisers in southeastern Florida who responded indicated that the *Hazelwood* decision had not influenced the status of the student newspaper at their schools. The authors surmised that the impact of *Hazelwood* was so limited because students were using self-censorship to avoid controversy.

Kopenhaver, Martinson, and Habermann noted that advisers in Dade County (Miami) schools supported press rights to a greater extent than did advisers at schools in the other three counties studied. From that determination, the authors concluded that "the level of freedom enjoyed by high school students will be impacted as much by the attitudes of the school district as a whole as by the individual administrator at a particular school."[71]

The three researchers also found in their Florida study that advisers took a more favorable position than administrators on 24 of 25 statements about press freedom, and in 18 cases differences were statistically significant.

They concluded that newspaper advisers and high school administrators view student press-related First Amendment issues quite differently. They decided that public school administrators support First Amendment freedoms but that they balance those freedoms against other concerns.

A quote by one south Florida administrator was representative of what other principals seemed to think: "Handled properly, with a good sponsor, conflict between discipline and freedom does not exist."[72]

Click and Kopenhaver (1990)

In the spring of 1989, J. William Click and Lillian Lodge Kopenhaver conducted a national study to get principals' and advisers' opinions about First Amendment issues.[73] The questions on the survey were similar to the ones they used in their 1984-85 study.

The researchers sent their 41-question survey to principals and advisers at the 531 public and private schools that were newspaper members of the Columbia Scholastic Press Association. The findings, therefore, are not necessarily representative of all U.S. high schools. In reporting their results, the authors did not differentiate between responses received from public and private schools. Unlike public schools, private schools do not have any First Amendment protection.

Click and Kopenhaver received responses from 41 percent of the principals (220) and 68 percent of the advisers (360). Just under 90 percent of the surveys returned were from public schools. As in Click and Kopenhaver's previous study, responses were based upon a seven-point scale. The two researchers omitted the three middle responses ("slightly agree," "neutral," and "slightly disagree") in their analysis. Their most relevant findings are reported in Table 9.6. In the table, however, all responses except "neutral" ones are reported.

Table 9.6: Percent of Columbia Scholastic Press Association Principals and Advisers with an Opinion Who Agreed with Statements about the Role of the Student Newspaper (Click and Kopenhaver, 1990)

	Principals	Advisers
It is more important to the school board for the school to have a good image than to have an uncensored student newspaper. (Principals: N=191; Advisers: N=324)	47%	30%
The student newspaper is more a learning tool than a vehicle for the expression of student opinion. (Principals: N=183; Advisers: N=313)	71%	40%
Guarantees of freedom of expression in the student newspaper outweigh public relations considerations. (Principals: N=202; Advisers: N=334)	51%	85%
Articles critical of the school board should not appear in the student newspaper. (Principals: N=202; Advisers: N=342)	29%	4%

	Principals	Advisers
School administrators should have the right to prohibit publication of articles they think harmful, even though such articles might not be legally libelous, obscene or disruptive. (Principals: N=202; Advisers: N=349)	71%	14%
The student newspaper should be allowed to print a story that it can prove is true even if printing the story will hurt the school's reputation. (Principals: N=205; Advisers: N=331)	55%	83%
The student newspaper adviser should review all copy before it is printed. (Principals: N=218; Advisers: N=349)	100%	92%
The adviser should correct factual inaccuracies in student copy before publication even if it is not possible to confer with the students involved. (Principals: N=209; Advisers: N=335)	82%	79%
Newspaper advisers who do not read copy of student newspapers before publication should be held personally responsible for any complaints about the newspapers. (Principals: N=214; Advisers: N=339)	92%	72%
The adviser should correct misspellings that students make in their copy. (Principals: N=209; Advisers: N=338)	89%	75%
If the adviser knows that the newspaper is going to publish something that will put the school in a bad light, the adviser has a professional obligation to see that that particular item is not published. (Principals: N=202; Advisers: N=335)	38%	13%
The faculty adviser is ultimately responsible for the content of the student newspaper rather than the student editors. (Principals: N=212; Advisers: N=342)	81%	51%
Controversial issues have no place in a student newspaper. (Principals: N=218; Advisers: N=360)	3%	1%
The adviser is obligated to inform the administration of any controversial stories before the newspaper goes to press. (Principals: N=211; Advisers: N=331)	90%	39%
Society has an obligation to protect the First Amendment rights of high school students. (Principals: N=202; Advisers: N=349)	88%	95%
If school officials do not exercise prior review over the content of the newspaper, they are not legally liable for its content. (Principals: N=188; Advisers: N=311)	12%	25%
A written editorial policy giving student editors final determination of the content of the newspaper has no effect following *Hazelwood*. (Principals: N=179; Advisers: N=314)	39%	44%

	Principals	Advisers
If student editors have clearly been given final authority over content decisions, or if the school has specifically designated the student publication as a forum, the *Hazelwood* decision does not apply and school officials will still be very limited in exercising censorship. (Principals: N=176; Advisers: N=318)	27%	50%

Role of the Newspaper. Whereas principals were more likely to agree that the student newspaper was a learning tool than that it was a means for student expression of opinion, advisers were more likely to disagree with that statement. The difference was statistically significant.

Extent of Press Freedom. Whereas a majority of principals and advisers with an opinion agreed that guarantees of freedom of expression in the student newspaper outweigh public relations considerations, advisers were far more likely to think so. The difference was statistically significant.

Prior Review. Whereas all principals and most advisers stated that the newspaper adviser should review all copy before it is printed, significantly more principals than advisers agreed with the position. Most principals with an opinion agreed with the statement that the adviser is obligated to inform the administration of controversial stories before the newspaper goes to press, but only a minority of advisers did. The difference in principals' and advisers' responses was statistically significant.

Prior Restraint. Whereas a majority of both groups thought that the student newspaper should be allowed to print a factual story even if it would hurt the school's image, significantly more advisers than principals agreed with the statement. In addition, significantly more advisers than principals expressed disagreement with the statement that articles critical of the school board should not appear in the student newspaper.

Advisers and principals disagreed over whether school administrators should have the right to prohibit publication of articles they thought were harmful, even if not libelous, obscene or disruptive. Most principals felt they should be allowed to prohibit such articles, but few of the advisers agreed. Most principals and editors thought that advisers should correct spelling and factual errors.

Understanding of the Law. Click and Kopenhaver found that a large number of principals and advisers were misinformed about important issues of student press law. For example, many of those who knew about the *Hazelwood* decision did not understand that they are not liable for the newspaper's content if they do not exercise prior review. Significantly more advisers than principals understood the law, however.

Principals and advisers also showed considerable misunderstanding of the *Hazelwood* ruling, though advisers were correct significantly more often than were principals.

Click and Kopenhaver concluded that it was unlikely that an adviser could use prior review without censoring the newspaper. To them, changing mistakes and correcting spelling both were censorship. They concluded, therefore:

> *From the results, it appears as if advisers see themselves as the last line of defense for the school and its administration before the newspaper is published; that is, they see themselves as editors who must review copy and correct misspellings and inaccuracies but not necessarily remove entire stories that will hurt the school's reputation.*[74]

The authors provided other results from their 1989 study in an article published in 1993.[75] In it, they reported that only one-fourth of the advisers and three-tenths of the principals who responded stated that prior restraint was used on their school newspapers. In addition, three-quarters of the advisers stated that prior restraint had not increased since the *Hazelwood* ruling.

NOTES ON CHAPTER 9

1. *Bethel School District #403 v. Fraser*, 478 U.S. 675, 106 S.Ct. 3159 (1986).

2. *Bethel*, at 3165, citing *Tinker*.

3. *Hazelwood School District v. Kuhlmeier*, 484 U.S. 260, 1988, cited in *Quill & Scroll*, February-March 1988: 12.

4. Student Press Law Center, *Law of the Student Press*, 15.

5. Cited in *Quill and Scroll*, February-March 1988, 13-14.

6. "Current Issues Memo Regarding the Supreme Court and Students' Rights—An Update," *Phi Delta Kappan*, February 1988, 1.

7. Dorothy Bowles, "*Hazelwood v. Kuhlmeier*: National Press Reaction to the Decision and Its Impact in Tennessee High Schools" (paper presented at the 1989 Midwinter Meeting of the Secondary Education Division of the Association for Education in Journalism and Mass Communication, St. Petersburg, FL, January 1989).

8. Richard M. Schmidt Jr., and N. Frank Wiggins, "Censoring Student Papers May Teach a Lesson That Will Return to Haunt the Mainstream Press," *The Bulletin of the American Society of Newspaper Editors*, February 1988, 4-8, quoted in Bowles: 15.

9. Fern Valentine, "Students Are Not Asking for License; They Are Asking for Press Freedom," *The Bulletin of the American Society of Newspaper Editors*, February 1988, pp. 4-8, quoted in Bowles: 15.

10. Bowles: 9.

11. *Ibid.:* 11.

12. *Ibid.:* 13.

13. Paula Renfro, Bruce Renfro, and Roger Bennett, "Expectations of Change in the High School Press after *Hazelwood*: A Survey of Texas High School Principals, Newspaper Advisers and Newspaper Editors," *Southwestern Mass Communication Journal 4* (1988): 64-65.

14. "When administrators have not exercised control over the content of student publications, the courts have refused to hold their schools responsible for libel appearing in such publications. If, however, administrators exercise the power of prior review, then the courts will

also hold them and their schools liable for the contents of such publications." Student Press Law Center, *Law of the Student Press*, 37-38.

15. Renfro, Renfro and Bennett, "Expectations of Change in the High School Press after *Hazelwood*": 67.

16. Bowles, "*Hazelwood v. Kuhlmeier*": 25.

17. "Finding: Student Journalists Need Guidance," *The American School Board Journal*, June 1988: 42.

18. *Ibid.*

19. Jean E. Brown, "The Relativity of Freedom," *Support for the Learning and Teaching of English Newsletter*, 13:1 (September 1988): 1.

20. Scott McNabb, "Censoring Student Newspapers Hurts Education," *Support for the Learning and Teaching of English Newsletter*, 13:1 (September 1988): 2.

21. Nathan L. Essex, "A Landmark Supreme Court Decision Grants School Authorities the Right to Censor School Sponsored Student Newspapers," *Contemporary Education*, 59:3 (Spring 1988): 140.

22. Louis E. Ingelhart, unpublished, "The *Hazelwood* Case Revisited," 1988.

23. *Ibid.*: 3.

24. *Ibid.*: 2.

25. Thomas Eveslage, "*Hazelwood v. Kuhlmeier:* A Threat and a Challenge to High School Journalism," *Quill and Scroll*, (February-March 1988): 9.

26. *Ibid.*

27. *New Jersey v. T.L.O.*, 469 U.S 325 (1985).

28. "Current Issues Memo Regarding the Supreme Court and Students' Rights": 2.

29. *Ibid.*: 7.

30. Mike Simpson, "Supreme Court Chills Student Press Rights," *NEA Today* (March 1988): 13.

31. *Ibid.*

32. *Ibid.*

33. Jack Dvorak and Jon Paul Dilts, "Academic Freedom v. Administrative Authority," *Journalism Educator* 47 (Autumn 1992): 5.

34. *Ibid.*: 3.

35. *Ibid.*

36. *Ibid.*: 4.

37. Max James, "Propaganda or Education? Censorship and School Journalism, *Arizona English Bulletin* 13:1 (October 1970): 37.

38. *Ibid.*

39. Louis A. Day and John M. Butler, "*Hazelwood School District v. Kuhlmeier:* A Constitutional Retreat or Sound Public Policy?" (paper presented at the convention of the Association for Education in Journalism and Mass Communication, Portland, OR, July 1988).

40. *Ibid.*: 2.

41. *Ibid.*: 5.

42. *Ibid.*: 39-40.

43. J. Marc Abrams and S. Mark Goodman, "End of an Era?: The Decline of Student Press Rights in the Wake of the Kuhlmeier Decision" (paper presented at the convention of the Association for Education in Journalism and Mass Communication, Portland, OR, July 1988).

44. *Ibid.*: 28.

45. *Perry Education Association v. Perry Local Educator's Association*, 460 U.S. 37, at 45-46 (1983).

46. Abrams and Goodman, "End of an Era," 33-34.

47. "Current Issues Memo Regarding the Supreme Court and Students' Rights," 1.

48. McNabb, "Censoring Student Newspapers Hurts Education," 2.

49. Ingelhart, "Press Law," *College Media Advisers Newsletter* (January 1989): 6-7.

50. Eveslage, "*Hazelwood v. Kuhlmeier:* A Threat and a Challenge to High School Journalism," 10.

51. Robert P. Knight, "High School Journalism in the Post-*Hazelwood* Era," *Journalism Educator* 43:2 (Summer 1988).

52. *Ibid.:* 43, 45.

53. Abrams and Goodman, "End of an Era?": 32.

54. *Ibid.:* 43.

55. *Ibid.:* 51.

56. Bowles, "*Hazelwood v. Kuhlmeier,*" 15-16.

57. Jane Peterson, "A Study of the Coorientation of High School Principals, Journalism Teachers, and Local Newspaper Editors in Selected Iowa Communities" (paper presented at the convention of the Association for Education in Journalism and Mass Communication, Portland, OR, July 1988).

58. Thomas Eveslage, "Teaching Free Speech Values to High School Students: Keys to Persevering Despite the Obstacles" (paper presented at the convention of the Association for Education in Journalism and Mass Communication, San Antonio, TX, August 1987).

59. Kay Phillips, "Freedom of Expression for High School Journalists: A Case Study of Selected North Carolina Public Schools" (paper presented at the convention of the Association for Education in Journalism and Mass Communication, Washington, DC, August 1989): 41.

60. *Ibid.:* 42.

61. Renfro, Renfro and Bennett, "Expectations of Change in the High School Press after *Hazelwood.*"

62. *Ibid.:* 73.

63. Bowles, "*Hazelwood v. Kuhlmeier.*"

64. *Ibid.:* 28.

65. Thomas V. Dickson, "Attitudes of High School Principals about Press Freedom after *Hazelwood,*" *Journalism Quarterly* 66:1 (Spring 1989): 169-173.

66. Thomas V. Dickson, "How Advisers View the Status of High School Press Freedom Following the *Hazelwood* Decision" (paper presented at the convention of the Association for Education in Journalism and Mass Communication, Washington, DC, August 1989).

67. Dickson, "Attitudes of High School Principals about Press Freedom after *Hazelwood*": 173.

68. *Ibid.*

69. Dickson, "How Advisers View the Status of High School Press Freedom Following the *Hazelwood* Decision": 13.

70. Lillian Lodge Kopenhaver, David L. Martinson, and Peter Habermann, "First Amendment Rights in South Florida: Views of Advisers and Administrators in Light of *Hazelwood*," *The School Press Review*, (Fall 1989): 17.

71. *Ibid.*

72. *Ibid.*

73. J. William Click and Lillian Lodge Kopenhaver, "Opinions of Principals and Newspaper Advisers toward Student Press Freedom and Advisers' Responsibilities Following *Hazelwood v. Kuhlmeier*" (paper presented at the convention of the Association for Education in Journalism and Mass Communication, Minneapolis, August 1990): 2.

74. *Ibid.*: 9.

75. J. William Click, Lillian Lodge Kopenhaver, and Larry Hatcher, "Attitudes of Principals and Teachers toward Student Press Freedom Following *Hazelwood v. Kuhlmeier*," *Journalism Educator* 48:1 (Spring 1993): 59-70.

Chapter 10

SCHOLASTIC PRESS FREEDOM IN THE '90s: HOW ADVISERS AND STUDENTS ARE COPING WITH HAZELWOOD

PART I: HAVE ADVISERS BECOME CENSORS?

Section Highlights

- Most advisers are somewhat more likely to state that the newspaper is a learning tool for students rather than that it is a means for student expression.

- Most advisers say that their newspaper is a public forum.

- The *Hazelwood* ruling did lead to more prior review by principals, but few principals read the newspaper before publication even after the ruling.

- The use of prior restraint did not increase significantly after the *Hazelwood* ruling.

- Stories that are not fair or balanced are most likely to result in both conflict between advisers and student journalists and to result in prior restraint.

- Advisers think student self-censorship did not increase because of the *Hazelwood* ruling.

- Most advisers did not think stories were more fair and balanced after the ruling.

- The advisers' experience as an adviser is the variable most related to differences in advisers' attitudes toward student press freedom.

As discussed in Chapter 9, all reported studies in the two years following the *Hazelwood* ruling indicated that prior restraint, while being used in some schools, had not increased much since the ruling. None of the studies, however, was based upon a random sample of all public high schools in the country.

With the financial support of Southwest Missouri State University, the staff support of the university's Office of Academic Computing, and the sponsorship of the Secondary Education Division of the Association for Education in Journalism and Mass Communication, we undertook a study of a random sample of all public high schools in the country. It was the largest reported survey of high school press freedom.

We not only wanted to ascertain the impact of the *Hazelwood* ruling on the public secondary school press, but also we wanted to establish benchmark data for a longitudinal study of advisers. Toward those ends, we tested variables that earlier studies had indicated were related to school press freedom. Some of those variables were investigated by Trager and Dickerson in 1980, Kristof in 1983, and Dickson in 1988 and 1989. Those studies are reported in Chapter 9.

In our study, conducted in 1990, we asked eight general research questions about press freedom:

1. Did the *Hazelwood* decision result in a significant increase in the principal's use of prior review of the student newspaper?

2. Did the *Hazelwood* decision result in a significant increase in the adviser's use of prior restraint of the student newspaper?

3. What was the reason for most adviser prior restraint?

4. Did the *Hazelwood* decision result in a significant increase in student journalists' use of self-censorship?

5. Were stories more fair and balanced following the *Hazelwood* ruling?

6. Were student newspapers less likely to contain stories about controversial topics following the *Hazelwood* ruling?

7. What were the biggest causes of student-adviser conflict?

8. What community/school and adviser characteristics are most related to the amount of press freedom in public secondary schools?

In the spring of 1990, we sent a 36-question survey to 1,600 public high schools (approximately 7 percent of the high schools in the country). We received responses from 32 percent of the schools (504). Of that number, 379 responses came from schools with a student newspaper. For the data reported below, we used chi square to determine statistical significance. Any correlation at the .05 level of confidence or above was considered statistically significant. Cramer's V, which can range from 0.0 to 1.0, was used to measure the strength of the association between variables: The higher the V score, the greater the strength of the association.

General Characteristics of the Sample

School and Community Size/Location. Just over four-tenths of the newspaper advisers responding were at small schools (defined as those with 500 or fewer students in grade 10 through 12). The remainder were about evenly divided between medium-sized and large schools. (See Graph 10.1.) Almost half of the schools with newspapers were in rural areas or communities with less than 10,000 population. Slightly under a third were in middle-sized communities (those with a population of 10,000-50,000), and about one-fifth were in larger cities (more than 50,000). (See Graph 10.2.) One-third of the schools were located in the Central region, about one-fourth each in the South and West, and about one-sixth in the Northeast.[1] (See Graph 10.3.)

Frequency of Publication. Monthly publication was the norm for newspapers in the sample. Nearly half of the advisers said that their newspapers were published about once a month. Slightly under one-third of the advisers said that their newspapers were published less often, and about one-fifth said that they were published more often than once a month. (See Graph 10.4.)

Graph 10.1

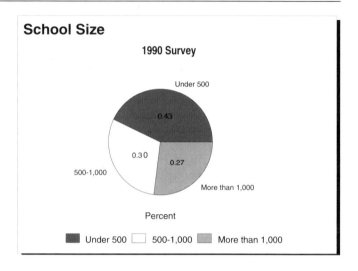

School Size

1990 Survey

Under 500

0.43

0.30

0.27

500-1,000

More than 1,000

Percent

◼ Under 500   ☐ 500-1,000   ▦ More than 1,000

Graph 10.2

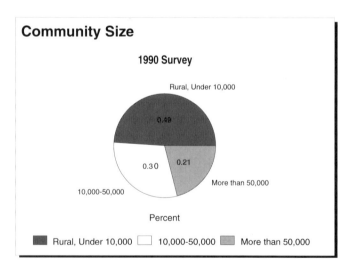

Community Size

1990 Survey

Rural, Under 10,000

0.49

0.30   0.21

10,000-50,000

More than 50,000

Percent

◼ Rural, Under 10,000   ☐ 10,000-50,000   ▦ More than 50,000

Graph 10.3

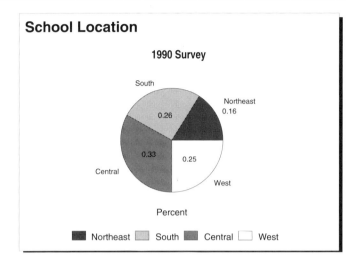

Graph 10.4

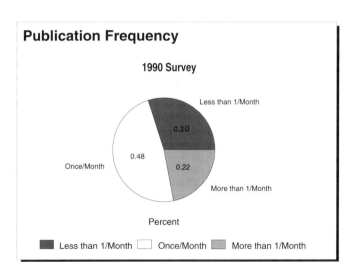

The Newspaper Staff. We found that a variety of procedures were used for determining who can work on the newspaper staff. About three-tenths of the advisers said that Journalism courses were not offered and that anyone in the appropriate grades could be on the staff. About one-quarter said that staff members must at least be enrolled in a beginning journalism course, and almost one-quarter said that staff members were not required to have taken a Journalism course even though courses were offered. A variety of other policies accounted for the rest of the responses. (See Graph 10.5.) About one-fourth of the advisers said that no credit was given for working on the newspaper staff.

Graph 10.5

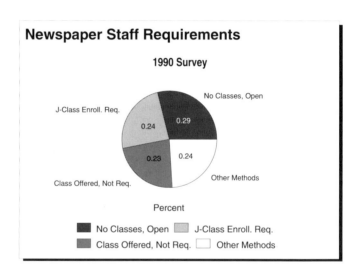

Purpose of the Newspaper. Nearly two-fifths of the advisers thought the newspaper's main purpose was to be "a means for journalism students to learn skills," and almost a third gave "a means for student expression" as the main purpose. The remainder responded that the newspaper's main purpose was to report both good and bad things about the school, to publicize school activities, or to promote positive things about the school. (See Graph 10.6.)

Graph 10.6

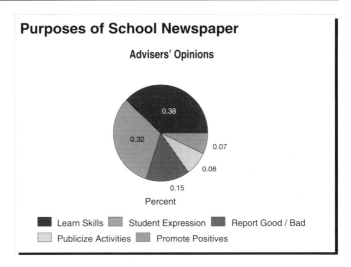

Purposes of School Newspaper

Advisers' Opinions

Percent

■ Learn Skills ▨ Student Expression ▨ Report Good / Bad
▨ Publicize Activities ▨ Promote Positives

Policies on Acceptable Content. Despite fears by some educators that the *Hazelwood* ruling would close the door on school press freedom, most advisers said that the newspaper was an open forum for all speech or for speech that had constitutional protection. Just under one-fourth said that the school policy stated that some subject matter should not go into the newspaper, even if it were constitutionally protected speech. A few advisers said there was no policy. (See Graph 10.7.)

Graph 10.7

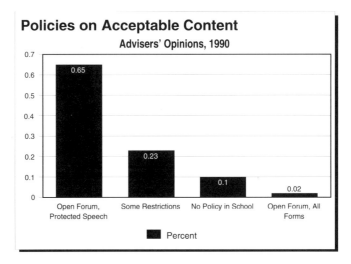

Policies on Acceptable Content

Advisers' Opinions, 1990

■ Percent

Answers to Research Questions Posed

Prior Review. In response to the first research question, we found that the ruling did lead to more principals using prior review. Only a small minority of advisers were submitting the paper to the principal for review in 1990. (See Table 10.1.) One-third of the advisers who had begun to submit the newspaper after the *Hazelwood* ruling said they had done so only as a precaution or as a courtesy, not because they were required to do so.

Table 10.1: Length of Time Adviser Had Been Submitting the Entire Newspaper to the Principal for Review (1990)

Adviser Doesn't Submit Newspaper to the Principal	84%
Adviser Began Doing So Before *Hazelwood* and Continued	9%
Adviser Began Doing So After *Hazelwood*	7%

Most of the advisers reported that they discussed potentially controversial items with their principals on occasion. Advisers were nearly four times more likely to have done so as a precaution rather than to have done so because they were asked. (See Table 10.2.)

Table 10.2: Reasons for Advisers to Consult with the Principal About Potentially Controversial Stories (1990)

As a Precaution	59%
Adviser Was Asked to Consult	15%
Adviser Does Not Consult	26%

Only a small minority of advisers stated that they had discussed potentially controversial items with their principals more often after the ruling than they had done before the ruling. Just over half of those who had done so more often said it was because the principal had told them to do so. (See Table 10.3).

Table 10.3: Reasons Advisers Discuss Potentially Controversial Items More Often Than before *Hazelwood* (1990)

Because Principal Has Told Adviser to Do So	10%
Because Principal Seems More Interested	7%
Because of Change in School Policy	2%
Adviser Doesn't Discuss Controversial Items More Often	81%

Prior Restraint. In response to the second research question, we found that the amount of prior restraint had not increased significantly. When we asked advisers whether more stories had been kept from publication in the previous 12 months than in that period of time before the *Hazelwood* ruling, most of the advisers stated that there had been no change in the number of stories kept from publication. (See Table 10.4.) The results were quite similar to what Click and Kopenhaver had found in their study of Columbia Scholastic Press Association advisers and principals a year earlier.

Just over one-third of the advisers said they had changed the wording of a story in the previous 12 months over the objections of the editor. Again, the findings were quite similar to what Click and Kopenhaver had found about use of prior restraint.

Table 10.4: Change in Amount of Prior Restraint by Adviser (1990)

No Change in Number of Rejections	82%
More Rejections	4%
Fewer Rejections	1%
Unknown	13%

Reasons for Prior Restraint. Concerning the third research question, we found that advisers were more likely to have rejected stories or editorials in the previous 12 months because they were not fair and balanced. They were next-most-likely to have rejected stories because they might embarrass students or invade their privacy, because of a controversial topic, or because the story had attacked a teacher. Having a possible legal problem was least likely to be a reason for rejecting a story. (See Table 10.5.)

Table 10.5: Reasons Why Advisers Had Rejected Newspaper Content (1990)

Not Fair or Balanced	37%
Embarrassing or Invaded Privacy	23%
Too Controversial	19%
An Attack against a Teacher	17%
Possible Legal Problems	7%

Advisers also were more likely to report multiple story rejections because of lack of fairness and balance. About one-fourth of all advisers reported rejecting stories for that reason between two and five times. Fewer than 3 percent of advisers reported more than five rejections in the previous year for any single reason.

Self-Censorship. In regard to our fourth research question, most advisers said that self-censorship had not increased. (We use the term self-censorship to mean that students hold back from writing some stories because they do not think they would be published.) Just under one-third of the advisers said that student journalists were less likely to write about controversial subjects. Most advisers stated that students had been about as likely to write about such subjects, and a few stated that students had been more likely to do so. (See Table 10.6.)

Table 10.6: How Likely Students Were to Have Written about Controversial Subjects since *Hazelwood,* According to Advisers (1990)

Much Less Likely to Write about Such Subjects	10%
Somewhat Less Likely to Write about Such Subjects	20%
About as Likely to Write about Such Subjects	63%
Somewhat More Likely to Write about Such Subjects	6%
Much More Likely to Write about Such Subjects	1%

Changes in Content. The fifth research question concerned whether newspapers were more likely to contain stories that were fair and balanced after *Hazelwood.* The Supreme Court had said that students could be held to a higher standard than was expected of professionals. If *Hazelwood*-type controls on the student press were necessary because unfair and biased stories were being printed, it seemed likely that stories would be more fair and balanced after the ruling. Few advisers thought that much change in fairness and balance of stories had taken place, however. (See Table 10.7.)

Table 10.7: Change in Fairness and Balance of Stories (1990)

	Stories	Editorials
More Fair and Balanced	6%	9%
Less Fair and Balanced	4%	2%
Can't Tell Much of a Difference	51%	53%
Don't Know	39%	36%

Controversial Subject Matter. The sixth research question concerned whether newspapers were less likely to contain stories about controversial topics following *Hazelwood*. Of the five types of potentially controversial story topics listed, most newspapers had run stories about alcohol or drug abuse. Just over half had run stories about teen-age sexuality, and slightly under half of the newspapers had run stories about AIDS. A small minority had run stories about divorce. (See Table 10.8.)

Table 10.8: Percent of Newspapers to Cover Various Types of Potentially Controversial Topics in the Previous 12 Months (1990)

Stories That Concerned Alcohol Abuse	73%
Stories That Concerned Drug Abuse	71%
Stories That Concerned Teen-Age Sexuality	54%
Stories That Concerned AIDS	44%
Stories That Concerned Divorce and Broken Homes	21%

Cause of Student/Adviser Conflict. The seventh research question concerned what the biggest causes of conflict were between the advisers and student journalists. Of the five choices provided, advisers were most likely to report that stories that were not fair or well-balanced were the greatest cause of conflict. About one-fifth of the advisers thought that stories that invaded privacy or embarrassed students had caused the most conflict. Stories that contained potential libel, stories that attacked a teacher, and stories that had obscenities or dirty language were at the bottom of the list. (See Table 10.9.)

Table 10.9: Cause of Most Student-Adviser Conflict, According to Advisers (1990)

Stories That Were Not Fair or Well-Balanced	55%
Stories That Invaded Privacy or Embarrassed Student	20%
Stories That Contained Potential Libel	11%
Stories That Attacked a Teacher	7%
Stories That Had Obscenities or Dirty Language	7%

Important School and Adviser Variables. In our eighth research question, we wanted to know what community/school and adviser characteristics were most related to differences in responses. We analyzed four types of community/school variables and three types of adviser characteristics. Community variables were location (region), community size, school size, and whether journalism courses were offered at the school. Advisers' variables were the number of college Journalism hours the adviser had taken, the number of years the adviser had been teaching Journalism or advising, and whether the adviser had state Journalism certification.

We found that the adviser's years of experience teaching journalism or advising accounted for the greatest overall average variance among respondents for all questions on the survey. It also accounted for the greatest variance for questions concerning the amount of change that had taken place since the *Hazelwood* ruling.

The school's enrollment accounted for the second-greatest overall variance and for the most variance for questions based upon the extent of press freedom at the school. City size ranked third overall for variance. Whether Journalism classes existed at the school ranked only fifth for overall variance, but it contributed the most variance for the questions concerning what advisers saw as the newspaper's purpose and concerning changes in content since the *Hazelwood* decision.

The following are the statistically significant findings when controlling for school/community and adviser characteristics:

Purpose of the Newspaper. Advisers in communities over 10,000 population were significantly more likely than those in smaller communities to state that the main purpose of the newspaper was as a means for student expression. Advisers in communities under 10,000 population, on the other hand, were significantly more likely to state that the purpose was to promote positive things about the school.

Policy on Acceptable Content. Controlling for schools with a policy, advisers in the South were significantly more likely than those in other regions to say that some subject matter was not allowed in the newspaper.

Prior Review. We found that the more teaching and advising experience the teacher had had, the less likely the adviser was to discuss the newspaper's contents with the principal before publication.

Change in Prior Review. The smaller the school, the more likely the adviser was to have submitted the newspaper to the principal before the *Hazelwood* decision and the more likely to have begun doing so after it.

Changing Wording. We found that advisers with less than 10 years of experience were significantly more likely than advisers with more experience to have changed wording over the objections of the editor.

Change in Prior Restraint. We found no differences among advisers with an opinion based upon any independent variables analyzed.

Change in Content. We found no differences among advisers with an opinion based upon any variable analyzed.

Controversial Subject Matter. The larger the school and the more teaching and advising experience the adviser had had, the more likely the newspaper was to have run stories on all types of controversial topics studies. Newspapers at schools in larger communities were more likely to have run stories about teen sexuality, AIDS, and divorce. Newspapers at schools with Journalism classes were more likely to have run stories about drug abuse and teen sexuality. Newspapers at schools with an adviser who had college journalism training were more likely to have run stories on teen sexuality and divorce, and newspapers at schools with advisers who were state-certified were more likely to have run stories on teen sexuality.

Change in Self-Censorship. We found no difference in the amount of change in student self-censorship based upon any variable analyzed.

Cause of Student-Adviser Conflict. Advisers in schools in cities larger than 10,000 were more likely than advisers in smaller schools to have conflicts with students over fairness and balance of stories. Advisers in schools under 10,000 were more likely than advisers in larger schools to have conflicts over invasion of privacy and attacks on teachers.

Advisers at schools at which Journalism classes were offered were significantly more likely than advisers at schools with no Journalism classes to state that stories that were not fair and balanced were the cause of the most conflict with students. Advisers at schools at which no Journalism classes were offered were more likely to state that stories that invaded privacy and stories with dirty language were the cause of most conflict.

Advisers who were state-certified in Journalism were significantly more likely than teachers who were not certified to state that potential libel was the cause of the most conflict with editors.

Conclusions

The survey was designed to answer questions about content changes and changes in the use of prior review and prior restraint by principals and advisers. We concluded from the study that the *Hazelwood* ruling had not made much of an impact on newspaper content or on the amount of prior review and prior restraint taking place. We found differences, however, based upon community, school, and adviser characteristics.

The apparent reason why so little prior restraint was taking place was that most advisers thought of their newspapers as public forums. It appeared that advisers did not find prior restraint necessary very often because they were doing what they were paid to do: advising rather than censoring.

We asked only a few questions about how students were coping with *Hazelwood*. It appeared that they were not doing things much differently, however. We found that advisers thought stories were no more fair and balanced and that the ruling had not resulted in making students less likely to tackle controversial topics.

Two major questions remained after the study. First, were advisers' perceptions about the amount of press freedom at the school the same as student editors' perceptions? Second, despite what advisers said, were students using self-censorship in order to avoid conflicts with their principals and advisers?

PART II. HAVE STUDENT JOURNALISTS BECOME THEIR OWN CENSORS?

Section Highlights

- Student self-censorship is being practiced most at smaller schools, at schools in smaller communities, at schools at which the newspaper is published less often, and at schools where the publications policy was established by the principal.

- Student self-censorship is being practiced least at schools in the West, at schools with a publication policy established by the students or by students and the adviser, and at schools with advisers who belong to journalism education organizations.

- The more experience with high school newspapers they have had and the more college Journalism hours they have taken, the more likely advisers are to think that student editors and reporters are practicing self-censorship.

- Prior restraint is greater at schools that have no public forum policy and at schools whose principal established the publication policy.

Research findings that the *Hazelwood* ruling had had little impact on the public high school press were contrary to what was expected. In addition, anecdotal information seemed to contradict what researchers had found. The Student Press Law Center, for example, reported that the number of calls for assistance had increased dramatically each of the first five years following the ruling. In addition, the American Society of Newspaper Editors reported in 1990 that journalism educators were convinced that student self-censorship was rampant. That anecdotal information caused some researchers to reach the same conclusion.[2]

In other studies following our 1990 research, however, we reached the same conclusion that we did then, that the *Hazelwood* ruling had not had much impact on the freedom of the high school press. For example, in a national study of high school principals and newspaper advisers in 1991, Larry Lain[3] found that a majority of school newspapers had run stories on a variety of controversial topics. Jack Dvorak[4] reported similar results after his national study in 1991. Dvorak found that more than eight of 10 advisers stated that they had "a great deal" or "almost complete" freedom in advising and that only one in 10 advisers stated that students had less freedom of expression because of the *Hazelwood* ruling. Researchers in other studies were to corroborate our findings.

Lorrie Crow (1991)

The first study of both high school principals and student editors was conducted in late 1991 by Lorrie Crow.[5] Crow sent out surveys using some of the questions from our 1990 study and some from Click and Kopenhaver's 1989 survey to principals and student editors at 240 high schools that were members of the Texas Interscholastic League Press Conference. She received responses from 93 editors (39 percent) and 85 principals (35 percent).

Crow found substantial agreement between student editors and principals concerning the extent of prior restraint that had taken place at the school. Table 10.10 reports some of her findings. Most principals and editors reported that no stories had been kept from publication for any reason. When differences existed, editors most often indicated more press freedom than did principals. Principals, however, were less likely than student editors to say that they had changed the words of an editorial or a news story.

Table 10.10: Responses of Texas Principals and Student Editors with an Opinion Concerning Press Freedom at Their Schools (Crow 1992)

	Principals	Editors
In the past 12 months, about how many times has the principal had to change the wording in an editorial or news story? (Principals: N=85; Student editors: N=90)		
Never	57%	41%
5 or fewer times	42%	49%
More than 5 times	1%	10%
In the past 12 months, about how many times has a story been kept from being published because it might embarrass a student or invade his/her privacy? (Principals: N=85; Student editors: N=91)		
Never	81%	80%
5 or fewer times	19%	19%
More than 5 times	0%	1%
In the past 12 months, about how many times has a story been kept from being published because its subject matter was too controversial? (Principals: N=83; Student editors: N=91)		
Never	80%	73%
5 or fewer times	20%	27%
More than 5 times	0%	0%
In the past 12 months, how many times has a story been kept from being published because it was an attack against a teacher? (Principals: N=85; Student editors: N=89)		
Never	99%	96%
5 or fewer times	1%	4%
More than 5 times	0%	0%
In the past 12 months, how many times has the principal suppressed a story from being published? (Principals: N=84; Student editors: N=90)		
Never	77%	72%
5 or fewer times	23%	28%
More than 5 times	0%	0%

	Principals	Editors
Has the principal become more interested in the content of the school newspaper since the *Hazelwood* decision? (Principals: N=74; Student editors: N=70)		
Yes	31%	23%
No	69%	77%

Despite agreement on what had happened at the school, principals and editors responded differently to a variety of opinion questions. Those responses are reported in Table 10.11. Principals and editors did agree on a number of opinion questions, however. For example, most principals and student editors thought that the adviser should review copy before publication, that maintaining discipline was more important than an uncensored press, and it is not censorship for administrators to read copy before publication. On the other hand, most principals said that administrators should have the right to prohibit publication of articles that they think might be harmful, but most student editors disagreed.

Table 10.11: Attitudes toward Student Press Freedom Held by Texas Principals and Student Editors Expressing an Opinion (Crow 1992)

	Principals	Editors
Advisers should review all copy before it is published? (Principals: N=85; Student editors: N=92)		
Agree	100%	91%
Disagree	0%	9%
Maintaining discipline in school is more important than an uncensored school press. (Principals: N=77; Student editors: N=86)		
Agree	86%	59%
Disagree	14%	41%
School administrators should have the right to prohibit publications of articles they think harmful, even though such articles might not be legally libelous, obscene, or disruptive. (Principals: N=85; Student editors: N=90)		
Agree	95%	28%
Disagree	5%	72%

	Principals	Editors
The student newspaper should be allowed to print a story that it can prove to be true even if printing the story will hurt the school's reputation. (Principals: N=84; Student editors: N=92)		
Agree	45%	76%
Disagree	55%	24%
It is more important for the school to function smoothly than for the student newspaper to be free from administrative censorship. (Principals: N=81; Student editors: N=88)		
Agree	78%	43%
Disagree	22%	57%
Newspaper editors sometimes fail to see how the paper can disrupt other aspects of the school. (Principals: N=84; Advisers: N=93)		
Agree	89%	63%
Disagree	11%	37%
Guarantees of freedom of expression in the student newspaper outweigh public relations consideration. (Principals: N=84; Student editors: N=92)		
Agree	25%	63%
Disagree	75%	37%
It is censorship for administrators to read copy before publication. (Principals: N=83; Student editors: N=93)		
Agree	27%	40%
Disagree	73%	60%
Controversial issues have no place in a student newspaper. (Principals: N=81; Student editors: N=93)		
Agree	11%	0%
Disagree	89%	100%

Crow concluded as follows:

> *The survey results indicate that the* Hazelwood *ruling did not "cut off the legs" of the First Amendment as some foresaw. The survey results do implicate [sic], though, that principals are*

still content to let advisers run the show as all agreed, along with the majority of the editors, that advisers should review all copy before it is published. The majority of principals said they reserved the right to prohibit publication of articles they think harmful, nevertheless. Under Hazelwood, *the potential for censorship is there, but the survey shows that principals claim they just haven't used their "rights."[6]*

Kathryn Stofer, 1992

In 1992, Kathryn Stofer studied 119 principals and 93 advisers at Nebraska public and parochial schools. Table 10.12 reports her major findings. She found that principals were significantly more likely than advisers to state that the principal had the final authority over the publication. She also found that principals were more likely than advisers to think that supervision of student publications at the school had increased during the previous five years and that administrators should have the right to prohibit publication of harmful articles. Advisers were more likely to support a state law protecting freedom of expression in public schools.

Table 10.12: Responses of Principals and Advisers at Nebraska Public and Parochial Schools Expressing an Opinion Concerning School Press Freedom (Stofer, 1992)

	Principals	Advisers
Does the adviser read all items before publication? (Principals: N=119; Advisers: N=92)		
Yes	93%	89%
No	7%	11%
Would you support a state law protecting students' freedom of expression? (Principals: N=101; Advisers:N=83)		
Yes	28%	75%
No	72%	25%
A student newspaper is more an educational tool than an outlet for the open expression of student opinion. (Principals: N=99; Advisers: N=79)		
Yes	81%	70%
No	19%	30%

	Principals	Advisers
It is the adviser's job to review all copy before it is printed. (Principals: N=115; Advisers: N=87)		
Yes	95%	92%
No	5%	8%
Student journalists are more likely to initiate stories about controversial topics than they were 10 years ago. (Principals: N=100; Advisers: N=76)		
Yes	71%	76%
No	29%	24%
School administrators should have the right to prohibit publication of any article they think harmful to the reputation of the school even if it is not obscene, libelous or disruptive. (Principals: N=106; Advisers: N=84)		
Yes	68%	32%
No	32%	68%
Supervision of the student publications in my school has increased in the last five years. (Principals: N=81; Advisers: N=69)		
Yes	40%	28%
No	60%	72%
The adviser should correct spelling errors in students' copy. (Principals: N=109; Advisers: N=86)		
Yes	78%	74%
No	22%	26%
School should have written policies defining student publications and students' freedom of expression in those publications. (Principals: N=95; Advisers: N=80)		
Yes	86%	85%
No	14%	15%
If responsibility for the newspaper is part of the adviser's job description, the adviser is not censoring students' freedom of expression by reading and editing their stories before publication. (Principals: N= 101; Advisers: N=83)		
Yes	86%	88%
No	14%	12%

Who has final authority on what may be published in your school newspaper?	Principals	Advisers
Principal	39%	21%
Adviser	15%	45%
Superintendent	20%	13%
Board of education	14%	6%
Principal and adviser	4%	8%
Other combination	8%	6%
Student editors	0%	1%

Most principals and advisers thought that it is the adviser's job to review all copy before publication, that advisers are not censoring when they read and edit student stories before publication, and that schools should have written policies defining press freedom. Most principals and advisers thought that student journalists were more likely to initiate stories about controversial topics than they were 10 years earlier and that the student newspaper is an educational tool more than an outlet for student expression. Stofer concluded the following from her study:

> The results of the study seem to suggest that there is some lack of communication between principals and advisers with regard to the assignment of responsibility for tasks such as proofreading and for actions such as determining when it is appropriate to consult higher authority. There is also a discrepancy between the perceptions of principals and advisers as to who is the final authority on what may be published.[8]

Stofer concluded that those uncertainties might be lessened if more schools had written guidelines covering the duties and responsibilities of administrators and students.

Self-Censorship and the Student Press

Most studies of school press freedom from the 1960s through 1992 looked at prior review and prior restraint. Only a few looked at self-censorship. The problem with early studies, Nicholas Kristof noted as early as 1983, was that researchers "focused exclusively on incidents where the principal or adviser forbade publication of an article and ignored intimidation and pressures that coerced the students themselves into altering or suppressing articles."[9]

Some researchers assumed that self-censorship had increased because of the *Hazelwood* ruling. Soon after the ruling, Kay Phillips suggested—much as the Kennedy Commission had—that considerable self-censorship was evident in all North Carolina high schools. She wrote:

> *In all schools, advisers exert subtle pressure and, in practice, most of them are censors by the definition applied in this study: both cutting controversial material and instituting a policy or atmosphere of intimidation that causes students to refrain from printing certain materials in the school newspaper. Clearly, persistent student editor deference to such authority has a stultifying effect on the student press.*[10]

In his study of school press freedom for the American Society of Newspaper Editors, David Zweifel also proposed that student journalists were using self-censorship and were avoiding a variety of controversial topics. He wrote:

> *A significant number of high school journalism educators are convinced that the U.S. Supreme Court's* Hazelwood v. Kuhlmeier *decision has turned too many high school newspaper staff members and their advisers into journalistic wimps.*[11]

He concluded that the biggest change in the secondary school press since the *Hazelwood* decision was in the newspaper's content. He noted that observers of high school journalism had concluded that "student staff members and their advisers are steering away from tackling controversies." Mark Goodman, executive director of the Student Press Law Center in Washington, D.C., told Zweifel that he felt not only that more censorship was taking place because of the *Hazelwood* decision, but also that "the biggest negative that has come out of *Hazelwood* is self-censorship."[12]

The position expressed by Kristof, Zweifel, and Goodman also was expressed by Olaye and Malandrino in 1992. They determined from anecdotal information that "publication content has suffered because advisers and students have been scared away from tackling controversial issues" and that "many publications have been restrained from covering issues of importance, controversy and interest to the school community."[13]

One reason censorship—and presumably self-censorship—was thought to have increased was a dramatic increase in the number of requests for help received by the Student Press Law Center. The center reported that the number of calls concerning threats of censorship or actual censorship increased each year from 1988 through 1992.[14] After receiving 548 requests for assistance in 1988, the number of requests rose to 615 in 1989, to 929 in 1990, to 1,376 in 1991. The total dropped slightly in 1992 to 1,364.

We wondered why the number of student complaints received by the Student Press Law Center were increasing at a time when studies indicated that the amount of censorship had not increased following the *Hazelwood* decision. (A reporting system implemented by the Student Press Law Center later in 1992 allowed the organization to track complaints. The SPLC determined that public high school students accounted for only 21 percent of the calls in 1992. Censorship-related calls accounted for 27 percent of all calls.)

We thought that the increase in student calls might be because the *Hazelwood* ruling had increased students' awareness of their loss of First Amendment rights. We also thought that the Student Press Law Center probably had gained greater visibility because of the ruling and because of the efforts of its executive director to spread the word about the law center's mission at national meetings of student journalists.

In addition to questions about the increase in student calls to the SPLC, we wondered how much self-censorship was taking place. If students were using self-censorship, we wanted to know whether student journalists were staying away from controversial issues because they did not think those issues belonged in the newspaper, because they doubted they would be printed if written, or because they were pressured by advisers to stay away from controversial issues. We also wanted to know to what extent publication policies were providing protection for student journalists after *Hazelwood*.

National studies since the *Hazelwood* ruling had been limited either to advisers or to principals and advisers, and researchers tended to look at prior review and prior restraint instead of at adviser pressure on students and student self-censorship. The only statewide study of student editors, Lorrie Crow's study in Texas, was not available until after our study was conducted. Because we wanted to confirm the conclusion from what advisers had told us in 1990 that self-censorship was not a major problem, we decided to undertake another study. Like the 1990 study, the 1992 survey was supported by a grant from Southwest Missouri State University, and the university's Office of Academic Computing provided additional assistance.

The sample, which consisted of 1,040 high schools, was randomly drawn from a list of all public high schools in the country. In April 1992, a cover letter, a 32-question survey addressed to the Student Newspaper Editor, and a self-addressed business reply envelope were sent to each school in the sample. A follow-up mailing was sent three weeks later.

A total of 426 surveys were returned (41 percent). Of that number, 323 were from student editors and were analyzed. A total of 103 returned surveys were from schools with no newspaper or were not usable and were not analyzed in this study.

In early May, 35-question surveys addressed to the Student Newspaper Adviser were sent to the same sample of 1,040 schools. A total of 387 surveys were returned (37 percent). Of that number, 270 were from advisers and were analyzed. A total of 117 were from schools with no newspaper or were otherwise unusable and were not analyzed.

We determined that some researchers after *Hazelwood* reported considerable censorship was taking place because their definition of the term differed from the definition other researchers were using. Indeed, a problem with the analysis of much previous research resulted because few researchers before 1990 defined "censorship" on their questionnaires, and their stated definitions of censorship varied considerably.

While the term most often was used by researchers in the 1960s and 1970s to mean "prior restraint," some researchers in the 1980s began using a broader definition. Some defined it as "any official interference by intimidation or coercion with student control of the newspaper" or "any official interference with student control of the newspaper"—whether by principal or adviser. Some researchers considered any prior review by the adviser or the principal to be censorship. Moreover, some researchers considered it censorship if the adviser fixed spelling errors or corrected errors of fact.

To avoid such confusion, we looked at several aspects of censorship and self-censorship: principal and adviser prior review and prior restraint, adviser pressure, and student intimidation, deference and self-restraint. We proposed two overall research questions:

1. Do student editors and advisers think that self-censorship and censorship are taking place at public high school newspapers very often and that school newspapers are avoiding important or controversial issues?

2. Are community/school, newspaper, or adviser/student characteristics most closely related to differences in the amount of self-censorship and newspaper censorship reported at public high schools?

We analyzed three community/school characteristics (region of the country, community size, and school size) and five newspaper characteristics (whether the newspaper was a credit or non-credit class, how often the newspaper was published, presence of a school publication policy, type of publication policy, and source of the publication policy).

We analyzed advisers' responses based upon four individual characteristics: gender, number of college journalism hours, years of journalism advising experience, and membership in journalism organizations. We analyzed students' responses based upon one individual characteristic—gender.

To help determine the reliability of the samples, advisers and student editors responding were compared to each other and to advisers in the sample we obtained in our 1990 study of advisers. We found no statistically significant difference between respondents in our 1990 survey and respondents in the two 1992 surveys based upon community or school size or region of the country.

We found no statistically significant difference between the 1992 editor and adviser samples based upon seven of the independent variables investigated: community size, enrollment, region of the country, whether the newspaper was part of a class or not, frequency of publication, whether a written publication policy existed, and the content of the school policy.

The largest number of schools in the sample had fewer than 500 students and were located in communities with under 10,000 population. Schools were most likely to be located either in the South or Central states. (See Graph 10.8.)

Graph 10.8

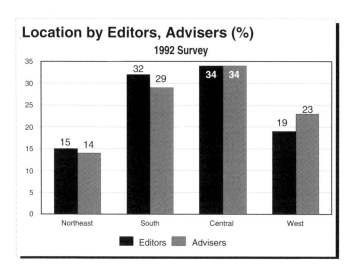

Just over half of the newspapers represented in the sample were printed once a month. (See Graph 10.9.) Most advisers and editors thought their school had an open-forum publications policy—open either to all student speech or to all student speech that is not libelous or obscene and doesn't advocate violence. (See Graph 10.10.). In most cases, the highest level of approval for the publications policy was either the adviser or the principal. (See Graph 10.11.)

Graph 10.9

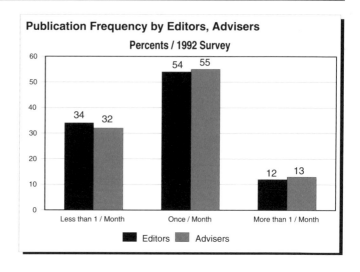

Publication Frequency by Editors, Advisers

Percents / 1992 Survey

Graph 10.10

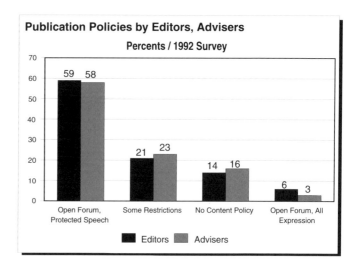

Publication Policies by Editors, Advisers

Percents / 1992 Survey

Graph 10.11

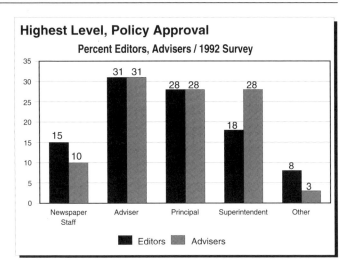

The only statistically significant difference between the advisers and student editors for any variable studied concerned the source of the publication policy. Student editors were more likely than advisers to think that students were the source of the policy; however, that difference likely can be attributed to students' misconceptions about policies put into effect in previous years.

Purpose of the Newspaper. Both advisers and editors listed "a means for student expression" as the most important purpose of the school newspaper. Advisers ranked "a means for journalism students to learn skills" second in importance and "a means for reporting good and bad things about the school" fourth. Student editors reversed the two rankings. Both advisers and editors ranked "a means for publicizing school events/activities" third.

Agreement with *Hazelwood*. As Table 10.13 shows, editors were more likely than advisers to disagree with the *Hazelwood* ruling, though slightly more editors than advisers did not have an opinion. Of respondents with an opinion, 81 percent of editors and 69 percent of advisers disagreed with the ruling, also a statistically significant difference.

Table 10.13: Advisers' and Editors' Opinion of the *Hazelwood* Ruling (1992)

Do you agree with the Supreme Court's *Hazelwood* ruling that gave the school board and the principal the right to control the content of student publications that are not public forums?

	Editors	Advisers
No	70%	62%
Yes	16%	27%
No strong opinion	14%	11%

(Cramer's V = .137, significant at .01 level of confidence.)

Censorship and Self-Censorship. We concluded that the answer to the first research question ["Do student editors and advisers think that self-censorship and censorship are taking place at public high school newspapers very often and that school newspapers are avoiding important or controversial issues?"] is "No." While we found some censorship and self-censorship, neither was taking place very often and neither appeared to keep most newspapers from covering important or controversial issues.

Table 10.14 compares editors' and advisers' responses to questions about principal and adviser prior review and prior restraint. Responses by both advisers and editors indicated that most advisers looked at the newspaper before publication, but most principals did not. Despite the use of prior review, prior restraint had been used in only a minority of schools surveyed, and at most schools it had not been used often.

Table 10.14: Comparison of Editors' and Advisers' Responses to Survey Questions Concerning Prior Review and Prior Restraint (1992)

	Editors	Advisers
PRIOR REVIEW		
Does the adviser read the contents of the newspaper before it is published? (Editors: N = 323; Advisers: N = 267)		
Never/a few times	5%	5%
Fairly/quite often	13%	6%
Always	82%	89%
(Cramer's V = .112, significant at .05 level of confidence)		
Does the principal read the contents of the newspaper before it is published? (Editors: N = 323; Advisers: N = 263)		
Never	62%	64%
A few times	21%	22%
Fairly often/quite often/always	17%	14%
(Cramer's V = .041, not significant at .05 level of confidence)		
PRIOR RESTRAINT		
Has the adviser told the editor he/she couldn't run a particular editorial? (Editors: N = 316; Advisers: N = 263)		
No	79%	73%
Yes	21%	27%
(Cramer's V = .072, not significant at .05 level of confidence)		
Has the adviser withheld an editorial from publication or required that it be substantially rewritten (other than for style and grammar mistakes or factual errors) because of the subject matter? (Editors: N = 320; Advisers: N = 264)		
No	63%	65%
Yes	37%	35%
(Cramer's V = .017, not significant at .05 level of confidence)		

	Editors	Advisers
Has the adviser told the editor he/she couldn't run a particular story? (Editors: N = 314; Advisers: N = 263)		
No	64%	70%
Yes	36%	30%
(Cramer's V = .056, not significant at .05 level of confidence)		
Has the adviser changed copy without telling the editor he/she was going to do so? (Editors: N = 315; Advisers: N = 265)		
No	76%	71%
Yes	24%	29%
(Cramer's V = .055, not significant at .05 level of confidence)		
Has the adviser withheld a news story from publication or required that it be substantially rewritten (other than for style and grammar mistakes or factual errors) because of the subject matter? (Editors: N = 317; Advisers: N = 262)		
No	74%	65%
Yes	26%	35%
(Cramer's V = .108, significant at .01 level of confidence)		
Has the adviser rejected advertising because of the subject matter? (Editors: N = 269; Advisers: N = 208)		
No	83%	67%
Yes	17%	33%
(Cramer's V = .186, significant at .001 level of confidence)		
Has the principal ever told the adviser or the editor that a story or editorial couldn't run or would have to be changed before it could run? (Editors: N = 318; Advisers: N = 262)		
No	66%	63%
Yes	34%	37%
(Cramer's V = .035, not significant at .05 level of confidence)		

In most schools, the adviser had not told the editor to withhold a story or an editorial and the adviser had not actually withheld a story or an editorial or rejected an advertisement because of subject matter. In addition, only a minority of advisers had changed copy without telling the editor. Moreover, the principal at most schools had not told the student editor or adviser that a story or editorial could not run or would have to be changed before it could run.

The difference between responses of advisers and student editors was statistically significant on three of nine questions about prior review and prior restraint: whether the adviser read the newspaper before publication, whether the adviser had withheld a story because of the topic and whether the adviser had rejected an ad because of topic. In all three cases, student editors were significantly less likely than advisers to indicate prior review or prior restraint had taken place. Thus, similar to what Crow found in Texas about student editors and principals, we found that student editors reported more freedom existed than did the advisers.

Table 10.15 compares students editors' and advisers' responses to questions concerning three things that likely would be involved in a student editor's decision not to publish particular articles or editorials: the amount of pressure applied, the extent to which the student editor felt intimidated, and the amount of deference the editor felt toward the adviser.

Table 10.15: Comparison of Editors' and Advisers' Responses to Survey Questions Concerning Pressure, Intimidation, and Deference (1992)

	Editors	Advisers
How much has the adviser stressed to the editor that stories about controversial subjects should not go into the newspaper? (Editors: N = 320; Advisers: N = 266)		
Not at all	45%	49%
Not much	40%	43%
Fairly much/quite a bit	15%	8%
(Cramer's V = .112, significant at .05 level of confidence)		

	Editors	Advisers
Has the adviser suggested that editor not publish an editorial because it was too controversial (without actually telling editor not to run it)? (Editors: N = 317; Advisers: N = 262)		
Never	67%	64%
A few times	31%	35%
Fairly/quite often	2%	1%

(Cramer's V = .032, not significant at .05 level of confidence)

	Editors	Advisers
Has the adviser suggested that editor not publish a story because it was too controversial (without actually telling editor not to run it)? (Editors: N = 316; Advisers: N = 263)		
No	66%	65%
A few times	33%	34%
Fairly/quite often	1%	1%

(Cramer's V = .005, not significant at .05 level of confidence)

	Editors	Advisers
Would the editor get into trouble with adviser or with school official for wanting to print something about a controversial topic? (Editors: N = 329; Advisers: N = 262)		
Yes, with adviser, and maybe with school officials	12%	12%
Yes, with school officials, but not adviser	39%	28%
No	49%	60%

(Cramer's V = .119, significant at .05 level of confidence)

	Editors	Advisers
When deciding whether to assign or use a story, how important is it to the editor whether the adviser will find it objectionable? (Editors: N = 318; Advisers: N = 263)		
Not important or not very important	32%	28%
Fairly important	47%	48%
Very Important	21%	24%

(Cramer's V = .053, not significant at .05 level of confidence)

	Editors	Advisers
How much does the adviser worry that the newspaper might include controversial stories? (Editors: N = 320; Advisers: N = 268)		
Not at all	21%	28%
Not much	51%	63%
Fairly much/quite a bit	28%	9%

(Cramer's V = .250, significant at .001 level of confidence)

Only a small percent of advisers and student editors reported pressure by the adviser. In about half the schools, advisers had stressed to some extent that controversial subject matter should not go into the newspaper, but at few schools was it stressed much. The adviser at a minority of schools had suggested that an editorial or story be withheld because it might be too controversial, and it did not happen often at many schools.

A considerable amount of intimidation was reported by student editors. About half of the editors stated that they would get into trouble if they wanted to print something about a controversial topic, but most of them thought the problem would be with school officials and not with the adviser.

Most student editors stated that it was important to them whether the adviser would find a story to be objectionable, an indication of deference. Most advisers, however, stated that they did not worry much that the newspaper might include controversial stories.

Response of advisers and editors to three questions were significantly different. For all three questions, editors were more likely than advisers to worry about controversial contents. Advisers were significantly less likely than editors to state that the adviser had stressed that stories about controversial subject should not go into the newspaper. Advisers also were significantly less likely to worry that the newspaper might include controversial stories than students thought was the case and were less likely than editors to state that the editor would get into trouble if the editor wanted to print something about a controversial topic.

Table 10.16 shows results of questions about students' actual use of self-restraint. Most advisers and editors stated that student reporters did not often hold off on controversial topics because they might be seen as objectionable by the adviser. Only a minority of editors had withheld a controversial story or editorial because they thought the topic was too controversial and few advisers or editors stated that the newspaper had failed to run important stories very often because editors thought they would not be allowed to print them. No statistically significant disagreement was found between advisers and editors concerning the amount of self-restraint being used.

Table 10.16: Comparison of Editors' and Advisers' Responses to Survey Questions concerning Self-Restraint (1992)

	Editors	Advisers
Do student reporters hold off from doing stories about potentially controversial subjects because such stories might be seen as objectionable by the adviser? (Editors: N = 319; Advisers: N = 262)		
Never	40%	35%
Once in a while	50%	55%
Fairly often/quite often	10%	10%
(Cramer's V = .050, not significant at .05 level of confidence)		
Has the editor withheld an editorial from publication because he/she thought the topic was too controversial? (Editors: N = 318; Advisers: N = 245)		
Never	76%	73%
A few times	23%	24%
Fairly/quite often	1%	3%
(Cramer's V = .034, not significant at .05 level of confidence)		

	Editors	Advisers
Has the editor withheld a story from publication because he/she thought the topic was too controversial? (Editors: N = 319; Advisers: N = 259)		
Never	79%	74%
A few times	20%	25%
Fairly/quite often	1%	1%
(Cramer's V = .065, not significant at .05 level of confidence)		
Has the newspaper failed to run important stories because editor didn't think he/she would be allowed to print them? (Editors: N = 320; Advisers: N = 266)		
Never	60%	58%
A few times	35%	38%
Fairly/quite often	5%	4%
(Cramer's V = .045, not significant at .05 level of confidence)		

Editors and advisers agreed about the type of subject matter that would cause the most conflict. For both groups of respondents, stories about sex ranked as being the most likely cause of problems between the editor and adviser, with stories about birth control and abortion ranking second and stories about drugs ranking third. According to editors, stories about divorce ranked fourth and stories about political issues ranked last. Advisers ranked political issues fourth and divorce last.

Even though they were asked only to rank the topics according to the amount of conflict they would cause, a number of the student editors and advisers reported stories on none of those topics would likely cause problems. Both student editors and advisers ranked stories with potential libel, stories that invaded privacy or embarrassed students, stories that were not fair or well-balanced or attacked someone, and stories that were poorly written or were not accurate as more likely to cause problems than stories about controversial subjects. Thus, journalistic issues were more likely than subject matter to be a source of conflict.

Differences between Respondents. The second research question was: "Are community/school, newspaper, or adviser/student characteristics most closely related to differences in the amount of self-censorship and newspaper censorship reported at public high schools?" (To answer the question, mean Cramer's V scores were calculated for independent variables based upon responses to questions concerning aspects of censorship and self-censorship. The higher the V score, the greater the difference in responses when controlling for that variable.)

For student editors, the highest mean V score was for source of publication policy, followed by type of policy, region of the country, school size, how often the newspaper was published, community size, whether class credit was given for being on the newspaper staff, and gender. For advisers, the highest mean V score was for type of policy, followed by source of policy, region, the number of professional organizations to which the adviser belonged, the amount of advising experience the adviser had had, school size, the number of college hours in journalism the adviser had had, community size, how often the newspaper was published, gender, and whether class credit was given for being on the newspaper staff.

Discussion here will refer only to independent variables found to be most significant: editors' responses when controlling for type and source of publications policy and advisers' responses when controlling for adviser characteristics other than gender. Gender was not statistically significant for any question, and school/community characteristics are not things that can be changed easily if at all.

Editors who stated that their school had a policy that the newspaper could not cover some subject matter were much more likely to state that they would get into trouble for running controversial stories and that the newspaper had failed to run important stories.

Editors at schools with restrictive policies were more likely to have withheld an editorial because the topic was controversial, to have been given a suggestion by the adviser that a story should not be published because it was too controversial, and to have had a news story withheld or required to be rewritten because of subject matter. The principal also was more likely to have told the editor or adviser at those schools that a story or editorial could not run or would have to be changed before it did run.

Type of publications policy did not make a difference in regard to whether the adviser read the newspaper before publication, whether the editor had withheld a controversial story from publication, whether the adviser had told the editor not to run a story, whether the adviser had changed copy without telling the editor, or whether the adviser had rejected advertising. In all those situations, very few editors reported self-censorship or censorship, and nearly all editors reported prior review.

Editors at schools with a publications policy established by the principal reported considerably more censorship and self-censorship than editors at schools with a policy established by someone other than the principal. For example, editors at schools at which the principal established the policy were most likely to think that they would get into trouble for wanting to print something controversial and that the newspaper had failed to run important stories because they might not be printed. The principals at those schools also were more likely to read the newspaper before it was published and were more likely to have said that a story or editorial could not be run or would have to be changed before it could run.

Editors at schools having a policy established by the principal, superintendent, or school board were more likely to state that the adviser had suggested that the editor not publish an editorial because it was too controversial.

In most cases, having a policy established by the adviser meant more press freedom than having one established by the principal. In some cases, however, that was not the case. Editors at schools having a policy set by the adviser as well as having one set by the principal meant that editors were more likely to state that reporters held off from doing stories because the adviser might see them as objectionable. Such editors also were more likely to state that the adviser had told the editor not to run a story and that the adviser worried that the newspaper might include controversial stories.

Three adviser characteristics were related to greater disagreement with the *Hazelwood* ruling: having taken more than six hours of college journalism classes, having more than five years of advising experience, and belonging to one or more journalism professional organizations. Advisers with those characteristics, however, were not always more likely to take a hands-off role with the newspaper.

The more advising experience the adviser had had, for example, the more likely the adviser was to have suggested that the editor not publish a story because it was too controversial, to have withheld a story because it was too controversial, and to have rejected an advertisement.

Advisers who had taken more college hours in journalism were more likely to state that student reporters held off from doing controversial stories because the adviser might object and to state that the editor had withheld a controversial story. In addition, the adviser was more likely to have rejected an advertisement because of subject matter.

Advisers who belonged to more than one journalism professional organization, on the other hand, were more likely to state that their editors would not get into trouble for wanting to print something controversial. Advisers with memberships in more than one journalism organization were less likely to think that it was important to the student editor whether the adviser would find a story to be objectionable and were less likely to have stressed to the editor that stories about controversial subjects should not go into the newspaper.

The more advising experience the adviser had had, the less likely the principal was to look at the newspaper before publication; however, the amount of college journalism credit and membership in journalism professional organizations were not statistically significant for that question.

Conclusions from Post-*Hazelwood* Studies

We undertook our 1990 and 1992 studies to determine whether the impact of the *Hazelwood* decision was as great as feared. Not only did advisers in the two studies agree the extent of censorship and self-censorship taking place was less than expected, but student editors agreed with advisers in nearly every instance.

Possibly the most important finding in the 1990 study was that nearly two-thirds of advisers stated that their newspaper had an open forum policy despite the *Hazelwood* ruling. The 1992 study found that almost the same percent of advisers and exactly the same percent of student editors said the same thing.

Ours and other studies found that the *Hazelwood* ruling had not caused many advisers to make more use of prior restraint than was the case before the ruling. Both our 1990 and 1992 studies found that most public high school newspapers were running a variety of stories about controversial topics. The 1992 study found that most editors were somewhat deferential to the adviser; however, editors and advisers agreed that only limited self-censorship was being practiced and that most newspapers had not failed to run important stories because of self-censorship. We found that the Supreme Court in *Hazelwood* only confirmed what most principals had thought—that they were the publisher of the newspaper and were responsible only to the superintendent and school board. We also found, however, that they did not ordinarily exercise that power.

Post-*Hazelwood* studies have shown what pre-*Hazelwood* studies had—that what principals want most is a responsible press, according to their definition of the term. It was not until the *Hazelwood* decision, however, that school administrators legally were given the power to enforce responsibility, unless they voluntarily give up that right. Supporters of the student press, of course, don't object to responsible journalism. They only object to school administrators having the right to enforce it.

The Supreme Court's solution to the conflict between administrators' right to determine what is appropriate speech at the school and student journalists' right to be free from governmental interference was to state that student newspapers are not public forums unless school officials say that they are. According to the Court, if school officials do not create forums, they are no more using censorship than the publisher of a newspaper is. That is also the position that many newspaper editors took when the *Hazelwood* decision was announced.

Our studies and others have shown that principals are not often using prior review or prior restraint. Most principals allow the adviser to oversee the student newspaper, but they expect to be notified of any potentially objectionable content. What advisers have done in most cases is to carry out the role of editor-in-chief by nearly always reading copy, advising student journalists about what is appropriate content, and sometimes changing copy if suggestion does not work.

In carrying out their perceived role, newspaper advisers have tended to use suggestion and the authority of their position to promote what they see as good and responsible journalism. Advisers try to steer student journalists away from potential problem areas, such as libel or privacy invasion, and sometimes are using prior restraint if that does not work. Thus, major conflict with student editors does not take place often.

PART III. SCHOOL PRESS FREEDOM IN THE 1990s

Section Highlights

- Directors of Scholastic Press Associations tend to think that journalism advisers and teachers are not adequately prepared to advise student publications and that student journalists need supervision in exercising their First Amendment rights.

- Press association directors are more likely than principals and advisers to think that the *Hazelwood* decision has had a negative effect on the secondary school press.

- Journalism education organizations state that prior review by advisers is advisable, but that prior review by administrators is not.

- Publications policies and publication boards help provide the student newspaper protection against prior restraint.

- State law can give more rights to the student press than the First Amendment.

Several advisers and editors responding to our 1992 surveys wrote about situations concerning press freedom at their schools. One incident, explained by an anonymous student editor, mentioned an incident involving a letter to the editor:

While our adviser does not find many controversial topics in need of censorship, our administration does at times. Just recently, for the first time, our administration found it necessary to censor a letter to the editor. The article was written by a student about the way the school's guidance counselors and some teachers seemed to show favoritism towards football players and lack of concern for other students.

No names were mentioned, but our principal found it necessary to censor because he thought since our paper gets into the community it would jeopardize their jobs and in his opinion it was untrue. He agreed to cross out what he did not like, and when he was through, there was no story left. We were also told that if we wrote the word "censor(ed)" where the article should have been, our paper would not be distributed.

Before the incident, our adviser did not mind printing controversial subjects. She is now more cautious. We may still write on controversial topics and so far all the rest have been printed without problems, although now our principal must read and check through our paper before it goes to the printer.

The letter did run, but with blank lines left where the deleted material would have been located. The next week, the newspaper interviewed students, asking the question: "Should school administrators censor student publications?"

A student editor from Vermont gave the following account of the situation at her school:

As editor of a newspaper at a fairly liberal school, I feel less pressure from the administrators and other school officials than most students in my position. Only the advisers see the newspaper before it is printed. They both support and encourage objective stories about controversial subjects.

However, as a reporter, I have felt that I am sometimes advised how to write my stories. When interviewing the principal and associate principal, I feel that they are almost trying to peek at what I am writing down. The principal has also tried literally to 'advise' me about my story angle.

While investigating a school break-in, the principal told me to try to report on more 'positive' issues next time. Janitors that I questioned declined to comment, saying it wasn't their job to speak for the school. I suspect that the janitors reacted so defensively because of a past incident in which they were threatened by the administration.

This indirect administrative censoring has also occurred through my advisers. After an unfavorable and revealing story was printed about a specific department, my advisers received several letters advising them to discourage this type of story. I think this story was well-written and objective.

In a recent incident, a poorly written story received direct reaction from administrators, in the form of letters to the editor. I was glad to see this open criticism rather than indirect pressure. However, I still suspect that administrators will try to do some indirect 'advising.'

Overall I feel lucky to be editing such an uncensored newspaper. Despite Supreme Court decisions like Tinker, school administrators contrive to control student expression." — R.H.

An anonymous adviser gave the following comments of his/her experiences:

We are in a fairly liberal inner city school. We have covered such issues as drunk driving, adoption, alcoholism, drug abuse, pro/con Desert Storm, child labor, etc. I do require the issues be well-researched and interviews included. Both sides should be presented — an editorial may accompany the article. If the principal does not like an article, he gives me the Big Chill for weeks; however, he is generally liberal.

I have been teaching for 20 1/2 years. I do not need my life to have more problems than it already has. Therefore, I stress the above requirements. I will be at the school long after these students (God willing). I don't want problems. No student has challenged me, ever. If this doesn't qualify me for Journalism Adviser of the Year, so be it.

What Student Newspapers Are Publishing

Several advisers and editors responding to our 1992 surveys also sent copies of their newspaper. An example of a school newspaper that tackles a variety of controversial topics is *The Norse Star* at Stoughton Senior High School in Stoughton, WI. The April 3, 1992, edition featured a costumed member of the Ku Klux Klan on the cover. The headline read: "A Kinder, Gentler KKK?" The words "Don't Bet on It" in 8-point type ran repeatedly across the page in the background.

The featured article, "Klan Tries to Revamp Image," analyzed the Klan's attempt to look less undesirable. The student reporter, Brooke Dilocker, went to the headquarters for the Wisconsin Knights of the Ku Klux Klan. Dilocker wrote:

"We are not the Klan of old. We just want to be able to speak and let people know where we're at," says Petersen, the heartbeat of Wisconsin's KKK chapter.

"Petersen and his friend Mike, a member from Madison, emphasize this point often throughout the interview. They want to dispel the idea that they are a lynch mob in bed sheets.

"The Klan is recruiting throughout Wisconsin in their effort to 'bring back' the Knights of the Ku Klux Klan. According to Petersen they've gotten 'a good response' from the residents of Stoughton. In a recent letter to the Stoughton *Courier Hub*, Peterson said, "We will be in Stoughton."

Opinion pages included a point/counterpoint on legalizing narcotics, student responses to the question "Should marijuana be legalized?" a letter to the editor from the KKK's Petersen about how well the interview was conducted, an article with interviews of the four candidates for school board positions, an article on 42 incidents of vandalism of cars in the school parking lot, and a series of articles on women in schools that included sex discrimination, women in sports, and sexism toward female teachers.

The Sept. 25, 1992, issue of the *Norse Star* included students' responses to the question "Do you think that condoms should be passed out in schools?" a column titled "Student Council: What's the

Point?" two points of view about freshman initiation, and a series of articles about the environment, including the top five environmental issues in Wisconsin.

A student news magazine that tackles the issues—local, national, and international—is the *Crest* of O.H. Cooper High School in Abilene, Texas. Its April 24, 1992, issue included three bylined editorials: "Student input should carry weight in teacher evaluation procedure" (which included a graphic for a student opinion survey on the subject), "Equality isn't promoted by double standard for minorities," and "People must wake up to end nightmare of secret racism." The edition also featured a news analysis concerning elections in South Africa, a story about why so few minorities were in gifted classes, and an article about child abuse.

In his article about a double standard for minorities, editor Nick Bell wrote:

> *Even at Cooper High School and in the modern educational community, there are a large number of processes and events that rather [than] eliminating racism, as was their goal, they only promote it.*
>
> *The Hispanic Seniors Banquet is one such example. Recognition of student excellence and encouraging people to stay in school is good, but when you recognize any single race's achievements alone, you only promote racist ideas and qualities, which is not at all the purpose. The purpose is to provide greater equality among the races. But in order to do this, a racially blind policy must be adopted, not one that promotes a single race.*

What Press Association Directors Say about the School Press

Most studies of high school press freedom have looked at principals and advisers, and a few have looked at student editors. In a recent survey, three researchers attempted to find out what press association directors think about student press freedom.

Olson, Van Ommeren, and Rossow (1993)

Lyle Olson, Roger Van Ommeren and Marshel Rossow surveyed 154 directors of state and national scholastic press associations and received responses from 50 percent of them.[15] The responses concerning press freedom are shown in Table 10.17.

Table 10.17: Responses of Scholastic Press Association Directors with an Opinion Concerning Student Press Freedom (Olson, Van Ommeren, and Rossow, 1993)

	Agree	Disagree
The *Hazelwood* decision has had a negative impact on high school journalism. (N=48)	69%	31%
Most high school journalism advisers and teachers in my state are adequately prepared to advise student publications. (N=66)	21%	79%
High School journalists do not have a complete understanding of the legal considerations and ethics of journalism. (N=69)	77%	23%
High school journalists should be given the freedom to report on any issue without supervision. (N=71)	31%	69%
High school journalists should exercise First Amendment rights on their publications only with the supervision of their advisers. (N= 63)	65%	35%
High school journalism adviser should review all copy before it is printed. (N=67)	76%	24%
It is censorship if a high school journalism adviser forbids publication of an article. (N=67)	87%	13%
It is censorship if a high school administrator forbids the publication of an article. (N=67)	87%	13%
School administrators should be able to prohibit the publication of articles they consider harmful, even though those articles may not be libelous, obscene, or disruptive. (N=73)	5%	95%

Who should exercise control over freedom of expression in high school newspapers?

Students	1st
Teachers/advisers	2nd
Courts	3rd
School administrators	4th
School board	5th
Parents	6th

The directors were much more likely to think that the *Hazelwood* decision had had a negative impact on high school journalism than to think otherwise. Most directors stated that student journalists did not have a "complete understanding" of journalism law and ethics and that journalism advisers and teachers were not adequately prepared to advise student publications.

Almost a third of the directors did not think high school journalists should be free to report on all issues without supervision, and most directors agreed that high school journalists should have the supervision of advisers when exercising their First Amendment rights. Most directors thought that the adviser should review all copy before it is printed, but most directors also agreed that it is censorship for advisers to forbid publication of an article.

Most directors considered it censorship for high school administrators to forbid the publication of an article, though a number of directors disagreed. Most of them also thought that administrators should not be able to prohibit the publication of constitutionally protected material that they consider to be harmful. Directors were most likely to state that students should exercise control over freedom of expression in high school newspapers, followed by teachers/advisers.

Hazelwood's Legacy

What the Supreme Court did in *Hazelwood v. Kuhlmeier* was to erect a series of barriers to prevent faculty and student speech from falling under the First Amendment. The Court said that "school officials may impose reasonable restrictions on the speech of students, teachers, and other members of the school community" if the officials have not "opened school facilities 'for indiscriminate use by the general public,' or by some segment of the public, such as student organizations." The Court stated that:

1. A public forum is not established by inaction or by permitting limited discourse. Instead, it happens only when the school intentionally opens a forum.

2. The First Amendment provides protection only if the censorship "has no valid educational purpose."

3. The school may set standards for a student newspaper that are higher than those demanded in the "real" world.

4. The emotional maturity of students may be taken into account when deciding whether to censor a publication or school play.

5. Schools may restrict "student speech that might reasonably be perceived to advocate drug or alcohol use, irresponsible sex, or conduct otherwise inconsistent with 'the shared values of a civilized social order,' or to associate the school with any position other than neutrality on matters of public controversy."

Potentially the most dangerous legacy of the *Hazelwood* decision is the broad power it gave administrators to suppress not only student speech but also faculty speech. Mike Simpson of the National Education Association's Office of General Counsel noted that it could be argued that a school has more interest in controlling what is said in a classroom or assigned for students to read than what is published in the newspaper. He stated about the implications of the case:

> *Although the case involved censorship of a school-sponsored paper, the Court's broad decision may adversely affect not just student press advisers but all teachers, threatening their ability to expose students to controversial ideas.*[16]

Jack Dvorak and Jon Paul Dilts also stated that *Hazelwood*'s legacy might well be the harm it does to academic freedom more than the harm done to the student press.[17] The two educators noted that whereas courts have not ruled that teachers have a greater right of academic freedom than other public employees or citizens, courts for years have supported a teacher's right to chose appropriate teaching methods, including promoting the classroom as a marketplace of ideas. *Hazelwood*, however, puts academic freedom in doubt. The Court stated that the role of the teacher was to instruct the student in democratic values, not open the student to a variety of opinions. Dvorak and Dilts, however, commented:

> *The distinction is that it is the teaching of a process for exploring and refining ideas, not the fixed doctrines of the*

moment, that is of most value and which most accurately describes the fundamental mission of a teacher.[18]

Dvorak and Dilts recommended that newspaper advisers protect themselves by making sure their actions can be defended as being based upon educationally sound principles.

Another First Amendment expert, Tom Eveslage, suggested that *Hazelwood*'s legacy could include some positive things. He also suggested that advisers take positive steps to ensure press freedom. He wrote:

> *First, push for a stronger journalism curriculum....The Court's mandate for curriculum excellence, along with the Court-imposed liability and responsibility that come with their new role of "publisher" should make administrators recognize the need for quality journalism programs.*

> *Second, establish a tradition of excellence in your program. A traditionally responsible publication with a record of solid reporting on controversial issues could effectively argue that a sudden decision to censor or restrict controversy is unreasonable and educationally unsound.*

> *Third, try to establish the student newspaper as a public forum....If the school board adopts a policy that acknowledges the rights of free expression or the role of the student newspaper as a forum for student ideas, you will be in a better position to oppose unreasonable administrative censorship.*

> *Fourth, broaden your base of support within and outside the school....*

> *Finally, be aware of legislative effort to assist you. The Supreme Court has ruled that states may offer their citizens more protection than the U.S. Constitution does.*[19]

Living with *Hazelwood*

Several means for overcoming the barriers that the Supreme Court set up have been suggested by other First Amendment experts. The Student Press Law Center, for example, gave suggestions to students for fighting censorship. The reasons the SPLC gave students for opposing *Hazelwood* were the same reasons the Supreme Court gave when it authorized censorship: because it "interferes with your ability to produce quality publications and to become well-trained student journalists." The SPLC told student journalists:

1. Don't begin censoring yourself in fear of what might happen at your school.

2. Establish your publication as a forum for student expression by policy.

3. Establish your publication as a forum for student expression by practice.

4. If you are censored, appeal.

5. Use public pressure to your advantage.

6. Call the Student Press Law Center or some other legal authority on student press issues if you are censored.

7. Remember alternative publications.

8. Make a push for legislation in your state to protect student press rights.

The best means for securing student press freedom is by making sure that the newspaper would be seen by the courts to be a public forum. At that point, presumably, the *Tinker v. Des Moines* standards would apply and only those limited *Tinker* barriers would remain. The speech would have to materially and substantially interfere with requirements for appropriate discipline in the operation of the school, and guidelines would have to be in place to ensure that students' First Amendment rights were not taken away.

Under *Hazelwood*, establishing a public forum is not as simple as stating in the newspaper's masthead that it is a public forum. As discussed more fully in Chapter 9, the Supreme Court in the *Hazelwood* case said that school facilities are public forums only if school authorities have "by policy or by practice" opened those facilities "for indiscriminate use by the general public," or for use by a segment of the public, such as student organizations.

The standard was not met by Hazelwood East High School even though the school district's policy stated that free expression within the rules of responsible journalism would not be restricted in student publications. The court concluded that the school board had not made the newspaper a public forum because the policy also stated that the newspaper was part of the school's curriculum. Students' claims that they could publish "practically anything" in the newspaper were dismissed as "not credible." It was clear to the court that the adviser at Hazelwood East had a great deal to say about the contents of the *Spectrum* and that the principal normally reviewed issues before publication.

The Supreme Court's standard for creating a public forum by practice presumably would be met if, for example, all school organizations were allowed free access to a certain amount of space in each issue. It presumably would not be met if only members of the staff or only journalism students were allowed access. It presumably also would not be met even if the newspaper published letters unless every letter was published, thus providing for "indiscriminate use." The Supreme Court did not address whether a limited public forum might exist because it published letters or because the newspaper was partially funded through advertising.

Presumably, a publications policy established by the newspaper staff would not be seen by courts as official, particularly if the adviser or principal normally had any say in the content or used prior review over materials. A policy set by an adviser most likely would not be sufficient to establish a forum unless the principal or school board policy has declared that a public forum does exist.

It appears that some action on the part of the principal or school board to open the publication to use by all students or student organizations or a long history of being opened to everyone would be required. The surest route to a public forum is to establish a school district policy. Law professor Benjamin Sendor noted soon after the *Hazelwood* ruling that educators should review their school systems' policies about what freedom is available for students and faculty members involved in curricular and extracurricular activities. He suggested that policies be much more specific than the vague Hazelwood East High School policy. He stated that policies should limit censorship to "legitimate educational purposes" while allowing for alternatives to censorship. He wrote:

> *In reviewing your school system's policies about student expression in school-sponsored publications and other curricular and extracurricular activities, it is important to understand that the Supreme Court in* Hazelwood *set only maximum bounds for school officials' control over student expression. School board certainly can give students more freedom than allowed by officials in* Hazelwood.[21]

Peter Habermann, Lillian Lodge Kopenhaver, and David Martinson concluded that publications policies can be "post-*Hazelwood* lifesavers." They commented about school district publications policies:

> *Guidelines for student publications, drawn up within a school district to protect press freedom, approved by the school board and enforced by the superintendent's office, may, in the last analysis in this post-*Hazelwood *era, be the best protection for students' First Amendment rights.*[22]

Lillian Lodge Kopenhaver, David L. Martinson, and Peter Habermann wanted to find out how much impact strong publications policies have on press freedom at a school.[23] They sent questionnaires to advisers in 62 public high schools in the four-county Miami metropolitan area and received responses from 40 of them.

The three researchers found that advisers in Dade County, which had a strong publications policy, had a more favorable position regarding school press freedom than did advisers in the other counties on 20 of 25 questions, and differences for 12 of the responses were statistically significant. On none of the questions were advisers in the other counties significantly more likely to give answers that were more favorable toward press freedom. The researchers suspected that the difference was due to the Dade County School Board policy. Thus, they concluded the following:

> *The fact that newspaper advisers in Dade County schools were more supportive of student press rights than advisers in the other three counties is a strong indication that the level of freedom*

enjoyed by high school students will be impacted as much by the attitudes of the school district as a whole as by the individual administrator at a particular school.[24]

Roy Mays and Julie Dodd surveyed advisers who were members of the Florida Scholastic Press Association to find out how many of them were located in school districts with a publications policy. Half of the 83 advisers who responded, representing 27 of 32 Florida school districts represented by the press association, stated that their school district had a written policy on student publications.[25] One-third of them stated no district policy existed, and nearly a fifth did not know or did not answer. Responses are not necessarily representative of the percent of all Florida school districts with policies, however.

The Student Press Law Center has drafted model guidelines for a school publications policy.[26] Guidelines include such things as a statement of policy (stating that students determine content), responsibilities of student journalists, and prohibited materials. The guidelines note that courts have ruled that matter which is obscene to minors, libelous, or likely to cause disruption is not protected speech even without the *Hazelwood* ruling.

An example of a school board policy that does not protect student and faculty rights is the Student Publications Policy for the Ladue, MO, School District—approved in 1970 and revised in 1976 and still in effect following *Hazelwood*. It notes that the publisher of student publications is the Board of Education. The policy states:

> *Final responsibility for the publications is vested in the Board of Education. Although the publications are primarily for the students and the readers, the staffs are finally responsible to the Board of Education and must conduct their work with the understanding that their authority to operate has been provided by the Board of Education, to the Superintendent of Schools, to the school principals, and to the advisers of the publications. With this authority, the staffs accept the responsibility of conducting themselves in such a manner so as not to jeopardize their authority to publish. They are accountable to the advisers of the publications for all activities related to school publications.*

A less-restrictive policy is the one established by the Hazelwood, MO, School Board. That policy, however, was not seen by the Supreme Court to give the newspaper public forum status. The Hazelwood School District's regulations state:

> *School sponsored student publications will not restrict free expression or diverse viewpoints within the rules of responsible journalism. School sponsored publications are developed within the adopted curriculum and its educational implications in regular classroom activities....*
>
> *No material shall be considered suitable for publication in student publications that is commercial, obscene, libelous, defaming to character, advocating racial or religious prejudice, or contributing to the interruption of the educational process.*

In stark contrast to the Ladue School District's restrictive policy and more protective of students' First Amendment rights than the Hazelwood School District's policy are the Rules of the School Board of Dade County (Miami), FL—which were put in place in 1983 and were not changed after the *Hazelwood* ruling. They state:

> *The right of free speech is extended to students through judicial interpretations of the First Amendment to the Constitution. As such, the principal is charged with the authority and responsibility to see that this right is exercised in a manner that is free from arbitrary censorship, compatible with responsible student behavior, and consistent with the needs of the institution.*

The rules also state that:

> *No teacher who advises a student publication will be fired, transferred or removed from the advisership for failure to exercise editorial control over the student publication or to otherwise suppress the rights of free expression of student journalists.*
>
> *No student publication, whether nonschool-sponsored or official, will be reviewed by school administrators prior to distribution.*

While not providing for complete freedom of the press, publications boards allow for public discussion of controversial issues and can insulate the adviser from repercussions from the principal for objectionable content. A well-formulated policy also can provide the student newspaper considerable freedom, particularly if approved by the principal. The following is an example of a typical publications board policy statement:

> *The purpose of the Publications Board of...High School is to advise the various publication staffs, their sponsors, the faculty and the administration when controversy arises or when an adviser feels he or she is too close to a situation and needs input from others....*

> *Advice may be sought on matters of legality or publication consequences or any other time when an adviser feels the need for support from people outside his/her particular staff....*

> *Since the Publications Board is to be advisory in nature, all suggestions should be written and a vote taken to see what the 'majority advises.'...*

> *Under no circumstances is this board to be used as a method of prior restraint nor a means of censorship. Its purpose is to help all controversial situations become learning experiences and to provide support for the adviser and staff in cases of adverse reaction to published works. Members should help the adviser and staff see the various possibilities open to them and possible repercussion of any action taken so that well-advised choices can be made.*

What State Courts Have Ruled since *Hazelwood*

Another means of protection from prior restraint for public school newspapers remains besides the limited protection provided by the First Amendment. State courts, beginning with courts in New Jersey, have ruled that the state constitution provides more protection for the student press than the First Amendment does.

Few cases concerning the rights of student journalists at school-sponsored publications have come to trial in the first four years following the *Hazelwood* ruling. One case should be of particular concern to publications advisers. In *Romano v. Harrington*[27] a newspaper adviser lost an appeal after being discharged when the newspaper published an editorial opposing Martin Luther King Jr. Day becoming a federal holiday. The appeals court stated that minimizing racial tensions at the school was a reasonable pedagogical concern.[28]

Another case involved advertising. In *Planned Parenthood of Southern Nevada v. Clark County School District*,[29] a court ruled that a school could keep Planned Parenthood's ads from running in school publications and sports programs. Citing *Hazelwood*, the court ruled that prohibiting the ads was reasonable because they were potentially controversial and offensive to some students.[30]

In addition to state courts, state free-speech laws can provide considerable protection to student publications. As of the fall of 1993, five states—California, Massachusetts, Iowa, Colorado, and Kansas—had passed such laws. Model legislation is available from the Student Press Law Center in Washington, D.C. (See footnote 26 for address.)

In addition, underground publications provide a means for publishing information that might not be allowed in school-sponsored publications. Such nonschool publications have full First Amendment protection and are protected by the *Tinker* guidelines when distributed on school property. In *Burch v. Barker*,[31] an appeals court ruled in favor of a student who had distributed an underground newspaper at a barbecue on the school grounds. The court cited *Tinker* and directed the school board to rewrite its policy requiring school officials to approve written material distributed on the school grounds.[32]

When Exactly Is Censorship in the 1990s?

Soon after the *Hazelwood* ruling, Robert Reynolds, the principal of Hazelwood East High School, debated David Hawpe, editor of the *Louisville Courier-Journal*. Reynolds said that he did not censor the *Spectrum*, the school newspaper. "As principal and as instructional leader of this school," he stated, "I acted in the role of the former journalism teacher, and thus became a part of the editing process."

Hawpe responded that it was "shameful that so many newspapers have fallen into lockstep with the Supreme Court decision," adding: "That's because they bought the metaphor. If you buy the metaphor of the principal as publisher, it is a very easy case to make.

But if you see that the metaphor is imperfect, that in fact what you have is...an official of government acting to exercise prior restraint, I think it is a much more difficult and disturbing case to make."[33]

Of course, the Supreme Court in the *Hazelwood* ruling stated that Principal Reynolds was correct in regard to Hazelwood East High School and to other schools whose newspapers are not found to be public forums. The ruling provided a legal basis for what principals at most public high schools always had thought they had a right to do: stop particularly objectionable material from being printed in school publications. If school officials had not taken action to open the newspaper for indiscriminate use by the community or students, essentially the only restriction on such action was that it must be "reasonably related to legitimate pedagogical concerns."

The principal's almost arbitrary power where a public forum does not exist puts advisers in a difficult position pedagogically and presents them with both legal and professional concerns. When a public forum is present, the adviser also has additional ethical dilemmas. Some possible questions advisers might ask in either situation are

—When advisers assign stories, are they interfering with students' rights to determine newspaper content?

—Does assigning stories lead to self-censorship by editors and reporters?

—When advisers read copy, is it censorship? Does it necessarily lead to student self-censorship?

—When advisers fix errors of fact or correct misspellings without the student editor's approval, is it censorship?

—Does reading copy make advisers responsible for all content? When they do not read stories, are they still responsible for content? And which is the most responsible position to take?

—Should advisers protect themselves by clearing potentially controversial content with the principal?

—When principals read articles before publication, is it censorship or does it lead to student self-censorship?

Some guidance in answering those and similar questions can be found in writings of journalism educators and in publications of journalism education organizations. The official "free press" answers were more obvious in *Tinker* days, when advisers were expected to read articles but only to advise students, not make changes. One pre-*Hazelwood* article stated that courts had defined the role of adviser as "advice-giver—when advice is sought." In the article, Mary Hartman wrote that

> *(T)hese same courts have removed the adviser from the role of censor, which perhaps, should be made clear in the guidelines. Realistically, most advisers have enough rapport with their students to blend some teaching with their advice-giving. This is a good-will relationship that doesn't have to be stipulated in writing.*"[34]

A handbook for advisers during the middle of the *Tinker* era explained that in the 1940s, 1950s, and most of the 1960s, high school journalism instructors "learned about working with school publications. Today they work with *student* publications and there is a subtle but essential distinction between the two." The handbook noted that there was little complaint of censorship when the principal read newspaper copy prior to publication. Things began to change in the 1970s, however, the article noted. It stated about that change:

> *Gradually, the courts made it clear that freedom of the press applies to student journalists in much the same way it applies to the professionals. Schools began to understand that there was little in the underground press that could not, that should not be dealt with in school newspapers as long as students understood the responsibilities that go with freedom. The courts have ruled that although schools may provide advisers, room, heat, light, equipment and subsidies for school publications, control belongs basically to the students.*[35]

As research has shown, prior review by publications advisers was commonly practiced by advisers before and after the *Hazelwood* decision. While there is unanimity among advocates of press freedom that prior review by school administrators should not take place, the use of prior review by advisers has not usually been seen as censorship. One change that can be attributed to *Hazelwood* is that actual editing by advisers, once seen as being a responsibility of the adviser, no longer is seen as appropriate by some student rights advocates.

John Bowen, chair of the Journalism Education Association's Scholastic Press Rights Commission, noted that prior review by administrators is not acceptable because it gives them the authority to decide what truth is and to withhold information that readers have a right to see. He wrote as follows:

> *Prior review negates the educational value of a trained, professional and active adviser working with students. The effect would be like telling the teacher and the students their education and their training did not actually matter, since someone else outside the advising process would have final say.*[36]

The Student Press Law Center's policy on prior review and prior restraint are given in its model legislation, available in the "SPLC *Hazelwood* Packet," published in 1992. The policy on administrative prior review states: "No student publication, whether school-sponsored or nonschool-sponsored, will be subject to prior review by school administrators."[37]

The prior restraint policy is stated in the SPLC's model guidelines for student publications. The guidelines state that the following prohibited material cannot be printed: anything obscene as to minors or libelous or which would cause "a material and substantial disruption of school activities." The prior review policy suggests that the school is not responsible for contents as long as administrators do not use prior review. The policy states:

> *No student publication, whether nonschool-sponsored or official, will be reviewed by school administrators prior to distribution or withheld from distribution. The school assumes no liability for the content of any student publication and urges all student journalists to recognize that with editorial control comes responsibility, including the responsibility to follow professional journalism standards.*[38]

The Student Press Law Center suggests that student journalists who have been subjected to prior restraint by the principal appeal the decision to the superintendent and, if the superintendent sides with the principal, to the school board itself.

The Journalism Education Association's policy on prior review, revised after the *Hazelwood* ruling, suggests that prior review by administrators is not acceptable, but prior review by advisers is acceptable as long as student editors agree with changes and constitutionally protected material is not censored. The policy states:

> *The Journalism Education Association strongly opposes prior review of student expression. Along with the Student Press Law Center, we believe no nonschool-sponsored or official publication, printed or electronic, should be reviewed by school administrators prior to distribution.*
>
> *Prior review by administrators, school officials or teachers other than publications advisers is illogical, journalistically inappropriate and educationally unsound.*
>
> *A journalism teacher working with students advises, counsels and supervises the editing process. Such internal discussions do not involve prior review, so long as protected speech is not tampered with and students make final content decisions....*
>
> *Prior review is but a weapon in the arsenal of censorship, and the Journalism Education Association opposes its use in America's schools.*[39]

The policy was changed slightly from the pre-*Hazelwood* policy on prior review. Rather than stating that the adviser "supervised the editing process," the previous policy stated that a journalism teacher's role involves counseling, advising and "editing."[40] According to John Bowen, chair of the JEA's Scholastic Press Rights Commission, the change came about because of *Hazelwood* and was approved by JEA's board of directors and the JEA membership. Bowen stated the following about the change:

> *"Supervised the editing process" was changed from "edits" for several very important reasons. First, if the adviser edits, why have editors?...(O)utcomes based education is improved by stu-*

dents performing the functions they have been taught. They must learn to make the critical decisions.

Secondly, to protect the validity of the forum function—and of student control—the editors must perform the editing function. The adviser is there to answer questions and, more importantly, to ask them.[41]

Bowen stated that he thought that prior review by advisers is OK as long as advisers do not make changes themselves. Instead, advisers should question and suggest to the editors what changes ought to be made. The Journalism Education Association policy on prior restraint states:

Student media shall not be subjected to prior restraints, review or censorship by faculty advisers, school administrators, faculty, school boards or any other individual outside the student editorial board, except as stated above, and only when these individuals can demonstrate legally defined justification. In addition, student journalists have the right to determine the content of their media.[42]

Bowen stated that "(l)egally, editing is an internal function and not a process of state control, so long as it is not arbitrarily carried out by the adviser, who is an agent of the state." He stated the following concerning whether advisers have a right to change content:

Changing wording for spelling, factual inaccuracies, etc., should ideally be carried out by student editors, with input from the adviser. Such "editing" is not censorship, in my mind, so long as the students and reporters fully understand the process and the responsibility. Also, I would argue, whenever possible, reporters should be involved in any changes in their copy, as in the coaching process.[43]

Bowen wrote that if students wanted to publish material that is constitutionally unprotected (anything libelous or obscene or likely to cause substantial disruption) that, as adviser, he would determine why they wanted to run the questionable material and present his objections. If the students decided to run the material anyway, he would ask them to consult a media attorney. If they insisted on running the material, he would note his objections and tell them that he would have to inform the principal of the students' decision, made against his advice and that of legal counsel. "I would advise the principal of our decisions, rationales and legal advice so he or she could take whatever steps he/she felt necessary," he wrote. "Once the administrator intervened, however, the administrator would bear the liability of any content." Bowen stated that the process he outlined "leaves intact the integrity of student decision-making and advising processes, yet can still act to protect the interests of the school system."[44]

To Censor or Not to Censor

Research has shown that advisers and student editors do not disagree very much about what good journalism is. Student journalists at most school newspapers are being allowed to cover controversial issues, but they are expected to do so in a fair, accurate, and responsible manner. Of course, editors of nonschool, adult publications expect the same thing of reporters. They just aren't employees of the state and, therefore, no First Amendment issues are involved.

A close parallel to the Supreme Court's image of the student press is the in-house college or university publication distributed by the office of public relations. Such publications are not public forums and the content is determined by the college's public relations director or publication editor. Instead of what the Court envisioned, however, newspapers at most secondary schools are operating more like something akin to public forums than to public relations newsletters.

Some researchers in the *Hazelwood* era have taken the libertarian position that any interference by non-students with the content of the school newspaper—even prior review by advisers—is censorship. The position against prior review by the adviser is not commonly accepted, however. In addition, only one federal appeals court has agreed that the First Amendment rights of the school press are identical to those of the nonschool press. In other federal circuits, school newspapers were operating under a type of social responsibility theory before the *Hazelwood* decision. Under court rulings during the *Tinker* era, prior restraint usually was allowed if procedural guidelines were followed and the restraint was reasonable—because of possible disruption or because of the maturity level of the audience.

Even the dissenters in the *Hazelwood* case took the position that restraint could be allowed if done in a less heavy-handed fashion. In addition, several decades of research have found that few school officials in any circuit before the *Hazelwood* decision would have stood aside and allowed the publication of material they saw as irresponsible, no matter what courts had ruled.

It seems somewhat unrealistic in the post-*Hazelwood* era to expect that advisers would not use prior review of school publications. Advisers would be expected to want the newspaper to have high journalistic standards, and they are expected by principals to make sure the newspaper lives up to those standards. Indeed, research shows that material that doesn't meet journalistic standards is more likely to be a problem than controversial material. If responsible journalism is practiced by students, little reason for prior restraint exists. The main problem is who determines what is responsible. It appears that, under *Hazelwood*, school officials have some responsibility to prohibit speech that is not constitutionally protected. That constitutionally protected speech that is harmful can be stopped was decided in *Hazelwood*. A decision to stop constitutionally protected material is something that should not be made without sufficient justification.

Though it did not mandate prior restraint, *Hazelwood* seems to have mandated that advisers in nonpublic-forum situations use prior review to see that legally dangerous copy is not printed. Whereas it could be argued before *Hazelwood* that school officials did not have responsibility for the newspaper's contents if they did not use prior review, it can be argued that school officials are responsible for nonpublic forum publications whether they review them or not.

Because anyone who is involved in the publication of a libelous statement or an article that invades a person's privacy (because of reporting methods or because it included private, embarrassing facts or put someone in false light) also is guilty, school officials who allow such statements to be published may be included in any legal action that results. School officials likely would be protected from lawsuits if the publication is a public forum and they had not exercised prior review. But because of *Hazelwood*, courts may find school officials liable at schools with nonpublic-forum newspapers even if prior review had not been used, on the assumption that responsible advisers and principals would ensure that articles without constitutional protection not be published.

It also might be questioned if student self-censorship always is incompatible with a free student press. Self-censorship might take place because of a variety of reasons: because of pressure or intimidation, because of deference to authority, because of a desire to follow accepted journalistic practices, or because of what the editor sees as insufficient news value. Self-restraint in not publishing something for ethical reasons is seen in the profession as being admirable professional conduct.

It also seems unrealistic to expect student journalists not to show some deference to a teacher concerning the newspaper content and not to show some self-restraint in what they write and publish out of a desire to do what the adviser expects of them. Indeed, all journalism students are in a learning situation, and most are participating in a classroom situation. Research has shown that student journalists tend to use self-restraint by practicing responsible reporting and not normally by failing to publish important stories because of fear of censorship. Self-censorship only becomes a problem when students fail to tackle important issues for fear of prior restraint or punishment.

Conclusions and Recommendations

It seems apparent from our 1992 study as well as other research that any attempt to increase school press freedom should be aimed first at newspaper publication policies. As our study showed, when schools have an expressed policy that the newspaper is an open forum, prior restraint and self-censorship are much less likely.

The study also showed that who establishes the publications policy influences the liberality of that policy. Press freedom was found to be greater at schools at which the students as well as the adviser had a part in forming the policy. Policies should be approved on the school district level, however, to provide maximum protection for the newspaper.

It also is apparent from ours and other studies that adviser characteristics are related to how much student press freedom is allowed. We and other researchers have found that advisers with more college journalism hours and with more advising experience were more likely to disagree with the *Hazelwood* ruling and that advisers with memberships in journalism education organizations tend to allow more student press freedom.

In looking at research on school press freedom, it is necessary to understand the researcher's determination of what censorship and self-censorship are. It is apparent from numerous studies over the years that most advisers read copy before publication. And, as we have said, it also might be argued that, because of the *Hazelwood* ruling, they are obligated to do so if the newspaper is not a public forum. If the adviser in nonforum situations does not question potentially libelous statements or errors of grammar or fact, the principal could conclude that the adviser was acting irresponsibly for not doing something about it. However, even in nonpublic-forum situations, the adviser has many tools other than censorship to use. If the adviser has good rapport with students, they are likely to heed suggestions that articles contain constitutionally unprotected speech.

Can the student newspaper be a means for student expression as well as a teaching tool and a means for publicizing school events? Can student press freedom coexist with press responsibility? It seems clear from three decades of research that few if any high schools have given the school newspaper complete freedom from "interference" by school officials; therefore, some coexistence would be necessary even without *Hazelwood v. Kuhlmeier*.

The *Hazelwood* ruling has not been an insurmountable barrier to scholastic press freedom or to producing student newspapers that are more than bland bulletin boards. With well-written publication policies, responsible students, well-educated and caring advisers, and principals dedicated to student rights as well as to student responsibility, press freedom and *Hazelwood* can coexist. While the ruling legitimizes restrictions by school officials on the content of the school press, it only gives them license to take away students' First Amendment freedoms. It does not require that they do so.

Addendum: Comments Received from Advisers and Student Editors

Advisers' Comments

"The only reason a story, editorial, or ad has been prevented from running is because of rejection from the principal. Ours is an extremely conservative community, and since the *Hazelwood* ruling, we have to send highly controversial stories to the principal for approval. I strongly disagree with this practice but, nevertheless, it is a rule I am obligated to follow." — L.W.

"While we have had no problems with censorship, neither have we been terribly assertive in the past. I don't really know what the limits are because we haven't pushed them severely." — K.J.

"I have been fortunate to have mature, experienced editors who investigate before making decisions. Legal constraints, in our case, are the only true restrictions we consider." — (Virginia)

"We had (an underground newspaper) erupt as a result of my having to punish students for censoring other students without the adviser or editor's knowledge." — D.R.

"We have no student editor. I act as editor but give students freedom if they would like to do a particular story or editorial. I wish they would get into controversial topics. Our main problem with what should/should not be printed revolves around the gossip column that has been a part of the paper for 25 years." — (New York state)

"My editors are generally pickier than I am. They have high quality standards and I really stress responsible journalism!

"I have met a lot of 'dingy, irresponsible' advisers. Perhaps *Hazelwood* might help that. By the same token, there are some real inept school board members and administrators who could potentially harm a publication and 'free press.'" — G.H. (Washington state)

"Because this is an extracurricular activity, it is difficult to get dedicated, responsible students with the basic skills needed to write. Students here do not know how to be editors and reporters, although they have been using these titles for years. They want to do gossip columns and 'The Enquirer Knows' stories. There is no written policy on controversial articles because there has been no writing on such topics!

"This is my first year in this school system. Perhaps in time things will change. At any rate, I would appreciate knowing about your results and how you plan to use them.— J.B. (Tennessee)

"P.S. I would also be grateful for any suggestions."

"I do not see censorship as a problem in our school. This is a very small school with a very 'tame' newspaper. It is written and published by the students for the students. It is not printed in a local newspaper, as some in the area are. Neither is it mailed to individuals.

"Most of the topics covered are upcoming events or results of past events. I do discourage 'gossip' columns or items that might be embarrassing to other students. We have had editorials from time to time, but I do ask that they be supported with facts, not just a place to 'gripe' about something the student doesn't like at the school.

"Generally, the students decide what articles they want to include." — (Anonymous)

Student Editors' Comments

"Although our paper has not been officially censored, it is reviewed by the...committee before it is published each month, and recently we were reprimanded for a story which the... committee did not censor. Although the story was completely factual, there was a quote in it which stated that our school would be better off without our principal. Usually, our principal edits the paper, but he was not here to edit this issue. Now he is hassling my adviser a lot. This year our school was assigned a whole new administration and there has been a lot of controversy over the capabilities of our new principal and although we have not yet been censored, we basically understand what is acceptable. Also, our principal stated that (if) he had seen the story he would have censored it." — (South Carolina)

"Our school newspaper is greatly controlled by the students on the staff. Our adviser reads the copy before it is put in, but finds only grammar and spelling errors. We have never had to fight her on a story or editorial that we wanted to put in and she had not. She has been behind us 100 percent and has put her faith into us. Our principal has done the same. He has never found a problem with a story that may be controversial. Our superiors have given us the ability to test the ground and publish well-written material that we believe in." — (Idaho)

"We have had great success in covering controversial issues in the newspaper at...High School. Our articles have included animal rights, sexual discrimination, drug and alcohol use, sexual activity, religion, violence, abortion, adoption, divorce, political issues—the list goes on and on.

"During the Gulf War, one student displayed a sign in her car window protesting the war. Even though it contained questionable language, we ran it with a thin line of tape over it. Many parents objected, but our principal backed us up. We have been lucky to receive such a large amount of support from (the) administration.

"Our staff and adviser are quite liberal and we feel it is important to cover all news, whether good and bad. The most protest we have heard of is from parents, and we believe this shows how uninformed many of them are of the trials teen-agers must face today. In our opinion, balanced coverage is a positive way of informing the public and spreading awareness." — (M.A.)

"I feel that a school press should have the same rights as any other newspaper. The object of a school paper is to inform the public of events (good and bad) happening inside the school system. If the students are not allowed to tell the controversial or bad things that are happening, the public is not getting a true picture of the school system." — J.T. (Missouri)

"In Colorado, we have Senate Bill 99, which overrules *Hazelwood*. We have complete freedom of speech." — (Colorado)

"As a journalism student, I have studied the *Hazelwood* case. I do not disagree with its ruling entirely, but I do not think that the school board should have a say-so in everything. We (journalism staff) work hard and do good reporting. Why should something that is true and reported carefully be denied printing? This is what I do not understand." — (Texas)

"There is no school written policy which regulates what goes into the newspaper. However, it is understood what can and can't be published. My adviser made that clear when I came to be on the staff two years ago. Sometimes I get frustrated because things that really need to be said can't be published because someone might be offended. I mean, how dare we say something about our wonderful school board? (Ha! Ha!) Nevertheless, I understand and respect my adviser's position even though I don't always agree with her decision." — (Georgia)

"Our school newspaper is under review because several years ago our editor published a letter about farting. This year, we got a new superintendent, who finds it necessary to complain about our paper and is constantly threatening to take it away." — J.B. (Indiana)

"The principal is given a copy of controversial issue stories when the paper goes to the printer—so she had advance 'warning' that she may receive calls. She has never censored anything. Our adviser would not stop any topic." — (Colorado)

"This year alone, the ... has published stories on date rape, date abuse, negative stories on school policies and racial issues concerning our community as well as our nation.

"Recently an underground newspaper charged us with attacks of too much intervention from the upper echelon of school administrators. To date, no story or editorial has been turned down due to the content of which they were written, and up until today the underground newspaper has not written an article that would not have been allowed in the....

"The ... staff decides as a whole whether an article would be overly offensive to one person or a group of people. Barely any intervention hinders the publication of the...." — J.J. (Pennsylvania)

"I would like to stress that our answers are not characteristic of the true nature of our newspaper. The enrollment at our high school is approximately 1,800, but we usually distribute fewer than 300 newspapers. Our adviser usually lets us publish what we please, but since our staff is so small (8 people), we normally don't carry many controversial stories or editorials.

"We have had a few instances when we've had to heed the advice of our adviser, but that was because our editorial board felt his advice was the best. We have run letters to the editor about homosexuality at our school, but never covered the topic, and have run columns that generated anger from other area schools that felt we were 'bashing' them, but no story in our paper has ever caused a major stir at school, at least not this year." — A.B. (Ohio)

"At my high school, we recently had a change in the administration. Saying good-bye to a liberal principal meant a change in the subject matter of our paper. We didn't want to upset or offend our new principal in the first few weeks of his 'reign.'

"Due to our principal's conservative views on teen sex, he 'discouraged' myself and my adviser from running a Planned Parenthood ad. While I didn't feel this was right, there wasn't much I could do.

"I feel sorry for the staff (I'm graduating) of next year's newspaper. Our school is taking a very conservative trend. I worry about what will happen to the paper." — (Missouri)

"In my opinion, controversy is a good thing, and when our newspaper prints something (mainly in editorials and columns) that causes controversy, we feel we are doing a good job. Every issue of our newspaper gets feedback, both negative and positive, and we always print all the letters to the editor that we receive. We never, under any circumstances, print anything that causes us to be liable or might incite violence." — J.C. (California)

"The principal and adviser of our newspaper both agree that the school newspaper is a production of the journalism class and that it is held responsible for all published material. The principal is usually happy with our subject matter and praises controversial articles for their balance. The adviser does just that—advises. He gives suggestions which I am able to accept or reject. I understand my responsibility and am proud to say that I have the trust and respect of the adviser and principal." — J.D. (Florida)

"Your survey is misleading, indicating that advisers and editors are at odds on what will and will not be published. Sure, we have disagreements, but this is something the staff discusses and decides on. Usually we work together to determine how things are covered. I would never describe it as conflict.

"We covered drugs and alcohol, sex, sexually transmitted diseases, and gangs this year. Each story told of our students in these areas. We spent hours and hours on these topics and got the full backing of our principal.

"If we do a good job, we can cover almost anything. It's the staffs that are careless with facts, libel, etc., that scare administrators." — (Anonymous)

"We, the editors of the ..., feel that our school board, principal, and adviser understand that we, as the staff, took on the responsibility of producing a paper that shows mature decisions from our staff. They understand that any controversial material will be dealt with by the editorial board." — A.P. and L.D.

"As far as controversial topics go, my adviser is fairly liberal in her thinking, and both she and I do not shy away from topics such as these. We have had several articles and polls on sex, rape, and abortion and dedicated much of our March 1992 issue to articles on discrimination. Don't limit yourself, when establishing your newspaper, to just covering school-related topics." — A.D.

"The reason the high authorities of the school censor the paper is because they believe the elderly people of the town will be offended." — (New Jersey)

"Concerning the *Hazelwood* ruling, our class discussed it and came to the general consensus that *Hazelwood* was wrong. The school paper was designed to be run by students. A little supervision is needed, though, to check for libel. Censoring of material should be an editorial decision, as in slander and controversial material!" — B.R. (Florida)

NOTES ON CHAPTER 10

1. NORTHEAST = Maine, New Hampshire, Vermont, Massachusetts, Rhode Island, New York, New Jersey, Pennsylvania, and Connecticut; SOUTH = Maryland, Delaware, District of Columbia, Virginia, West Virginia, Kentucky, Tennessee, North Carolina, South Carolina, Georgia, Florida, Alabama, Mississippi, Louisiana, Arkansas, Oklahoma, and Texas; CENTRAL = Ohio, Indiana, Michigan, Illinois, Wisconsin, Minnesota, North Dakota, South Dakota, Iowa, Missouri, Nebraska, and Kansas; WEST = Arizona, New Mexico, Colorado, Wyoming, Idaho, Nevada, Montana, Utah, California, Oregon, Washington, Alaska, and Hawaii.

2. Imafidon M. Olaye and Lynne E. Malandrino, "Contextual First Amendment Rights: Perceptions of Teachers and Administrators in the Age of *Hazelwood*" (paper presented at the convention of the Association for Education in Journalism and Mass Communication, Montreal, Canada, August 1992).

3. Larry Lain, "A National Study of High School Newspaper Programs: Environmental and Adviser Characteristics, Funding and Pressures on Free Expression" (paper presented at the convention of the Association for Education in Journalism and Mass Communication, Montreal, Canada, August 1992).

4. Jack Dvorak, "Secondary School Journalism in the United States," *High School Journalism Institute Insight*, April 1992.

5. Lorrie Ronae Crow, "The Impact of Texas High School Students' and Principals' Perceptions of Student Press Freedom Following the *Hazelwood v. Kuhlmeier* Supreme Court Decision" (unpublished M.A. thesis, University of Oklahoma, 1992).

6. *Ibid.:* 62-63.

7. Kathryn T. Stofer, "Life after *Hazelwood*: Journalism Programs in Nebraska Schools 1992" (paper submitted to the Scholastic Journalism Division for presentation at the convention of the Association for Education in Journalism and Mass Communication, Kansas City, MO), August 1993).

8. *Ibid.:* 26-27.

9. Nicholas B. Kristof, *Freedom of the High School Press* (Lanham, MD: University Press of America, 1983): 9.

10. Kay Phillips, "Freedom of Expression for High School Journalists: A Case Study of Selected North Carolina Public Schools" (paper presented at the convention of the Association for Education in Journalism and Mass Communication, Washington, DC, August 1989): 42.

11. David Zweifel, "Self-Censorship Is Flourishing at High School Newspapers," *The Bulletin of the American Society of Newspaper Editors* (March 1990): 19.

12. *Ibid.:* 22.

13. Olaye and Malandrino, "Contextual First Amendment Rights": 15.

14. "Student Press Law Center Calls Up Over 143 Percent since 1988 *Hazelwood* Case," *Student Press Law Center Report*, January 4, 1993: 3.

15. Lyle D. Olson, Roger Van Ommeren, and Marshel Rossow, "The Nation's Scholastic Press Association Directors Describe the State of High School Journalism," *Communication: Journalism Education Today,* (Spring 1993): 10-12.

16. Mike Simpson, "Supreme Court Chills Student Press Rights," *NEA Today* (March 1988): 13.

17. Jack Dvorak and Jon Paul Dilts, "Academic Freedom vs. Administrative Authority," *Journalism Educator 47*, 3 (Autumn 1992): 3-12.

18. *Ibid.:* 5

19. Tom Eveslage, "*Hazelwood v. Kuhlmeier;* A Threat and a Challenge to High School Journalism," *Quill and Scroll* (February-March 1988): 10.

20. Student Press Law Center, "What to Do if It Happens to You: Fighting Censorship after *Hazelwood*," 1992.

21. Benjamin Sendor, "Managing the Student Press: Consider Carefully before You Unsheath (sic) the Censor's Scissors," *The American School Board Journal* (April 1988): 25.

22. Peter Habermann, Lillian Lodge Kopenhaver, and David Martinson, "Publication Polices: Post-*Hazelwood* Lifesavers," *Student Press Law Center Report* (Fall 1989): 43.

23. Lillian Lodge Kopenhaver, David L. Martinson, and Peter Habermann, "First Amendment Rights in South Florida: Views of

Advisers and Administrators in Light of *Hazelwood*," *The School Press Review* (Fall 1989).

24. *Ibid.:* 17.

25. Roy Mays and Julie Dodd, "The Impact of the *Hazelwood v. Kuhlmeier* (1988) Decision on the Development or Revision of School Publication Policies" (paper presented at the Mid-Winter Meeting of the Secondary Education Division of the Association for Education in Journalism and Mass Communication, Atlanta, January 1993).

26. Student Press Law Center model publications guidelines are available in the "SPLC *Hazelwood* Packet," from the Student Press Law Center, 1735 Eye St. NW, Suite 504, Washington, DC 20006-2402. Tel: (202) 466-5242; FAX (202) 466-6326. The SPLC also has a legal guide, *Law of the Student Press*, that is available for $7.50 from Quill and Scroll, School of Journalism and Mass Communication, University of Iowa, Iowa City, IA 52242. Other useful information can be found in *From the School Newsroom to the Courtroom*, published by the Constitutional Rights Foundation (48 pages, $4.95), 601 S. Kingsley Drive, Los Angeles, CA 90005.

27. 725 F.Supp. 687.

28. Ann Gynn, "*Hazelwood*: Four Years Later" (paper prepared for presentation to the Scholastic Journalism Division at the Convention of the Association for Education in Journalism and Mass Communication, Montreal, Canada, August 1992): 13.

29. 941 F.2d 817.

30. Gynn, "*Hazelwood*: Four Years Later": 14.

31. 861 F.2d 1149.

32. Gynn: 13.

33. *The Dow Jones Newspaper Fund Adviser Update*, Winter, 1988: 5.

34. Mary Hartman, "Official Guidelines and Editorial Policies: Remedying the Confusion," *Scholastic Editor* (April/May 1978): 5.

35. Robert L. Button, *Managing Publications: A Handbook for Advisers* (Iowa City, IA: Quill and Scroll Foundation/University of Iowa, 1982): 32.

36. John Bowen, "Fighting Prior Review," *Communication: Journalism Education Today* (Fall 1990): 2.

37. *SPLC Hazelwood Packet:* 12.

38. *Ibid.:* 11.

39. Letter, John Bowen to Tom Dickson, Oct. 7, 1993.

40. "JEA's Policy on Prior Review," *Communication: Journalism Education Today* (Fall 1990): 4.

41. Letter, John Bowen to Tom Dickson, Oct. 14, 1993.

42. Journalism Education Association, "Student Press Rights Position" (undated).

43. Letter, John Bowen to Tom Dickson, Oct. 14, 1993.

44. John Bowen, "Our Job as Advisers Is Self-Explanatory," *Communication: Journalism Education Today* (Fall 1990): 6.

WE DON'T JUST MAKE IT UP AS WE GO ALONG

We began by talking about the isolation felt by so many journalism teachers and publication advisers. By now it should be evident that the isolation is only apparent; in fact, there is an immense network of colleagues available to us in almost every high school and college in the country, in administrative offices, in the commercial press throughout the country. The bibliography that concludes this book is a catalogue of hundreds of books, articles and papers written by scores of people from junior high school teachers to Ph.D.s at prestigious universities, authors with one specific end in mind: to make it possible for each of us to do our jobs a little better. While journalism teachers may not have a lot of support or understanding in their own buildings, there is surely no other teaching field that has at its heart such an extensive and collegial chain of help and support. The extent to which this book can be another link in that chain is the measure of its success and completeness.

There is a final issue to address, one that is perhaps more often shared with our teaching colleagues in other areas. The concern was articulated by a student of one of the authors, a young woman who hopes to teach high school journalism one day. "My boyfriend is an engineering major, and he doesn't think we do *anything* in education," she said recently. "He thinks all we take are 'cake' classes."

Teachers grow weary of such thinking. There's surely more to the world than rocket science—and besides: Even the rocket scientists had teachers who *taught* them. If it does nothing else (and our

365

hope, of course, is that it does a great deal more!) the overview of the literature of the field of journalism education contained in these pages suggests that there exists an abundant amount of research done over a period of many years. That research has provided us with a solid intellectual and empirical base from which we can improve and develop our field.

Certainly journalism is not the only area that is able to draw on an important base of research. But those underpinnings demonstrate clearly its significance in the curriculum. In these pages we have seen the important outcomes of journalism education in improved test scores and classroom performance. We have seen the way in which the writing skills, organizational skills, and, indeed, *thinking* skills that are an intrinsic part of journalism education transfer to other areas of students' academic and personal lives.

America is built on principles of democracy and capitalism, two qualities which also are foundational to our press system. If we purport to teach these principles to our students, it is imperative that they be permitted to practice them. And to do that both they and their teachers must understand them. The law itself, as it has been interpreted by the courts, is an area journalism teachers simply cannot know too much about. The links between income and the amount of freedom students have is an important emerging subject for study. The censorship of the school press by administrators, advisers or students themselves is an area that needs constant monitoring. It is not enough for only academicians to be interested in these issues; the teachers working each day with the young people who will someday be leading this democracy and driving its economy must also remain aware of the growth of knowledge and understanding of these concerns.

If...

...through its review of some of the important recent work in our field;

...through its extensive bibliography of other studies and useful publications;

...through its showing the broad range of people and backgrounds that are part of journalism education;

...through providing resources, suggestions, and encouragement to our fellow journalism educators

this book has made our colleagues feel less alone and given them a new arsenal of information with which to do their important work all the better, then this book has met its objective. We don't just make it up as we go along! The research base for journalism education is deep and rich, and a knowledge of what grows in those fertile fields will yield important fruit for our students and for us.

BIBLIOGRAPHY IN
SECONDARY SCHOOL JOURNALISM

Selected references below have been classified by subject and arranged in reverse chronological order. Where possible, ERIC access numbers and annotations have been provided.

Journalism's Role in Academics

Olman, Gloria Grove. "Value of Journalism Education Touted," *JEA Newswire* 21,2 (January 1993):1.

AU: Olson,-Lyle-D.
TI: Effect of News Writing Instruction in English Composition Classes.
PY: 1992
JN: Journalism-Educator; v47 n2 p50-56 Sum 1992
DE: Higher-Education; Writing-Research
DE: *Freshman-Composition; *News-Writing; *Student-Attitudes; *Writing-Ability; *Writing-Attitudes
AB: Examines the effect of news writing instruction on the attitudes and writing performance of students in English composition classes. Finds the only significant difference between treatment and control groups is students' perception of the practicality of the writing instruction they received. (SR)

Shepard, Lenore. "Students Analyze Classics, Contemporary Literature," *C:JET (Communication: Journalism Education Today)* 26 (Winter 1992):21-22.

AN: EJ435828
AU: Stuart,-Judy-L.
TI: Class Notes for "Class-Y-News."
PY: 1991
JN: Teaching-Exceptional-Children; v24 n1 p52-53 Fall 1991
AV: UMI
DE: Elementary-Secondary-Education; Newsletters-; News-Writing; Special-Classes; Student-Projects
DE: *Disabilities-; *Parent-School-Relationship; *Student-Publications; *Writing-for-Publication

AB: A self-contained class of students with mild to moderate disabilities published a monthly newsletter which was distributed to students' families. Students became involved in writing, typing, drawing, folding, basic editing, and disseminating. (JDD)

AN: EJ425389
AU: Dvorak,-Jack
TI: Charting the Facts.
PY: 1991
JN: Communication:-Journalism-Education-Today-(C:JET); v24 n3 p5-8 Spr 1991
DE: Communication-Research; Higher-Education; High-Schools; Surveys-
DE: *College-Freshmen; *Curriculum-Evaluation; *English-Instruction; *Journalism-Education; *Student-Attitudes; *Writing-Instruction
AB: Describes a survey of college freshmen on how to improve high school language arts instruction. Reports that students favored (1) placing greater emphasis on basic writing skills and language use; (2) developing and encouraging various writing styles; and (3) assigning much writing. Notes that students rated high school journalism courses as superior to English courses in several respects. (SG)

AN: EJ411550
AU: Dvorak,-Jack
TI: College Students Evaluate Their Scholastic Journalism Courses.
PY: 1990
JN: Journalism-Educator; v45 n1 p36-46 Spr 1990
AV: UMI
DE: College-Curriculum; College-Students; Communication-Skills; Critical-Thinking; English-Instruction; Higher-Education; High-Schools; Secondary-School-Curriculum
DE: *Curriculum-Evaluation; *Journalism-Education; *Skill-Development; *Student-Attitudes
AB: Evaluates college students' attitudes concerning their high school English and journalism courses and their college-level journalism instruction. Reports students' belief that high school journalism provided their best training in many of the 29 language arts competencies studied. (SG)

Bennett, Ron. "Journalism vs. English," *C:JET (Communication: Journalism Education Today)* 23 (Fall 1989):16,18.

AN: EJ398770
AU: Cole,-Judy
TI: Writing: The Key to Success.
PY: 1989
JN: Communication:-Journalism-Education-Today-(C:JET); v23 n1 p9-10 Fall 1989
DE: Course-Descriptions; Journalism-Education; Secondary-Education; Student-Projects; Teaching-Methods; Writing-Improvement
DE: *Advanced-Placement-Programs; *English-Instruction; *Local-History; *News-Writing; *Student-Publications; *Writing-Instruction
AB: Describes how an intensive journalistic writing course motivated students by combining journalistic writing with a school-history research project. (MM)

AN: EJ419864
AU: Dvorak,-Jack
TI: Publications Experience as a Predictor of College Success.
PY: 1989

JN: Journalism-Quarterly; v66 n3 p702-06 Fall 1989 DE: E d u c a t i o n a l - R e s e a r c h; Extracurricular-Activities; Higher-Education; High-Schools; School-Newspapers; Yearbooks-

DE: *Academic-Achievement; *College-Freshmen; *Predictive-Measurement

AB: Investigates whether participation on high school newspaper or yearbook staffs leads to higher grades in freshman college English and a higher overall freshman grade point average. Finds that such out-of-class accomplishments are not good predictors of college outcomes. Finds the ACT composite score to be a good predictor of first collegiate English grade. (RS)

Engleman, Tom. "Building Respect for Journalism: A New High School English Course in Intensive Journalistic Writing," *C:JET (Communication: Journalism Education Today)* 23 (Fall 1989):2-4.

Hollenbeck, Carol, "Intensive Journalistic Writing for the AP," *C:JET (Communication: Journalism Education Today)* 23 (Fall 1989):5-8, 18.

Lange, Carol. "Intensive Journalistic Writing Methods Add Spice to English Classes," *C:JET (Communication: Journalism Education Today)* 23 (Fall 1989):19.

AU: Peterson,-Jane-W.
TI: High School Principals and the High School Journalism Program.
PY: 1989
PG: 22
DE: High-School-Students; Questionnaires-; Student-Rights; Value-Judgment
DE: *Administrator-Attitudes; *High-Schools; *Journalism-Education; *Principals-; *Student-Publications
AB: A study asked selected high school principals to respond to statements about the value of high school journalism to the high school student and about the rights and responsibilities of the high school journalist. These responses were then checked against such information as whether or not the high school principal had worked on a high school publication and how the principal valued that experience. Subjects were 43 high school principals (a response rate of 67%) from communities in the central and north central sections of Iowa selected so that all the principals represented high schools where there is a certified journalism teacher. Questionnaires which covered demographics, questions about the school, the journalism program and the principals' own high school journalism background, the value of high school journalism to the high school student, and the rights and responsibilities of the student journalist (and also asked the principals to evaluate the statements on a 5-point scale) were mailed to each principal. Results indicated that years as a principal cannot be used to predict a principal's response to the rights of the student journalist; knowing whether the principal worked on a high school publication can help predict how the principal values high school journalism 20% of the time; knowing how principals rate their own high school publication experience can help predict how they value high school journalism today 16% of the time and how supportive they are of high school student rights 10% of the time. (Seventeen tables of data are included.) (RAE)

Weber, Diane. "Writing Project Survives Many Obstacles in Alabama," *C:JET (Communication: Journalism Education Today)* 23 (Fall 1989):17.

AN: EJ383930
AU: Smith,-Gregory-A.
TI: The Media Academy: Engaging Students in Meaningful Work.

PY: 1989
JN: Educational-Leadership; v46 n5 p38-39 Feb 1989
AV: UMI
DE: Journalism-Education; Secondary-Education; Student-Developed-Materials; Student-Projects; Writing-for-Publication
DE: *Extracurricular-Activities; *High-Risk-Students; *School-Newspapers; *Student-Motivation; *Student-Publications
AB: One California high school is motivating at-risk students by giving them the opportunity to produce school publications. (Author/TE)

AN: EJ379958
AU: Clemons,-Molly-J.
TI: When Will Principals Have No Need to Worry about Publications?
PY: 1988
JN: NASSP-Bulletin; v72 n511 p9-10 Nov 1988
AV: UMI
DE: Freedom-of-Speech; Secondary-Education; Student-Rights
DE: *Administrator-Role; *Principals-; *School-Policy; *Student-Publications; *Student-Responsibility
AB: Describes a midwestern high school's serious student publications program. Over the past 20 years, students here have published major stories on incest, homosexuality, teen pregnancy, cheating, divorce, fatal illness, and other topics without prepublication scrutiny by the principal. Recommendations are provided to ensure fair coverage, relevant content, and excellent writing. (MLH)

AN: ED295219
AU: Dvorak,-Jack
TI: College Student Attitudes toward High School Journalism and Other Language Arts Experiences.
PY: 1988
NT: 47 p.; Paper presented at the Annual Meeting of the Association for Education in Journalism and Mass Communication (71st, Portland, OR, July 2-5, 1988).
PR: EDRS Price - MF01/PC02 Plus Postage.
DE: Curriculum-Evaluation; Higher-Education; High-Schools; Journalism-Education; Minimum-Competencies; Surveys-; Writing-Instruction; Writing-Skills DE: *College-Students; *Instructional-Effectiveness; *Language-Arts; *Student-Attitudes
AB: Examining high school language arts experiences, a study surveyed 2,687 randomly selected students from 18 colleges in 14 Midwestern states who had taken the American College Testing (ACT) tests in high school. Responses were received from 558 students (a 21% response rate), with a high ratio of generally academically superior and non-minority female students. Respondents answered a 29-item survey concerning 29 essential competencies considered crucial to the language arts programs in secondary schools (including the ability to organize writing for a specific purpose, and the ability to edit the writing of others). For each of the competencies, students were asked to rate their experiences in the three areas that applied to their high school language arts classes—standard (required) English, journalism courses, and other English electives (speech, drama, creative writing, etc.). Students also responded to an open-ended question asking for suggestions for high school language arts teachers. Results revealed that, when compared to students with no high school journalism experience, students who took at least one journalism course rated it as fulfilling the general language arts competencies better in 16 of the 29 competencies. When the competencies were collapsed into six categories, students rated journalism courses superior in four of them: writing, editing,

gathering/use of sources, and affective domain. On the open-ended question, among the most-mentioned of college students' suggestions for high school language arts teachers were to: (1) teach basic writing skills; (2) develop and encourage various writing styles; and (3) assign more writing. (Four tables of data are included, and a survey cover letter, sample survey, and 20 footnotes are appended.) (MM)

AU: Green,-Nancy-L.
TI: Journalism Offers Life Skills.
PY: 1988
JN: Communication:-Journalism-Education-Today-(C:JET); v22 n1 p2-3 Fall 1988
DE: News-Reporting; News-Writing; Secondary-Education
DE: *Daily-Living-Skills; *Journalism-; *Journalism-Education; *News-Media
AB: Asserts that journalism education provides students with important life skills. Suggests reasons why journalism education is so effective in preparing students for the future. (MS)

AU: Iorio,-Sharon-Hartin; Garner,-R.-Brooks
TI: What High School Teachers Want in University Journalism Programs.
PY: 1988
JN: Journalism-Quarterly; v65 n4 p990-95 Win 1988
DE: Educational-Research; Higher-Education; High-Schools
DE: *College-Programs; *Curriculum-Development; *Journalism-Education; *Secondary-School-Teachers; *Student-Needs; *Teacher-Attitudes
AB: Addresses demographic changes in secondary education in relation to the composition of university programs for scholastic journalism. Suggests that university programs be targeted toward specific groups which comprise segments of the scholastic journalism market. (RS)

AN: EJ368674
AU: Jao,-Greg
TI: The Impact of Involvement.
PY: 1988
JN: Communication:-Journalism-Education-Today; v21 n3 p15 Spr 1988
AV: UMI
DE: Editing-; Information-Sources; News-Reporting; News-Writing; School-Newspapers; Secondary-Education; Student-Publications; Writing-for-Publication
DE: *Journalism-Education
AB: Discusses the experiences associated with being involved in scholastic journalism and in researching the book "Voice of Conflict and Voices of Hope." Finds the value of scholastic journalism lies in its potential to train reporters and editors to seek the hidden experiences of student life that the "professional" media cannot investigate. (JK)

AN: EJ379959
AU: McPhillips,-Dorothy
TI: ACT Research Report Validates Journalism in the Curriculum.
PY: 1988
JN: NASSP-Bulletin; v72 n511 p11-16,18 Nov 1988
AV: UMI
DE: Higher-Education; Secondary-Education
DE: *Academic-Achievement; *College-Freshmen; *Curriculum-Enrichment; *Journalism-; *Student-Publications
AB: American College Testing Program (ACT) research evidence supports the inclusion of an academic-based journalism course (coordinated with publications) in every high

school's curriculum. ACT results show that college students who studied journalism or worked on school newspapers or yearbooks perform better during their freshman year. Includes recommendations and four tables. (MLH)

AU: Peterson,-Jane-W.
TI: A Study of the Coorientation of High School Principals, Journalism Teachers, and Local Newspaper Editors in Selected Iowa Communities.
PY: 1988
PG: 49
DE: High-Schools; High-School-Students
DE: *Editors-; *Journalism-Education; *News-Media; *Principals-; *School-Newspapers
AB: A study investigated the extent to which high school journalism teachers, principals, and local newspaper editors in selected Iowa communities have a common understanding of each other and the issues of high school journalism. A questionnaire sent to 187 newspaper editors, high school principals, and journalism teachers was returned by 118 respondents. The questions were constructed to prompt responses on the value of high school journalism, the rights and responsibilities of the high school journalist, and the roles of partners in high school journalism partnerships. Results indicated that principals and editors are in agreement on the issues of the value of high school journalism, the rights and responsibilities of the high school journalist, and the roles of high school journalism partnerships. Teachers were found to value high school journalism more highly than do the principals or editors. All three groups agreed on the role of journalism partnerships. (Twenty-one tables of data and three figures are included; 25 references are attached.) (RS)

AN: EJ345140
TI: ACT Research Shows High School Publications Experience Influences College Writing, Career.
PY: 1987
JN: Quill-and-Scroll; v61 n2 p11-13 Dec-Jan 1987
AV: UMI
DE: Higher-Education; Secondary-Education; Writing-Skills
DE: *Academic-Achievement; *Career-Choice; *Journalism-Education; *School-Newspapers; *Student-Publications; *Yearbooks-
AB: Summarizes a study that concluded beginning college freshmen with high school publications experience are better writers and are more likely to major in a communication-related field than those who were not on newspaper or yearbook staffs. (SRT)

AN: EJ385137
AU: Dvorak,-Jack
TI: ACT Survey Shows Some Top College Freshmen Find Journalism Class Fulfills Language Arts Competencies.
PY: 1987
JN: Quill-and-Scroll; v62 n1 p14-16 Oct-Nov 1987
AV: UMI
DE: College-Freshmen; Competence-; Educational-Research; Graduate-Surveys; Higher-Education; High-Schools; Journalism-; Secondary-Education; Student-Attitudes; Summative-Evaluation
DE: *English-Instruction; *Journalism-Education; *Language-Arts
AB: Reports on an American College Testing Program survey of academically superior college freshmen. Indicates that they found high school journalism classes to have fulfilled language arts competencies better than required or elective English courses. (SR)

374

AN: EJ373872
AU: Dvorak,-Jack
TI: High School Journalism Research: Community College Program Implications.
PY: 1987
JN: Community-College-Journalist; v15 n4 p2-5 Fall 1987
AV: UMI
DE: Comparative-Analysis; High-Schools; Journalism-; Outcomes-of-Education; Scores-
DE: *Extracurricular-Activities; *High-School-Students; *School-Newspapers; *Writing-Skills
AB: Reviews findings from a Journalism Education Association study comparing the American College Testing (ACT) Program standardized scores, writing samples, and Language Arts Survey responses of students who were involved in high school journalism programs with students who were not. Urges community college Journalism Educators to support high school journalism. (AYC)

AN: EJ349006
TI: High School Journalism Confronts Critical Deadline, A Report by the Journalism Education Association Commission on the Role of Journalism in Secondary Education.
PY: 1987
JN: Communication:-Journalism-Education-Today-(C:JET); v20 n3 p1-25 Spr 1987
AV: UMI
NT: A digest of the full report prepared by the Journalism Education Association Commission on the Role of Journalism in Secondary Education. The digest and full report are available from JEA, Kedzie Hall 103, Kansas State University, Manhattan, KS 66506-1505.
DE: Language-Arts; Newspapers-; Professional-Associations; Program-Content; Writing-Instruction; Yearbooks-
DE: *Educational-Research; *Faculty-Advisers; *Journalism-Education; *Secondary-Education; *Student-Publications
AB: Examines the value of journalism education at the secondary level. Concludes that journalism effectively develops language arts competency. Also identifies the characteristics of outstanding journalism programs and provides model guidelines and a job description for publications advisers. (FL)

AN: ED292081
TI: High School Journalism Confronts Critical Deadline. A Report by the Journalism Education Association Committee on the Role of Journalism in Secondary Education.
CS: Journalism Education Association.
PY: 1987
AV: Journalism Education Association, JEA, Kedzie Hall 103, Kansas State University, Manhattan, KS 66506-1505.($8.50, $5.00 for JEA members; a digest is $3.50, $2.50 for JEA members).
NT: 138 p.; For related document, see CS 211 021.
PR: EDRS Price - MF01 Plus Postage. PC Not Available from EDRS.
DE: High-Schools; School-Newspapers; Secondary-Education; Writing-Composition; Writing-Skills; Yearbooks-
DE: *Journalism-; *Journalism-Education; *Student-Publications
AB: In response to a resolution adopted by the Journalism Education Association (JEA) which requested a study of both the strengths and problems of scholastic journalism, this report analyzes various aspects of and specific programs in high school journalism, affirming the importance of journalism in secondary education. Summaries of adviser hearings conducted by the Commission on the Role of Journalism in Secondary

375

Education are furnished in the report, and several examples of successful high school newspaper and yearbook programs are examined. The report also discusses responses to an American Society of Newspaper Editors (ASNE) questionnaire, which revealed that high school journalism influences professionals. The report then presents results of a study which compared college grades, American College Testing (ACT) scores, and high school grades between students with and students without high school newspaper or yearbook experience—students with journalism experience achieve higher scores and grades than their counterparts. The relationship of journalism school and teacher education is reviewed in the report, and proposed standards for state-approved teacher education are presented. The report closes with sections on survey conclusions and recommendations for the strengthening of high school journalism education as well as a discussion of model guidelines for publication advisers. A list of additional resources and related readings is also provided. (MM)

AN: ED292082
TI: High School Journalism Confronts Critical Deadline. A Report by the Journalism Education Association Commission on the Role of Journalism in Secondary Education.
CS: Journalism Education Association.
PY: 1987
NT: 28 p.; For a related document, see CS 211 001.
PR: EDRS Price - MF01/PC02 Plus Postage.
DE: School-Newspapers; Secondary-Education; Student-Attitudes; Writing-Skills; Yearbooks-
DE: *Journalism-; *Journalism-Education; *Student-Publications; *Writing-Composition
AB: In cooperation with the American College Testing (ACT) Program, the Journalism in Education Association conducted a 2-year study to explore the status of high school journalism and, in particular, to determine factual data concerning the values of journalism in secondary education by comparing students with high school journalism/publication experience with those having no such experience. The study was divided into three parts. The first part, which compared college grades, ACT scores, and high school grades between students with and without high school newspaper or yearbook experience, examined 19,249 students enrolled in 10 colleges and universities who had completed at least one year of college. Results indicated that the 4,798 students who had served on their high school newspaper or yearbook scored higher than their counterparts without publications experience. The second part examined 1,204 students who had taken the ACT Assessment tests and the ACT COMP Prospectus Writing test segment, in order to compare the collegiate writing samples of students with and without high school newspaper/yearbook experience. Results revealed that students with publications experience scored significantly higher than those without such experience. Finally, the third part surveyed 558 students with high school publications experience to detect influences of a journalism credit course per se in relationship to all other language arts courses that students took for credit, with results indicating the importance of journalism education as a route to good writing. (MM)

AU: Krendl,-Kathy-A.; Dodd,-Julie
TI: Assessing the National Writing Project: A Longitudinal Study of Process-Based Writing.
PY: 1987
PG: 38
DE: Elementary-Secondary-Education; Instructional-Improvement; Language-Arts; Parent-Attitudes; Student-Attitudes; Teacher-Attitudes; Teacher-Improvement; Writing-Evaluation; Writing-Processes; Writing-Research

DE: *Process-Education; *Program-Effectiveness; *Program-Evaluation; *Writing-Improvement; *Writing-Instruction

AB: To evaluate the effectiveness of a new writing curriculum in the Oak Ridge Schools (Tennessee), modeled after the process-oriented National Writing Project, a three-year study of student writing was conducted. The study consisted of evaluating writing samples collected from 90 students in grades 3 through 12 over 3 consecutive years, and surveying by means of annual questionnaires the writing attitudes of students, parents, and teachers. Results from the student attitude surveys show an increase over the second and third year in students' interest in learning about writing, in their level of confidence, and in their association of self-esteem with good writing. A decrease was observed in students' feelings of discomfort about completing writing assignments and in their feelings that they do not write well and that writing is difficult. At the end of the study, students at each grade level were better writers than were previous students in that grade level. Students in classrooms with teachers trained according to the National Writing Project approach performed better on the writing sample than did students in the classrooms of untrained teachers. The teacher survey showed few differences between trained and untrained teachers in attitudes about writing, ranking of writing problems, and assessment of language arts priorities. Some significant differences were found between parent and teacher attitudes. (Recommendations of the writing committee are included, and writing assignments and assessment rubrics are appended.) (JG)

AN: ED269787
AU: Dvorak,-Jack
TI: Comparisons of College Grades, ACT Scores and High School Grades between Those with and Those without High School Newspaper or Yearbook Experience.
PY: 1986
NT: 24 p.; Paper presented at the Annual Meeting of the Association for Education in Journalism and Mass Communication (69th, Norman, OK, August 3-6, 1986).
PR: EDRS Price - MF01/PC01 Plus Postage.
DE: Comparative-Analysis; Extracurricular-Activities; Higher-Education; High-Schools; High-School-Students; Journalism-; Journalism-Education; School-Newspapers; Student-Publications; Yearbooks
DE: *Academic-Achievement; *College-Freshmen; *Educational-Experience; *Grades-Scholastic; *School-Publications; *Scores-

AB: To determine if any significant differences existed between secondary school students who had been on the staff of a school newspaper or yearbook and those students who had no publication experience, a study examined 19,249 college students who had completed their college freshman year in 1984 and who had taken the ACT Assessment as high school students during the 1982-1983 testing period. The following data were also obtained: Interest Inventory and Student Profile Section scores; final grades in the last high school courses in English, social studies, mathematics, and science; college freshman cumulative grade point averages; and first college English course grades. Findings showed that in 10 of 12 statistical comparisons, those students who had completed at least one year of college and who had been on the staff of a high school newspaper or yearbook earned significantly higher scores than their counterparts who were not involved in publications. The 10 significantly higher comparisons were found in cumulative college freshman grade point average; first collegiate English course; ACT Composite score; ACT English score; ACT Social Studies score; and mean score and final score of four high school courses in English, social studies, mathematics, and natural science. In only one of 12 comparisons—the ACT Mathematics score—did the group with high school publications experience show a significant negative difference. (Author/HOD)

AN: EJ342414
AU: Holbrook,-Hilary-Taylor
TI: ERIC/RCS Report: Journalism in the English Classroom.
PY: 1986
JN: English-Journal; v75 n7 p70-72 Nov 1986
AV: UMI
DE: Education-; Secondary-Education
DE: *English-Instruction; *Journalism-; *Student-Publications; *Teaching-Methods; *Writing-Composition
AB: Presents a rationale for the use of journalism in teaching English. Drawing from sources in the ERIC database, surveys journalistic aspects and sources that are closely related to and useful for the teaching of writing, critical reading, and production of a student literary magazine. (JK)

AN: EJ327789
AU: Moore,-Michael; Kohlmann,-Kristin
TI: Learning More than We Ever Wanted to Know about High School Journalism.
PY: 1986
JN: English-Journal; v75 n1 p56-59 Jan 1986
AV: UMI
DE: Extracurricular-Activities; Faculty-Advisers; Journalism-Education; Secondary-Education; Student-Experience; Student-Participation; Teacher-Student-Relationship; Writing-for-Publication
DE: *School-Newspapers; *Student-Publications
AB: A faculty adviser and his student associate editor chronicle their first year of producing the high school newspaper. Discusses problems that arose, including the interpretation of school news and the selection of articles. (EL)

AN: ED253879
AU: Arts; *Writing-Instruction
AB: Through a review of literature, this paper notes that journalism has been fulfilling several elements considered crucial in the language arts program for many years, more richly and more understandably for students than many traditional English composition courses and other writing classes. In view of this, and in light of the many educational reform commissions' directives, a one- or two-semester journalism course should be considered a worthy writing course in either the college bound or the general curriculum. The paper then examines several concerns raised by the commissions about language arts, writing's role in learning, writing competencies fulfilled in journalism courses, research related to journalistic writing, problems with English education, programs for English educators, and the reform movement and nonwriting journalistic competencies. In conclusion, the paper recommends that the credibility of journalism as a vital part of the language arts curriculum needs to be studied and that evidence supporting that part needs to be widely disseminated; that high school journalism classes need to attract and keep good teachers; and that press associations on all levels need to become active in disseminating research and concerns of Journalism Educators to influential groups and decision makers. (FL)

Bowen, John. "More Than a Basic." *School Press Review* (Winter 1984):20.

AN: EJ297962
TI: Former High School Journalism Students Speak.
PY: 1984
JN: Communication:-Journalism-Education-Today-(C:JET); v17 n4 p9-15 Sum 1984

AV: UMI
DE: Secondary-Education
DE: *Educational-Benefits; *Education-Work-Relationship; *Journalism-Education; *Student-Attitudes
AB: Graduates from four high schools across the United States, some journalism majors in college and some not, discuss their high school journalism experiences and the value of those experiences to their professional lives. (HTH)

AN: EJ297959
AU: Hall,-H.-L.
TI: Will Scholastic Journalism Survive?
PY: 1984
JN: Communication:-Journalism-Education-Today-(C:JET); v17 n4 p2-3 Sum 1984
AV: UMI
DE: Secondary-Education; Teaching-Methods; Writing-Exercises
DE: *Course-Content; *English-Curriculum; *Journalism-Education; *Writing-Instruction
AB: Recommends teaching journalism as an English course or in combination with an English course to ensure the continuation of journalism education in the face of more stringent graduate requirements. Describes such a course, which includes literature, a research paper, and regular composition assignments. (HTH)

AN: EJ297961
AU: Hall,-Lynlea
TI: Is High School Journalism Worth Keeping?
PY: 1984
JN: Communication:-Journalism-Education-Today-(C:JET); v17 n4 p5-7 Sum 1984
AV: UMI
DE: Educational-Quality; English-Curriculum; School-Publications; Secondary-Education; Teacher-Certification
DE: *Educational-Improvement; *Journalism-Education; *Teacher-Qualifications
AB: Examines the role of certification of journalism instructors in improving the quality of journalism education and of high school publications. Discusses the relationship of journalism to the English curriculum. (HTH)

AN: EJ297960
AU: Weyen,-Wendy
TI: Benefits of a Strong Journalism Program.
PY: 1984
JN: Communication:-Journalism-Education-Today-(C:JET); v17 n4 p3-4 Sum 1984
AV: UMI
DE: Higher-Education; Secondary-Education; Teacher-Attitudes
DE: *Educational-Benefits; *Journalism-Education; *Student-Attitudes; *Student-Needs
AB: Defends the value of the high school journalism course, examining the attitudes of students and college instructors. Discusses the importance of journalism in a well-rounded liberal arts education. (HTH)

National Commission for Excellence in Education. *A Nation at Risk: The Imperative for Educational Reform.* Washington, D.C.: U.S. Department of Education, 1983.

Blinn, John Robert. "A Comparison of Selected Writing Skills of High School Journalism and Non-Journalism Students." Ph.D. dissertation, Ohio University, 1982.

AN: EJ259327
AU: Johnson,-Linda
TI: Journalism Students Develop Writing Skills through Positive Experiences.
PY: 1982
JN: Quill-and-Scroll; v56 n3 p9-13 Feb-Mar 1982
AV: Reprint: UMI
DE: Secondary-Education; Student-Publications; Teacher-Role; Writing-Instruction
DE: *Journalism-Education; *Student-Attitudes; *Student-Motivation; *Teaching-Methods; *Writing-Skills
AB: Suggests students achieve greater success in writing through a program set up so that both journalism and composition students write for publication. (HOD)

Bloom, Benjamin S., ed. *Taxonomy of Educational Objectives I: Cognitive Domain.* New York: David McKay Company, Inc., 1956.

Sherwood, H.N., "Value of High School Publications," *Educational Review* 67 (January 1924):20-21.

Characteristics of Schools, Journalism Programs and Educators

Death by Cheeseburger: High School Journalism in the 1990s and Beyond. Arlington, VA: The Freedom Forum, 1994.

Dvorak, Jack. "Job Satisfaction and Working Conditions of Today's High School Journalism Educator," *Communication: Journalism Education Today* 26 (Spring 1993):2-5.

Ortman, Sarah. "Are you the adviser or the editor-in-chief?" JAOS Journal (Winter 1993):6.

Lain, Laurence B. "A National Study of High School Newspaper Programs: Environmental and Adviser Characteristics, Funding and Pressures on Free Expression." (Paper presented to the Secondary Education Division of the Association for Education in Journalism and Mass Communication, Montréal, Québec, 5 August 1992.)

Irby, Janet R. "Creating the Culture of Journalism," (paper presented to the Secondary Education Division at the convention of the Association for Education in Journalism and Mass Communication, Montreal, Canada, August 1992.)

Peterson, Jane W. "Secondary Journalism Research: Bridging the Gaps," (paper presented to the Secondary Education Division at the convention of the Association for Education in Journalism and Mass Communication, Montreal, Canada, August 1992.)

AN: ED344214
AU: Dvorak,-Jack
TI: Secondary School Journalism in the United States. Indiana High School Journalism Institute Insight. Research Report.
CS: Indiana Univ., Bloomington. High School Journalism Inst.
PY: 1992
NT: 11 p.; Type in tables and figures may be too small for legibility.
PR: EDRS Price - MF01/PC01 Plus Postage.
DE: High-Schools; High-School-Students; National-Surveys; School-Surveys; Student-Publications
DE: *Journalism-; *Journalism-Education; *School-Newspapers; *Yearbooks-
AB: A study investigated media-related activities in U.S. secondary schools. A seven-page survey was completed by 834 high school personnel from around the country. Topics

addressed included the extent and type of media outlets and classes; journalism credit; recruitment of students; participation by students from multicultural backgrounds; and the working conditions, attitudes, and characteristics of high school journalism teachers and advisers. Results indicated that: (1) 94% of all U.S. high schools have some type of media activity or outlet; (2) 93% publish yearbooks and 79% have newspapers; (3) more than half a million high school students are enrolled in journalism classes; (4) nearly three-quarters of a million students are on school media staffs; (5) 28% of journalism teachers and advisers hold state certification in journalism, and 8% earned a journalism major; and (6) 84% of advisers reported "a great deal" or "almost complete" freedom in advising. (Twenty-four notes are included.) (SR)

Lain, Laurence B. "A National Study of High School Newspaper Programs: A Preliminary Report." (Paper presented to the Mid-Winter Meeting of the Secondary Education Division of the Association for Education in Journalism and Mass Communication, Nashville, Tenn., January 1992.)

AN: ED339035
AU: Everton,-Muriel; Butler,-John-M.
TI: A Twenty-Five Year Slice of the Secondary Education Division's Historical Pie.
PY: 1991
NT: 37 p.; Paper presented at the Annual Meeting of the Association for Education in Journalism and Mass Communication (74th, Boston, MA, August 7-10, 1991).
PR: EDRS Price - MF01/PC02 Plus Postage.
DE: Communication-Skills; Educational-Trends; Secondary-Education; Student-Publications; Teacher-Associations; Teacher-Certification
DE: *Educational-History; *Journalism-Education
AB: An honors lecture has been given each year since 1973 by a person chosen by the Secondary Education Division members of the Association for Education in Journalism and Mass Communication (AEJMC). Several lecturers have provided insights into each decade of scholastic journalism and its relationship to society. Lecturers have discussed four major points as current problems: recruitment of dedicated students, help and support for advisers, language skills, and the need for research in scholastic journalism. Conclusions drawn from advice given by the lecturers and analysis made of their suggestions indicate that Division members: (1) took the lead in preparing teachers of journalism who achieved much during the past 25 years; (2) wrote extensively in various publications about scholastic journalism; (3) remained on the cutting edges of computer instruction and graphic design principles and practices; (4) developed a stronger relationship with other divisions of AEJMC; (5) led the fight for teacher accreditation; (6) improved activities at summer workshops; and (7) studied ways to improve communication skills in word usage, sentence structure, and facts. (Sixteen references are attached.) (RS)

AU: Iorio,-Sharon-Hartin
TI: Threats to Scholastic Journalism.
PY: 1991
JN: Communication:-Journalism-Education-Today-(C:JET); v24 n3 p18-20 Spr 1991
DE: Communication-Research; High-Schools; Surveys-
DE: *Courses-; *Course-Selection-Students; *Journalism-Education; *School-Newspapers; *Student-Attitudes
AB: Describes a survey of Oklahoma high school journalism teachers and advisers. Notes that 71 percent of respondents reported that enrollment in journalism and publication production classes had either remained the same or increased. Suggests that noneduca-

tional factors such as student interest impact more heavily on enrollment than do educational factors. (SG)

AN: ED322527
AU: Arnold,-Mary
TI: Mapping the Territory: A Conceptual Model of Scholastic Journalism.
PY: 1990
NT: 60 p.; Paper presented at the Annual Meeting of the Association for Education in Journalism and Mass Communication (73rd, Minneapolis, MN, August 1-4, 1990).
PR: EDRS Price - MF01/PC03 Plus Postage.
DE: Censorship-; Content-Analysis; Ethics-; Secondary-Education
DE: *Journalism-; *Journalism-Education; *Models-; *School-Newspapers; *Secondary-Schools
AB: Intended to provide a comprehensive conceptual framework to serve as a scaffold for past, present, and future research on "scholastic journalism" (journalism in the secondary school), a topical content analysis of the Association for Education in Journalism and Mass Communication (AEJMC) Secondary Education Division research, teaching, and issues sessions for the years 1977 to 1989 was undertaken. Papers or teaching sessions were placed into one or more of 13 categories, including censorship and legal and ethical issues, electronic media/technology, established media, financial concerns, publication production, and visual content. A list of 182 primary and secondary subject headings was developed, based on indexing practices in a number of existing electronic databases, to serve as key words for a newsletter indexing program. The categories derived from the AEJMC program topical content analysis were compared to the 37 masters theses and doctoral dissertations in the "high school media" category of "Journalism Abstracts" for the same period. Results indicated that legal and ethical issues were the primary conceptual area for scholastic journalism researchers. Results also indicated that history and cultural diversity were two conceptual areas that were slighted by researchers. (Thirty-nine footnotes, five tables and four figures of data, and a figure representing a conceptual model of scholastic journalism are included; 116 references, a list of dissertations and theses, the newsletter indexing key word list, and a list of studies concerned with secondary school journalism are attached.) (RS)

Gallinger, Nancy. "Still Captive Voices? High School Journalism in New England Needs Help." *Newspaper Research Journal* 11,2 (Spring 1990):12-27.

Hawthorne, Bobby. *Job Satisfaction and Dissatisfaction Among Texas High School Journalism Teachers.* Austin, Texas: Interscholastic League Press Conference, January 1990.

AN: EJ419783
AU: McCallie,-Franklin-S.
TI: One Principal's View: Educators Must "Stimulate—Not Stifle" Students' Ideas.
PY: 1990
JN: Communication:-Journalism-Education-Today-(C:JET); v24 n1 p23 Fall 1990
DE: Administrator-Role; Journalism-Education; Secondary-Education
DE: *Principals-; *School-Newspapers
AB: Discusses the administration's view of student journalism and the student press, as presented by one high school principal. Recognizes the value of journalism as an effective teaching/learning tool and recommends that educators stimulate rather than stifle students' ideas. (KEH)

Messenger, Jennifer, and Arnold, Mary Peterson. *Researching Scholastic Journalism.* Iowa City: Iowa Center for Communication Study, 1990.

Willis, Jim. *Journalism: State of the Art.* New York: Praeger Publishers, 1990.

Weaver, Marilyn. "A Summary of Journalism Certification Requirements: A National Assessment," Paper presented at the Mid-winter Meeting of the Secondary Education Division, Association for Education in Journalism and Mass Communication, Knoxville, Tenn., Jan. 16, 1988.

AN: EJ379792
AU: Clemons,-Molly-J.
TI: An Administrator's View of Student Publications.
PY: 1988
JN: Communication:-Journalism-Education-Today-(C:JET); v22 n1 p4-5 Fall 1988
AV: UMI
DE: Administrative-Policy; Administrative-Principles; Administrator-Attitudes; Censorship-; Controversial-Issues-Course-Content; Journalism-Education; Leadership-; Peer-Relationship; School-Administration; School-Newspapers; Secondary-Education; Student-School-Relationship
DE: *Administrator-Role; *Communication-Skills; *Principals-; *Student-Publications
AB: Emphasizes that strong communication skills and daily communication with teachers, staff, students, school board members, and the public are necessary for principals to survive. Suggests that principals need not be publications censors since they support the right of students to learn and to practice communication in classes, in co-curricular events, and in school publications. (MS)

AN: EJ379958
AU: Clemons,-Molly-J.
TI: When Will Principals Have No Need to Worry about Publications?
PY: 1988
JN: NASSP-Bulletin; v72 n511 p9-10 Nov 1988
AV: UMI
DE: Freedom-of-Speech; Secondary-Education; Student-Rights
DE: *Administrator-Role; *Principals-; *School-Policy; *Student-Publications; *Student-Responsibility
AB: Describes a midwestern high school's serious student publications program. Over the past 20 years, students here have published major stories on incest, homosexuality, teen pregnancy, cheating, divorce, fatal illness, and other topics without prepublication scrutiny by the principal. Recommendations are provided to ensure fair coverage, relevant content, and excellent writing. (MLH)

AN: EJ379793
AU: Hall,-Homer
TI: An Overview of Scholastic Journalism in the 1980s and into the 1990s.
PY: 1988
JN: Communication:-Journalism-Education-Today-(C:JET); v22 n1 p6-8 Fall 1988
AV: UMI
DE: Critical-Thinking; English-Instruction; High-Schools; Secondary-Education
DE: *Journalism-Education; *Student-Publications
AB: Discusses the status and future of high school journalism. (MS)

Peterson, Jane. "A Study of the Coorientation of High School Principals, Journalism Teachers, and Local Newspaper Editors in Selected Iowa Communities" (paper presented at the convention of the Association for Education in Journalism and Mass Communication, Portland, Ore., July 1988).

AN: EJ377393
AU: Vilsack,-Christie
TI: A Five-Step Plan for Laying a Journalism Program Foundation and Improving Public Relations between Elementary, Junior and Senior High Teachers.
PY: 1988
JN: Quill-and-Scroll; v62 n3 p20-22 Feb-Mar 1988
AV: UMI
DE: Administrators-; Elementary-Secondary-Education; High-Schools; Program-Design; Public-Relations; Recruitment-; Teachers-; Yearbooks-
DE: *Extracurricular-Activities; *Faculty-Advisers; *Journalism-Education; *School-Newspapers
AB: Promotes a plan for laying the foundation of a journalism program, including making contacts with junior high advisers, sending newspaper staff to junior high and grade school classrooms, and approaching administrators with a plan. (MS)

AN: EJ348967
AU: Disselhorst,-Frances-L.
TI: The Other Side of the Table, An Administrator's Perspective.
PY: 1987
JN: Quill-and-Scroll; v61 n3 p4-7 Feb-Mar 1987
AV: UMI
DE: Decision-Making; Nonverbal-Communication; Problem-Solving; Secondary-Education; Speech-Communication; Verbal-Communication
DE: *Administrator-Role; *Creative-Thinking; *Critical-Thinking; *Humor-; *Journalism-Education; *Student-Publications
AB: Discusses the importance of thinking, communication, and laughter to a successful and useful student publications program. (SRT)

AN: EJ342372
AU: Ferentinos,-Nick
TI: How One Award-Winning Newspaper Reports the Big Story Responsibly.
PY: 1986
JN: Communication:-Journalism-Education-Today-(C:JET); v20 n1 p5-8 Fall 1986
AV: UMI
DE: News-Writing; Secondary-Education; Student-Publications
DE: *Ethics-; *Journalism-Education; *News-Reporting; *School-Newspapers
AB: Discusses the school newspaper of Westlake High School in Austin, Texas, which regularly features "hard" news stories and how, as a result, the students have learned the responsibility and honesty involved in ethical journalism. (SRT)

AN: EJ349110
AU: Hawthorne,-Bobby
TI: A Judge Gives Today's Newspapers a Critique.
PY: 1986
JN: C.S.P.A.A.-Bulletin; v4 n1 p3-8 Sum 1986
AV: UMI
DE: Content-Analysis; Educational-Objectives; Educational-Research; Faculty-Advisers; Secondary-Education; Teacher-Attitudes
DE: *Journalism-Education; *School-Newspapers; *Student-Publications
AB: Assesses how well student newspapers "inform and entertain"—the goal most often cited in a survey of Texas newspaper advisers. Notes that most fail to meet this goal. (HTH)

AN: EJ334117
AU: Melingagio,-John
TI: Central Newspaper to Observe Centennial.
PY: 1986
JN: Quill-and-Scroll; v60 n4 p4-7 Apr-May 1986
AV: UMI
DE: Journalism-; Secondary-Education
DE: *Journalism-Education; *School-Newspapers; *Student-Publications; *Student-Research
AB: Reports on the efforts of a school newspaper staff to prove that the newspaper at Omaha Central High School is 100 years old and discusses the students' opinions of the paper throughout its history. (DF)

AN: EJ339918
AU: Paschal,-James-F.
TI: The Adviser's Role—An Historic View.
PY: 1986
JN: C.S.P.A.A.-Bulletin; v43 n4 p8-13 Spr 1986
AV: UMI
DE: Educational-History; Secondary-Education; Student-Publications
DE: *Faculty-Advisers; *Journalism-Education; *Professional-Development; *Teacher-Role
AB: Chronicle's the editor's career as scholastic press and yearbook adviser, noting that advising is one of the most important, exciting, challenging, and rewarding careers one can have, and that one can grow professionally in a chosen field by being an adviser. (HTH)

AN: EJ311524
AU: Colasurdo,-Anthony-P.
TI: The Literary Magazine as Class Project. PY: 1985
JN: English-Journal; v74 n2 p82-84 Feb 1985
AV: UMI
DE: Editing-; Journalism-Education; Secondary-Education
DE: *Class-Activities; *English-Instruction; *Periodicals-; *Student-Publications; *Writing-for-Publication
AB: Deals with organizing, editing, and producing a literary magazine as a class project. Suggests steps to be taken and pitfalls to be avoided. (RBW)

AN: EJ325083
AU: Haggerty,-Donna
TI: SNAP—High School Newspaper Advisory Program.
PY: 1985
JN: Communication:-Journalism-Education-Today-(C:JET); v19 n1 p2-3 Fall 1985
AV: UMI
DE: Journalism-; Layout-Publications; School-Business-Relationship; Secondary-Education; Writing-Instruction
DE: *Journalism-Education; *Newspapers-; *Student-Publications
AB: Explains the Students Newspaper Advisory Program (SNAP) at the Call-Chronicle Newspapers in Pennsylvania that provides area high school staffs the opportunity to use the Call-Chronicle's technical equipment and professional guidance to produce publications. (DF)

AN: EJ313614
AU: Hale,-Ann
TI: Verbal and Visual—Together.

PY: 1985
JN: Communication:-Journalism-Education-Today-(C:JET); v18 n3 p13-15 Spr 1985
AV: UMI
DE: Faculty-Advisers; Journalism-Education; Secondary-Education; Writing-Instruction
DE: *Editing-; *Guidelines-; *Student-Publications; *Teacher-Student-Relationship
AB: Advises faculty editors to have a written set of guidelines for all materials submitted to a literary magazine to avoid alienating contributors. (CRH)

AN: EJ325084
AU: Hicks,-Irene
TI: Herald's Program Helps Young Journalists.
PY: 1985
JN: Communication:-Journalism-Education-Today-(C:JET); v19 n1 p4-5 Fall 1985
AV: UMI
DE: Journalism-; Layout-Publications; School-Business-Relationship; Secondary-Education; Writing-Instruction
DE: *Journalism-Education; *Newspapers-; *Student-Publications
AB: Discusses the benefits of having high school students produce an issue of their school paper at the office of the "Pierce County (Washington) Herald," using its equipment and following the advice of professionals. (DF)

AN: EJ313619
AU: Keyser,-Christine-L.
TI: Public Relations and the High School Press.
PY: 1985
JN: Quill-and-Scroll; v59 n3 p8-12 Feb-Mar 1985
AV: UMI
DE: Administrator-Attitudes; Newspapers-; Secondary-Education; Student-Attitudes; Teacher-Attitudes
DE: *Journalism-Education; *Morale-; *Publicity-; *Public-Relations; *Student-Publications
AB: A series of guidelines for generating positive relationships between publications' staff and the student body, faculty, administration, school board, and community. (CRH)

AN: EJ325085
AU: Lesher,-Dean-S.
TI: Lesher Publications High School Classroom.
PY: 1985
JN: Communication:-Journalism-Education-Today-(C:JET); v19 n1 p6 Fall 1985
AV: UMI
DE: Graphic-Arts; Journalism-; Layout-Publications; School-Business-Relationship; Secondary-Education; Writing-Instruction
DE: *Journalism-Education; *Newspapers-; *Student-Publications
AB: Describes a one-semester high school journalism course taught in the building of the "Contra Costa Times" in Walnut Creek, California. (DF)

AN: EJ313609
AU: Perry,-Sue; Watterson,-Bruce
TI: Literary and Journalistic—Both.
PY: 1985
JN: Communication:-Journalism-Education-Today-(C:JET); v18 n3 p2-3 Spr 1985
AV: UMI
DE: English-Instruction; Literary-Styles; Secondary-Education; Standards-
DE: *Journalism-Education; *Student-Publications; *Teacher-Responsibility

AB: Explains the problems of and the school's responsibility for putting out a quality literary magazine. (CRH)

AN: EJ313616
AU: Vahl,-Rod
TI: Dissecting Leadership: Within the Staff.
PY: 1985
JN: Communication:-Journalism-Education-Today-(C:JET); v18 n3 p17 Spr 1985
AV: UMI DE: Faculty-Advisers; Journalism-Education; Opinions-; Secondary-Education; Teacher-Attitudes
DE: *Morale-; *School-Newspapers; *Student-Attitudes; *Teacher-Student-Relationship
AB: Emphasizes people, professionalism, and pride as aspects of leadership that must emerge from within a staff of school newspapers. (CRH)

AN: EJ325086
AU: Valentine,-Fern
TI: Publications Board Supervises Editorial Policy.
PY: 1985
JN: Communication:-Journalism-Education-Today-(C:JET); v19 n1 p7-8 Fall 1985
AV: UMI
DE: Editing-; Journalism-; Layout-Publications; News-Writing; School-Business-Relationship; Secondary-Education; Student-Publications; Writing-Instruction
DE: *Journalism-Education; *Newspapers-
AB: Explains an editorial policy for a high school newspaper that requires using the editor of the local professional newspaper as publications chair. (DF)

AN: EJ316575
AU: Willis,-Tony
TI: What an Adviser Wants from the Staff.
PY: 1985
JN: Quill-and-Scroll; v59 n4 p9 Apr-May 1985
AV: UMI
DE: Secondary-Education; Student-Publications; Student-Responsibility
DE: *Guidelines-; *Journalism-Education; *Student-Behavior; *Teacher-Response
AB: Lists of behavioral guidelines for sliding staff members. (CRH)

AN: ED243151
AU: Dodd,-Julie-E.
TI: High School Principals' and Newspaper Advisers' Evaluations of the Important Characteristics for Newspaper Advisers.
PY: 1984
NT: 26 p.; Paper presented at the Annual Meeting of the Association for Education in Journalism and Mass Communication (67th, Gainesville, FL, August 5-8, 1984).
PR: EDRS Price - MF01/PC02 Plus Postage.
DE: Comparative-Analysis; Educational-Research; Media-Research; School-Newspapers; Secondary-Education; Teacher-Role
DE: *Faculty-Advisers; *Journalism-Education; *Occupational-Surveys; *Principals-; *Role-Perception; *Teacher-Characteristics
AB: More than 200 high school principals and 175 school newspaper advisers responded to a survey that examined the similarities and differences in the two groups' evaluations of the important characteristics for newspaper advisers. The respondents supplied information concerning their schools and newspapers, their journalism training, and conflicts that had occurred between advisers and principals during the past year. In addition, they

ranked personality characteristics and interpersonal communication skills on a specially prepared scale. Results indicated that (1) neither the adviser's nor principal's background in journalism affected his or her perception of the importance of advisers being certified in journalism; (2) advisers with journalism training were more likely to have conflicts with their publication staff members than those with no such training; (3) the more college journalism training an adviser had, the greater likelihood that he or she would have conflicts with the school administration; (4) in ranking training characteristics for advisers, principals ranked teaching certification and college grades as much more important than did the advisers, who gave higher rankings to skills they would actually use in advising a newspaper staff, and (6) in ranking personality traits, principals selected "supports school philosophy" and "understands community mores" as most important, while advisers chose "assertiveness" as most important. (FL)

AN: EJ308178
AU: Lambert,-Bryce
TI: Advising at Private School Differs from Public.
PY: 1984
JN: Communication:-Journalism-Education-Today-(C:JET); v18 n2 p15-16 Win 1984
AV: UMI
DE: News-Writing; Private-Schools; Production-Techniques; Secondary-Education
DE: *Faculty-Advisers; *Journalism-Education; *Program-Descriptions; *School-Newspapers; *Student-Publications
AB: Describes the advantages of working with students in a boarding school on newspaper production in staff selection, preliminary dummy layout, distribution, and staff training. (CRH)

AN: EJ291492
AU: Shenkman,-Lynn
TI: Publications Advisers—What Are Their Competencies, Skills?
PY: 1984
JN: NASSP-Bulletin; v68 n468 p75-78 Jan 1984
AV: UMI
DE: Censorship-; Freedom-of-Speech; Legal-Responsibility; Secondary-Education
DE: *Faculty-Advisers; *Journalism-Education; *Student-Publications; *Student-Rights
AB: Advisers to student-run publications should be professionals with knowledge of journalistic ethics. The author outlines responsibilities and concerns, pointing out that administrators need to treat journalism as a legitimate academic subject. (MD)

AN: EJ309830
AU: Walling,-Donovan-R.
TI: It's Time to Consider a School Magazine.
PY: 1984
JN: Clearing-House; v58 n3 p116-17 Nov 1984
AV: UMI
DE: Information-Dissemination; Secondary-Education
DE: *Journalism-Education; *Periodicals-; *Public-Relations; *School-Community-Relationship; *School-Newspapers; *School-Publications
AB: Stresses the role school magazines play in providing the community with on-going information about the school. (HOD)

AN: EJ279397
AU: Daggett,-Sondy
TI: Building Staff Unity, Morale Takes Time, Total Effort.

388

PY: 1983
JN: Quill-and-Scroll; v57 n4 p4-6 Apr-May 1983
AV: Reprint: UMI
DE: Organizational-Climate; Secondary-Education
DE: *Conflict-Resolution; *Group-Unity; *Journalism-Education; *Morale-; *Student-Publications; *Teamwork-
AB: Suggests that building unity and pride through activities, social events, and professionalism will prevent destructive conflicts among the staff members of student publications. (JL)

AN: ED230964
AU: Sparks,-Mary-Kahl
TI: The Grading Systems of Award-Winning High School Journalism Teachers in Production-Oriented Classes.
PY: 1983
NT: 28 p.; Paper presented at the Annual Meeting of the Association for Education in Journalism and Mass Communication (66th, Corvallis, OR, August 6-9, 1983).
PR: EDRS Price - MF01/PC02 Plus Postage.
DE: Educational-Research; School-Surveys; Secondary-Education; Teacher-Role
DE: *Faculty-Advisers; *Grading-; *Journalism-Education; *School-Newspapers; *Student-Evaluation; *Writing-Evaluation
AB: Twenty-seven school journalism teachers who have been honored as "outstanding" by the Newspaper Fund in the last 3 years responded to a survey about how they grade students in production oriented classes. The teachers reported using a variety of grading systems, including subjective decision making, a combination grading system, self-evaluation, peer evaluation, and point systems. Most agreed that meeting deadlines was an important area in determining grades. However, there was less agreement on the importance of spelling, grammar, and the use of string books. Among the incentives besides grades cited by teachers for attracting and retaining good students were the reputation of the school publications, giving by-lines, having an occasional staff party, attending journalism conferences, and allowing student editors to be in charge. (Appendixes contain copies of student evaluation sheets used by various teachers.) (FL)

Vornberg, James A.; Zukowski, James J.; Gipson, Vance W.; Southern, J. Stephen. "A Model for Organizing Your School's Activity Program." *NASSP Bulletin* 67,465 (October 1983):86-90.

Blick, Thomas Edward, Jr. "High School Newspapers: Factors Significant in Achieving High Ratings." Paper presented at the Annual Meeting of the Association for Education in Journalism, Athens, Ohio, August 1982.

AN: EJ271085
AU: Hallaian,-Dorothy
TI: The Principle behind the Principal.
PY: 1982
JN: Communication:-Journalism-Education-Today-(C:JET); v16 n2 p18-19 Win 1982
AV: Reprint: UMI
DE: Secondary-Education; Student-Publications
DE: *Faculty-Advisers; *Journalism-Education; *Principals-; *Teacher-Administrator-Relationship
AB: Describes the kind of principal supportive of publications advisers and recommends strategies for keeping him or her. (JL)

AN: EJ261488
AU: Jankowski,-Laurence-J.
TI: GLIPA Surveys School Newspapers.
PY: 1982
JN: Communication:-Journalism-Education-Today-(C:JET); v15 n4 p24-26 Sum 1982
AV: Reprint: UMI
DE: Production-Techniques; Secondary-Education
DE: *Journalism-Education; *School-Newspapers; *School-Surveys; *Student-Publications
AB: Presents data gathered in a survey of 56 midwestern schools concerning various aspects of school newspaper production. (AEA)

AN: EJ259329
AU: Rasmussen,-Patricia-A.
TI: Ten Tips for Building a Better Journalism Program.
PY: 1982
JN: Quill-and-Scroll; v56 n3 p19-20 Feb-Mar 1982
AV: Reprint: UMI
DE: Secondary-Education
DE: *Administrator-Role; *Faculty-Advisers; *Journalism-Education; *Program-Design; *School-Newspapers
AB: Offers helpful tips for school newspaper advisers to pass to administrators in order to build a better scholastic journalism program and to move the administration toward detente with the student press. (HOD)

AN: EJ257643
AU: Rataiczak,-Thomas-E.
TI: Yearbooks Become a History Reference.
PY: 1982
JN: Communication:-Journalism-Education-Today-(C:JET); v15 n3 p20-21 Spr 1982
AV: Reprint: UMI
DE: Secondary-Education
DE: *Journalism-Education; *School-Publications; *Social-History; *Yearbooks-
AB: Advocates creating a reference room stocked with yearbooks, school newspapers, scrapbooks, pictures, programs, athletic records, and films in order to preserve a school's history. (FL)

Benedict, Mary. "Two Views of the High School Newspaper: A Comparative Study of the Perceptions of the Role of the High School Newspaper in Nine States." Paper presented to the Secondary Education Division of the Association for Education in Journalism Annual Convention, East Lansing, Mich., 11 August 1981.

AN: EJ254914
AU: Claussen,-Dane-S.
TI: 40 Tips for High School Editors.
PY: 1981
JN: Scholastic-Editor; v61 n1 p28-30 Sep 1981
AV: Reprint: UMI
DE: Job-Performance; Journalism-Education; Secondary-Education
DE: *Job-Skills; *Student-Publications; *Writing-Skills
AB: Provides guidelines for high school editors to help improve their paper's operation, image, and content, including devising a style manual and covering school board, faculty, parent, and administration activities. (HTH)

AN: EJ264195
AU: Hale,-Ann
TI: The Care and Feeding of Your Principal.
PY: 1981
JN: C.S.P.A.A.-Bulletin; v39 n3 p4-6 Win 1981-82
AV: Reprint: UMI
DE: Attitude-Change; Change-Strategies; Journalism-Education; Secondary-Education; Student-Publications
DE: *Administrator-Attitudes; *Faculty-Advisers; *Teacher-Administrator-Relationship
AB: Proposes ways by which publications advisers can win over school administrators: keeping administrators informed, giving them good news about the publication staff, and letting them know that they are appreciated. (RL)

AU: Knight,-Robert-P.
TI: Scholastic Journalism Comes of Age.
PY: 1981
JN: School-Press-Review; v57 n4 p8-12 Nov 1981
DE: High-Schools; Journalism-; School-Publications
DE: *History-; *Journalism-Education
AB: A review of the advances that have been made in scholastic journalism over the past 25 years. (RL)

AN: ED237991
AU: Winitch,-Vera
TI: The Study of Newspaper Journalism in the High Schools. Centering On.
CS: New York City Teacher Centers Consortium, NY.
PY: 1981
AV: New York City Teacher Centers Consortium, 260 Park Ave. South, New York, NY 10010 ($1.75).
NT: 49 p.
PR: EDRS Price - MF01/PC02 Plus Postage.
DE: Layout-Publications; News-Reporting; Secondary-Education; Student-Participation
DE: *Class-Activities; *English-Instruction; *Journalism-Education; *News-Writing; *School-Newspapers; *Student-Publications
AB: Intended as an introduction to the study of journalism in an English class, this booklet is divided into two sections, the first of which focuses on the purpose and importance of newspapers in a free thinking democratic society. In addition to considering the purpose of newspapers, the first section discusses responsibilities of journalists, a code of journalism standards, approaches to writing news, slanted reporting, objective reporting, elements of news stories, the "5 w's" and "how" in news stories, news leads, news story structure, feature stories, techniques of interviewing, a checklist for news stories, and a checklist for feature stories. The second section presents guidelines for community-focused student journalism projects. It is arranged into suggestions for selecting a topic, organizing a folder, using resources, conducting specific lessons, forming project groups, writing summary reports, doing layouts, discussing problems, and getting a story. The booklet concludes with a checklist for student reporters; a discussion of problems and pitfalls; ideas for extra credit, field trips and trip activities; and a bibliography. (HOD)

Eveslage, Thomas. "A Research Agenda for Journalism in the Secondary Schools." Paper presented to the Secondary Education Division of the Association for Education in Journalism and Mass Communication Annual Convention, Boston, Mass., August 1980.

Ingelhart, Louis E., "A Look at Captive Voices," *NASSP Bulletin*. 59 (February 1975).

Johns, Richard P. "Prescription for Administrators, Advisers: Accountability of Scholastic Journalism," *National Association of Secondary School Principals Bulletin*, 59 (February 1975).

Sellmeyer, Ralph L., and Billy I. Ross, "Realities of Scholastic Journalism," *NASSP Bulletin*, 59 (February 1975).

Nelson, Jack, ed. Commission of Inquiry into High School Journalism. *Captive Voices*. New York: Schocken Books, 1974.

Pettibone, John. "Summer Workshops Offer Training for Nation's Publications Advisers," *Quill and Scroll* 44,4 (April-May 1970):8-9.

Robbins, Jerry H. and Williams Jr., Stirling B. *Student Activities in the Innovative School*. Minneapolis: Burgess Publishing Co., 1969.

Atwood, E. Erwin, and Malcolm S. MacLean Jr., "How Principals, Advisers, Parents and Pupils View Journalism," *Journalism Quarterly*, 44 (Spring 1967), pp. 71-78.

Horine, D.R. "How Principals, Advisers, and Editors View the High School Newspaper." *Journalism Quarterly* 43,2 (Summer 1966): 339-345.

Boyd, John A. "High School Journalism Instruction in Indiana." *Journalism Quarterly* 37,4 (Autumn 1960):586-587.

Kimball, Penn T., and Samuel Lubell, "High School Students' Attitudes Toward Journalism as a Career: II," *Journalism Quarterly*, 37 (Summer 1960), pp. 413-422.

Campbell, Laurence R. "Training Sponsors for High School Journalism." *Journalism Quarterly* 16,4 (December 1939):366-370.

Fretwell, Elbert K. *Extra-Curricular Activities in Secondary Schools*. Boston: Houghton Mifflin Co., 1931.

McKown, Harry C. *Extracurricular Activities*. New York: Macmillan Co., 1927.

Whipple, Guy Montrose, ed. *Twenty-Fifth Yearbook of the National Society for the Study of Education, Part II: Extra-Curricular Activities*. Bloomington, Ill.: Public School Publishing Co., 1926.

Roemer, Joseph and Allen, Charles Forrest. *Readings in Extra-Curricular Activities*. Richmond, Va: Johnson Publishing Co., 1929.

Foster, Charles R. *Extra-Curricular Activities in the High School*. Richmond, Va: Johnson Publishing Co., 1925.

Rohrbach, Quincy Alvin W. *Non-Athletic Student Activities in the Secondary School*. Philadelphia: Westbrook Publishing Co., 1925.

Fretwell, E.K. and O'Neil, Marion. "Bibliography on High School Publications," *Teachers College Record* 26 (September 1924): 59-73.

Curriculum—Computers and Computing

AN: EJ426884
AU: Geske,-Joel
TI: Hypercard Another Computer Tool.

PY: 1991
JN: Communication:-Journalism-Education-Today-(C:JET); v24 n4 p14-17 Sum 1991
DE: Secondary-Education
DE: *Class-Activities; *Computer-Assisted-Instruction; *Courseware-; *Hypermedia-; *Journalism-Education; *Student-Publications
AB: Describes "Hypercard," a computer application package usable in all three modes of instructional computing: tutor, tool, and tutee. Suggests using Hypercard in scholastic journalism programs to teach such topics as news, headlines, design, photography, and advertising. Argues that the ability to access, organize, manipulate, and comprehend information may be Hypercard's most important function. (SG)

AN: EJ386983
AU: Rodewald,-Pam
TI: Computer Information Retrieval for Journalists.
PY: 1989
JN: Quill-and-Scroll; v63 n3 p8-9 Feb-Mar 1989
AV: UMI
DE: Computers-; Costs-; High-Schools; Journalism-Education
DE: *Databases-; *Information-Retrieval; *Information-Services; *Online-Searching
AB: Discusses the use of computer information retrieval (on-line electronic search methods). Examines advantages and disadvantages of on-line searching versus manual searching. Offers questions to help in the decision to purchase and use on-line searching with students. (MS)

AU: Oates,-Rita-Haugh
TI: "Software Tools" to Improve Student Writing.
PY: 1987
JN: Quill-and-Scroll; v61 n3 p14-16 Feb-Mar 1987
DE: Computer-Software-Reviews; Computer-Uses-in-Education; Grammar-; Punctuation-; Readability-Formulas; Spelling-
DE: *Authoring-Aids-Programing; *Computer-Software; *Journalism-Education; *Readability-; *Writing-Instruction
AB: Reviews several software packages that analyze text readability, check for spelling and style problems, offer desktop publishing capabilities, teach interviewing skills, and teach grammar using a computer game. (SRT)

AU: Oates,-Rita-Haugh
TI: Computer-Mediated Communication for High School Classroom.
PY: 1987
JN: Quill-and-Scroll; v61 n2 p8-10 Dec-Jan 1987
DE: Ethics-; Information-Networks; Secondary-Education
DE: *Computers-; *Electronic-Mail; *Interpersonal-Communication; *Journalism-Education; *Telecommunications-
AB: Focuses on computer-mediated communication and its integration into the high school journalism classroom. (SRT)

AU: Oates,-William-R.; Oates,-Rita-Haugh
TI: Going beyond Word Processing: A Survey of Computer-Based Approaches for Writing Instruction.
PY: 1987
PG: 21
DE: Computer-Software-Reviews; Elementary-Secondary-Education; Prewriting-; Revision-Written-Composition; Theory-Practice-Relationship; Writing-Research; Writing-Skills

DE: *Computer-Assisted-Instruction; *Computer-Uses-in-Education; *Instructional-Improvement; *Word-Processing; *Writing-Instruction

AB: Noting that (1) current research suggests that technology may contribute to improved instruction in writing but it does not do so automatically, and (2) while teachers may successfully employ computers with their writing students, their choices of methods remain critical, this paper surveys computer approaches and appropriate software for effective writing instruction. These include: prewriting software, composing tools, editing and revising approaches, and instructional software for writing skills. In addition, the paper briefly reviews new areas related to computer technology—desktop publishing, telecommunications, and electronic bulletin boards. The methods presented represent a composite of approaches developed by national leaders in computer writing instruction from the National Council of Teachers of English and the Association for Education in Journalism and Mass Communication. (Author/SKC)

AN: EJ332981
AU: Bear,-James-A.
TI: Computers: Small School, Small Budget, Small Yearbook and Paste-Up.
PY: 1986
JN: Quill-and-Scroll; v60 n2 p4-7 Dec-Jan 1986
AV: UMI
DE: Secondary-Education; Yearbooks-
DE: *Computer-Assisted-Instruction; *Computers-; *Journalism-Education; *Production-Techniques; *School-Publications
AB: Describes a high school yearbook paste-up project that used phototypesetting by means of a computer connected to a typesetting firm. (FL)

AN: EJ331853
AU: Riedl,-Richard
TI: CompuServe in the Classroom.
PY: 1986
JN: Computing-Teacher; v13 n6 p62-64 Mar 1986
DE: Costs-; Information-Sources; Information-Utilization; Learning-Activities; Online-Systems; Periodicals-; Program-Descriptions; Secondary-Education DE: *Information-Retrieval; *Journalism-; *Student-Projects
AB: Describes a student magazine publishing project in which the participating junior high school students accessed the information utility, CompuServe, to gather current and accurate background information for their magazine articles. Student use of CompuServe is described, and the value and costs of using CompuServe are discussed. (MBR)

AN: EJ346107
AU: Schleifer,-Neal
TI: Making the Leap to Desktop Publishing.
PY: 1986
JN: Classroom-Computer-Learning; v7 n3 p39-41 Nov-Dec 1986
AV: UMI
DE: Microcomputers-; Newspapers-; School-Publications; Secondary-Education; Teaching-Methods
DE: *Computer-Assisted-Instruction; *Computer-Uses-in-Education; *Journalism-Education; *School-Newspapers; *Student-Publications
AB: Describes one teacher's approach to desktop publishing. Explains how the Macintosh and LaserWriter were used in the publication of a school newspaper. Guidelines are offered to teachers for the establishment of a desktop publishing lab. (ML)

AN: EJ316574
AU: Kay,-Lois
TI: Computer Opens a New World.
PY: 1985
JN: Quill-and-Scroll; v59 n4 p7-8 Apr-May 1985
AV: UMI
DE: Faculty-Advisers; Journalism-Education; Opinions-; Secondary-Education; Writing-for-Publication
DE: *Computer-Assisted-Instruction; *Editing-; *Microcomputers-; *Student-Publications; *Word-Processing
AB: Outlines the advantages of computerization for both individual writers on staff and for the journalism teacher and adviser. (CRH)

AU: Oates,-Rita-Haugh
TI: Computer Software for Scholastic Journalism.
PY: 1985
PG: 20
DE: Computer-Graphics; Evaluation-Criteria; Grammar-; Layout-Publications; Secondary-Education; Writing-Skills
DE: *Computer-Assisted-Instruction; *Courseware-; *Educational-Games; *Journalism-Education; *News-Writing; *Teaching-Methods
AB: Four commercially available instructional software programs for high school journalism students are examined in this paper, which also contains suggestions on their use. The four programs reviewed in the paper provide (1) practice in finding the best interview sources in a newsgathering simulation (Super Scoop); (2) review and reinforcement of grammar skills in a news-editorial game setting (The Grammar Examiner); (3) use of a utility program—a tool—to create computer graphics and actual layouts of 8 1/2 x 11- or 8 1/2 x 14-inch pages (The Newsroom); and (4) review of general knowledge in areas such as American history, government, and literature in a game format (Knowledge Master series). (HOD)

AN: EJ325087
AU: Wilson,-Jack
TI: Students Typeset Copy at Newspaper Plant.
PY: 1985
JN: Communication:-Journalism-Education-Today-(C:JET); v19 n1 p9 Fall 1985
AV: UMI
DE: Computer-Literacy; Editing-; Learning-Processes; News-Writing; Program-Content; School-Business-Relationship; Secondary-Education; Student-Publications; Writing-Instruction
DE: *Journalism-Education; *Newspapers-; *Printing-
AB: Outlines a program that allows high school students to produce their school newspaper in the offices of the "Bellevue Journal American." (DF)

AN: EJ337857
AU: Overbeck,-Wayne
TI: Of Mice and Minicomputers: Computer Alternatives for Student Publications.
PY: 1984
JN: Community-College-Journalist; v12 n1 p2-6 Win 1984
AV: UMI
DE: Community-Colleges; Costs-; Needs-Assessment; Two-Year-Colleges; Word-Processing
DE: *Computer-Software; *Journalism-Education; *Microcomputers-; *Student-Publications

AB: Considers the advantages and disadvantages of various microcomputer hardware and software alternatives for the campus newspaper staff. Looks at hardware factors such as cost, speed, expandability, and software availability. Assesses choices in word processing and business applications software. (AYC)

AN: EJ296603
AU: Strause,-Lynn
TI: Yearbook by Computer: Surviving the Battle of the Byte.
PY: 1984
JN: Communication:-Journalism-Education-Today-(C:JET); v17 n3 p11-13 Spr 1984
AV: UMI
DE: Electronic-Equipment; Secondary-Education; Student-Experience
DE: *Journalism-Education; *Microcomputers-; *School-Publications; *Telecommunications-; *Yearbooks-
AB: Describes how a small town high school yearbook and newspaper staff successfully made the transition to computerized production using the Typestar 2000 system, developed by Inter-Collegiate Press and Data Basic of Mt. Pleasant, MI. (AEA)

AN: EJ296602
AU: Wilson,-Jack
TI: Not All Bliss in Computer Newspapers.
PY: 1984
JN: Communication:-Journalism-Education-Today-(C:JET); v17 n3 p8-10 Spr 1984
AV: UMI
DE: Computers-; Electronic-Equipment; Newspapers-; School-Business-Relationship; School-Community-Relationship; Secondary-Education
DE: *Journalism-Education; *Microcomputers-; *School-Newspapers; *Telecommunications-
AB: Recounts the unsuccessful attempts of a high school newspaper staff to transmit news stories over a telephone modem to a professional typesetter and the subsequent cooperation of a local newspaper with the high school staff. (AEA)

AN: EJ279298
AU: Kennedy,-Jack
TI: Computers Revolutionize Journalism Production.
PY: 1983
JN: Communication:-Journalism-Education-Today-(C:JET); v16 n4 p2-5 Sum 1983
AV: Reprint: UMI
DE: Secondary-Education
DE: *Computers-; *Journalism-Education; *Production-Techniques; *Student-Publications
AB: Reviews the many uses for computers in journalism education. (FL)

Curriculum — Content of Student Publications

AN: EJ426937
AU: Ricchiardi,-Sherry
TI: Student Press Responds with Barrage of Stories Ranging from Tearjerkers to Editorials about the Gulf Crisis.
PY: 1991
JN: Quill-and-Scroll; v65 n4 p4-6 Apr-May 1991
AV: UMI
DE: Secondary-Education; Student-Reaction
DE: *Journalism-; *Journalism-Education; *School-Newspapers

AB: Describes how the student press across the United States responded to the Gulf War with a barrage of stories ranging from tearjerkers about alumni who died to editorials condemning anti-Arab sentiment. (SR)

AN: EJ406828
AU: Benedict,-Mary
TI: Rating Your Story's EQ: Ethics Quotient.
PY: 1990
JN: Quill-and-Scroll; v64 n3 p4-5 Feb-Mar 1990
AV: UMI
DE: High-Schools; Secondary-Education
DE: *Ethics-; *Journalism-Education; *News-Reporting; *News-Writing; *School-Newspapers
AB: Offers six questions intended as an ethics guide to help school newspaper writers review their motivation for writing the story and the methods used in gathering and packaging the information. (SR)

AN: EJ406764
AU: Frischmann,-Bob
TI: Students Can Serve Readers Just as Professionals Do.
PY: 1989
JN: Communication:-Journalism-Education-Today-(C:JET); v23 n2 p15 Win 1989
DE: Journalism-Education; News-Writing; Secondary-Education
DE: *News-Reporting; *Student-Publications
AB: Discusses how service journalism has limitless possibilities in the scholastic press in terms of topics and angles for news stories. (MM)

AN: EJ406762
AU: Knight,-Robert-P.
TI: Building a Reputation for Service Journalism.
PY: 1989
JN: Communication:-Journalism-Education-Today-(C:JET); v23 n2 p13 Win 1989
DE: Journalism-Education; News-Writing; Secondary-Education
DE: *Administrator-Guides; *News-Reporting; *Student-Publications
AB: Provides suggestions for building a reputation for service journalism, including (1) how to get started; (2) how to build service journalism once it is started; and (3) how to maintain service journalism. (MM)

AN: ED317441
AU: Zombory,-Chris
TI: Covering the Global Village: A Handbook for the Student Press.
CS: Youth Communication, Washington, DC.
PY: 1989
NT: 62 p.
PR: EDRS Price - MF01/PC03 Plus Postage.
DE: Elementary-Secondary-Education; Guides-; International-Organizations; News-Media; Social-Studies; Student-Participation; Student-Projects; World-Affairs; World-Problems
DE: *Developing-Nations; *Global-Approach; *News-Reporting; *News-Writing; *Student-Publications
AB: Geared to student journalists and their advisers, this handbook demonstrates how different journalism techniques can be used to cover developing nations issues locally. News briefs are timely, short stories that give an overview or summary of a news topic. A news

event is similar to a news brief in that the event being covered must be current and the coverage should be thorough in as short a story as possible. A profile is a description of a program, group, or business. This type of story does not need to be timely. A personality portrait uses a person as a window on societies and living conditions. An in-depth story is one that requires a news hook and coverage of all sides of an issue. The explanations of how to write these types of stories are accompanied by sample stories, that illustrate the important points. Instructions are given for setting up an issues forum and for interviewing. A resource list is included of 81 international organizations that may be contacted for information on such topics as children in difficult circumstances, child survival and world health, the environment, population, foreign aid and trade, hunger and poverty, women in development, community-based resources and speakers, and development in general. The handbook also contains a glossary and additional model stories that fit into the news brief category. (JB)

AN: EJ383710
AU: Craghead,-Kathy
TI: Handling Sensitive Issues in the Yearbook.
PY: 1988
JN: Communication:-Journalism-Education-Today-(C:JET); v22 n2 p21,24 Win 1988
NT: Themed Issue: Sensitive Issues.
DE: Journalism-Education; Secondary-Education; Student-Publications
DE: *Death-; *Yearbooks-
AB: Discusses how sensitive issues should be approached in a school yearbook, focusing on suggestions for covering the death of a student or faculty member. (MM)

AN: EJ383705
AU: Boyle,-Diane
TI: Preparing a Sensitive Issue—From Beginning to End.
PY: 1988
JN: Communication:-Journalism-Education-Today-(C:JET); v22 n2 p9-10 Win 1988
NT: Themed Issue: Sensitive Issues.
DE: School-Newspapers; Secondary-Education; Teacher-Administrator-Relationship
DE: *Journalism-Education; *News-Writing; *Student-Publications; *Teacher-Responsibility; *Teacher-Role
AB: Presents guidelines for student reporters when writing about sensitive issues. Notes that journalism teachers are responsible for teaching the importance of accuracy, and for ensuring that students handle sensitive issues maturely and professionally. Stresses the need to establish a good relationship with the school principal. (MM)

AN: EJ383707
AU: Hathaway,-Susan
TI: A Sensitive Case Study: Senior Superlatives.
PY: 1988
JN: Communication:-Journalism-Education-Today-(C:JET); v22 n2 p13 Win 1988
NT: Themed Issue: Sensitive Issues.
DE: Journalism-Education; School-Newspapers; Secondary-Education
DE: *Student-Interests; *Student-Publications
AB: Suggests ways to deal with "senior superlatives" in newspaper supplements devoted to high school graduating classes. Reports that superlatives should be positive (as in "Most Likely to Succeed") and that results should be published only with the written consent of each "winner." Provides a sample release form for "senior superlatives." (MM)

AN: EJ383706
AU: Perkins,-Candy
TI: Annual Event, Homecoming, Turns Controversial.
PY: 1988
JN: Communication:-Journalism-Education-Today-(C:JET); v22 n2 p11-12 Win 1988
NT: Themed Issue: Sensitive Issues.
DE: Dress-Codes; Journalism-Education; News-Reporting; School-Activities; Secondary-Education
DE: *School-Newspapers; *Student-Publications; *Student-Reaction; *Student-School-Relationship
AB: Describes a high school's controversial homecoming celebration, and reports how the school newspaper covered the controversy. (MM)

AN: EJ383708
AU: Taylor,-George
TI: Community Coverage Deserves Accuracy, Fairness, Foresight, Thoroughness, Persistence.
PY: 1988
JN: Communication:-Journalism-Education-Today-(C:JET); v22 n2 p14-17 Win 1988
NT: Themed Issue: Sensitive Issues.
DE: Journalism-Education; Secondary-Education; Student-Publications
DE: *Local-Issues; *News-Reporting; *School-Community-Relationship; *School-Newspapers
AB: Asserts that coverage of community issues is essential to a student publication. Discusses the importance of accuracy, fairness, foresight, thoroughness, and persistence when reporting on community issues. Describes and reports on community response to several controversial stories in a high school newspaper. (MM)

AN: EJ368673
TI: Teens and Media.
PY: 1988
JN: Communication:-Journalism-Education-Today; v21 n3 p2-14 Spr 1988
AV: UMI
DE: Media-Selection; Newspapers-; News-Reporting; Nonprint-Media; Secondary-Education; Student-Publications; Telecommunications-
DE: *Mass-Media; *News-Media
AB: Teenage consumers question the priorities of the media. They: (1) regard the media as another institution against young people; (2) avoid it because they find it depressing, (3) challenge time allocated for sports and weather, (4) question emphasis on violence, and lack of concern for details and fairness; and (5) advocate a reversal in the role of the media. (JK)

AN: EJ368604
AU: Johnston,-Margaret
TI: Student Activities Coverage by College Newspaper.
PY: 1987
JN: Communication:-Journalism-Education-Today; v21 n2 p6-7 Win 1987
AV: UMI
DE: Content-Area-Writing; Editing-; Expository-Writing; News-Reporting; News-Writing; Secondary-Education; Writing-for-Publication
DE: *School-Newspapers; *Student-Publications
AB: Offers examples of how the Red and Black, an independent student newspaper at the University of Georgia, covers student activities. (JK)

AN: EJ368607
AU: Walker,-Hilda
TI: Front Page Push Promotes Participation.
PY: 1987
JN: Communication:-Journalism-Education-Today; v21 n2 p12-13 Win 1987
AV: UMI
DE: Extracurricular-Activities; Secondary-Education; Student-Participation
DE: *News-Reporting; *Publicity-; *School-Newspapers; *Student-Publications
AB: Presents an effective way of helping to publicize a big school activity and increase student interest and participation. (JK)

AN: EJ313613
AU: Perry,-Sue; Watterson,-Bruce
TI: Policy and Procedures—For Content.
PY: 1985
JN: Communication:-Journalism-Education-Today-(C:JET); v18 n3 p11-12 Spr 1985
AV: UMI
DE: Journalism-Education; Secondary-Education; Visual-Arts
DE: *Assignments-; *Student-Publications; *Thematic-Approach; *Writing-for-Publication
AB: Recommends avoiding cliches, overly long statements, and label themes for a literary magazine and coming up with tailor-made themes through staff brainstorming. (CRH)

AN: EJ319700
AU: Vahl,-Rod
TI: Leadership within the School.
PY: 1985
JN: Communication:-Journalism-Education-Today-(C:JET); v18 n4 p16 Sum 1985
DE: Secondary-Education
DE: *Journalism-Education; *School-Newspapers; *Student-Leadership
AB: Explains how high school journalists can serve as powerful leaders within the school by recognizing at least four journalistic functions of a newspaper: informing, explaining, analyzing, and persuading. (DF)

Sokoloff, Harris. "Integrating Thinking Skills into Content Areas." *Media & Methods* 31,3 (November 1984):25, 44.

AN: EJ297909
AU: Peterson,-Paul
TI: Plagiarism: It Can Happen to You!
PY: 1984
JN: Quill-and-Scroll; v58 n4 p15 Apr-May 1984
AV: UMI
DE: Credibility-; Faculty-Advisers; Higher-Education; Journalism-Education; Secondary-Education
DE: *Plagiarism-; *Student-Publications; *Teacher-Role; *Writing-Composition
AB: Suggests that preventative measures, such as proper instruction in basic journalism classes, are not always enough to prevent plagiarism. Urges publications that have discovered they have printed a plagiarized piece to admit their error frankly to their readers. (MM)

AN: EJ293089
AU: Daggett,-Sondy
TI: Controversial Issues Possible in Student Press.
PY: 1983

JN: Communication:-Journalism-Education-Today-(C:JET); v17 n2 p8-10 Win 1983
AV: UMI
DE: Alcoholism-; High-School-Students; Homosexuality-; Secondary-Education; Student-Experience; Suicide-
DE: *Journalism-Education; *School-Newspapers; *Social-Problems; *Student-Development
AB: Offers examples of controversial topics that had been covered successfully by a high school newspaper staff. (AEA)

AN: EJ282586
AU: Vacha,-John
TI: Burden of Death: How the School Press Covered the Assassination of John F. Kennedy.
PY: 1983
JN: C.S.P.A.A.-Bulletin; v41 n1 p12-19 Sum 1983
AV: Reprint: UMI
DE: Crime-; Journalism-; Journalism-Education; Secondary-Education; Student-Publications
DE: *Death-; *News-Reporting; *School-Newspapers; *United-States-History
AB: Examines the accounts of President John Kennedy's assassination in several high school newspapers. Notes the transition of most school papers from superficial school-related reporting to in-depth journalism. (HTH)

AU: Oates,-Rita-Haugh
TI: How Can Your Publication Avoid Sexist Content?
PY: 1982
JN: Communication:-Journalism-Education-Today-(C:JET); v15 n3 p4-5 Spr 1982
DE: Secondary-Education
DE: *Journalism-Education; *Language-Usage; *School-Publications; *Sex-Bias; *Sex-Stereotypes
AB: Offers examples of sexist language that often appear in school publications and suggests ways of avoiding such language. (FL)

AU: Dodd,-Julie
TI: Better Sports Pages Can Make a Major Contribution to Today's School Newspaper.
PY: 1981
JN: School-Press-Review; v57 n4 p2-4 Oct 1981
DE: High-Schools; Layout-Publications; Student-Publications
DE: *Athletics-; *Media-Research; *News-Reporting; *School-Newspapers
AB: A survey of 23 high school newspapers revealed factors contributing to a "winning" sports section, including methods of game coverage and the use of a sports column and sports features. (RL)

AU: Oates,-Rita-Haugh
TI: Understanding News Values: Secret to Good Public Relations.
PY: 1981
JN: English-Journal; v70 n8 p38-41 Dec 1981
DE: English-Instruction; High-Schools
DE: *News-Media; *Public-Relations; *School-Community-Relationship; *Teacher-Role
AB: Explains the news values that journalists use. Shows English teachers and administrators how they can apply this knowledge of news media to improve public relations between the school and the community. (RL)

AN: EJ254909
AU: Prentice,-Tom

TI: Editorials Need Facts to Convince.
PY: 1981
JN: Scholastic-Editor; v61 n1 p5-6 Sep 1981
AV: Reprint: UMI
DE: Journalism-Education; Newspapers-; Persuasive-Discourse; Secondary-Education; Writing-Skills
DE: *Editorials-; *Journalism-; *Press-Opinion; *School-Newspapers
AB: Discusses the elements of quality editorial writing. Briefly follows the development of the editorial page through U.S. history and offers strategies to ensure concise, persuasive student editorials. (HTH)

Birmingham, John, ed. *Our Time Is Now: Notes from the High School Underground.* New York: Praeger Publishers, 1970.

Curriculum—News Gathering, Reporting Techniques

AN: EJ421234
AU: Massy,-Susan
TI: Back to the Basics.
PY: 1990
JN: Communication:-Journalism-Education-Today-(C:JET); v24 n2 p2-3 Win 1990
DE: Editing-; Secondary-Education
DE: *News-Reporting; *News-Writing; *School-Newspapers
AB: Maintains that good news reporting requires hard work, careful research, and even more careful verification. Notes that there is nothing old fashioned about news reporting, except that, like fine antiques, good news reporting in scholastic publications is hard to find. (RS)

AN: EJ435618
AU: Mosier,-Joel
TI: Interviewing Coaches and Athletes.
PY: 1990
JN: School-Press-Review; v65 n4 v66 n1 p16-17 Sum-Fall 1990
AV: UMI
DE: Journalism-Education; School-Newspapers; Secondary-Education; Writing-for-Publication
DE: *Athletics-; *Interviews-; *News-Reporting; *Student-Publications
AB: Offers advice to student sports reporters on how to get the best interviews with coaches and athletes. States that good sports interviewing should start before the game, and follow up with an in-depth interview as soon as possible once the game is over. (MG)

AU: Puntney,-Linda
TI: Just Ask Me Anything.
PY: 1990
JN: Communication:-Journalism-Education-Today-(C:JET); v24 n2 p4-6 Win 1990
DE: Communication-Skills; News-Writing; Secondary-Education
DE: *Interviews-; *News-Reporting
AB: Presents tips to make the interviewing process more effective and comfortable for the reporter and the interviewee. Reviews the "standard pointers" for interviews as well as pointers to make the interview more of a personal conversation. (RS)

AN: EJ435617
AU: Wells,-Terrance-D.

TI: Be Ready for the Unexpected.
PY: 1990
JN: School-Press-Review; v65 n4 v66 n1 p14-15 Sum-Fall 1990
AV: UMI
DE: Journalism-Education; Questioning-Techniques; Secondary-Education; Writing-for-Publication
DE: *Interviews-; *School-Newspapers; *Student-Publications
AB: Offers advice to high school newspaper reporters on how to be ready for the unexpected when conducting interviews. Suggests that reporters get better quotes by using follow-up questions during a conversation with the interviewee than through use of preplanned questions. (MG)

AN: EJ397640
AU: Hadnot,-Ira-J.
TI: Professional Responsibility vs Personal Ethics.
PY: 1989
JN: Quill-and-Scroll; v64 n1 p8-10 Oct-Nov 1989
AV: UMI
DE: High-School-Students; Secondary-Education; Student-Writing-Models
DE: *Ethics-; *Journalism-Education; *News-Reporting; *School-Newspapers; *Student-Publications
AB: Discusses how to approach journalistic situations in which professional responsibility and personal ethics collide. (SR)

AN: EJ385121
AU: Strentz,-Herb
TI: When Is the Use of Anonymous Sources Permissible?
PY: 1989
JN: Quill-and-Scroll; v63 n2 p8-9 Dec-Jan 1989
AV: UMI
DE: Editors-; Secondary-Education; Student-Publications
DE: *Ethics-; *Journalism-; *Journalism-Education; *News-Reporting
AB: Argues that anonymity is granted too often by high school journalists. Lists guidelines to help high school reporters and editors decide when anonymity for a news source is appropriate. (MS)

AN: EJ383709
AU: Irby,-Janet
TI: International Reporting Requires Care, Fortitude.
PY: 1988
JN: Communication:-Journalism-Education-Today-(C:JET); v22 n2 p18-20 Win 1988
NT: Themed Issue: Sensitive Issues.
DE: Cultural-Interrelationships; Culture-Contact; Developing-Nations; Foreign-Countries; Journalism-Education; School-Newspapers; Secondary-Education; Student-Publications
DE: *Cultural-Context; *News-Reporting
AB: Discusses problems faced when interviewing people from different cultures. Describes several situations encountered when student journalists traveled to the Dominican Republic. Presents seven guidelines for international reporting, developed from the author's experiences in developing nations. (MM)

AN: EJ377448
AU: Kovas,-Marcia
TI: Use Networking to Improve Coverage.

PY: 1988
JN: Quill-and-Scroll; v63 n1 p7-10 Oct-Nov 1988
AV: UMI
DE: Secondary-Education
DE: *Journalism-Education; *News-Reporting; *School-Newspapers; *Student-Publications
AB: Describes eight "networking" strategies to uncover leads for high school reporters: (1) follow the local media; (2) use magazine approaches; (3) borrow ideas from exchange papers; (4) brainstorm together; (5) try a first-hand account; (6) investigate yourself; (7) tackle tough issues; and (8) provide your staff with inside information. (SR)

AN: EJ383703
AU: Wilson,-Jack
TI: School Survey Lists Sensitive Issues to Pursue.
PY: 1988
JN: Communication:-Journalism-Education-Today-(C:JET); v22 n2 p2-5 Win 1988
NT: Themed Issue: Sensitive Issues.
DE: Adolescents-; High-School-Students; Journalism-Education; News-Reporting; School-Newspapers; Secondary-Education; Student-Publications; Student-Research
DE: *School-Surveys; *Student-Interests
AB: Reports on a high school survey, conducted by the school's newspaper staff, concerning issues of importance in students' lives. Notes that drug/alcohol abuse was the most frequently cited issue; other issues included AIDS, teen sex, college, and peer pressure. Provides a table of survey results. (MM)

AN: EJ368603
AU: Walker,-Hilda
TI: Information for Copy; News Stories Come from Many Sources.
PY: 1987
JN: Communication:-Journalism-Education-Today; v21 n2 p3-5 Win 1987 AV: UMI
DE: Content-Area-Writing; Editing-; Expository-Writing; Information-Sources; Journalism-Education; News-Reporting; News-Writing; Secondary-Education; Writing-for-Publication
DE: *School-Newspapers; *Student-Publications; *Yearbooks-
AB: Presents ways of finding news sources for newspaper and yearbook reporters. Suggests how to work the "Beat System." (JK)

AN: EJ368602
AU: Walker,-Hilda
TI: Open Communication Improves Activities Coverage.
PY: 1987
JN: Communication:-Journalism-Education-Today; v21 n2 p2 Win 1987 AV: UMI
DE: Cooperation-; Feedback-; News-Reporting; School-Newspapers; Secondary-Education
DE: *Group-Dynamics; *Interpersonal-Communication; *Organizational-Communication; *Student-Publications
AB: Discusses the importance of open communication between the publication staffs and those involved in organizing school events. (JK)

AN: EJ309782
AU: Arnold,-George-T.
TI: A Realistic Approach for Sportswriters.
PY: 1985
JN: Quill-and-Scroll; v59 n2 p4-7 Dec-Jan 1985
AV: UMI

DE: Journalism-; News-Media; News-Writing; Secondary-Education
DE: *Athletics-; *Journalism-Education; *News-Reporting; *Student-Publications
AB: Identifies the advantages students have over community media persons in covering high school athletics and encourages writers to work with rather than compete with local media. (CRH)

AN: EJ269718
AU: Reque,-John
TI: Use a Feedback Form!
PY: 1982
JN: Quill-and-Scroll; v57 n1 p9-11 Oct-Nov 1982
AV: Reprint: UMI
DE: Secondary-Education; Student-Publications
DE: *Information-Sources; *Journalism-Education; *News-Reporting; *School-Newspapers
AB: Recommends using a feedback form to help student reporters solve problems relating to the accuracy of direct or indirect quotation of sources. (JL)

AN: EJ276127
AU: Sullivan,-Dolores-P.
TI: How to Develop Better Student Opinion Polls.
PY: 1982
JN: C.S.P.A.A.-Bulletin; v40 n3 p7-11 Win 1982-83
AV: Reprint: UMI
DE: School-Newspapers; Secondary-Education
DE: *Attitude-Measures; *Journalism-Education; *Opinions-; *Student-Attitudes; *Student-Publications
AB: Gives a brief history of the polling phenomenon and step-by-step instructions for conducting a reliable poll for a high school newspaper. (HTH)

Curriculum—General

Eveslage, Thomas. "Strengthening Scholastic Journalism Through Goals Shared With the Social Studies." *Communication: Journalism Education Today* 26 (Spring 1993):6-9.

Grusin, Elinor Kelley and Stone, Gerald C. "The Newspaper in Education and New Readers: Hooking Kids on Newspapers Through Classroom Experiences," *Journalism Monographs* 141 (October 1993).

AN: EJ444264
AU: Owen,-Betsy
TI: Critiques: Required Reading for All Staffers.
PY: 1992
JN: Communication:-Journalism-Education-Today-(C:JET); v25 n4 p20 Sum 1992
DE: Secondary-Education
DE: *Evaluation-Criteria; *Evaluation-Methods; *Journalism-Education; *Student-Publications
AB: Maintains that all staff—not just editors and advisers—should read and learn from judges' critiques of their publication. Describes a process for doing so. (SR)

Wanta, Wayne and Brierton, Patricia. "The Newspaper in Education Program: Types of Activities and Later Reading Habits," (paper presented to the Secondary Education Division at the convention of the Association for Education in Journalism and Mass Communication, Montreal, Canada, August 1992.)

English, Earl; Hach, Clarence and Rolnicki, Tom. *Scholastic Journalism*. 8th ed. Ames: Iowa State University Press, 1990.

AN: EJ414658
AU: Shuman,-Jim
TI: Help for the New Yearbook Adviser: No One Should Have to Suffer through the First Year Alone.
PY: 1990
JN: Communication:-Journalism-Education-Today-(C:JET); v23 n4 p12-13 Sum 1990
DE: Journalism-Education; Secondary-Education; Teaching-Methods
DE: *Faculty-Advisers; *School-Newspapers; *Student-Publications; *Yearbooks-
AB: Presents advice for new yearbook advisers planning and production of a yearbook. (RS)

AN: EJ411515
AU: Vahl,-Rod
TI: The Writing Teacher, the Photography Teacher Teaming Up to Provide the Best of Everything.
PY: 1990
JN: Quill-and-Scroll; v64 n4 p4-7 Apr-May 1990
AV: UMI
DE: Cooperation-; High-School-Students; Layout-Publications; Secondary-Education; Teacher-Effectiveness; Teaching-Methods
DE: *Journalism-Education; *Photojournalism-; *School-Newspapers; *Student-Publications; *Teamwork-
AB: Describes how a writing teacher and a photography teacher teamed up to provide opportunities for high school students to combine their skills in the production of the school newspaper. (MG)

Boyd, John A. "Responsibility: The Key to Scholastic Journalism. *NASSP Bulletin* 72,511 (November 1988):19-20.

AN: EJ379957
AU: Green,-Nancy-L.
TI: Journalism Training: Preparation for Student Success.
PY: 1988
JN: NASSP-Bulletin; v72 n511 p5-6,8 Nov 1988
AV: UMI
DE: Secondary-Education; Success-
DE: *Academic-Achievement; *Basic-Skills; *College-Students; *Communication-Skills; *Journalism-; *Student-Publications
AB: Interviewing, fact checking, writing, research, analysis, meeting deadlines—all are necessary skills gained from journalism training. The Journalism Education Association recently reported that students taking high school journalism courses and working on student publications performed better in college than students without such training. Suggestions for improving journalism courses are provided. (MLH)

AN: ED294186
TI: Language Arts.
CS: Arkansas State Dept. of Education, Little Rock.
PY: 1987
NT: 46 p.
PR: EDRS Price - MF01/PC02 Plus Postage.

DE: Basic-Skills; Course-Content; Curriculum-Development; Language-Arts; Public-Schools; Secondary-Education; Skill-Development; Speech-Communication; State-Curriculum-Guides; Writing-Instruction

DE: *Course-Objectives; *English-Curriculum; *Journalism-Education; *Speech-Curriculum

AB: The language arts course content guides presented in this manual cover English, oral communications, and journalism in grades 9-12 and provide a framework from which a curriculum can be built. Within each subject area and at each grade level, skills are identified at three instructional levels: basic, developmental, and extension. The basic skills are skills which all students should master; developmental skills, going beyond the basic level, should be introduced and taught, but not mastered by all students; extension skills, for learners who have mastered the required basic and recommended developmental skills, stress the higher order thinking, processing, and problem solving skills. Subject areas for English consist of capitalization, punctuation, writing numbers (grade 9), syllabication (grade 9), usage, elements of the sentence, semantics, spelling, reference skills, literature, and composition. For the oral communications curriculum, subject areas include universal dimensions of all oral communications efforts, intrapersonal communication, interpersonal communication, listening and critical thinking, nonverbal communication, group discussion, public speaking, parliamentary procedure, oral interpretation, and debate. Journalism subject areas include an introduction to journalism, history of journalism, terminology, news writing, feature writing, editorials, publication production, ethics, advertising, and careers in journalism. (MM)

AN: ED273992
AU: Deluzain,-Edward, Ed.
TI: Florida's Centers of Excellence in English.
CS: Florida Council of Teachers of English.
PY: 1986
JN: Florida-English-Journal; v22 spec iss Mar 1986
AV: National Council of Teachers of English, 1111 Kenyon Rd., Urbana, IL 61801 (Stock No. 17511, $5.00 member, $5.50 nonmember).
NT: 77 p.
PR: EDRS Price - MF01/PC04 Plus Postage.
DE: Debate-; Drama-; Elementary-Secondary-Education; Journalism-Education; Program-Descriptions
DE: *English-Curriculum; *English-Instruction; *Language-Arts
AB: The eight English language arts programs in the six Florida public schools included among the 150 Centers of Excellence in English selected by the National Council of Teachers of English are described in this focused journal issue. Following an introductory essay by coeditor Edward Deluzain describing the Centers of Excellence selection procedure, the titles and authors of the articles are as follows: (1) "The Drama Program of South Plantation High School" (Patricia F. Cook); (2) "The Debate Program at Twin Lakes High School" (Barbara Dale McCall); (3) "Journalism Motel; or, Time Reaps Rewards at South Plantation High School" (Alyce Culpepper); (4) "The Mass Media Program of Cooper City High School" (Mary McClintock); (5) "Creative Writing for Hearing Impaired Students at South Plantation High School" (Susan S. Steege and Mary Lou Ridge); (6) "The Language Arts Program of Hialeah High School" (Gail Kelly); (7) "English at Mowat Junior High School: Real Reading, Real Writing, Real People" (Beth Owens Deluzain, Alyne Pitman Farrell, and Gloria Treadwell Pipkin); (8) "English and the Language Arts at David Fairchild Elementary School" (Alice Warren). The journal concludes with a complete list of the Centers of Excellence in the United States and Canada. (HTH)

AN: EJ343674
TI: Newspaper Lesson Aids.
PY: 1986
JN: Communication:-Journalism-Education-Today-(C:JET); v20 n2 p2-22 Win 1986
AV: UMI
DE: Advertising-; Grading-; Interviews-; Lesson-Plans; School-Newspapers; Secondary-Education
DE: *Class-Activities; *Journalism-Education; *News-Writing; *Student-Publications
AB: Provides photocopy-ready lesson aids on story ideas, interviewing, inverted pyramid writing style, newswriting, sports/scavenger hunt, finding feature material, identifying feature leads, feature lead selection, evaluating feature leads, compiling survey material, cutlines, headlines, paste-up rules, advertising, final semester project, newspaper evaluation, specific issue evaluation, and grading. (SRT)

AN: EJ334129
TI: Literature Packets for the Journalism Class.
PY: 1986
JN: Communication:-Journalism-Education-Today-(C:JET); v19 n4 p13-18 Sum 1986
AV: UMI
NT: Thematic Issue: Journalism as Literature: Literature as Journalism
DE: Integrated-Activities; Literary-Criticism; Secondary-Education
DE: *English-Curriculum; *Journalism-Education; *Literature-Appreciation
AB: Lists the literature selections included in packets for use in journalism classes entitled "Personality Sketch," "Newswriting," "Informative Feature," "Interpretive Writing," "Personal Experience," "Sports," "Editorial/Opinion," "Letters," "The Critical Review," "Humor and Satire," "Readings for Women," "The Family," "Education," "Photography," "Words and Writing," and "Being Black." (DF)

AN: EJ334128
TI: Sources for a Literature Program for Journalists.
PY: 1986
JN: Communication:-Journalism-Education-Today-(C:JET); v19 n4 p12 Sum 1986
AV: UMI
NT: Thematic Issue: Journalism as Literature: Literature as Journalism
DE: Bibliographies-; English-Curriculum; Secondary-Education
DE: *Curriculum-Development; *Journalism-Education; *Literature-Appreciation; *Reading-Materials
AB: Lists 26 sources of literature from the California Reading List. (DF)

AN: EJ334127
TI: Major Authors in the California Reading List.
PY: 1986
JN: Communication:-Journalism-Education-Today-(C:JET); v19 n4 p11 Sum 1986
AV: UMI
NT: Thematic Issue: Journalism as Literature: Literature as Journalism.
DE: Course-Content; Curriculum-Development; English-Curriculum; Secondary-Education
DE: *Authors-; *Integrated-Activities; *Journalism-Education; *Literature-Appreciation; *Reading-Materials
AB: Lists 128 authors whose work is included in the reading program approved for use in journalism classes in California, including Woody Allen, Pearl S. Buck, Jesse L. Jackson, and George Orwell. (DF)

AN: EJ334126
TI: Develop Your Own Program.
PY: 1986
JN: Communication:-Journalism-Education-Today-(C:JET); v19 n4 p10 Sum 1986
AV: UMI
NT: Thematic Issue: Journalism as Literature: Literature as Journalism.
DE: Literary-Criticism; Literature-; Secondary-Education
DE: *English-Curriculum; *Integrated-Activities; *Journalism-Education; *Literature-Appreciation; *Program-Development; *Teacher-Role
AB: Lists five steps in developing a literature program for a journalism class, including knowing what you want to find in literature and sharing results of the program with other teachers. (DF)

AN: EJ334125
TI: Step-by-Step through a Literature Packet.
PY: 1986
JN: Communication:-Journalism-Education-Today-(C:JET); v19 n4 p8-10 Sum 1986
AV: UMI
NT: Thematic Issue: Journalism as Literature: Literature as Journalism.
DE: Course-Content; English-Curriculum; English-Instruction; Literary-Criticism; Literature-; Secondary-Education
DE: *Integrated-Activities; *Journalism-Education; *Literature-Appreciation; *Teaching-Methods
AB: Thoroughly discusses teaching strategies for a literature packet entitled "Personality Sketch." (DF)

AN: EJ334124
TI: Strategies for Teaching Literature in Journalism.
PY: 1986
JN: Communication:-Journalism-Education-Today-(C:JET); v19 n4 p7-8 Sum 1986
AV: UMI
NT: Thematic Issue: Journalism as Literature: Literature as Journalism.
DE: English-Curriculum; English-Instruction; Integrated-Activities; Literary-Criticism; Literature-; Secondary-Education
DE: *Journalism-Education; *Literature-Appreciation; *Reading-Writing-Relationship; *Teaching-Methods
AB: Cites three strategies for teaching literature in journalism classes, including using literature packets as a class project and having students receive grades for the work they do on the literature packets. (DF)

AN: EJ334123
TI: For the Journalism Class Itself: What a Good Reading Program Can Do.
PY: 1986
JN: Communication:-Journalism-Education-Today-(C:JET); v19 n4 p6 Sum 1986
AV: UMI
NT: Thematic Issue: Journalism as Literature: Literature as Journalism.
DE: English-Curriculum; High-School-Students; Literature-Appreciation; Reading-Writing-Relationship; Secondary-Education
DE: *Class-Activities; *Integrated-Activities; *Journalism-Education; *Reading-Programs
AB: Lists four benefits to a journalism class of a good reading program, including proving academic worthiness for a class in jeopardy and aligning journalism classes with the nationwide requirement of reading across the curriculum. (DF)

AN: EJ334122
TI: For the High School Journalist: What a Good Reading Program Can Do.
PY: 1986
JN: Communication:-Journalism-Education-Today-(C:JET); v19 n4 p5 Sum 1986
AV: UMI
NT: Thematic Issue: Journalism as Literature: Literature as Journalism.
DE: English-Curriculum; High-School-Students; Secondary-Education
DE: *Integrated-Activities; *Journalism-Education; *Literature-Appreciation; *Reading-Programs; *Reading-Writing-Relationship
AB: Lists five benefits to high school journalists as a result of a good reading program, including adding to students' store of information and providing students with reading practice. (DF)

AN: EJ334121
TI: How the Literature Program Was Created.
PY: 1986
JN: Communication:-Journalism-Education-Today-(C:JET); v19 n4 p2-4 Sum 1986
AV: UMI
NT: Thematic Issue: Journalism as Literature: Literature as Journalism.
DE: Literary-Criticism; Literature-; Secondary-Education; Units-of-Study
DE: *English-Curriculum; *Integrated-Activities; *Journalism-Education; *Literature-Appreciation; *Program-Content; *Program-Development
AB: Traces the development of a literature program for use in high school journalism classes in California. Contains a synopsis of the program units. (DF)

AN: EJ331180
AU: Downs,-William-D., Jr.
TI: 121 Tips on Advising High School Publications.
PY: 1985 JN: C.S.P.A.A.-Bulletin; v43 n3 p2-9 Fall 1985
AV: UMI
DE: Faculty-Advisers; Newspapers-; Program-Improvement; Secondary-Education; Student-Motivation; Teacher-Role; Yearbooks-
DE: *Journalism-Education; *Student-Publications
AB: Lists 121 suggestions for advisers of high school publications, including making it clear to students that most readers are lazy and have to be motivated to read, sending letters to parents praising the work of their children, and maintaining a positive attitude. (DF)

AU: Hines,-Barbara; Nunamaker,-Anne
TI: High School Journalism Textbooks, 1980-1985: An Overview of Content.
PY: 1985
PG: 30
DE: Comparative-Analysis; News-Reporting; Secondary-Education
DE: *Content-Analysis; *Journalism-Education; *Mass-Media; *Skill-Development; *Textbook-Content; *Textbook-Research
AB: To determine how high school journalism textbooks published from 1980 to 1985 deal with mass media and to what extent they deal with journalistic skills versus historical and theoretical content, a content analysis was made of nine comprehensive textbooks published during that period. Specific content areas that were analyzed in the historical and theoretical context were news understanding, the individual's use of the media, mass media in society, journalism history, press law/First Amendment freedom, functions of newspapers, responsibility, new technology, careers, and ethics. Among the journalistic skills analyzed were newsgathering, news reporting, proofreading, copyediting, production processes, and news writing. The analysis showed that current high school journal-

ism textbooks tend to cover similar information for student development of skills. However, the analysis of the coverage of the historical and theoretical content showed a disparity among books. A content checklist for the books and a bibliography of texts reviewed are included. (HOD)

AN: ED288197
TI: Language Arts. Suggested Learner Outcomes, Grades 9-12.
CS: Oklahoma State Dept. of Education, Oklahoma City.
PY: 1985
NT: 45 p.; For "Reading, Grades 9-12," see CS 008 963.
PR: EDRS Price - MF01/PC02 Plus Postage.
DE: Communication-Skills; Critical-Thinking; Drama-; Grammar-; Interpersonal-Communication; Journalism-Education; Listening-Skills; Reading-Skills; Secondary-Education; Speech-Instruction; Spelling-Instruction; State-Curriculum-Guides; Student-Educational-Objectives; Vocabulary-Development; Writing-Instruction; Writing-Skills
DE: *Curriculum-Development; *English-Curriculum; *Language-Arts; *Secondary-School-Curriculum; *Speech-Curriculum
AB: Noting that language skills such as thinking, listening, reading, writing, and speaking are basic to education, this guide for Oklahoma schools contends that school curricula should emphasize the role that language arts play in understanding all subjects, achieving success in life, and in communicating with people. Following a discussion of the philosophy behind the language arts curriculum, the guide presents instructional goals for grades 9 through 12 in the following subject areas: (1) language arts skills; (2) literature; (3) composition; (4) grammar; (5) spelling and vocabulary; (6) handwriting; (7) speech/drama; and (8) journalism (including a journalism skills chart). Preceding the section on speech/drama are scope and sequence charts for literature, composition, grammar, handwriting, listening, and speaking. (SKC)

Educational Excellence for Iowa. Final Report of the Joint Committee on Instructional Development and Academic Articulation in Iowa. Des Moines: Iowa State Board of Regents and the Department of Public Instruction, 1984.

AU: Kopenhaver,-Lillian-Lodge
TI: Guidelines Help Press Advisers in High Schools.
PY: 1984
JN: Journalism-Educator; v39 n2 p40-42 Sum 1984
DE: Educational-Philosophy; Journalism-; Legal-Responsibility; News-Writing; Secondary-Education; Writing-for-Publication
DE: *Constitutional-Law; *Journalism-Education; *School-Supervision AB:
Recognizes the opportunity for journalism departments to develop and institute courses for scholastic journalism teachers and to develop guidelines for the student press based on the most recent research. (CRH)

AN: EJ281631
AU: Glass,-Marlys-A.
TI: Media Studies in the Classroom.
PY: 1983
JN: Education-Canada; v23 n1 p21-25,20 Spr 1983
AV: Reprint: UMI
DE: Foreign-Countries; Journalism-; Secondary-Education
DE: *Classroom-Techniques; *Discriminant-Analysis; *English-Curriculum; *Media-Research; *Teaching-Methods

AB: Students need to be taught how to use the media effectively if they are to operate intelligently in a society that is highly media oriented. In order to deal with media, students must understand why media operate as they do and what the attendant consequences are. (BRR)

AN: ED249512
AU: Christensen,-Linda, Ed.; And-Others
TI: A Guide to Integrating Language Arts.
CS: Wisconsin Univ., Madison. School of Education.
PY: 1982
AV: Wisconsin Writing Project, 556c Teacher Education Building, University of Wisconsin, 225 North Mills St., Madison, WI 53706 ($2.50).
NT: 52 p.; For other guides in this series, see CS 208 608-609, CS 208 611-612, and ED 220 864-865.
PR: EDRS Price - MF01/PC03 Plus Postage.
DE: Creative-Dramatics; Curriculum-Development; Elementary-Secondary-Education; News-Reporting; Silent-Reading; Teaching-Methods; Television-Viewing; Writing-Composition; Writing-Processes
DE: *English-Curriculum; *Integrated-Activities; *Integrated-Curriculum; *Language-Arts; *Listening-
AB: Two model programs for integrating the language arts and specific lessons that integrate language arts activities for kindergarten through grade 12 are described in this booklet. The two programs are (1) the New Brunswick Comprehensive Reading/Language Arts Program, which has five critical experiences as the core of the program: sustained silent reading, oral and written composing, reading aloud to children, responding to literature, and investigating and mastering basic skills; and (2) the Wisconsin Writing Project, which provides a process model of writing for unifying the language arts through composition. The descriptions of integrated language arts activities include those for webbing (i.e., mapping a variety of experiences that are related to one theme, topic, book, or concept), television viewing, news reporting, and creative dramatics. The booklet concludes with teaching strategies and activities for integrating listening into the language arts. (HOD)

AN: EJ271081
AU: Pasqua,-Tom
TI: Teaching Ethics, A Risky Venture.
PY: 1982
JN: Communication:-Journalism-Education-Today-(C:JET); v16 n2 p2-9 Win 1982
AV: Reprint: UMI
DE: Journalism-; Moral-Values; Newspapers-; Secondary-Education
DE: *Codes-of-Ethics; *Ethical-Instruction; *Journalism-Education; *Student-Publications; *Values-Education
AB: Points out the problems of teaching ethics to journalism students and describes codes and guidelines that can assist the teacher in doing so. (JL)

AN: EJ271082
AU: Russell,-Luana
TI: Recycle the Blunders to Teach Ethics.
PY: 1982
JN: Communication:-Journalism-Education-Today-(C:JET); v16 n2 p10-12 Win 1982
AV: Reprint: UMI
DE: Codes-of-Ethics; Journalism-; Newspapers-; Secondary-Education; Student-Publications

DE: *Ethical-Instruction; *Journalism-Education; *Moral-Values; *Values-Education
AB: Emphasizes that learning ethical principles is an ongoing process rather than a unit of study, since trial and error generate understanding of journalistic ethics. (JL)

AN: EJ276126
AU: Stano,-Randy
TI: The School Yearbook is No Longer a Joke!
PY: 1982
JN: C.S.P.A.A.-Bulletin; v40 n3 p4-5 Win 1982-83
AV: Reprint: UMI
DE: Journalism-Education; News-Reporting; Secondary-Education
DE: *Student-Publications; *Yearbooks-
AB: Examines the journalistic characteristics of many recent high school yearbooks. (HTH)

AN: ED219771
AU: Brunton,-Max, Ed.
TI: Language Arts Curriculum Guide. Second Edition.
CS: Parkrose Public Schools, Portland, Ore.
PY: 1981
NT: 67 p.
PR: EDRS Price - MF01/PC03 Plus Postage.
DE: Drama-; Elementary-Secondary-Education; Humanities-Instruction; Journalism-Education; Listening-; Middle-Schools; Novels-; Poetry-; Reading-Instruction; Short-Stories; Speech-Instruction; Spelling-Instruction
DE: *Course-Objectives; *English-Curriculum; *Language-Arts; *Language-Skills; *Literature-Appreciation; *Writing-Instruction
AB: Language arts course statements for grades 7 through 12 are presented in this curriculum guide. Content areas for each grade level are as follows: grade 7—reading, writing, and spelling, with certification required in reading; grade 8—reading, writing, and spelling; grade 9—writing, speaking, and listening, with certification required in each area; grade 10—writing (description, narrative, and exposition); grade 11—writing (exposition and third person form); and grade 12—writing and literature. Course statements are provided for the following areas: reading and writing analysis, speech, drama, basic skills, journalistic writing, the novel, the short story, poetry, language study, college preparatory English, senior English, Shakespeare, school yearbook, school newspaper, global studies, humanities, reading, and writing. The statements indicate grade level, length of course, term hours, and prerequisites and provide course overviews and goals. (HOD)

AU: Rolnicki,-Tom
TI: Career Aspirations for College Journalists.
PY: 1981
JN: Communication:-Journalism-Education-Today-(C:JET); v15 n1 p11-12 Fall 1981
DE: High-Schools; Higher-Education
DE: *Career-Choice; *Career-Planning; *Careers-; *Journalism-; *School-Publications
AB: Two college journalism students offer advice for high school students who want a career in journalism. (FL)

AN: ED205997
TI: From Newsroom to Classroom: An Introduction to the Newspaper. Fifth Edition.
CS: Palm Beach Newspapers, Inc., West Palm Beach, Fla.
PY: [1980]
NT: 21 p.

PR: EDRS Price - MF01/PC01 Plus Postage.
DE: Elementary-Secondary-Education; Journalism-Education; Teaching-Guides; Teaching-Methods
DE: *Class-Activities; *Learning-Activities; *Newspapers-; *Student-Publications
AB: Intended for use with students at all grade levels, this booklet contains activities for incorporating newspaper study into the classroom. The first section of the booklet contains a week-long teaching unit designed to familiarize students with the format and style of newspapers. The remaining sections of the booklet contain activities designed to teach students how to (1) use the newspaper in conjunction with television and radio, (2) write letters to the editor, and (3) use the advertisements. Suggestions are also provided for devising spelling and grammar lessons from the newspaper and for creating a class newspaper. A copy of a class newspaper is included. (FL)

AN: ED205995
AU: Hanson,-Phebe; And-Others
TI: The Newspaper in Secondary English and Language Arts: A Teaching Guide of Suggested Classroom Newspaper Activities.
CS: Minneapolis Public Schools, Minn. Curriculum Div.; Minneapolis Star and Tribune Co., Minn.
PY: 1977
AV: Minneapolis Tribune, 425 Portland Ave., Minneapolis, MN 55488 ($4.00).
NT: 66 p.; For related document see CS 206 549.
PR: EDRS Price - MF01 Plus Postage. PC Not Available from EDRS.
DE: Listening-Skills; Reading-Skills; Secondary-Education; Teaching-Guides; Writing-Skills
DE: *Class-Activities; *English-Instruction; *Journalism-Education; *Language-Arts; *Learning-Activities; *Newspapers-; *Student-Publications
AB: Intended for use with students in secondary school English and language arts classes, this guide provides a number of ways to use newspapers in the classroom. The guide is designed to help teachers and students with ways for starting newspaper activities; with reading, writing, speaking, listening, and thinking opportunities; and with possibilities for making newspaper reading an enjoyable experience. The guide provides approximately 45 activities, including (1) writing found poems, (2) preparing a newspaper collage, (3) getting the reader's interest, (4) writing picture captions, (5) writing parodies, (6) detecting sex role stereotyping, (7) preparing an advertising campaign, and (8) using humor. An activities index and a glossary of newspaper terms are appended. (FL)

Arnold, Edmund C., and Krieghbaum, Hillier. *Handbook of Student Journalism: A Guide for Staff and Advisers.* New York: New York University Press, 1976.

Campbell, Laurence R. "The Role of the High School Newspaper." *Quill and Scroll* 45,3 (February-March 1971):22.

Student Newspaper, The. Washington, D.C.: American Council on Education, 1970.

Krathwohl, David R.; Bloom, Benjamin S.; and Masia, Bertram B. *Taxonomy of Educational Objectives II: Affective Domain.* New York: David McKay Company, Inc., 1964.

Dressel, Paul L. *Liberal Education and Journalism.* New York: Columbia University Bureau of Publications, 1960.

Tarlow, Milton. "The 3 'P's' of School Publications." *School Activities* 23,9 (May 1952):278-280.

Mann, James W. *The Student Editor.* New York: Macmillan Co., 1938.

Harrington, H.F. *Writing for Print.* Boston: D.C. Heath & Co., 1922.

Perry, Frances M. "School Publications," *English Journal* 8 (May 1919):299-308.

_____. "The Supervision of School Publications," *English Journal* 8 (December 1919): 617-622.

Curriculum—Magazines: Literary and Journalistic

AN: EJ426920
AU: Carbaugh,-James-Christopher
TI: Using the Literary Journal for More than Literary Writing.
PY: 1989
JN: Civic-Perspective; v2 n2 p3-4 Spr 1989
DE: Secondary-Education; Teaching-Methods; Writing-Ability; Writing-Instruction
DE: *Civics-; *Student-Publications; *Writing-Composition; *Writing-for-Publication; *Writing-Skills
AB: Describes how the school literary journal can be used to publish students' writing about public affairs to add new dimensions to the journal and transform it to a comprehensive display of students' interests and writing abilities. (MG)

AN: EJ376097
AU: Locklear,-J.-Grady
TI: The Magazine: Its History and Present Status.
PY: 1988
JN: Quill-and-Scroll; v62 n4 p4-6 Apr-May 1988
AV: UMI
DE: Art-; High-Schools; Journalism-Education; Literary-Styles; Photojournalism-; Secondary-Education; Student-Developed-Materials; Student-Publications
DE: *Periodicals-
AB: Presents the history and present status of the high school literary art feature magazine. Contends that high school magazines must become contemporary to survive. (MS)

AN: EJ327780
AU: Smith,-Jayne-R.
TI: How to Put Out a Literary Magazine: A Survivor's Guide for Beginners.
PY: 1986
JN: English-Journal; v75 n1 p27-31 Jan 1986
AV: UMI
DE: Communication-Skills; English-Instruction; Extracurricular-Activities; Faculty-Advisers; Journalism-; School-Publications; Secondary-Education; Writing-Composition; Writing-Skills
DE: *Creative-Writing; *Production-Techniques; *Student-Publications; *Teacher-Role
AB: Tells how to produce a literary magazine, including picking a staff, selling the magazine, getting entries, typing and proofing, laying out and illustrating, cutting and pasting, and distributing the magazine. (EL)

Curriculum—Visuals, Graphics, Photojournalism, Typography

Olman, Gloria. "Yearbook DTP Course Meets Traditional Goals," *C:JET (Communication: Journalism Education Today)* 26 (Winter 1992):16-18.

Smith, David E. "The Good and the Ugly of Digitized Photography," *C:JET (Communication: Journalism Education Today)* 26 (Winter 1992):8-11.

AN: EJ411516
AU: Widmer,-Laura
TI: Finding Ways to Overcome the Predictable and Ordinary in the Portrait Section.
PY: 1990
JN: Quill-and-Scroll; v64 n4 p8-10 Apr-May 1990
AV: UMI
DE: Cooperation-; Feature-Stories; High-School-Students; School-Publications; Secondary-Education; Teamwork-
DE: *Journalism-Education; *Layout-Publications; *Photojournalism-; *Student-Publications; *Yearbooks-
AB: Shares methods of making the portrait section of a school yearbook more interesting by combining design, feature writing, and photography ideas. Stresses the need for photo-journalists and reporters to work together on the product. (MG)

AN: EJ406831
TI: Yearbook Judges Identify Qualities of Excellence.
PY: 1990
JN: Quill-and-Scroll; v64 n3 p14-16 Feb-Mar 1990
AV: UMI
DE: Journalism-; Journalism-Education; Secondary-Education; Student-Publications
DE: *Graphs-; *Illustrations-; *Photographs-; *Yearbooks-
AB: Offers guidelines summarizing the major points of judges in the 1989 Yearbook Excellence Contest regarding: (1) visual impact; (2) visual readability; (3) appropriateness of illustrations and graphics to the verbal content; and (4) writing quality. (SR)

AN: EJ406759
AU: Hall,-H.-L.
TI: Serving Readers through Infographics.
PY: 1989
JN: Communication:-Journalism-Education-Today-(C:JET); v23 n2 p7-9 Win 1989
DE: Journalism-Education; Secondary-Education; Visual-Aids
DE: *Graphic-Arts; *Layout-Publications; *Student-Publications; *Surveys-
AB: Discusses how to use information graphics successfully. Describes how to conduct a survey and transform the results into an information graphic. (MM)

AN: EJ349112
AU: Rard,-Johnny
TI: Former Yearbook Editor Suggests How to Avoid Those Terrible Photographs!
PY: 1986
JN: C.S.P.A.A.-Bulletin; v4 n1 p17-20 Sum 1986
AV: UMI
DE: Secondary-Education
DE: *Journalism-Education; *Photography-; *Photojournalism-; *School-Newspapers; *Student-Publications; *Yearbooks-

AB: Offers five steps for eliminating poor quality photographs in student publications: plan in advance, understand photographic techniques, understand photography quality, make assignments with care, and understand photographers. (HTH)

AN: EJ329468
TI: Yearbooks, Magazines, Newspapers.
PY: 1986
JN: Communication:-Journalism-Education-Today-(C:JET); v19 n3 p2-16 Spr 1986
AV: UMI
DE: Captions-; Headlines-; Higher-Education; Journalism-; School-Publications; Secondary-Education
DE: *Design-; *Layout-Publications; *Periodicals-; *School-Newspapers; *Yearbooks-
AB: Provides photographs and descriptions of attention-getting layouts used in high school and college yearbooks, magazines, and newspapers. (DF)

AN: EJ313612
AU: Bartholomew,-Ann
TI: Unity and Versatility—Theme.
PY: 1985
JN: Communication:-Journalism-Education-Today-(C:JET); v18 n3 p9-10 Spr 1985
AV: UMI
DE: Assignments-; Secondary-Education; Writing-for-Publication
DE: *Graphic-Arts; *Journalism-Education; *Layout-Publications; *Photographs-; *Student-Publications; *Visual-Arts
AB: Offers tips on effectively and cheaply incorporating student graphics and photography into a literary magazine. (CRH)

AN: EJ313610
AU: Kranes,-Carol
TI: Consistent and Varied—Design.
PY: 1985
JN: Communication:-Journalism-Education-Today-(C:JET); v18 n3 p4-5 Spr 1985
AV: UMI
DE: Secondary-Education; Visual-Aids
DE: *Graphic-Arts; *Journalism-Education; *Layout-Publications; *Student-Publications; *Visual-Arts
AB: Explains good graphic design and gives examples using the student literary magazine "Runes." (CRH)

AN: EJ316573
AU: Cutsinger,-John; Coolidge,-Judi
TI: Yearbook Staffs Wanting More Should Examine Mini-Themes.
PY: 1985
JN: Quill-and-Scroll; v59 n4 p4-6 Apr-May 1985
AV: UMI
DE: Secondary-Education
DE: *Graphic-Arts; *Journalism-Education; *Layout-Publications; *Student-Publications; *Thematic-Approach; *Yearbooks-
AB: Describes how unifying concepts for yearbook sections can provide a fresh look at activities and keep the attention of the contemporary reader. (CRH)

AN: EJ309783
AU: Hoyt-Biga,-Evelyn

TI: Color, Color, Color, Color.
PY: 1985
JN: Quill-and-Scroll; v59 n2 p8-11 Dec-Jan 1985
AV: UMI
DE: Journalism-; Production-Techniques; School-Newspapers; Secondary-Education; Student-Publications; Technological-Advancement
DE: *Color-; *Color-Planning; *Journalism-Education; *Printing-
AB: Describes the advantages and problems of using new color printing technology in student newspapers. (CRH)

AN: EJ294673
AU: Sullivan,-Dolores-P.
TI: The Graphic Journalist Comes of Age.
PY: 1984
JN: Quill-and-Scroll; v58 n3 p8-11 Feb-Mar 1984
AV: UMI
DE: Design-; Headlines-; Journalism-Education; News-Reporting; Photography-; Secondary-Education; Student-Publications
DE: *Graphic-Arts; *Layout-Publications; *School-Newspapers
AB: Presents a formula for structural page design that can help the student journalist create graphically pleasing pages that emphasize news content. (MM)

AN: EJ271084
AU: Arrigo,-Jim
TI: Four Ways to Crop for Effective Pictures.
PY: 1982
JN: Communication:-Journalism-Education-Today-(C:JET); v16 n2 p16-17 Win 1982
AV: Reprint: UMI
DE: Production-Techniques; Secondary-Education
DE: *Journalism-; *Journalism-Education; *Layout-Publications; *Photography-; *Student-Publications
AB: Presents guidelines for cropping photographs for student publications. (JL)

AN: EJ259328
AU: Hepker,-Robyn
TI: Troubleshooting in the Darkroom.
PY: 1982
JN: Quill-and-Scroll; v56 n3 p16-18 Feb-Mar 1982
AV: Reprint: UMI
DE: Layout-Publications; Secondary-Education
DE: *Journalism-Education; *Photography-; *Production-Techniques; *Student-Publications; *Yearbooks-
AB: Highlights six photographic errors that are commonly found in yearbooks and urges that photos be double-checked in the darkroom. (HOD)

AN: EJ262994
AU: Mills,-Steve
TI: The State of the Art in Graphics and Design: No Longer Such a "Mixed Bag."
PY: 1982
JN: Quill-and-Scroll; v56 n4 p7-9 Apr-May 1982
AV: Reprint: UMI
DE: Photography-; Secondary-Education
DE: *Graphic-Arts; *Journalism-Education; *Layout-Publications; *Yearbooks-

AB: Suggests that yearbook designers streamline their designs to maintain the elegance of simplicity. (HOD)

Curriculum—Writing and Editing

Dodd, Julie E. and Robinson, Judy L., "Use of Commercial Newspapers in Florida High Schools and Middle Schools," (paper presented to the Scholastic Journalism Division at the convention of the Association for Education in Journalism and Mass Communication, Kansas City, Mo., August 1993.)

AN: EJ439067
AU: Harkrider,-Jack
TI: Teaching and Advising.
PY: 1991
JN: Communication:-Journalism-Education-Today-(C:JET); v25 n2 p16-19 Win 1991
AV: UMI
DE: Journalism-Education; Secondary-Education
DE: *Student-Publications; *Writing-for-Publication; *Writing-Instruction; *Writing-Processes
AB: Discusses writing instruction with student publications, teaching higher order thinking skills, developing a production schedule, process writing elements, and revision. (MG)

AN: EJ435641
AU: Hawthorne,-Bobby
TI: Writing That Captures the Action (Sports).
PY: 1991
JN: Student-Press-Review; v66 n4 p28-33 Sum 1991
DE: Journalism-Education; Secondary-Education; Student-Publications
DE: *Athletics-; *News-Reporting; *School-Newspapers; *Writing-for-Publication
AB: Suggests ways for student reporters to correctly use the medium they have at their disposal and reach their audience more effectively than the daily professional newspaper, radio, or television. Discusses how to cover the games; how to get the advance, postgame, and in-depth stories; how to use photography effectively; and other areas. (MG)

AN: EJ419781
AU: Brown,-Donal
TI: Redwood Bark.
PY: 1990
JN: Communication:-Journalism-Education-Today-(C:JET); v24 n1 p18-20 Fall 1990
DE: Journalism-Education; News-Reporting; Secondary-Education; Student-Writing-Models
DE: *News-Writing; *School-Newspapers; *Student-Rights
AB: Describes the organization, effectiveness, and readership of one particular school newspaper in California. Includes two articles about student rights, carefully researched and written by student reporters. (KEH)

AN: EJ397641
AU: Chesney,-Bob
TI: Writing Award Winning Feature Stories.
PY: 1989
JN: Quill-and-Scroll; v64 n1 p12-15 Oct-Nov 1989
AV: UMI

DE: High-School-Students; Secondary-Education; Student-Writing-Models
DE: *Journalism-Education; *News-Writing; *School-Newspapers; *Student-Publications
AB: Presents advice for writing award-winning feature stories for high school newspapers. (SR)

Knudtson, Judy. "Teaching Writing Involves Many Curriculum Changes," *C:JET (Communication: Journalism Education Today)* 23 (Fall 1989):11-14.

AN: EJ397639
AU: McCartney,-John
TI: Dynamic Yearbook Copy.
PY: 1989
JN: Quill-and-Scroll; v64 n1 p4-7 Oct-Nov 1989
AV: UMI
DE: High-School-Students; Journalism-Education; News-Reporting; Secondary-Education; Student-Writing-Models; Writing-Skills
DE: *News-Writing; *Student-Publications; *Yearbooks-
AB: Maintains that the challenge of writing vibrant yearbook copy means accepting the risk of self-exposure, doing extensive preliminary research, asking pointed questions during interviews, and double-checking quotes prior to publication. (SR)

AN: EJ376101
AU: Hutchison,-Marian
TI: The Stringbook: An Easy Means of Grading the Publication Staff.
PY: 1988
JN: Quill-and-Scroll; v62 n4 p15-16 Apr-May 1988
AV: UMI
DE: Journalism-; Newspapers-; Secondary-Education; Student-Publications
DE: *Grading-; *Journalism-Education; *Student-Evaluation
AB: Discusses how a journalism teacher can grade the newspaper staff on its production efforts in a fair and consistent manner. Proposes a point system for students to earn a grade in newspaper production that places the burden on students to keep track of their work. (MS)

AN: EJ391837
AU: Pitts,-Beverly
TI: Improving Writing for Student Publications.
PY: 1988
JN: Journal-of-Teaching-Writing; v7 n2 p205-14 Fall-Win 1988
DE: Interdisciplinary-Approach; Secondary-Education; Teaching-Methods
DE: *Journalism-Education; *Newspapers-; *Student-Publications; *Writing-Instruction
AB: Suggests ways to improve publications writing by alleviating time constraints on advisers and taking advantage of the skills of the publications staff, faculty, and other students. Suggests: (1) building on already gained writing experience; (2) selecting models and posting them for students; and (3) using a formula sheet for gathering information. (MM)

AN: EJ368605
AU: Adams,-Julian
TI: Writing a Series of Stories.
PY: 1987
JN: Communication:-Journalism-Education-Today; v21 n2 p8 Win 1987
AV: UMI

DE: Expository-Writing; Journalism-Education; News-Reporting; Periodicals-; School-Newspapers; Secondary-Education; Writing-for-Publication; Written-Language
DE: *News-Writing; *Student-Publications; *Writing-Skills
AB: Presents ways to develop a series of stories on a single topic. Suggests that a writer must develop fresh facts or a fresh angle for each issue. (JK)

AN: EJ345138
AU: Jungblut,-Joseph-A.
TI: Using your Head(line) to Control Your Module.
PY: 1987
JN: Quill-and-Scroll; v61 n2 p4-7 Dec-Jan 1987
AV: UMI
DE: Secondary-Education; Student-Publications
DE: *Headlines-; *Journalism-Education; *Layout-Publications; *School-Newspapers
AB: Describes five common headline styles, how to place them properly, and their advantages and disadvantages. (SRT)

AN: EJ339916
AU: Hawthorne,-Bobby
TI: "Writing the Season Summary."
PY: 1986
JN: C.S.P.A.A.-Bulletin; v43 n3 p1-4 Win 1985-86
AV: UMI
DE: News-Media; Secondary-Education
DE: *Athletics-; *Journalism-Education; *News-Reporting; *News-Writing; *Student-Publications
AB: Observes that, in summarizing the school sports season, the reporter must look at the performances of the season in the context of the player/coach/team expectations. Offers guidelines for writing season summaries and scoreboard information, and includes sample summaries. (HTH)

AN: EJ349111
AU: McKeen,-William
TI: As A Teacher...I Find Myself Serving As That Editing Partner with My Students.
PY: 1986
JN: C.S.P.A.A.-Bulletin; v4 n1 p8-10 Sum 1986
AV: UMI
DE: Editing-; Faculty-Advisers; Secondary-Education; Writing-Processes
DE: *Cooperation-; *Journalism-Education; *School-Newspapers; *Student-Publications; *Teacher-Student-Relationship; *Teaching-Methods
AB: Advocates a collaborative relationship between student reporters and faculty editors, preserving editorial involvement during the writing process rather than after the story has been written. (HTH)

AN: EJ316577
AU: Lindemer,-Kristen; Seehuus,-Richard
TI: Richard Smyser, Oak Ridge Editor, Cites Good Reporter Qualities.
PY: 1985
JN: Quill-and-Scroll; v59 n4 p13-15 Apr-May 1985
AV: UMI
DE: Opinions-; Secondary-Education; Standards-; Student-Publications
DE: *Guidelines-; *Journalism-Education; *News-Reporting; *Writing-for-Publication

AB: Lists criterion that award winning editor Smyser declares are important for becoming a good reporter. (CRH)

AN: EJ313611
AU: LoCascio,-Joe
TI: Beyond Poetry and Fiction.
PY: 1985
JN: Communication:-Journalism-Education-Today-(C:JET); v18 n3 p6-9 Spr 1985
DE: Secondary-Education; Student-Publications; Writing-Skills
DE: *Assignments-; *Journalism-Education; *Literary-Styles; *School-Newspapers; *Writing-for-Publication
AB: Describes the standard student contribution to the literary magazine and offers substitute writing assignments. (CRH)

AN: EJ313618
AU: Turner,-Ralph-J.
TI: Don't Write Heads that Bite the Dust!
PY: 1985
JN: Quill-and-Scroll; v59 n3 p4-6 Feb-Mar 1985
AV: UMI
DE: Reading-Habits; Secondary-Education; Teaching-Methods; Writing-Instruction
DE: *Headlines-; *Journalism-Education; *School-Newspapers; *Writing-for-Publication
AB: Summarizes guidelines for writing effective and prize-winning headlines. (CRH)

AN: EJ308227
AU: Arnold,-George-T.
TI: Stick Your Neck Out! Write a Better Headline.
PY: 1984
JN: C.S.P.A.A.-Bulletin; v42 n3 p1-4 Fall 1984
AV: UMI
DE: Secondary-Education; Student-Publications
DE: *Headlines-; *Journalism-Education; *School-Newspapers; *Writing-Improvement
AB: Discusses some of the pitfalls inherent to writing news headlines. Distinguishes between feature and editorial headlines and news headlines. (HTH)

Cripe, Dennis Alan. "We Are What We Write." *School Press Review* (Winter 1984):21.

Maeroff, Gene I. "Teaching of Writing Gets New Push." *The New York Times Education Winter Survey*, 8 January 1984, sec. 12, p. 1, 36.

AN: EJ296679
AU: Schrader,-Vincent-E.
TI: Teaching Journalism on the Micro.
PY: 1984
JN: English-Journal; v73 n4 p93-94 Apr 1984
AV: UMI
DE: Production-Techniques; Revision-Written-Composition; Secondary-Education; Student-Publications
DE: *Computer-Assisted-Instruction; *Journalism-Education; *Microcomputers-; *School-Newspapers; *Word-Processing; *Writing-Instruction
AB: Outlines the advantages of using microcomputers in producing high school newspapers—word processors permit the generation of columnar newspaper copy and encourage student revision—and suggests three necessary characteristics in computer

hardware—a large memory, good software, and reliable technical assistance for handling problems. (MM)

AN: EJ288082
AU: Sheffield,-L.-Curtis
TI: Better Yearbook Copy.
PY: 1983
JN: C.S.P.A.A.-Bulletin; v41 n2 p1-4 Fall 1983
AV: UMI
DE: Literary-Styles; News-Reporting; Secondary-Education
DE: *Journalism-Education; *Student-Publications; *Writing-Improvement; *Yearbooks-
AB: Discusses the problems that usually plague high school yearbook writing. Offers 12 rules of style that can help improve feature and news writing in yearbooks. (HTH)

AN: EJ276128
AU: McKeen,-William
TI: Taking Them by the Collar on to Better Feature Leads.
PY: 1982
JN: C.S.P.A.A.-Bulletin; v40 n3 p12-13 Win 1982-83
AV: Reprint: UMI
DE: Secondary-Education; Student-Publications
DE: *Journalism-Education; *School-Newspapers; *Writing-Skills
AB: Offers suggestions for putting personal excitement into feature stories. Includes examples of "classic" feature story leads. (HTH)

Financing and Advertising

Mueller, Barbara and Wulfemeyer, K. Tim. "Commercial Speech and Captive Minds: Regulating Advertising in Public High Schools," (paper presented at the convention of the Association for Education in Journalism and Mass Communication, Montreal, Canada, August 1992.)

Perkins, Candace. "Unit Covers Pros, Cons of Media Advertising," *C:JET (Communication: Journalism Education Today)* 26 (Winter 1992):19-20.

Lain, Larry. *ASK: The Advertising Survival Kit.* 2nd ed. Iowa City: Quill and Scroll Foundation, 1992.

AN: EJ435581
AU: Duncan,-Tom
TI: Sell a Campaign, Not Just an Ad.
PY: 1991
JN: Communication:-Journalism-Education-Today-(C:JET); v25 n1 p8-9 Fall 1991
NT: Special Issue: Advertising.
DE: High-School-Students; Journalism-Education; Secondary-Education
DE: *Advertising-; *Salesmanship-; *School-Newspapers
AB: Presents nine basic steps to teach students to sell advertising campaigns (not just one ad), thus bringing in more advertising revenue for the school paper by selling in quantity. (SR)

Fried, Alan. "Advertising: Use Research Techniques to Transform Your Amateur Peddlers into a Professional Sales Staff." *Quill & Scroll* 65,2 (December-January 1991):7-11.

Melton, Rob and Stautz, *Sunny. Advertising A-Z*. Portland, Ore.: Rob Melton and Company, 1991.

AN: EJ435583
AU: Shaver,-Mary-Alice
TI: Selling Your Newspaper: Tips for Ad Sales.
PY: 1991
JN: Communication:-Journalism-Education-Today-(C:JET); v25 n1 p12-13 Fall 1991
NT: Special Issue: Advertising.
DE: Higher-Education; Journalism-Education; Secondary-Education
DE: *Advertising-; *Salesmanship-; *School-Newspapers
AB: Presents tips for selling ads in school newspapers. Discusses getting started in sales, the sales call, after the sale, and beyond the basics. (SR)

Wardrip, Jon P. "Learning About Advertising: A Do-It-Yourself Guide." *Communication: Journalism Education Today* 25,1 (Fall 1991):2-4.

AN: EJ435615
AU: Speidel,-Jane-W.
TI: Professional Ad Sales for Student Publications.
PY: 1990
JN: School-Press-Review; v65 n4 v66 n1 p6-9 Sum-Fall 1990
AV: UMI
DE: Corporate-Support; Journalism-Education; School-Support; Secondary-Education
DE: *Advertising-; *Salesmanship-; *School-Business-Relationship; *Student-Publications
AB: Suggests five strategies to use when working with corporations and businesses to cement good relationships and bring positive cash flow into school publication budgets. (MG)

AN: EJ385122
AU: Kovas,-Marcia-A.
TI: Why Not Develop a Parent Booster's Club?
PY: 1989
JN: Quill-and-Scroll; v63 n2 p10-11 Dec-Jan 1989
AV: UMI
DE: Fund-Raising; Journalism-Education; Secondary-Education
DE: *Financial-Support; *Parent-Role; *Parent-School-Relationship; *School-Newspapers
AB: Describes the role parents can play in helping with the expenses involved in running a school newspaper. Lists dos and don'ts for developing a Booster Club. (MS)

AN: EJ391889
AU: Levy,-Joseph-R.
TI: Advertising: Try It, You'll Like It, but First Learn the Rules.
PY: 1989
JN: Quill-and-Scroll; v63 n4 p14-16 Apr-May 1989
AV: UMI
DE: Budgeting-; Faculty-Advisers; High-Schools; Publishing-Industry DE:
    *Advertising-; *Journalism-Education; *School-Newspapers; *Student-Publications
AB: Suggests advertising as a strategy to increase school publication budgets. Offers rules for student publication advertising. (MS)

AU: Plopper,-Bruce
TI: Building an Ethical Advertising Operation.
PY: 1989

JN: Quill-and-Scroll; v63 n3 p10-12 Feb-Mar 1989
DE: Ethical-Instruction; High-Schools; Journalism-Education; Mass-Media; Publications-
DE: *Advertising-; *Ethics-; *Student-Publications
AB: Discusses three of the more significant ethical problems related to the advertising opera-
      tion of student and commercial publications: (1) explaining circulation to potential
      advertisers; (2) negotiating special deals; and (3) following through with quality and dis-
      tribution. (MS)

Ross, Billy I., and Sellmeyer, Ralph L. *School Publications: The Business Side.* Branson, Mo.:
Molatx Press, 1989.

AN: EJ379963
AU: Watterson,-C.-B.
TI: Rx for Journalism Departments and Their Budgets—DTP.
PY: 1988
JN: NASSP-Bulletin; v72 n511 p30-32,34-37 Nov 1988
AV: UMI
DE: Secondary-Education
DE: *Computer-Assisted-Instruction; *Computer-Software; *Journalism-; *Microcomputers-;
      *Student-Publications
AB: One way to entice students into high school journalism courses is to integrate desktop
      publishing (via microcomputers) as a vehicle for type-setting, design, and pagination of
      school publications. Desktop publishing also saves time, cuts costs, and provides voca-
      tional training. (MLH)

Adams, Julian. "Staffs Make Money While Promoting Activities." *Communication: Journalism
Education Today* 21,2 (Winter 1987):15.

AN: EJ342397
AU: Hinman,-Sheryl
TI: Grant Writing: An Overlooked Source of Publishing Money.
PY: 1986
JN: Quill-and-Scroll; v61 n1 p4-5 Oct-Nov 1986
AV: UMI
DE: Financial-Support; Higher-Education; Program-Proposals; Secondary-Education
DE: *Financial-Needs; *Fund-Raising; *Grants-; *School-Newspapers
AB: Suggests that school newspapers with tight budgets and limited advertising money try to
      obtain financial support by applying for educational grants and offers tips on writing
      grant proposals. (SRT)

AN: ED268577
AU: Lain,-Laurence-B.
TI: The Funding of Secondary School Newspapers in Ohio.
PY: 1986
NT: 33 p.; Paper presented at the Annual Meeting of the Association for Education in
      Journalism and Mass Communication (69th, Norman, OK, August 3-6, 1986).
PR: EDRS Price - MF01/PC02 Plus Postage.
DE: Curriculum-Development; Faculty-Advisers; High-Schools; School-Publications;
      School-Surveys; Student-Publications
DE: *Educational-Research; *Financial-Support; *Journalism-Education; *School-
      Newspapers
AB: A study identified the principal ways in which high school newspapers are funded in
      Ohio, particularly with respect to the public or private nature of the schools, the paper

size, frequency of publication, the methods by which papers are printed, and the sorts of staffs that publish them. Of the 1,080 high schools listed for the state, 228 completed the survey, 160 of which reported publishing a newspaper. The results indicated that school size was related to the presence or absence of school newspapers, although there was no clear relationship between community size and publication of a paper. Public schools were more likely to sponsor student newspapers than were private or parochial schools. The most common publication cycle for papers was monthly, but nearly 40% of respondents published less often. Offset printing was the most popular means of reproduction, and the likelihood of using offset increased with the size of the school. Only 8% of the papers were printed in a school or district print shop. Overall, the greatest percentage of the high school newspaper budget came from single copy sales. Advertising and administration grants were also important sources of income, with fund raising, subscription sales, and student activities reported as less important sources. More than half the papers were published by classes receiving academic credit for the work. The results suggest that high school newspapers are not being published frequently enough, due in part to funding. The long-range problem of financing the newspaper will not be solved until journalism takes a more prominent place in the curriculum, thus also attracting advisers trained in journalism. (HTH)

AN: EJ332983
AU: Winski,-Tom
TI: Boost Your Budget and School Spirit with Special Editions.
PY: 1986
JN: Quill-and-Scroll; v60 n2 p20-21 Dec-Jan 1986
AV: UMI
DE: Morale-; Secondary-Education
DE: *Fund-Raising; *Journalism-Education; *Production-Techniques; *School-Newspapers
AB: Explains how a high school newspaper staff raised money by preparing and selling special editions whenever a school team or organization was involved in a special event. (FL)

AN: EJ331181
AU: Burns,-Norma
TI: Business Management and Advertising in a Student Publication.
PY: 1985
JN: C.S.P.A.A.-Bulletin; v43 n3 p10-11 Fall 1985
AV: UMI
DE: Newspapers-; Salesmanship-; School-Business-Relationship; Secondary-Education; Standards-; Yearbooks-
DE: *Advertising-; *Journalism-Education; *Student-Publications
AB: States that the business staff and business editor are important positions on a high school publication and suggests ways of improving their effectiveness, such as making appointments with advertisers, having effective procedures for collecting bills, and teaching students to look and behave professionally. (DF)

Heaston, Frank. "Are Your Ad Rates Adequate?" *CSPAA Bulletin* 42,3 (Fall 1984):12-14.

Heaston, Frank. *A Practical Guide to Advertising in Scholastic Publications.* Norman, Okla.: American Student Press Institute, 1984.

AN: EJ280531
AU: Luft,-Roger-L.
TI: Promoting Business Education through School Newspapers and Bulletins.

PY: 1983
JN: Business-Education-Forum; (1983 Yearbook Issue: Promoting Business Education) v37 n8 p86-89 Apr-May 1983
AV: Reprint: UMI
DE: Public-Relations; School-Publications; Secondary-Education
DE: *Bulletins-; *Business-Education; *Journalism-; *Publicity-; *School-Newspapers; *Writing-Instruction
AB: Discusses the use of school publications for promoting business education. Gives specific suggestions on writing news articles. (JOW)

AN: EJ269717
AU: Dieleman,-Merle
TI: With that Little Extra, Yearbook Staffs Can Double Advertising Sales.
PY: 1982
JN: Quill-and-Scroll; v57 n1 p5-8 Oct-Nov 1982
AV: Reprint: UMI
DE: Secondary-Education
DE: *Advertising-; *Fund-Raising; *Journalism-Education; *Student-Publications; *Yearbooks-
AB: Advises that good ad design, student and advertiser incentives, sales team organization, and hard work can help school yearbook staffs raise more money. (JL)

AN: ED213039
AU: Dvorak,-Jack
TI: High School Newspaper Financing: An Assessment.
PY: 1982
NT: 27 p.; Paper presented at the mid-winter Meeting of the Secondary Education Division of the Association for Education in Journalism (Norman, OK, January 1982).
PR: EDRS Price - MF01/PC02 Plus Postage.
DE: Costs-; High-Schools; Production-Techniques; School-Publications; State-Surveys
DE: *Financial-Support; *Journalism-Education; *Media-Research; *School-Newspapers
AB: Eighty schools that were members of the Iowa High School Press Association responded to a questionnaire about the school newspaper's financial status in light of public school budget cuts. The collected data indicated that nearly half of the respondent schools published newspapers at no cost and in cooperation with a community newspaper. Sixty school papers had subsidies from the school of $500 or less; the majority of these did not accept advertising, and neither subscriptions nor individual sales of newspapers made up the revenues. Responses in other categories indicated that school newspaper personnel were attempting to economize, in that many schools had typesetting equipment and 80% of the schools did their own paste-up and darkroom work. Other responses indicated a healthy physical situation for newspapers in that over half published twice or more per month. A cross-tabulation of the total budget with the printing method showed that as budget size increased, the schools tended to publish independently. As circulation increased to about 1,900, schools tended to accept advertising, but only a fraction of those with a circulation of 2,000 or more accepted advertising. Those with a per issue cost tended to have offset printing and typesetting. Based on this study, the economic stability of school newspapers appears sound. (HTH)

AN: EJ264197
AU: Jankowsky,-Lawrence-J.
TI: The Future of High School Publications.
PY: 1981
JN: C.S.P.A.A.-Bulletin; v39 n3 p15-16 Win 1981-82

AV: Reprint: UMI
DE: Costs-; High-Schools; Journalism-Education; Occupational-Surveys; Prediction-; Regional-Attitudes
DE: *Educational-Trends; *Futures-of-Society; *School-Publications; *Teacher-Attitudes
AB: Offers comments from high school publications advisers on the effects of increased publishing costs and on what to expect in the future of school publications. (RL)

Smoot, Marie. "Can the high school newspaper pay for itself?" *Quill and Scroll* 53 (October-November 1978):13-14

Jerome, A.E. "Increasing your Advertising Revenue." 8-part series in *Scholastic Editor*, 1976.

Lain, Larry. "Mind Your Business" *Quill and Scroll* 49,2 (December-January 1975):16-19.

Nixon, O.F. "The Cost and financing of Student Publications," *School Review* 31 (March 1924):204-212.

Lewin, W. "The Business of Running a School Paper," *English Journal* 11 (January 1922):8-13.

Legal Issues Related to *Hazelwood*

Click, J. William; Kopenhaver, Lillian Lodge; and Hatcher, Larry. "Following *Hazelwood v. Kuhlmeier:* Attitudes of Principals and Teachers Toward Student Press Freedom," *Journalism Educator* 48 (Spring 1993):59-70.

Dickson, Thomas V. "Have Student Journalists Become 'Journalistic Wimps'?" *C:JET (Communication: Journalism Education Today)* 26 (Spring 1993):13-16.

Mays, Roy P., and Julie E. Dodd, "The Impact of the *Hazelwood v. Kuhlmeier* (1988) Decision on the Development or Revision of School Publication Policies" (paper presented at the midwinter meeting of the Secondary Education Division of the Association for Education in Journalism and Mass Communication, Atlanta, 1993).

Olson, Lyle D.; Van Ommeren, Roger; and Rossow, Marshel. "A Paradigm for State High School Press Freedom Laws" (paper presented to the Scholastic Journalism Division at the convention of the Association for Education in Journalism and Mass Communication, Kansas City, Mo., August 1993.)

Stofer, Kathryn T. "Life After Hazelwood: Journalism Programs in Nebraska Schools 1992" (paper submitted to the Scholastic Journalism Division for presentation at the convention of the Association for Education in Journalism and Mass Communication, Kansas City, Mo., August 1993.)

Trager, Robert and Russomanno, Joseph A., "Free Speech for Public School Students: A 'Basic Educational Mission,'" (paper presented to the Scholastic Journalism Division at the convention of the Association for Education in Journalism and Mass Communication, Kansas City, Mo., August 1993.)

Crow, Lorrie Ronae. "The Impact of Texas High School Students' and Principals' Perceptions of Student Press Freedom Following the *Hazelwood v. Kuhlmeier* Supreme Court Decision" (unpublished M.A. thesis, University of Oklahoma, 1992).

Dvorak, Jack and Dilts, Jon Paul. "Legacy of *Hazelwood v. Kuhlmeier:* Academic Freedom vs. Administrative Authority." *Journalism Educator*, 47(Autumn 1992): 3-12.

Olaye, Imafidon M., and Lynne E. Malandrino, "Contextual First Amendment Rights: Perceptions of Teachers and Administrators in the Age of *Hazelwood*" (paper presented at the convention of the Association for Education in Journalism and Mass Communication, Montreal, Canada, August 1992).

AN: EJ425390
AU: Dickson,-Tom
TI: Exploring New Territory.
PY: 1991
JN: Communication:-Journalism-Education-Today-(C:JET); v24 n3 p9-11 Spr 1991
DE: Educational-Research; High-Schools; Surveys-
DE: *Court-Litigation; *Freedom-of-Speech; *High-School-Students; *Journalism-Education; *School-Newspapers
AB: Discusses a survey of press freedom at American high school newspapers, as judged by newspaper advisers and teachers. Explains that most respondents indicated that the Supreme Court's *Hazelwood* ruling has produced little change in the fairness of high school newspaper stories. Notes significant differences between responses from Journalism Education Association members and nonmembers. (SG)

AN: ED341056
AU: Dvorak,-Jack; Dilts,-Jon-Paul
TI: Post-Hazelwood Considerations for High School Publications Advisers.
PY: 1991
NT: 70 p.; Paper presented at the Annual Secondary Division Meeting of the Association for Education in Journalism and Mass Communication (Miami, FL, January 5-6, 1991).
PR: EDRS Price - MF01/PC03 Plus Postage.
DE: Academic-Freedom; Administrators-; High-Schools; Legal-Problems
DE: *Court-Litigation; *Freedom-of-Speech; *Journalism-Education; *School-Newspapers; *Student-Publications
AB: Even though the high school publications adviser in the Hazelwood East High School Supreme Court case of 1983 was named as a petitioner with school officials, some litigation and much research indicates that advisers have often encountered administrators in an adversarial role. Because "Hazelwood" ruled that the school newspaper is part of the curriculum, an examination of federal and state court decisions focused on several issues: (1) the role of federal courts in content-control of school curricula; (2) the marketplace of ideas concept and the notion of academic freedom as applied to high school teachers; (3) the authority of schools in controlling the curriculum; (4) the conflicts that occur when school authorities' decisions conflict with teacher academic freedom; and (5) due process rights for teachers. From a teacher's point of view, the publication by journalistic tradition is a curricular tool for the practice of journalism, which includes protections provided by the First Amendment and the Constitution generally. When an administrator decides to censor such a curricular vehicle, it means that the state seems to be both violating its mandated curriculum and implementing a practice violative of the First Amendment, which it has been charged to protect in the schools. Designation of "Spectrum" (the student newspaper involved in the "Hazelwood" decision) as part of the curriculum might afford teacher-advisers a more substantial and reasonable First Amendment claim. (One-hundred eighty-two notes are included.) (Author/RS)

AN: EJ434293
AU: Click,-J.-William; Kopenhaver,-Lillian-Lodge
TI: Few Changes since "Hazelwood."
PY: 1990
JN: School-Press-Review; v65 n2 p12-27 Win 1990

AV: UMI

DE: Court-Litigation; Court-Role; Educational-Change; Educational-Research; Journalism-; Secondary-Education

DE: *Freedom-of-Speech; *Journalism-Education; *School-Newspapers; *Student-Publications; *Writing-for-Publication

AB: Surveys Columbia Scholastic Press Association member newspapers to explore the influence of the Supreme Court's ruling in the Hazelwood case. Finds a great deal of control is being exerted over student newspapers across the country. Finds that the clear majority of student newspapers across the United States are functioning as forums for student expression. (MG)

AN: ED327877

AU: Dickson,-Tom

TI: How Advisers View Changes in the High School Press in the Post-Hazelwood Era.

PY: 1990

NT: 94 p.; Paper presented at the Annual Meeting of the Secondary Education Division of the Association for Education in Journalism and Mass Communication (Tampa, FL, December 1990).

PR: EDRS Price - MF01/PC04 Plus Postage.

DE: Media-Research; Public-Schools; School-Surveys

DE: *Administrator-Role; *Freedom-of-Speech; *High-Schools; *Journalism-; *School-Newspapers; *Student-Rights

AB: In Hazelwood v. Kuhlmeier, The United States Supreme Court ruled that school administrators "need not tolerate" student speech deemed inconsistent with a school's educational mission. To study the effects of the ruling, a 36-question survey was mailed to a random sample of just under 1,600 American public high school English/Journalism departments. Questions addressed the following issues: demographic information; each school's newspaper and its purpose and content; school policy about content; changes in content since the Hazelwood decision; the type of prepublication review carried out; censorship; and student-adviser conflict. There was no majority position on the purpose of the newspaper, but nearly two-thirds of respondents identified the paper as an open forum for student speech that was not libelous or obscene or did not advocate violence. Little change in school administrators' treatment of the papers as a result of the Hazelwood decision was reported. Over half of respondents indicated that advisers objected to student stories most often because they were seen as unfair or unbalanced. The findings suggest that the Hazelwood decision was not the disaster many people in journalism education feared, and that student press freedom can co-exist with the Supreme Court ruling. (Fifty tables are included; a sample questionnaire is attached.) (SG)

AU: Click,-J.-William; Kopenhaver,-Lillian-Lodge

TI: Opinions of Principals and Newspaper Advisers toward Student Press Freedom and Advisers' Responsibilities following Hazelwood v. Kuhlmeier.

PY: 1990

PG: 20

DE: High-Schools; Journalism-Education; Surveys-

DE: *Administrator-Attitudes; *Censorship-; *Principals-; *School-Newspapers; *Student-Publications

AB: A study examined the opinions of high school principals and advisers regarding a free student press and adviser role to determine whether opinions and practices had changed since the Hazelwood v. Kuhlmeier decision. A survey was sent to both the newspaper adviser and the principal at 531 schools throughout the United States during the spring semester of 1989, just one year after the court's decision. Responses were received from 220 principals and 360 advisers. Respondents were asked to indicate on a seven-point scale the intensity of their agreement or disagreement for statements regarding role of the student newspaper, control by the administration, responsibility of the adviser, controversial issues, First Amendment rights, and the Hazelwood decision. Results revealed significant shifts in intensity in all seven points from the 1985 J. W. Click and L. L. Kopenhaver survey and indicated a more alarming extent of censorship than had been hypothesized. Findings suggest that advisers clearly see their role as requiring review of student copy and correction of factual inaccuracies and misspellings, even if the student cannot be told about them before publication. More research into the increased censorship conditions appears to be called for. (Five tables containing the complete results of replies and intensity measures are included.) (KEH)

AN: EJ411517
AU: Gomez,-Tony
TI: The Day Hazelwood Struck.
PY: 1990
JN: Quill-and-Scroll; v64 n4 p12-15 Apr-May 1990
AV: UMI
DE: High-School-Students; Local-Issues; Moral-Issues; News-Writing; Racial-Discrimination; Secondary-Education; Student-Experience; Student-Responsibility
DE: *Censorship-; *Journalism-Education; *News-Reporting; *School-Newspapers; *Student-Publications
AB: Shares the events leading up to the publication of several articles on discrimination in a high school newspaper in Arizona. (MG)

AN: EJ419778
AU: Henry,-Fran
TI: The Little Guy Can Win. PY: 1990
JN: Communication:-Journalism-Education-Today-(C:JET); v24 n1 p14-15 Fall 1990
DE: Freedom-of-Speech; Journalism-Education; School-Publications; Secondary-Education
DE: *Censorship-; *School-Newspapers; *State-Legislation
AB: Describes the driving force and the political network and coalition which led to the passage of a Colorado bill guaranteeing student free expression rights at the state level. (KEH)

AN: EJ406829
AU: Ricchiardi,-Sherry
TI: Despite the Chilling Effect, There Is Life after Hazelwood.
PY: 1990
JN: Quill-and-Scroll; v64 n3 p6-8 Feb-Mar 1990
AV: UMI
DE: Faculty-Advisers; High-Schools; Journalism-; Journalism-Education; Secondary-Education
DE: *Censorship-; *School-Newspapers; *Student-Publications
AB: Reviews the state of the high school press two years after the United States Supreme Court's Hazelwood decision which limited First Amendment protections for school publications. Finds mixed results, with some schools experiencing a chilling effect on reporting and others finding hidden benefits. (SR)

AN: EJ391874
AU: Adams,-Julian
TI: Brennan's Dissenting Opinion in Hazelwood Case Offers Insight.

PY: 1989
JN: Communication:-Journalism-Education-Today-(C:JET); v22 n4 p13-14 Sum 1989
AV: UMI
DE: Administrators-; Court-Litigation; Faculty-Advisers; Public-Education; Secondary-Education
DE: *Censorship-; *Freedom-of-Speech; *Journalism-Education; *Student-Publications
AB: Discusses Supreme Court Justice William J. Brennan Jr.'s dissenting opinion in the Hazelwood v. Kuhlmeier decision in order to help advisers and editorial staffs who are preparing arguments intended to impress administrators with the value of student publications. (MS)

AN: ED301884
AU: Bowles,-Dorothy
TI: Hazelwood v. Kuhlmeier: National Press Reaction to the Decision and Its Impact in Tennessee High Schools.
PY: 1989
NT: 39 p.; Paper presented at the Midwinter Meeting of the Secondary Education Division Association for Education in Journalism and Mass Communication (St. Petersburg, FL, January 5-7, 1989).
PR: EDRS Price - MF01/PC02 Plus Postage.
DE: Editorials-; High-Schools; High-School-Students; Professional-Associations; Secondary-Education
DE: *Faculty-Advisers; *Journalism-Education; *News-Media; *School-Newspapers; *Student-Publications
AB: On January 13, 1988, the U.S. Supreme Court announced its decision in "Hazelwood School District v. Kuhlmeier," giving educators the right to exercise "editorial control over the style and content of student speech in school-sponsored expressive activities so long as their actions are reasonably related to legitimate pedagogical concerns." A study explored the immediate reaction to "Hazelwood v. Kuhlmeier" from professional press associations, journalism reviews, and newspaper editorials and used the results of a mail survey of high school advisers to assess the current level of prepublication review and controversial content and anticipated impact of the case on student publications in Tennessee. The study also reported survey results on the amount of attention the case received in schools, the advisers' perceptions of attitudes of student staff members, faculty, and other adults in the community, and the advisers' own attitudes about the outcome of the case. Survey results indicate that "Hazelwood" had no immediate effect on Tennessee high school publications and few advisers anticipate changes in their publishing situations, a third of which (53% of newspapers) are already subject to prepublication review by school administrators. Professional and editorial reaction to the decision was mixed. (Two tables of data and 63 notes are included.) (MS)

AN: ED308524
AU: Dickson,-Tom
TI: How Advisers View the Status of High School Press Freedom Following the Hazelwood Decision.
PY: 1989
NT: 20 p.; Paper presented at the Annual Meeting of the Association for Education in Journalism and Mass Communication (72nd, Washington, DC, August 10-13, 1989).
PR: EDRS Price - MF01/PC01 Plus Postage.
DE: High-Schools; Journalism-; Journalism-Education; Public-Schools; Questionnaires-; Student-Publications; Teacher-Role
DE: *Court-Litigation; *Freedom-of-Speech; *School-Newspapers

432

AB: To examine how the Hazelwood decision (Hazelwood School District versus Kuhlmeier) affected high school advisers' views of their role in controlling content in their school newspapers and what they see as objectionable content, a study surveyed 100 Missouri high school advisers randomly selected from a list of 573 Missouri public high schools (with a 56% response rate). Each respondent was sent a cover letter and a 34-item questionnaire. Results indicated that schools have a variety of means for controlling newspaper content, but that there was no significant difference between advisers at small and large schools on the questions concerning how advisers oversee their newspapers' content. School size did appear to be related to the type of controversial articles that appeared in school papers, however. In addition, findings indicated that the Hazelwood decision would not affect the content of school publications. A table provides responses of advisers to 16 of the survey questions. (MM)

AN: EJ398888
AU: Dickson,-Thomas-V.
TI: Attitudes of High School Principals about Press Freedom after Hazelwood.
PY: 1989
JN: Journalism-Quarterly; v66 n1 p169-73 Spr 1989
DE: Censorship-; Court-Litigation; High-Schools; Secondary-Education
DE: *Administrator-Attitudes; *Freedom-of-Speech; *Principals-; *Student-Publications
AB: Surveys high school principals in Missouri to examine how they have responded to their new authority over the student press following the Supreme Court's Hazelwood decision. Reports that while principals say that student newspapers are open forums, most also say that they would censor certain types of material. (MM)

AN: EJ389794
AU: Gynn,-Ann
TI: Supreme Court Deals Blow to Student Journalists.
PY: 1989
JN: Social-Education; v53 n3 p175-76 Mar 1989
AV: UMI
DE: Controversial-Issues-Course-Content; Higher-Education; High-School-Students; Intellectual-Freedom; Journalism-; Journalism-Education; Personal-Narratives; Secondary-Education; Social-Studies; Student-Publications; United-States-Government-Course
DE: *Censorship-; *College-Students; *Freedom-of-Speech; *School-Newspapers
AB: Covers the U.S. Supreme Court decision in Hazelwood School District v. Kuhlmeier, which gave principals the right to censor school publications. In "One Student's Pursuit of Journalism," Alexandra Salas relates one student journalist's experience, including internships, from high school through the end of college. (LS)

Kopenhaver, Lillian Lodge, David L. Martinson, and Peter Habermann, "First Amendment Rights in South Florida: Views of Advisers and Administrators in Light of *Hazelwood,*" *The School Press Review*, Fall 1989.

AN: EJ392960
AU: Morocco,-Maria
TI: Hazelwood One Year Later.
PY: 1989
JN: Update-on-Law-Related-Education; v13 n2 p48-50 Spr 1989
DE: Civil-Liberties; Court-Litigation; Journalism-Education; Secondary-Education; Social-Studies; Student-Publications

DE: *Censorship-; *Constitutional-Law; *Freedom-of-Speech; *Law-Related-Education; *School-Newspapers

AB: Discusses the effects of the U.S. Supreme Court's decision not to enunciate a broad First Amendment protection for student journalists. Examines the decision and provides comments of legal experts and political leaders relative to the impact of the decision in the courts and state legislatures. Reports on teacher and student reactions. (KO)

AU: Phillips,-Kay-D.
TI: Freedom of Expression for High School Journalists: A Case Study of Selected North Carolina Public Schools.
PY: 1989
PG: 50
DE: Case-Studies; Editors-; Journalism-; Principals-; Public-Schools; Student-Publications
DE: *Censorship-; *Faculty-Advisers; *Freedom-of-Speech; *High-Schools; *School-Newspapers
AB: A study examined the freedom of the high school press in North Carolina to determine whether publication guidelines should be in place, and if so, what those guidelines should contain. High school newspaper advisers, high school principals, and high school newspaper editors from large and small, urban and rural, eastern and western high schools were interviewed on several occasions. The nine advisers interviewed for this study attended the North Carolina Scholastic Press Association Workshop at the University of North Carolina at Chapel Hill in June, 1987 and to that extent are not representative of the generality of North Carolina high school newspaper advisers, most of whom are untrained and have never attended a journalism workshop. But, although better informed than average, results indicate that few of the study advisers are well informed on matters of journalistic importance (North Carolina has no certification requirements for secondary journalism teachers), all practice prior review, and all censor student writing by cutting controversial material and instituting an atmosphere of intimidation that causes students to refrain from printing certain materials in the school newspaper. Findings suggest that most of the problems that confront the high school newspaper adviser and staff can be avoided if every high school adopts a clear, legally explicit set of guidelines and if advisers are required to be well-trained. (Ninety-seven notes are attached.) (RS)

AN: ED317474
AU: Rosenblum,-Warren; And-Others
TI: From the School Newsroom to the Courtroom. Lessons on the Hazelwood Case and Free Expression Policy Making in the Public Schools.
CS: Constitutional Rights Foundation, Los Angeles, Calif.
PY: 1989
NT: 38 p.
PR: EDRS Price - MF01/PC02 Plus Postage.
DE: Censorship-; Constitutional-Law; Due-Process; High-Schools; High-School-Students; Law-Related-Education; Lesson-Plans; Newspapers-; News-Writing; Public-Schools; Role-Playing; School-Districts; School-Policy; Secondary-Education; Simulation-; United-States-Government-Course; Units-of-Study
DE: *Court-Litigation; *Freedom-of-Speech; *Journalism-Education; *School-Newspapers; *Student-Rights
AB: The purpose of this lesson packet is to raise issues about student rights of free expression in public schools. Included are preparatory reading material and two classroom simulation activities. The lessons are based on the U.S. Supreme Court case of Hazelwood v. Kuhlmeier, in which a Missouri high school principal and school district were sued by

students for censoring controversial feature articles in a school newspaper. Part 1 presents the legal background of the Hazelwood case, discussing the U.S. Constitution and various court decisions regarding free expression, due process, and the rights of schools and the local, state and federal governments. Part 2 gives the background of the Hazelwood case, and discusses the development of relevant legal issues such as "public forum" and "compelling interest." Part 3 presents a simulation exercise, a moot court activity in which teams of students represent attorneys for petitioners and respondents, and Supreme Court justices. Part 4 summarizes the arguments presented by both the majority and the dissenting justices in the Hazelwood case. Part 5 presents a simulation activity in which students engage in a policy debate on the rights of student journalists. Included in the packet are profiles of former Hazelwood East High School student Leslie Smart and principal Robert E. Reynolds, and a teacher's guide to the lessons. (AS)

AN: EJ392961
AU: Shah,-Dorothie-C.
TI: Individual Rights: Freedom of the Press.
PY: 1989
JN: Update-on-Law-Related-Education; v13 n2 p51-53 Spr 1989
DE: Censorship-; Court-Litigation; Instructional-Materials; Journalism-Education; Lesson-Plans; Secondary-Education; Social-Studies
DE: *Constitutional-Law; *Freedom-of-Speech; *Law-Related-Education; *School-Newspapers
AB: Outlines a lesson plan for discussing the civil rights of public school students. Uses the U.S. Supreme Court decision in Hazelwood School District v. Kuhlmeier as a basis for discussing freedom of expression protected by the First Amendment. Provides materials for student use and detailed directions for implementation of the lesson. (KO)

Abrams, J. Marc, and S. Mark Goodman, "End of an Era?: The Decline of Student Press Rights in the Wake of the Kuhlmeier Decision" (paper presented at the convention of the Association for Education in Journalism and Mass Communication, Portland, Ore., July 1988).

AN: EJ371776
AU: Adams,-Julian
TI: Cleaning the Slate: Hazelwood Decision Leaves Student Editorial Staffs with Questions.
PY: 1988
JN: Communication:-Journalism-Education-Today-(C:JET); v21 n4 p22-23 Sum 1988
AV: UMI
DE: Journalism-Education; School-Policy; Secondary-Education
DE: *Censorship-; *Court-Litigation; *Freedom-of-Speech; *Student-Publications; *Student-Rights
AB: Discusses the U.S. Supreme Court ruling on Hazelwood School District v. Kuhlmeier, dealing with school publication censorship. Suggests that although school officials may impose some restrictions on the speech of students, teachers, and other members of the school community, several ways exist to protect the vitality of school-sponsored student publications. (MM)

AN: EJ434288
AU: Brennan,-William-J.
TI: Dissent of Justice Brennan.
PY: 1988
JN: School-Press-Review; v63 n2 p11-19 Win 1988
AV: UMI
NT: Special pull-out section paginated separately.

DE: Court-Judges; Journalism-; School-Newspapers; Secondary-Education; Student-Publications

DE: *Court-Litigation; *Court-Role; *Freedom-of-Speech; *Journalism-Education; *Writing-for-Publication

AB: Presents the dissent of Justice Brennan, with whom Justice Marshall and Justice Blackmun join, dissenting, in the Hazelwood School District versus Kuhlmeier case. (MG)

AN: EJ434290
AU: Burlingham,-Nelly
TI: Hazelwood Comes Home to Roost.
PY: 1988
JN: School-Press-Review; v63 n2 p22-25 Win 1988
AV: UMI
NT: Special pull-out section paginated separately.
DE: Court-Judges; Court-Role; Educational-Change; Journalism-; Secondary-Education; Student-Publications
DE: *Court-Litigation; *Freedom-of-Speech; *Journalism-Education; *School-Newspapers; *Writing-for-Publication
AB: Provides reactions from principals, journalism advisers, and journalism students to the Supreme Court decision in the Hazelwood case. (MG)

AN: EJ376098
TI: California Law Protects Student Journalists in Censorship Test!
PY: 1988
JN: Quill-and-Scroll; v62 n4 p8-9 Apr-May 1988
AV: UMI
DE: Acquired-Immune-Deficiency-Syndrome; Faculty-Advisers; High-Schools; Journalism-Education; Secondary-Education
DE: *Censorship-; *Editorials-; *Freedom-of-Speech; *School-Newspapers
AB: Recollects the events surrounding the decision on whether a California high school would be able to print a story on AIDS. Discusses the role the Hazelwood decision played in the censorship of the story and its effect on other states. (MS)

"Current Issues Memo Regarding the Supreme Court and Students' Rights — An Update," *Phi Delta Kappan*, February 1988.

Day, Louis A., and John M. Butler, "Hazelwood School District v. Kuhlmeier: A Constitutional Retreat or Sound Public Policy?" (paper presented at the convention of the Association for Education in Journalism and Mass Communication, Portland, Ore., July 1988.)

Essex, Nathan L. "A Landmark Supreme Court Decision Grants School Authorities the Right to Censor School Sponsored Student Newspapers," *Contemporary Education*, 59:3 (Spring 1988).

AN: EJ377391
AU: Eveslage,-Thomas
TI: Hazelwood v. Kuhlmeier: A Threat and a Challenge to High School Journalism.
PY: 1988
JN: Quill-and-Scroll; v62 n3 p9-10 Feb-Mar 1988
AV: UMI
DE: Faculty-Advisers; Freedom-of-Speech; High-Schools; Secondary-Education
DE: *Censorship-; *Journalism-Education; *School-Newspapers

AB: Analyzes potential problems the Hazelwood decision may present. Warns faculty advisers and staffs to consider protective measures. (MS)

AN: EJ434289
AU: Goodman,-Mark
TI: Reaction: Student Press Law Center.
PY: 1988
JN: School-Press-Review; v63 n2 p20-21 Win 1988
AV: UMI
NT: Special pull-out section paginated separately.
DE: Court-Judges; Court-Role; Educational-Change; Journalism-; Secondary-Education; Student-Publications
DE: *Court-Litigation; *Freedom-of-Speech; *Journalism-Education; *School-Newspapers; *Writing-for-Publication
AB: Provides a reaction from the Student Press Law Center to the Hazelwood School District versus Kuhlmeier decision. Urges student journalists and advisers to continue to do their best to produce quality, intelligent publications and to educate school administration and community about the importance of a free student press. (MG)

AN: EJ379795
AU: Goodman,-Mark
TI: The Push by Educators for Student Press Freedom.
PY: 1988
JN: Communication:-Journalism-Education-Today-(C:JET); v22 n1 p12-15 Fall 1988
AV: UMI
DE: Court-Litigation; Educational-Policy; High-Schools; Secondary-Education; Student-School-Relationship
DE: *Administrators-; *Censorship-; *Freedom-of-Speech; *Journalism-Education; *Student-Publications
AB: Discusses the effects of the Hazelwood School District v. Kuhlmeier decision involving the First Amendment rights of high school journalists and the thrust by Journalism Educators to insure student press freedom. (MS)

AN: EJ379964
AU: Goodman,-Mark
TI: Student Press Freedom: One View of the "Hazelwood" Decision.
PY: 1988
JN: NASSP-Bulletin; v72 n511 p38,40-44 Nov 1988
AV: UMI
DE: Secondary-Education
DE: *Censorship-; *Court-Litigation; *Freedom-of-Speech; *Student-Publications; *Student-Rights
AB: Reviews the "Hazelwood v. Kuhlmeier" U.S. Supreme Court decision upholding a principal's right to censor the content of a school-sponsored student publication. Explains why teachers oppose this decision, discusses liability issues, and argues for a free, uncensored student press. Includes eight legal references. (MLH)

AN: EJ373186
AU: Knight,-Robert-P.
TI: High School Journalism in the Post-Hazelwood Era.
PY: 1988
JN: Journalism-Educator; v43 n2 p42-47 Sum 1988
AV: UMI

DE: Higher-Education; Journalism-; Journalism-Education; Professional-Associations; School-Policy; Secondary-Education

DE: *Censorship-; *Court-Litigation; *Freedom-of-Speech; *Student-Publications; *Student-Rights

AB: Discusses the U.S. Supreme Court ruling on Hazelwood School District v. Kuhlmeier, dealing with school publication censorship. Outlines implications for college-level journalism, and suggests actions that professional journalism organizations can take to support student publications. (MM)

Renfro, Paula, Bruce Renfro, and Roger Bennett, "Expectations of Change in the High School Press after Hazelwood: A Survey of Texas High School Principals, Newspaper Advisers and Newspaper Editors," *Southwestern Mass Communication Journal*, 4 (1988).

AN: ED298534
AU: Robbins,-Jan-C.
TI: Student Press and the "Hazelwood" Decision. Fastback 274.
CS: Phi Delta Kappa Educational Foundation, Bloomington, Ind.
PY: 1988
AV: Phi Delta Kappa, Eighth and Union, Box 789, Bloomington, IN 47402 ($.90).
NT: 41 p.; Fastback sponsored by the University of Northern Iowa Chapter of Phi Delta Kappa.
PR: EDRS Price - MF01/PC02 Plus Postage.
DE: Faculty-Advisers; Federal-Courts; High-Schools; Secondary-Education
DE: *Censorship-; *Court-Litigation; *Freedom-of-Speech; *Journalism-Education; *School-Newspapers
AB: This fastback examines Hazelwood School District v. Kuhlmeier (1988), the first high school student press case ever to reach the United States Supreme Court. The pamphlet reviews the background and implications of the Hazelwood decision and speculates as to how it will be applied to student expression in the public high schools. Chapters include: (1) "Student Press and the Public Forum Doctrine"; (2) "Whatever Happened to Tinker?"; (3) "Strict Scrutiny v. Rational Relationship"; and (4) "Applying Hazelwood in the Public Schools." The fastback concludes that official censorship of the student press, and of student expression generally, seems to have been reborn with Hazelwood, because it now governs all student expression in curriculum-related or other school-sponsored activities. (MS)

Hazelwood v. Kuhlmeier, 108 S.Ct. 562 (1988).

AN: EJ434287
TI: Opinion.
PY: 1988
JN: School-Press-Review; v63 n2 p1-10 Win 1988
AV: UMI
NT: Special pull-out section paginated separately.
DE: Court-Judges; Journalism-; Secondary-Education; Student-Publications; Writing-for-Publication
DE: *Court-Litigation; *Court-Role; *Freedom-of-Speech; *Journalism-Education; *School-Newspapers
AB: Presents the opinion of the Supreme Court on the Hazelwood School District versus Kuhlmeier case delivered by Justice White. (MG)

AN: EJ377392
TI: Hazelwood Decision: The Complete Text of the Jan. 13 U.S. Supreme Court 5-3 Decision.
PY: 1988
JN: Quill-and-Scroll; v62 n3 p11-18 Feb-Mar 1988
AV: UMI
DE: Court-Litigation; Editorials-; Faculty-Advisers; Freedom-of-Speech; High-Schools; Journalism-; Secondary-Education
DE: *Censorship-; *Journalism-Education; *School-Newspapers
AB: Reprints the complete text of the January 13, 1988, United States Supreme Court decision on Hazelwood School District versus Kuhlmeier, which concerns educators' editorial control over the content of a high school newspaper produced as part of a school's journalism curriculum. (MS)

Schmidt Jr., Richard M., and N. Frank Wiggins, "Censoring Student Papers May Teach a Lesson That Will Return to Haunt the Mainstream Press," *The Bulletin of the American Society of Newspaper Editors*, February 1988, pp. 4-8.

Simpson, Mike. "Supreme Court Chills Student Press Rights," *NEA Today*, March 1988.

AN: EJ434286
AU: Sullivan,-Edmund-J.
TI: Six Messages in Hazelwood Decision.
PY: 1988
JN: School-Press-Review; v63 n2 p2-5 Win 1988
AV: UMI
NT: Special pull-out section paginated separately.
DE: Court-Judges; Court-Role; Educational-Change; Secondary-Education; Student-Publications; Writing-for-Publication
DE: *Court-Litigation; *Freedom-of-Speech; *Journalism-; *Journalism-Education; *School-Newspapers
AB: States the six messages sent from the Supreme Court in the Hazelwood School District versus Kuhlmeier decision. Comments on the messages sent to federal judges, public school administrators, public school teachers, student journalists, professional press, and to the "education reform movement." (MG)

Legal Issues (General)

Dickson, Tom. "How Goes the Great Debate? A Study of 'Censorship' and 'Self-Censorship' and Their Effect on the Content of the Scholastic Press" (paper presented to the Scholastic Journalism Division at the convention of the Association for Education in Journalism and Mass Communication, Kansas City, Mo., August 1993.)

Eveslage, Thomas. "The Federal Courts and Educational Policy: Paternalism, Political Correctness and Student Expression," (paper presented to the Secondary Education Division at the convention of the Association for Education in Journalism and Mass Communication, Montreal, Canada, August 1992.)

AU: Martinson,-David-L.; Kopenhaver,-Lillian-Lodge
TI: High School Newspaper Advisers, Public School Administrators View First Amendment Issues Differently.
PY: 1992
JN: Quill-and-Scroll; v66 n3 p7-11 Feb-Mar 1992

DE: Comparative-Analysis; High-Schools; Public-Schools; School-Surveys; Student-Publications; Student-Rights
DE: *Administrators-; *Freedom-of-Speech; *School-Newspapers
AB: Presents the results of a survey that shows the difference between how school administrators and school newspaper advisers view First Amendment issues. Finds that advisers are fully supportive of presenting possibly controversial material whereas administrators are primarily concerned with maintaining a safe environment. (PA)

Tantillo, Susan Hathaway. "Lessons on Law, Ethics Establish Checkpoints," *C:JET (Communication: Journalism Education Today)* 26 (Winter 1992):12-14.

AN: EJ403651
AU: Thiele,-Norma
TI: Staff Uses Even-Handed, Mature Approach to Report about Teacher Indictment in Dealing with Sensitive Issues.
PY: 1990
JN: Quill-and-Scroll; v64 n2 p7-8 Dec-Jan 1990
AV: UMI
DE: Secondary-Education
DE: *Controversial-Issues-Course-Content; *High-Schools; *Journalism-Education; *News-Reporting; *School-Newspapers
AB: Describes how a high school newspaper handled a sensitive issue (in this case the arrest and indictment of a teacher), choosing to face undesirable news by getting the facts correctly, explaining them, and putting a stop to speculative stories. (SR)

AN: EJ403652
AU: Vahl,-Rod
TI: Legal vs Ethical News-Gathering Methods.
PY: 1990
JN: Quill-and-Scroll; v64 n2 p20-21 Dec-Jan 1990
AV: UMI
DE: High-School-Students; Legal-Problems; Plagiarism-; Secondary-Education
DE: *Ethics-; *High-Schools; *Journalism-Education; *News-Reporting; *School-Newspapers
AB: Discusses legal and ethical issues surrounding methods of news-gathering, including undercover reporting, misrepresentation of the reporter's identity, fabrication, and plagiarism. Maintains that high school reporters should search out and follow guidelines for their information-seeking methods. (SR)

Zweifel, David. "Self-Censorship Is Flourishing at High School Newspapers," *The Bulletin of the American Society of Newspaper Editors*, March 1990.

AN: EJ391875
AU: Adams,-Julian
TI: Censorship of Off-Campus Publications Violates First Amendment Rights.
PY: 1989
JN: Communication:-Journalism-Education-Today-(C:JET); v22 n4 p15-16 Sum 1989
AV: UMI
DE: Federal-Courts; Secondary-Education
DE: *Censorship-; *Court-Litigation; *Freedom-of-Speech; *Journalism-Education; *Student-Publications

AB: Reviews Burch v. Barker, in which the Ninth Circuit Court of Appeals ruled that school administrators' prior review of an alternative or off-campus publication, destined for distribution on the school campus, is in violation of the First Amendment. (MS)

Brown, Jean E. "The Relativity of Freedom," *Support for the Learning and Teaching of English Newsletter*, 13:1 (September 1988).

AN: EJ373187
AU: Click,-J.-William; Kopenhaver,-Lillian-Lodge
TI: Principals Favor Discipline More than a Free Press.
PY: 1988
JN: Journalism-Educator; v43 n2 p48-51 Sum 1988
AV: UMI
DE: Discipline-; Freedom-of-Speech; Journalism-; Journalism-Education; Secondary-Education; Surveys-
DE: *Censorship-; *Principals-; *School-Policy; *Student-Publications; *Student-Rights
AB: Summarizes a national survey of high school principals and newspaper advisers concerning their opinions on freedom of the high school press. Reports that, although most principals and advisers believe in a free press, they also believe that maintaining discipline is more important than an uncensored press. (MM)

AN: EJ379961
AU: Eveslage,-Thomas
TI: Publications Guidelines: A Way to Avoid Conflict and Courtrooms.
PY: 1988
JN: NASSP-Bulletin; v72 n511 p21-22,24-26 Nov 1988
AV: UMI
DE: Secondary-Education
DE: *Guidelines-; *Journalism-; *Legal-Responsibility; *Stress-Variables; *Student-Publications; *Student-Rights
AB: To minimize antagonism and enhance the educational process, schools should consider adopting student publications guidelines that clearly outline the legal parameters of protected expression, the system for regulating speech, and procedures for administrative policies. (MLH)

AN: EJ376099
AU: Heintz,-Ann
TI: What Might a Principal Consider "Inappropriate"?
PY: 1988
JN: Quill-and-Scroll; v62 n4 p9-10 Apr-May 1988
AV: UMI
DE: Acquired-Immune-Deficiency-Syndrome; Editorials-; Faculty-Advisers; Freedom-of-Speech; High-Schools; Journalism-; Secondary-Education
DE: *Censorship-; *Principals-; *School-Newspapers
AB: Considers the questions surrounding a principal's decision to censor a controversial story. Depicts an improvised drama of this problem and relates the reactions of an audience of attorneys, a school superintendent, and their own colleagues during the drama. (MS)

McNabb, Scott. "Censoring Student Newspapers Hurts Education," *Support for the Learning and Teaching of English Newsletter*, 13:1 (September 1988), p. 2.

AN: EJ377447
AU: Thiele,-Norma
TI: Mock Libel Trial Provides Unique Educational Experience.
PY: 1988
JN: Quill-and-Scroll; v63 n1 p4-6 Oct-Nov 1988
AV: UMI
DE: Secondary-Education; Student-Publications
DE: *Journalism-Education; *School-Newspapers
AB: Describes a mock libel trial held at North Side High School in Fort Wayne, Indiana, involving a question of whether a school newspaper may properly comment on a teacher's performance. Describes how the mock trial was integrated into various subjects, such as journalism, social studies, English, physics, art, and business. (SR)

Valentine, Fern. "Students Are Not Asking for License; They Are Asking for Press Freedom," *The Bulletin of the American Society of Newspaper Editors*, February 1988.

AN: EJ368609
AU: Adams,-Julian
TI: Is There Liability When Reporting about Activities?
PY: 1987
JN: Communication:-Journalism-Education-Today; v21 n2 p16 Win 1987
AV: UMI
DE: Journalism-Education; News-Reporting; Secondary-Education; Student-Publications
DE: *Faculty-Advisers; *Insurance-; *Legal-Responsibility; *School-Newspapers
AB: Discusses the matter of liability and insurance coverage of staff members when they are reporting about activities. (JK)

Eveslage, Thomas. "Teaching Free Speech Values to High School Students: Keys to Persevering Despite the Obstacles" (paper presented at the convention of the Association for Education in Journalism and Mass Communication, San Antonio, Texas, August 1987).

AN: EJ359124
AU: Goodman,-Mark
TI: First Amendment Must Be Real.
PY: 1987
JN: Communication:-Journalism-Education-Today-(C:JET); v21 n1 p4 Fall 1987
AV: UMI
DE: Citizen-Participation; Journalism-Education; Newspapers-; Secondary-Education; Student-Publications
DE: *Censorship-; *Freedom-of-Speech
AB: Advocates showing by example the principles of the First Amendment by curbing censorship of student publications to better prepare students to function as journalists and as informed citizens. (HTH)

AN: EJ359123
AU: Hall,-Carol-Ann
TI: To Whom? For What?
PY: 1987
JN: Communication:-Journalism-Education-Today-(C:JET); v21 n1 p2-3 Fall 1987
AV: UMI
DE: Administrator-Responsibility; Censorship-; Court-Litigation; News-Reporting; School-Responsibility; Secondary-Education; Student-Rights; Student-School-Relationship

DE: *Freedom-of-Speech; *Journalism-Education; *Newspapers-; *Student-Publications; *Student-Responsibility
AB: Explores the responsibility incumbent upon student journalists, the school administration, and the community for upholding the First Amendment. (HTH)

AN: EJ359126
AU: Hastings,-Nancy
TI: Seeks Prior Approval.
PY: 1987
JN: Communication:-Journalism-Education-Today-(C:JET); v21 n1 p6-7 Fall 1987
AV: UMI
DE: Secondary-Education; Student-School-Relationship
DE: *Board-of-Education-Policy; *Faculty-Advisers; *Journalism-Education; *Newspapers-; *Student-Publications; *Student-Rights
AB: Recounts an adviser's successful efforts to mobilize support and educate the school board on the First Amendment and student press rights, thereby circumventing a board-proposed publications policy requiring that news items be approved prior to publication. (HTH)

AN: EJ359127
AU: McDaniel,-Chanda; Collins,-Katie
TI: Working Journalists' Reasons, Opinions Differ on Views of Scholastic Press Rights.
PY: 1987
JN: Communication:-Journalism-Education-Today-(C:JET); v21 n1 p9-10 Fall 1987
AV: UMI
DE: Privacy-; Secondary-Education; Student-Rights; Student-School-Relationship
DE: *Censorship-; *Court-Litigation; *Journalism-Education; *Newspapers-; *Student-Publications
AB: Discusses the pending "Hazelwood School District vs. Kuhlmeier" censorship case and why some working journalists are siding with the school administration. (HTH)

AN: EJ359128
AU: Simpson,-Stephanie
TI: Principal Favors "Safety Net" for Administrators.
PY: 1987
JN: Communication:-Journalism-Education-Today-(C:JET); v21 n1 p11 Fall 1987
AV: UMI
DE: Censorship-; Secondary-Education; Student-Rights
DE: *Administrator-Role; *Faculty-Advisers; *Journalism-Education; *Newspapers-; *Student-Publications
AB: Notes that administrators must appease both the community and the student press rights. Suggests that advisers inform the administration of any story that may not be legal or may pose problems, and the principal can then exercise "publisher's" rights if he or she concurs, subject to student appeal. (HTH)

AN: EJ359129
AU: Weisenburger,-Dave
TI: Controversy.
PY: 1987
JN: Communication:-Journalism-Education-Today-(C:JET); v21 n1 p12 Fall 1987
AV: UMI
DE: News-Reporting; Secondary-Education; Student-Rights
DE: *Journalism-Education; *Student-Publications; *Yearbooks-

AB: Notes that many school yearbooks are now covering what may be considered "controversial" topics. Discusses the merits of an editorial policy for yearbooks, and notes that First Amendment rights and responsibilities also apply to publishing a yearbook. (HTH)

AN: EJ343675
AU: Adams,-Julian
TI: Press Freedom Column: When Ads Contain Political Opinions.
PY: 1986
JN: Communication:-Journalism-Education-Today-(C:JET); v20 n2 p23-24 Win 1986
AV: UMI
DE: Court-Litigation; Ethics-; Secondary-Education
DE: *Advertising-; *Freedom-of-Speech; *Journalism-Education; *Political-Issues; *School-Newspapers
AB: Discusses the responsibility of public school newspapers to carefully review the political advertising considered for publication because as a public forum paper, the school newspaper must represent a variety of political viewpoints. (SRT)

AN: EJ334130
AU: Adams,-Julian
TI: Districts 'Jump the Gun' on Prior Restraint Rules.
PY: 1986
JN: Communication:-Journalism-Education-Today-(C:JET); v19 n4 p19-20 Sum 1986
AV: UMI
NT: Thematic Issue: Journalism as Literature: Literature as Journalism
DE: Elementary-Secondary-Education; Journalism-Education; School-Publications
DE: *Administrator-Responsibility; *Administrators-; *Censorship-; *Court-Litigation; *Legal-Responsibility; *School-Newspapers
AB: Debates the federal court decision in the case of "Kuhlmeier v. Hazelwood School District," which found that the school newspaper was an integral part of the school curriculum and was therefore subject to administrative control and censorship. (DF)

AN: EJ329470
AU: Adams,-Julian
TI: Who Pays for Libel in School Newspapers?
PY: 1986
JN: Communication:-Journalism-Education-Today-(C:JET); v19 n3 p18-19 Spr 1986
AV: UMI
DE: Court-Litigation; Faculty-Advisers; Higher-Education; Secondary-Education; Teacher-Role
DE: *Journalism-Education; *Legal-Responsibility; *School-Newspapers
AB: Discusses the possibilities of who may be held responsible in cases of libel in school newspapers and offers seven defenses against charges of libel, including the truth, retraction, and consent. (DF)

AU: Click,-J.-William; Kopenhaver,-Lillian-Lodge
TI: Principals' and Newspaper Advisers' Attitudes toward Freedom of the Student Press in the United States.
PY: 1986
PG: 23
NT: Paper presented to the Secondary Education Division of the Association for Education in Journalism and Mass Communication, Norman, Okla.
DE: Administrator-Responsibility; Administrator-Role; Censorship-; Discipline-; High-Schools; Journalism-Education; Social-Problems

DE: *Administrator-Attitudes; *Faculty-Advisers; *Freedom-of-Speech; *Principals-; *School-Newspapers; *Teacher-Attitudes

AB: The opinions of principals and newspaper advisers toward high school student press freedom were surveyed in a random sample of principals and newspaper advisers at 502 high schools in all 50 states. Subjects completed a 39-statement instrument on which they indicated levels of agreement or disagreement on the following concerns: control and disruption, role of student newspapers, censorship, responsibilities of advisers, role of administrators, controversial issues, and freedom of expression in general. Usable responses were received from 191 school newspaper advisers and 144 high school principals. Among the findings were the following: (1) 58.8% of the principals, but only 22.5% of the advisers, agreed that school administrators should have the right to prohibit publication of articles they think harmful, even though such articles might not be libelous, obscene, or disruptive; (2) 58.5% of the principals agreed that maintaining discipline in the school is more important than publishing a newspaper free from administrative censorship, while 74% of the advisers disagreed; (3) 96.5% of the principals and 89% of the advisers agreed that student newspaper advisers should review all copy before it is printed; and (4) 46.5% of the principals disagreed that the student newspaper should be allowed to print a story it can prove is true even if printing the story will hurt the school's reputation, while 44.5% of the advisers agreed that such an article should be published. (HOD)

AU: Martinson,-David-L.
TI: College/High School Advisers Hold Similar Views on Most—But Not All—Student Press, First Amendment Issues.
PY: 1986
JN: C.S.P.A.A.-Bulletin; v43 n3 p5-10 Win 1985-86
DE: Administrator-Role; Comparative-Analysis; Higher-Education; High-Schools; Student-Publications; Teacher-Attitudes
DE: *Censorship-; *Faculty-Advisers; *Freedom-of-Speech; *Journalism-Education; *Media-Research; *Student-Rights
AB: Reports on a survey of high school newspaper advisers' attitudes toward student press rights and the adviser's role, indicating that most support a free and independent press, but, unlike college advisers, high school advisers were neutral concerning faculty/administration control where a potentially damaging article was concerned. (HTH)

AN: EJ332224
AU: Abrams,-J.-Marc
TI: The Curious Case of the Student Press.
PY: 1985
JN: Update-on-Law-Related-Education; v9 n3 p10-12 Fall 1985
DE: Court-Litigation; Freedom-of-Speech; Higher-Education; Journalism-Education; Secondary-Education
DE: *Legal-Education; *School-Newspapers; *Student-Rights; *Teacher-Rights
AB: Discussed is a court case in which a journalism teacher filed suit against a two year college alleging that the students' civil rights had been violated because the college had eliminated the student newspaper. The court allowed the teacher third-party standing to defend the rights of the students. (RM)

AN: EJ326457
AU: Adams,-Julian
TI: Libel Is Rare in Secondary School Newspapers, but the Study of It Is an Absolute Necessity.
PY: 1985

JN: Communication:-Journalism-Education-Today-(C:JET); v19 n2 p14-15 Win 1985
AV: UMI
DE: Court-Litigation; Faculty-Advisers; Secondary-Education; Teacher-Role
DE: *Journalism-Education; *Legal-Responsibility; *School-Newspapers
AB: Discusses the necessity of being aware of what constitutes libel in secondary school pub-
lications and offers examples of materials that may be libelous, including letters to the
editor, quotations, photographs, headlines, and picture captions. (DF)

AN: EJ313620
AU: Bowen,-John
TI: Captive Voices: What Progress, Change Has Occurred in 10 Years?
PY: 1985
JN: Quill-and-Scroll; v59 n3 p14-16 Feb-Mar 1985
AV: UMI
DE: Conflict-; Educational-Research; School-Surveys; Secondary-Education; Teacher-
Administrator-Relationship
DE: *Censorship-; *Educational-Philosophy; *Freedom-of-Speech; *Journalism-Education;
*Student-Publications
AB: Conclusions drawn from a new survey indicate that student editors are less willing to
tackle sensitive topics, that administrators will honor first amendment rights until there
is a conflict, and that advisers continue to support students' rights. (CRH)

AN: EJ311620
AU: Cramer,-Jerome
TI: Learn to Avoid a Mess with the Student Press.
PY: 1985
JN: Executive-Educator; v7 n1 p28-30,33 Jan 1985
AV: UMI
NT: Includes two brief "boxed" articles by the same author: "Use Care in Crafting Press
Policies" and "Select the Right Newspaper Adviser."
DE: Censorship-; Due-Process; Elementary-Secondary-Education; Faculty-Advisers;
Journalism-; Press-Opinion; Student-Publications
DE: *Constitutional-Law; *Freedom-of-Speech; *School-Newspapers; *Student-Rights
AB: The First Amendment protects editors of school newspapers. Accordingly, school policy
should offer students due process rights, and the newspaper adviser, who is instrumental
in controlling the content of student publications, should be chosen with care. (TE)

Eveslage, Thomas. *The First Amendment: Free Speech & a Free Press.* A Curriculum Guide for
High School Teachers. Philadelphia: School of Communications and Theater, Temple
University, 1985.

AN: EJ313467
AU: Hale,-Ann
TI: Let's Score One for Our Side!
PY: 1985
JN: C.S.P.A.A.-Bulletin; v42 n3 p4-5 Win 1984-85
AV: UMI
DE: Censorship-; Faculty-Advisers; Journalism-Education; School-Administration; School-
Newspapers; Secondary-Education; Student-School-Relationship
DE: *Administrator-Role; *Freedom-of-Speech; *Student-Publications; *Student-Rights
AB: Reviews an article in the January 1985 issue of "The Executive Educator" that contains
sound advice to administrators on the responsibilities of and restrictions to their role

with the student press. Urges journalism teachers and advisers to obtain a copy of the article for support of student press rights. (HTH)

AN: EJ308179
AU: Adams,-Julian
TI: Press Law—Obscenity: A First Amendment Outlaw.
PY: 1984
JN: Communication:-Journalism-Education-Today-(C:JET); v18 n2 p18-19 Win 1984
AV: UMI
DE: Constitutional-Law; High-School-Students; Laws-; Secondary-Education; Student-Publications
DE: *Court-Litigation; *Freedom-of-Speech; *Journalism-; *Obscenity-; *School-Newspapers
AB: Describes court cases with which news writers and reporters can make decisions about material they may question as being obscene. (CRH)

AU: Hines,-Barbara; Saville,-Anita
TI: Editors' and Advisers' Perceptions of Scholastic Press Freedom in Maryland Public Schools.
PY: 1984
PG: 40
DE: Censorship-; High-Schools; Media-Research; Student-Publications; Student-Teacher-Relationship
DE: *Faculty-Advisers; *Freedom-of-Speech; *School-Newspapers; *Student-Attitudes; *Student-Rights; *Teacher-Attitudes
AB: To test whether a positive relationship exists between perceptions of school press function and acceptance of First Amendment protection for school journalists, high school newspaper advisers in the public schools of an east coast state were surveyed concerning their understanding of and attitudes toward both student press freedom and student press function. Student editors were also questioned about their views toward student press freedom. The results gave no indication that advisers' understanding of student press law affected their attitude toward students' First Amendment rights or their attitudes toward student press function. It was not apparent from the analysis that advisers' experience, education, or attitudes influenced their perception of student press role. Both objective and subjective data indicated that student newspaper editors tended to have a narrower idea of student press freedom than did their advisers. While both advisers and editors overwhelmingly supported the coverage of controversial topics in the student press, both groups appeared to feel that such items may also be banned if they are "in poor taste" or do not represent "good journalism." Censorship occurred least where advisers and editors worked closely together to determine material suitability. The results showed a continuing trend toward improved recognition of student journalists' rights. However, it is also apparent that both philosophically and in practice, advisers and editors do not recognize the full measure of First Amendment press freedoms the courts have granted to student journalists. (A copy of the survey questionnaire is included.) (HTH)

AN: ED243100
AU: Newton,-Ray
TI: Student Press Freedoms: Rights and Responsibilities.
PY: 1984
NT: 23 p.; Paper presented at the Annual Meeting of the Western Speech Communication Association (Seattle, WA, February 18-21, 1984).
PR: EDRS Price - MF01/PC01 Plus Postage.

DE: Constitutional-Law; Freedom-of-Speech; Guidelines-; Higher-Education; School-Newspapers; Secondary-Education; Student-School-Relationship

DE: *Academic-Freedom; *Censorship-; *Court-Litigation; *Journalism-; *Student-Publications; *Student-Rights

AB: First Amendment court decisions have generally been consistent in affirming the rights of students against administrative censorship. Despite these decisions, a review of scholastic and collegiate journals indicates that the constitutional rights of students and their journalism advisers or instructors are clearly and frequently being violated. Educational officials often mandate that material submitted by students for newspapers or other media for student expression must be subject to prior review. At the heart of the conflict are administration fears that student expression may not reflect positively upon the school and that the school may be held liable in litigation over libel or slander. In spite of several books and reports on the subject, confusion about student press law prevails. Although guidelines such as editorial policy or codes of ethics are not necessarily a safeguard for either students or administrators, the National Council of College Publications Advisers recommends that at least some guidelines be in effect at institutions so that students, faculty, and administrators may have common ground on which to base discussions of freedom of expression and the First Amendment. (Examples of cases involving First Amendment litigation and a quiz on student press rights are included.) (HTH)

AN: EJ304066
AU: Osborn,-David-R.
TI: Confessions of a High School Newspaper Adviser.
PY: 1984
JN: English-Journal; v73 n6 p64-66 Oct 1984
AV: UMI
DE: Intellectual-Freedom; Journalism-Education; Sanctions-; Secondary-Education; Student-Responsibility; Teacher-Attitudes; Teacher-Morale; Teacher-Rights; Writing-for-Publication
DE: *Academic-Freedom; *Censorship-; *Freedom-of-Speech; *School-Newspapers; *Student-Rights
AB: Describes how a last issue of the school newspaper carrying senior class wills offended some faculty members and how the issue of censorship was raised and dealt with. (CRH)

Student Press Law Center, *Law of the Student Press* (Washington, D.C.: Student Press Law Center, 1984).

AN: EJ293087
AU: Brown,-Donal
TI: Free Student Press Strengthens Democracy.
PY: 1983
JN: Communication:-Journalism-Education-Today-(C;JET); v17 n2 p4-5 Win 1983
AV: UMI
DE: Democratic-Values; Journalism-Education; Secondary-Education
DE: *Censorship-; *Freedom-of-Speech; *School-Newspapers; *Student-Rights
AB: Reports the update of a 1970 censorship case and offers reasons why the student press should be permitted to report controversial stories. (AEA)

AN: EJ293088
AU: Duling,-Dennis
TI: A Case History in Press Freedom.
PY: 1983

JN: Communication:-Journalism-Education-Today-(C:JET); v17 n2 p6-7 Win 1983
AV: UMI
DE: Administrator-Role; School-Administration; Secondary-Education
DE: *Censorship-; *Freedom-of-Speech; *Journalism-Education; *School-Newspapers;
      *Student-Rights
AB: Describes how a high school newspaper adviser and his staff dealt with administrative
      censorship. (AEA)

Kirstof, N.D. *Freedom of the High School Press.* Lanham, Md.: University Press of America,
1983.

AN: EJ269793
AU: Eveslage,-Thomas
TI: Are Model Guidelines Possible Through State?
PY: 1982
JN: Communication:-Journalism-Education-Today-(C:JET); v16 n1 p16-17 Fall 1982
AV: Reprint: UMI
DE: Journalism-; Secondary-Education; State-Agencies
DE: *Freedom-of-Speech; *Guidelines-; *Journalism-Education; *News-Reporting; *State-
      Surveys; *Student-Publications
AB: Reports on a survey conducted by the Journalism Education Association to determine
      how states regulate the behavior of student journalists, the responses to which suggest
      the development of guidelines should be made at a local level. (HOD)

Trager, Robert and Dickerson, Donna L. "Prior Restraint in High School: Law, Attitudes and
Practice." *Journalism Quarterly* 57,1 (Spring 1980):135-138.

Broussard, E. Joseph, and C. Robert Blackmon, "Advisers, Editors and Principals Judge First
Amendment Cases," *Journalism Quarterly*, 55 (Winter 1978), pp. 797-799.

Driscoll, Carol K. *First Amendment and the High School Press Adviser.* Report by the Journalism
Education Association, January 1976.

Campbell, Laurence R. "Principals' Attitudes Toward Student Journalism and Freedom of the
Press." Quill and Scroll Society, 1976.

James, Max H. "Propaganda or Education? Censorship and School Journalism," *Arizona
English Bulletin*, 13:1 (October 1970), pp. 37-41.

Tinker v. Des Moines Independent School District. 89 S.Ct. 733, 393 U.S. 503 (1969).

Minorities in Journalism

Arnold, Mary. "Inner City High School Newspapers: An Obituary?" (paper presented to the
Scholastic Journalism Division at the convention of the Association for Education in
Journalism and Mass Communication, Kansas City, Mo., August 1993.)

Minder, Lisa. "The Whole Elephant: A Case Study of a High School Newspaper and
University Partnership," (paper presented to the Scholastic Journalism Division at the conven-
tion of the Association for Education in Journalism and Mass Communication, Kansas City,
Mo., August 1993.)

Novek, Eleanor M. "Buried Treasure: The Theory and Practice of Communicative Action in
an Urban High School Newspaper," (paper presented to the Scholastic Journalism Division at

the convention of the Association for Education in Journalism and Mass Communication, Kansas City, Mo., August 1993.)

Arnold, Mary. "Teaching Strategies for the Multicultural Classroom," *C:JET (Communication: Journalism Education Today)* 26 (Fall 1992):2-3.

Arnold, Mary and Fuller, Njeri. "When It All Began: Journalism Minority Recruiting and High School Students," (paper presented to the Secondary Education Division at the convention of the Association for Education in Journalism and Mass Communication, Montreal, Canada, August 1992.)

Arnold, Mary and Fuller, Njeri, eds. *Breakthrough: A Multi-cultural Guide to High School Journalism.* Iowa City, Iowa: The University of Iowa School of Journalism and Mass Communication. May 1992.

Bernard, Jim. "Multicultural Student Journalism Awards Enhance Minority Interest," *C:JET (Communication: Journalism Education Today)* 26 (Fall 1992):12-13.

AN: EJ437387
TI: Breakthrough: A Multicultural Guide for High School Journalism Ready for Spring 1992 Distribution.
PY: 1992
JN: Quill-and-Scroll; v66 n2 p20-21 Dec-Jan 1991-92
AV: UMI
DE: Journalism-; Secondary-Education
DE: *Journalism-Education; *Multicultural-Education; *School-Newspapers; *Student-Publications
AB: Presents a guide to help prepare secondary education journalism teachers create opportunities for greater minority involvement in scholastic journalism. (SR)

Engleman, Thomas E. "What It Takes to Attract the Attention...and the Dollars...for Journalism Education, Multicultural Students," *C:JET (Communication: Journalism Education Today)* 26 (Fall 1992):14-15.

Greenman, Robert. "Removing Barriers to School Newspaper Staff Diversity," *C:JET (Communication: Journalism Education Today)* 26 (Fall 1992):4-9.

Kovas, Marcia. "Making Diversity Count: A 10-Step Plan to Encourage Minority Involvement on Your Staff," *C:JET (Communication: Journalism Education Today)* 26 (Fall 1992):18-20.

McDuff, Celia. "Programs Involve Few Minority Students," *C:JET (Communication: Journalism Education Today)* 26 (Winter 1992):23-24.

Novek, Eleanor M. "Newsmaking, a Tool for Self-Determination: Urban Secondary School Journalism Students Publish a Community Newspaper," (paper presented to the Secondary Education Division at the convention of the Association for Education in Journalism and Mass Communication, Montreal, Canada, August 1992.)

O'Donoghue, Steve. "Journalism as a Dropout Prevention Program: A Basic Structure to Aid At-Risk Students, Foster Diversity and Restructure Schools," *C:JET (Communication: Journalism Education Today)* 26 (Fall 1992):16-17.

Rios, J.A. "A Personal Statement: One Adviser's Experiences Recruiting and Teaching a Multicultural Staff," *C:JET (Communication: Journalism Education Today)* 26 (Fall 1992):10-11.

Arnold, Mary. "Reaching Out to Minority Students." *C:JET (Communication: Journalism Education Today)* 23 (Spring 1990):12-13.

Cormeny, Sara. "The Mentor Program: One Approach to Parity in the Newsroom." *Communication: Journalism Education Today (C:JET)* 23 (Spring 1990):10-11, 22.

Curry, George. "A Minority Journalist Who's Been There Reaches Back to Help Others." *Communication: Journalism Education Today (C:JET)* 23 (Spring 1990):8-9.

AN: EJ408430
AU: Dvorak,-Jack
TI: New Scholarship Program Assists Minorities in Indiana.
PY: 1990
JN: Communication:-Journalism-Education-Today-(C:JET); v23 n3 p14-15 Spr 1990
DE: Corporate-Support; Higher-Education; Professional-Education
DE: *Journalism-Education; *Minority-Groups; *Scholarship-Funds
AB: Describes the recent formation, program of study, and benefits of the Foellinger Foundation Minority Scholarships at Indiana University, a program for minority students seeking degrees in journalism. Notes that this scholarship program addresses the lack of minority representation in newsrooms, an underlying problem in professional journalism. (KEH)

AU: Hines,-Barbara
TI: Cooperative Efforts Needed to Nurture Young Journalists.
PY: 1990
JN: Communication:-Journalism-Education-Today-(C:JET); v23 n3 p16-17,22 Spr 1990
DE: Mass-Media; Professional-Associations; Secondary-Education; Student-Experience; Workshops-
DE: *Career-Planning; *Cooperative-Programs; *High-School-Students; *Journalism-Education; *Minority-Groups; *School-Business-Relationship
AB: Describes cooperative efforts by Howard University and seven media and professional organizations in Washington, DC, to provide minority high school students with the necessary guidance and assistance to pursue careers in journalism. Provides information on how to organize similar consortiums to help minority students in other parts of the country. (KEH)

Morales, Sharon. "Students Who Don't 'Fit the Mold' Become One Teacher's Success Stories." *Communication: Journalism Education Today (C:JET)* 23 (Spring 1990):18-19.

Nelson, Linda Waller. "Newspaper Fund Plays Important Role in Minority Education in Journalism," *Communication: Journalism Education Today (C:JET)* 23 (Spring 1990):4-7.

AN: EJ414655
AU: O'Donoghue,-Steve
TI: Inner-City Journalism: Why It's Bad, How to Cope, What Can Be Done to Build a Quality Newspaper Program.
PY: 1990
JN: Communication:-Journalism-Education-Today-(C:JET); v23 n4 p3-6,16 Sum 1990
DE: Journalism-Education; Journalism-History; Secondary-Education; Teaching-Methods; Urban-Education
DE: *Faculty-Advisers; *Inner-City; *Journalism-; *Program-Development; *School-Newspapers

AB: Looks at current conditions inhibiting the growth and sustenance of quality journalism programs in inner-city areas. Examines some practical steps journalism advisers in these schools can take to better advance the talents and desires of their students. (RS)

AN: EJ391888
AU: Dvorak,-Jack
TI: Ann Christine Heintz.
PY: 1989
JN: Quill-and-Scroll; v63 n4 p10-12 Apr-May 1989
AV: UMI
DE: High-Schools
DE: *Journalism-Education; *Minority-Groups
AB: Recalls the accomplishments of Sister Ann Christine Heintz, an educator who devoted her career to identifying the best and brightest young minority people, and encouraging them to get involved in journalism. (MS)

AN: EJ371501
AU: Norris,-Frances
TI: MOSAIC: South Boston High's Bridge between Equity and Art.
PY: 1988
JN: Equity-and-Choice; v4 n2 p9-13 Win 1988
DE: Exhibits-; Journalism-; Multicultural-Education; Racial-Attitudes; Student-Publications
DE: *Art-; *Cultural-Awareness; *Equal-Education; *Secondary-Education; *Urban-Education
AB: "Mosaic" is a program that shows positive aspects of South Boston High School in the wake of its poor desegregation reputation. A community studies magazine is produced with writing and photographs that examines life in Boston and documents the lives of former students. It is used to teach multicultural education. (VM)

Secondary School Press Associations and Other Resources

McFarlin, Diane, ed. "Rescuing High School Journalism." A Report by Education for Journalism Committee, American Society of Newspaper Editors. Reston, Va.: ASNE Foundation, 1993.

Olson, Lyle O.; Van Ommeren, Roger; and Rossow, Marshel, "The State of High School Journalism," *C:JET (Communication: Journalism Education Today)* 27 (Spring 1993):10-12.

AN: EJ444261
AU: Dickey,-Beth
TI: Promoting Excellence in Evaluations.
PY: 1992
JN: Communication:-Journalism-Education-Today-(C:JET); v25 n4 p17,21 Sum 1992
DE: Evaluation-Criteria; Journalism-Education; Secondary-Education
DE: *Evaluation-Methods; *Evaluation-Problems; *Student-Publications
AB: Describes the Southern Interscholastic Press Association's (SIPA) evaluation service for student publications. (SR)

Hall, H.L. "Commission Gives Exams at National Conventions: Teachers Across Country Become Certified," *C:JET (Communication: Journalism Education Today)* 26 (Winter 1992):2-3.

Hall, H.L. "Teachers Give Reasons for Seeking Certification," *C:JET (Communication: Journalism Education Today)* 26 (Winter 1992):4-7.

AN: EJ444257
AU: Hawthorne,-Bobby
TI: Living with Your Critique.
PY: 1992
JN: Communication:-Journalism-Education-Today-(C:JET); v25 n4 p5-6 Sum 1992
DE: Secondary-Education
DE: *Evaluation-Criteria; *Evaluation-Problems; *Journalism-Education; *Student-Publications
AB: Discusses difficult aspects of the evaluation of student publications, in which the judge's analysis is often pitted against the adviser's aspirations for praise. (SR)

AN: EJ444260
AU: Hudnall,-John
TI: Publication Swap.
PY: 1992
JN: Communication:-Journalism-Education-Today-(C:JET); v25 n4 p16 Sum 1992
DE: Evaluation-Criteria; Journalism-Education; Secondary-Education
DE: *Evaluation-Methods; *Student-Publications
AB: Describes a new cooperative venture between the Kansas Scholastic Press Association and the Nebraska High School Press Association, in which adviser-judges from one state evaluate publication from the other. (SR)

AN: EJ444259
AU: Johns,-Richard
TI: Evaluation as a Cooperative Study.
PY: 1992
JN: Communication:-Journalism-Education-Today-(C:JET); v25 n4 p10-12 Sum 1992
DE: Journalism-Education; School-Newspapers; Secondary-Education
DE: *Evaluation-Criteria; *Evaluation-Methods; *Student-Publications
AB: Discusses the special qualities of Quill and Scroll Society's evaluation service for student newspapers, which includes requiring advisers and staffs to analyze their own publications. (SR)

AN: EJ444263
AU: Konkle,-Bruce
TI: Covering All the Bases.
PY: 1992
JN: Communication:-Journalism-Education-Today-(C:JET); v25 n4 p19 Sum 1992
DE: Evaluation-Criteria; Journalism-Education; Secondary-Education
DE: *Evaluation-Methods; *Student-Publications
AB: Offers four strategies to press association directors on how to structure an evaluation service. (SR)

Olson, Lyle D.; Van Ommeren, Roger; and Rossow, Marshel. "The Nation's Scholastic Press Association Directors Describe the State of High School Journalism," (paper presented to the Secondary Education Division at the convention of the Association for Education in Journalism and Mass Communication, Montreal, Canada, August 1992.)

AN: EJ444256
AU: Ortman,-Sarah
TI: Different Hats Provide Different Views.
PY: 1992
JN: Communication:-Journalism-Education-Today-(C:JET); v25 n4 p2-4 Sum 1992

DE: Secondary-Education
DE: *Evaluation-Criteria; *Evaluation-Problems; *Journalism-Education; *Student-Publications
AB: Discusses the evaluation of student publications from the author's various perspectives as adviser, teacher, judge, and press association director. (SR)

AN: EJ444262
AU: Pell,-Cheryl
TI: Reflecting Changing Trends and Times.
PY: 1992
JN: Communication:-Journalism-Education-Today-(C:JET); v25 n4 p18 Sum 1992
DE: Journalism-Education; Secondary-Education
DE: *Evaluation-Methods; *Evaluation-Problems; *Student-Publications
AB: Maintains that scholastic press associations must listen to their advisers, students, and judges to make sure the evaluation service is meeting needs. (SR)

AU: Hines,-Barbara
TI: Resource Directory for High School Journalism Teachers and Publications Advisers.
PY: 1990
JN: Communication:-Journalism-Education-Today-(C:JET); v23 n3 p20-21 Spr 1990
DE: Career-Planning; Secondary-Education
DE: *Educational-Opportunities; *Educational-Resources; *Journalism-Education; *Minority-Groups; *Professional-Associations
AB: Lists addresses and descriptions of programs and services for 27 organizations which assist minority students interested in study opportunities and careers in journalism. (KEH)

AN: EJ434291
AU: Duval,-Tom
TI: The 20 Most-Asked Questions about the CSPA's Judging.
PY: 1988
JN: School-Press-Review; v63 n2 p16-19 Win 1988
AV: UMI
NT: Special pull-out section paginated separately.
DE: Journalism-; Journalism-Education; Judges-; Secondary-Education; Student-Publications
DE: *School-Newspapers; *Writing-for-Publication
AB: Identifies the 20 most-asked questions regarding the judging of student publications by the Columbia Scholastic Press Association. Provides answers to help clarify these matters. (MG)

AU: Iorio,-Sharon-Hartin; Garner,-R.-Brooks
TI: Scholastic Journalism Enrollment Changes and Attendance at University Programs for High School Students.
PY: 1988
PG: 29
DE: College-School-Cooperation; Higher-Education; High-Schools; Journalism-; Media-Research; School-Publications; School-Surveys
DE: *Enrollment-; *Faculty-Advisers; *Journalism-Education; *Teacher-Attitudes
AB: Almost from its beginning, scholastic journalism, in a number of schools, has fought an up-hill battle against the stereotype of academic orphan relegated to a low priority position in the curriculum, the perception of administration, and fiscal allocation. In order to address the status of scholastic journalism, a study surveyed the attitudes of high school

teacher-advisers toward changes in enrollment in high school journalism classes and attendance at university programs directed toward scholastic journalism. Subjects were 281 high school and/or mid-high journalism teachers from the Oklahoma public school system who responded to a questionnaire mailed to a total sample of 487. Findings showed that (1) over 73% of teacher-adviser respondents reported that enrollment in journalism classes and publication production classes had either remained the same or had decreased; (2) increased graduation requirements in basic courses appear to be the most detrimental factor influencing secondary journalism educational enrollment; (3) at the schools studied, scheduling of classes, student interest, and the person selected to teach/advise journalism can either help or hinder high school journalism; (4) experienced teacher-advisers and those certified seem to be more successful in increasing enrollment than their counterparts who are inexperienced or not certified; and (5) there is a need for university programs that would serve a wider scholastic journalism constituency. (Six tables of data and 25 notes are included.) (MS)

AU: Plopper,-Bruce-L.
TI: The Usefulness of University-Sponsored Workshops as Aids for High School Journalism Advisers in A Rural State: A Descriptive Analysis.
PY: 1988
PG: 22
DE: High-Schools
DE: *Faculty-Advisers; *Journalism-; *Journalism-Education; *Rural-Schools; *Student-Publications; *Workshops-
AB: Advising high school publications is a difficult task that makes it necessary to ascertain the needs and perceptions of high school journalism teachers and advisers. In an attempt to identify problems faced by high school journalism advisers in Arkansas and to determine what would prevent these advisers from using just one of the common aids available to them, the university-sponsored workshop, a study surveyed the opinions of journalism advisers. Subjects, 94 high school journalism advisers (76% in schools of less than 700 students), responded to a questionnaire about problems relating to student publications and the possibility of attending journalism workshops. Their responses indicated that their major problems concerned students' poor newswriting skills; lack of money and resources; photography; lack of time; inability to meet deadlines; students' lack of motivation and commitment; and students' lack of layout and design skills. Schedule conflicts, as well as lack of money, time, and administrative approval, were identified as the reasons most likely to prevent them from taking their students to journalism workshops. Results show that a need for traditional "skills" workshops for high school journalism students still exists, but that there also is a need for workshops which will help advisers solve time and money problems, as well as difficulties involving student commitment and motivation. (Six tables of data 13 notes are included, and one appendix is attached.) (MS)

AN: EJ379965
AU: Sullivan,-Edmund; Siver,-Kenson-J.
TI: Scholastic Press Associations: A Valuable Resource for Teachers and Students.
PY: 1988
JN: NASSP-Bulletin; v72 n511 p45-48,50-51 Nov 1988
AV: UMI
DE: Secondary-Education
DE: *Censorship-; *Journalism-; *Student-Participation; *Student-Publications
AB: Principals can ensure the accuracy and excellence of student publications by enrolling the advisers and student staff members in at least one scholastic press association. These

groups welcome student participation, set publication and instructional standards, and offer many services, including planning workshops, evaluating publications, and recognizing excellence. (MLH)

AN: EJ359207
AU: Blick,-Eddie
TI: Periodicals, Workshops, Conventions Can Assist Publication Improvement.
PY: 1987
JN: Quill-and-Scroll; v62 n1 p10-12 Oct-Nov 1987
AV: UMI
DE: Publications-; Secondary-Education; Statistical-Analysis; Teacher-Role; Teacher-Workshops; Teaching-Methods; Workshops-
DE: *Faculty-Advisers; *Instructional-Improvement; *Journalism-Education; *Newspapers-; *School-Publications; *Student-Publications
AB: Offers faculty advisers suggestions for improving student publications, such as attending workshops and returning with new ideas, enrolling in college journalism courses, and interning with a professional newspaper during the summer. (JC)

AN: ED292112
AU: Dodd,-Julie-E.
TI: Editors' and Publishers' Handbook for Helping High School Journalism Programs.
PY: 1987
NT: 51 p.; Prepared for the Journalism Education Committee, Southern Newspaper Publishers Association.
PR: EDRS Price - MF01/PC03 Plus Postage.
DE: Editors-; Education-Work-Relationship; High-Schools; Publishing-Industry; Secondary-Education
DE: *Journalism-Education; *School-Community-Relationship
AB: Noting the benefits of high school journalism training, this guidebook familiarizes commercial newspaper editors and publishers with high school journalism programs and publications and helps them become more involved in such programs. Following a look at the positive influence of high school journalism courses on student performance and motivation, the guide discusses various threats to high school journalism programs, including curricular constraints, lack of certification for faculty advisers, student press rights, and funding. Next, the guide discusses the state of high school newspapers and yearbooks, and how they have evolved in the last 20 years. The guide then explores ways in which newspapers can help high school journalism programs, including: (1) meeting the journalism teachers and publication advisers in the area; (2) providing guest speakers and tours of the newspaper plant; (3) publishing school newspapers or school pages in commercial newspapers; (4) training high school journalism students and journalism instructors and advisers; (5) funding college courses for teachers and advisers; (6) sponsoring a publication awards program and awards for individual students; (7) funding scholarships; (8) providing part-time student internships; and (9) contacting legislators and policy-makers in support of journalism programs. (Appended is a list of organizations and publications available for high school journalism programs, and 14 references are included.) (HTH)

AN: EJ359125
AU: Eveslage,-Tom
TI: Help Where You Least Expect It: Tapping the Ivory Tower
PY: 1987
JN: Communication:-Journalism-Education-Today-(C:JET); v21 n1 p5 Fall 1987
AV: UMI

DE: Higher-Education; Secondary-Education

DE: *College-School-Cooperation; *Journalism-Education; *Newspapers-; *Student-Publications

AB: Explodes some of the misconceptions about college journalism departments, providing tips for using college departments as a resource for secondary school journalism programs. (HTH)

AU: Iorio,-Sharon-Hartin; Garner,-R.-Brooks

TI: A Needs Assessment of High School Journalism Teacher-Advisers Concerning Types of University Programs Most Beneficial to Scholastic Journalism Education.

PY: 1987

PG: 33

DE: Attendance-; Educational-Needs; Educational-Research; Faculty-Advisers; Higher-Education; High-Schools; Needs-Assessment; Program-Evaluation; Workshops-

DE: *College-School-Cooperation; *Journalism-Education; *Program-Attitudes; *Program-Effectiveness; *Teacher-Attitudes

AB: To determine high school journalism teacher/advisers' attitudes toward the effectiveness of current university programs directed toward high school scholastic journalism instruction, a study surveyed 291 Oklahoma teacher advisers employed during the 1986-87 school year. Responses were analyzed according to teaching certification, experience, school size, and publication type (yearbook or newspaper). Results showed, among other things, that about half of the respondents sent their journalism students to summer workshops and one-day university programs and about half of them attended with their students. From those schools that do utilize university programs now offered, most reported 10 or fewer students attending during a given summer. It was also found that high school journalism students and their teacher/advisers generally seek benefits that are not now being offered by universities and that by far the most preferred instructor for workshops and one-day programs was someone currently teaching/advising secondary school journalism. Overall, respondents rated as very helpful workshops in several locations around the state, workshops for teacher/advisers, individual student writing competitions and one-day skill workshops at universities. (Several recommendations are made based on these findings. Tables of data and 28 footnotes are included.) (JD)

AN: EJ313621

AU: Currence,-Cindy

TI: Youth News Service: An Idea Whose Time Has Come.

PY: 1985

JN: Quill-and-Scroll; v59 n3 p22-23 Feb-Mar 1985

AV: UMI

DE: Secondary-Education; Writing-for-Publication

DE: *Journalism-Education; *Online-Systems; *Student-Organizations; *Student-Publications

AB: Describes a computerized student press association that allows members to use news from its correspondents in communities across the country. (CRH)

AN: EJ313615

AU: Lange,-Carol

TI: Yes or No—The Critique.

PY: 1985

JN: Communication:-Journalism-Education-Today-(C:JET); v18 n3 p15-16 Spr 1985

AV: UMI

DE: Guidelines-; Journalism-Education; Secondary-Education; Teacher-Response

DE: *Competition-; *Evaluation-Criteria; *News-Media; *Professional-Associations; *Student-Publications

AB: Explains how a national press association review of a school publication is beneficial even if a low score is given and provides a brief overview of associations. (CRH)

AN: EJ294672
AU: Arnold,-Mary
TI: Summer Workshops: Learning Basics, New Ideas, Discovering Solutions.
PY: 1984
JN: Quill-and-Scroll; v58 n3 p5-7 Feb-Mar 1984
AV: UMI
DE: Improvement-Programs; Journalism-Education; Layout-Publications; Secondary-Education; Student-Publications
DE: *Cooperation-; *Photography-; *Summer-Programs; *Workshops-; *Yearbooks-
AB: Describes how a high school yearbook workshop helped student photographers and editors learn to work together to produce unique and interesting yearbooks. (MM)

AN: EJ297908
AU: Dodd,-Julie-E.; Hume,-Katherine-C.
TI: Press Associations Need to Exchange Ideas, Programs.
PY: 1984
JN: Quill-and-Scroll; v58 n4 p11-14 Apr-May 1984
AV: UMI
DE: Higher-Education; Journalism-; News-Media; Newspapers-; Secondary-Education; Workshops-; Yearbooks-
DE: *Journalism-Education; *Organizational-Change; *Professional-Associations; *Student-Publications
AB: Urges the need for improved communication among advisers of state and regional press associations. Presents a table detailing results of a survey of association membership, management structure, activities and services, problems, and major accomplishments. Offers suggestions for improving cooperation among advisers of state and regional press associations. (MM)

AN: ED248540
AU: Dvorak,-Jack
TI: Rating the Raters: Some Characteristics of Quill and Scroll's Newspaper and Newsmagazine Judges.
PY: 1984
NT: 20 p.; Paper presented at the Mid-winter Meeting of the Association for Education in Journalism and Mass Communication (Baton Rouge, LA, January 1984).
PR: EDRS Price - MF01/PC01 Plus Postage.
DE: Faculty-Advisers; School-Newspapers; Secondary-Education
DE: *Evaluation-Criteria; *Individual-Characteristics; *Journalism-Education; *Judges-; *Media-Research; *School-Publications
AB: To prepare a profile of Quill and Scroll's newspaper and newsmagazine judges, questionnaires were sent to all 57 judges involved in the 1982 competition. Analysis of the 39 responses indicated that the typical judge (1) is female and has judged for two or more years, (2) has taught high school for five or more years, (3) holds certification to teach journalism, (4) has earned 30 or more semester hours of journalism credit, (5) moderately disagrees that knowing a newspaper's previous year's score would help in evaluations, (6) slightly disagrees that there is too much emphasis on graphics and design in the evaluations, (7) agrees that schools with large budgets tend to finish high in contests, (8) agrees that business practices should be part of newspaper evaluations, (9) strongly

agrees that a qualified adviser is the single most important factor in producing an award winning publication, and (10) most strongly agrees that she or he is an exacting, thorough, and conservative judge. Other findings showed that the judge knew the previous year's score of each publication evaluated, while statistical comparisons of the years 1980 through 1983 showed no significant differences when previous years' scores were either known or not known. (Author/FL)

AU: Hines,-Barbara
TI: The Emergence and Changing Role of Scholastic Press Associations.
PY: 1984
PG: 24
DE: Educational-Research; Higher-Education; High-Schools; Institutional-Role; Organizational-Effectiveness; School-Role
DE: *Journalism-; *Journalism-Education; *National-Surveys; *Organizational-Change; *Student-Organizations
AB: Recognizing that scholastic press associations at the regional, state, and national levels enhance and encourage high school journalism, a study was conducted to update a 1980 survey of scholastic journalism/press associations in the United States. Of the 122 organizations originally polled, 54 were reevaluated either by telephone, personal interview, or a review of the literature provided by the organization. Among the findings were the following: (1) most of the organizations are based at a college or university, usually under the aegis of a journalism school or department of communications; (2) among the services universities provide are mailing services, speakers, contest judges, and printing facilities; (3) most of the organizations are headed by a part-time director who has other college related duties; (4) many press association executives feel that the success (or failure) of an association could be directly attributable to the support provided by the chairman or dean of the school where the association is housed; (5) association activities and services are varied, but the most popular service is student workshops and conventions followed by ratings and writing contests; (6) half of the university based associations sponsor journalism teacher training programs through special workshops or regularly scheduled university courses; and (7) press associations serving only the collegiate press seem to have problems remaining solvent. (HOD)

AN: EJ305281
AU: Jeanne,-Rita
TI: Financial History One of Ups and Downs.
PY: 1984
JN: Communication:-Journalism-Education-Today-(C:JET); v18 n1 p3 Fall 1984
AV: UMI
DE: Financial-Problems; History-; Secondary-Education
DE: *Financial-Needs; *Journalism-Education; *Money-Management; *Professional-Associations; *Resources-
AB: Describes the financial history of the Journalism Education Association from its inception in 1924 to the present. (CRH)

AN: EJ297963
AU: Prentice,-Tom
TI: How Good Is It Journalistically? Papers Try Using More Pflash, Pizzaz.
PY: 1984
JN: Communication:-Journalism-Education-Today-(C:JET); v17 n4 p16-19 Sum 1984
AV: UMI
DE: Graphic-Arts; Secondary-Education

DE: *Evaluation-Criteria; *Journalism-Education; *Layout-Publications; *Standards-; *Student-Publications
AB: Laments the emphasis on packaging, marketing, and graphics characterizing many award-winning school publications. Calls for a return to the realm of more substantive journalism in evaluating school publications. (HTH)

AN: EJ253726
AU: Hall,-H.-L.
TI: An Inside Look.
PY: 1981
JN: Communication:-Journalism-Education-Today-(C:JET); v15 n2 p8-11 Win 1981
AV: Reprint: UMI
DE: Evaluation-; Production-Techniques; School-Publications; Secondary-Education
DE: *Evaluators-; *Guidelines-; *Journalism-Education; *Yearbooks-
AB: Reviews yearbook production guidelines prepared by the national rating services. Notes some differences and many similarities in the various guidelines. (FL)

INDEX

ow Do Journalists Think?

Proposal for the Study of Cognitive Bias in Newsmaking

S. Holly Stocking and Paget H. Gross

oomington, Indiana: ERIC/Clearinghouse on Reading, English, and
ommunication, 1989

4.95

hy do Dan and Tom and Connie sometimes get it so wrong on the 6 o'clock
ws, and even Charles on Sunday morning?

ore importantly, how do they decide what to talk about and what slant to take?

ow Do Journalists Think?—a trailblazing study by a team made up of a communi-
tion researcher and a cognitive psychologist, is a diagram of the structure of logic
the news reporter's cognitive processes. Stocking and Gross discuss categoriza-
n, theory generation and testing, information selection and integration, and the
rseverance of biases despite claims of fairness and objectivity. Notwithstanding the
ct-gathering power of the major networksm, error is inevitable.

> Stocking and Gross...take 200 years of additional thought [beyond I.
> Kant] on the subject of rose colored glasses and apply it to the way
> journalists filter reality through the myriad perceptual and cognitive
> prisms with which all human are born. There's no getting away from
> those prisms....Are journalists dupes of their own senses? I suspect the
> authors don't think so. The book implies that rose colored glasses can
> be pushed down one's nose. And occasionally, we may see over the
> rims—if we'll try.
>
> *—Tom Grimes, Assistant Professor of Journalism and Mass*
> *Communication, University of Wisconsin-Madison*

> Holly Stocking is a journalism professor at Indiana University who has
> worked for the L.A. Times, the Minneapolis Tribune, and the
> Associated Press.
>
> *—Paget Gross, formerly a psychology professor at Columbia*
> *University, is now studying the law.*

heir book is a rejoinder for those who wonder how human information processing
esearch can be applied. Stocking and Gross depart from the bulk of traditional
esearch to understand news reporting in terms of the reporters' cognitive processes.

If you are interested in ordering these or other publications, or if you would like a copy of
our catalogue, call us (812) 855-5847 or TOLL-FREE at 1-800-759-4723.

A High School Student's Bill of Rights

by Stephen S. Gottlieb; foreword by John J. Patrick, Director, ERIC/ChES

Co-published by ERIC/REC (the Clearinghouse on Reading, English, and Communication) and ERIC/CHeSS (the Clearinghouse for Social Studies/Social Science Education)

$14.95

A High School Student's Bill of Rights, by Stephen S. Gottlieb, an Indiana district attorney, puts into perspective the erties and limitations under the law of high-school students and other legal minors. Students, like grown-ups, are citizens with rights, but students' rights are limited so long as they are "underaged" and under the care of their parents and school authorities. They have freedom of speech in school assembly, but not completely; their lockers are protected from search and seizure, but not entirely; they have the right to publish their opinions in the school newspaper, but not if the principal says no.

Gottlieb draws on three major documents in testimony to our basic rights: The U.S. Constitution and its "Bill of Rights," the Northwest Ordinance of 1787, and the U.N. Declaration of Universal Human Rights. He interprets these basic statements according to the process of judicial refinement that has arisen in the courts through lawsuits and other contests over civil rights.

- Must students be "Mirandized"?
- May students be frisked in the hall?
- May a student speaker talk dirty in the school assembly?
- Do teachers have the right to paddle school kids?
- Who controls which books go into the school library?

- Is religion really outlawed in schools?
- May the principal abridge freedom of the school press?
- What are the rights of a student who has been suspended?
- What is the legal status of Black v. White at school?
- Do we really have to go to school?

A High School Student's Bill of Rights is a book for all classes. Gottlieb has redesigned lesson plans drawn from the ERIC database, actual exercises that have been tried and tested by classroom teachers from all over the country, study outlines that have proved themselves effective. In each lesson, Gottlieb addresses both teacher and student, making suggestions on how to teach and what to learn.

Gottlieb lays out in thought-provoking ways the basic concepts of republican democracy, the governmental structures, and the legal traditions that underpin our constitutional rights—an excellent workbook for civics classes. He focuses c three of the main historical documents of human liberty and on court cases that were decided at the pitch of crisis in historic struggles to define and preserve our rights—a real-life workbook for history classes.

He structures an approach to all this history, law, and concern for rights and freedoms in terms of critical reading, critical thinking, and critical writing—an across-the-curriculum workbook for English teachers and reading-and-writing specialists.

A High School Students Bill of Rights is a volume in the TRIED series (Teaching Resources In the ERIC Database).